ASVAB®

THE ARMED SERVICES VOCATIONAL APTITUDE BATTERY

Ninth Edition

KAPLAN

PUBLISHING

New York

Published by Kaplan Publishing, a division of Kaplan, Inc.
395 Hudson Street, 4th Floor
New York, NY 10014

Printed in the United States of America

10 9 8 7 6 5 4 3 2 1

ISBN-13: 978-1-60714-878-4

Kaplan Publishing books are available at special quantity discounts to use for sales promotions, employee premiums, or educational purposes. For more information or to purchase books, please call the Simon & Schuster special sales department at 866-506-1949.

TABLE OF CONTENTS

Part Three: Review of Technical ASVAB Subtests

Part Four: ASVAB Practice Tests

HOW TO USE THIS BOOK

This book provides you with everything you need to ace the ASVAB. We've included this section with some tips on how to make sure you make the most of your prep time.

Step One: Familiarize Yourself with the ASVAB

The first chapter of this book, The ASVAB Challenge, covers the basics of the test: what's on it, who it's for, and the various formats it appears in. Once you get a sense of what's on the test, you're ready to get a sense of yourself as a test taker. Additionally, the first chapter gives you Kaplan's exclusive test-taking strategies. Read this chapter carefully to learn Kaplan's proven methods for increasing your score on this challenging exam.

Step Two: Take the Diagnostic Test (Practice Test I)

This book contains three simulated full-length ASVAB tests with explanations. We've designed this book to allow you to take one of these tests early in your preparation and get a sense of where you're scoring now, and what score you're shooting for on test day. As you work through your diagnostic exam, pay especially close attention to the areas in which you perform best. Particular attention should be given to the two math and the two verbal sections. These four sections form the AFQT, which is the qualifying part of this armed services exam (more on the AFQT in chapter 1). Strength in these areas will provide you with the bulk of your points on the actual exam. Also make note of your problem areas. You will need to shore up your knowledge in your problem areas to maximize your performance on the test.

With a clear sense of your strengths and weaknesses, you will be ready to tackle the content chapters that form the bulk of this book.

Step Three: Work Through the Material So That You Reinforce Strengths and Shore Up Weaknesses

Each content chapter focuses on a specific subject as it is tested on the ASVAB. Based on your performance on the Diagnostic Test, you should have a good sense of which areas you are strongest in, and which areas need the most reinforcement. Each chapter includes quizzes to help you test yourself on the content just covered.

Develop a study plan that devotes roughly equal time to all of the chapters. Aim to complete all the content two weeks prior to your exam date. The last two weeks should be spent working through the second and third practice tests and reviewing your notes.

Step Four: Conclude Your Preparation with Practice Tests II and III

Your preparation with this book should conclude with the second and third simulated full-length ASVAB tests. After completing these exams, work through the explanations that follow them. Be sure to review the explanations for questions you got right as well as for those you got wrong. This will serve as a good review of the wide range of topics covered on the exam. After completing the exams, continue to refer to the content chapters to make sure you are familiar with everything we cover in this book.

Use this game plan to prepare for test day. Then, right before the exam, relax. You can rest easier because you're ready for the ASVAB. With some hard work and a little forward thinking, you're going to get a great score!

Part One

GETTING STARTED

CHAPTER ONE

The ASVAB Challenge

WHAT IS THE ASVAB?

The ASVAB (Armed Services Vocational Aptitude Battery) is the most widely used multiple-aptitude test battery in the world. It measures a test taker's suitability to enlist in the Unites States Armed Forces and his or her abilities to be trained in specific civilian or military jobs.

Depending upon your reasons for taking the ASVAB and the stage you are at in the career decision-making process, you will take on one of the following three versions of the test battery:

Enlistment Testing Program ASVAB

This version of the ASVAB, sometimes referred to as the *Production Version*, is used for enlistment purposes only and is administered to potential enlistees in all branches of the military. A potential recruit's performance on the ASVAB subtests is used to determine whether the candidate has the necessary aptitudes to enlist in a desired branch of service, and for which military jobs the candidate is best suited.

THE ASVAB IS NOT AN IQ TEST!

The ASVAB does not purport to measure intelligence. The battery of tests is supposed to measure an individual's aptitude to be trained in specific jobs. But it's not an aptitude test either, because you can improve your score on the ASVAB greatly by studying this book. What the ASVAB truly measures is your ability and preparedness to take the ASVAB, nothing more or less.

The ASVAB is administered at all 65 Military Entrance Processing Stations (MEPS) located across the United States and Puerto Rico as well as at a number of Military Entrance Test (MET) sites. If you take the ASVAB at a MEPS, it will be administered as the computer version of the ASVAB, called the CAT-ASVAB. CAT stands for Computer Adaptive Test. If you take the ASVAB at a MET, you'll likely be administered the paper and pencil version of the test.

Almost 90 percent of recruits take the CAT-ASVAB, so there is good chance you will, too. The question types are identical to the paper and pencil version, but the timing and number of questions differ. The CAT also has ten subtests compared to the paper and pencil version's nine—it splits the Auto and Shop Information (AS) subtest into two separate subtests. However, it combines them into one single score, labeled (AS). The order in which the subtests are administered on the ASVAB never varies, and is as follows:

Subtest	Questions/ Time Limit in Minutes (CAT-ASVAB)	Questions/ Time Limit in Minutes (Paper & Pencil)	What's Tested
General Science (GS)	16 questions/8 minutes	25 questions/11 minutes	Knowledge of general concepts from life, earth, and physical sciences
Arithmetic Reasoning (AR)	16 questions/ 39 minutes	30 questions/36 minutes	Ability to answer word problems that involve basic arithmetic calculations
Word Knowledge (WK)	16 questions/8 minutes	35 questions/11 minutes	Ability to recognize synonyms of words
Paragraph Comprehension (PC)	11 questions/ 22 minutes	15 questions/13 minutes	Ability to answer questions based on short passages (of 30–120 words)
Mathematics Knowledge (MK)	16 questions/ 20 minutes	25 questions/24 minutes	Knowledge of math concepts, including applied arithmetic, algebra, and geometry
Electronics Information (EI)	16 questions/8 minutes	20 questions/9 minutes	Knowledge of electronic principles and terminology, and basic electronic circuitry
Auto and Shop Information (AS)*	11 questions/7 minutes; and 11 questions/ 6 minutes	25 questions/11 minutes	Knowledge of automobiles, and of tool and shop practices and terminology
Mechanical Comprehension (MC)	16 questions/ 20 minutes	25 questions/19 minutes	Knowledge of basic mechanical and physical principles
Assembling Objects (AO)	16 questions/ 16 minutes	25 questions/ 15 minutes	Ability to determine how a disassembled object will look when it is put back together
Totals	145 questions/ 154 minutes	225 questions/ 149 minutes	

*On the CAT-ASVAB, this is split into two parts, but one score is reported.

Career Exploration Program ASVAB

This is a paper and pencil, eight-subtest version of the ASVAB that is administered along with an interest inventory to high school and postsecondary students as part of the Department of Defense's Career Exploration Program. The content and format of this ASVAB are the same as the enlistment paper and pencil version, with two exceptions: the Assembling Objects subtest is not given, and the Auto Information subtests are combined into one subtest.

A student's results on the battery and inventory can be used to help the student recognize particular civilian and military career aptitudes. If a student scores high enough on the four subtests used to determine basic qualification for enlistment (see *What Is the AFQT*), he or she may use these scores to enlist within two years.

Armed Forces Classification Test (AFCT)

Also known as the "In-Service" ASVAB, the AFCT is identical to the paper and pencil version and is administered to those already in the military who are looking to switch jobs within the military.

WHAT IS THE AFQT?

Your score on the AFQT, or the Armed Forces Qualification Test, determines your eligibility in all branches of the Armed Services. The ASVAB does not have an "overall" score. When someone talks about getting a score of, say, a 75 or 80 on the ASVAB, he or she is really talking about the AFQT score, not the overall ASVAB score.

The AFQT score is derived from your performance on just the verbal and math subtests of the ASVAB, or to be more specific: Word Knowledge, Paragraph Comprehension, Arithmetic Reasoning, and Mathematics Knowledge. You should also realize that your verbal sections are doubly counted, while the math sections are only counted once. Scoring on the AFQT is a rather complicated affair, so let's break it down piece by piece.

The military determines your AFQT score by first adding your Word Knowledge and Paragraph Comprehension scores together to get your "Verbal Expression" or "VE" score. The formula to derive the AFQT "raw score" is 2VE + AR (Arithmetic Reasoning) + MK (Mathematics Knowledge) = AFQT score. The percentile score that is your final AFQT score tells you how well you did on the AFQT compared to other test takers. (See "How to Read Your ASVAB Scores" later in this chapter.)

In order to join the **Air Force,** one needs a minimum AFQT score of 36. Those who hold a GED rather than a regular high school diploma must have a minimum score of 65 to join.

NOT ALL QUESTIONS ARE WORTH THE SAME

ASVAB questions are weighted. Harder questions result in more points than easy ones. There is no particular order of difficulty on the ASVAB subtests. In other words, easy and difficult questions can appear in any order on any subtest.

Army recruits must score at least 31 on the AFQT, with no more than ten percent per year being high school dropouts. GED holders must score a 50 percent or better to be eligible (although waivers are possible).

Marine Corps recruits must score at least 32, with no more than five percent being high school dropouts. GED holders must score at least 50 on the AFQT (although waivers are possible).

Navy recruits must score at least 35. Additionally, high school dropouts must be at least 19 years of age, and show a proven work history. GED holders must score at least 50 on the AFQT. Female applicants to the Navy must also score at least a 50, because of the limited availability of female accommodations on Navy vessels.

Like the Air Force, **Coast Guard** recruits must also score at least 36 points on the AFQT. For the very few who will be allowed to enlist in the Coast Guard with a GED, the minimum AFQT score is 50, and these recruits must have 15 hours of college credit.

These scores are subject to change without notice.

RETAKING THE ASVAB

ASVAB results are valid for two years. After taking an initial ASVAB Test (any school-administered ASVAB doesn't count as an initial test), one may retake the ASVAB after 30 days. After the retest, one must wait at least six months before taking the test again.

THE COMPUTERIZED TEST VERSUS THE PAPER TEST

Computer-adaptive testing, or CAT for short, has recently become a staple among big test givers. Computer-adaptive testing is really just a fancy way of saying that the difficulty of the questions you get on the test adapts based on your performance up to that point.

For example, the first question you receive on any particular CAT-ASVAB subtest will be of medium difficulty. If you answer it correctly, the next question you get will be pulled from a bank of above-average difficulty questions. If you get the question wrong, your next question will be of a lower difficulty level. This process is repeated throughout the test, so that the test can more precisely zero in on your exact performance level on the exam.

NO DISTRACTIONS

One advantage of taking the CAT-ASVAB is that it gives you the chance to work methodically on one question at a time with no other questions there to distract you.

Studies have shown that, overall, people perform the same on the ASVAB whether they take the paper or CAT version of the test. There are, however, some individuals who will tend to do better on one version of the test than the other. If you do have a choice as to which version of the test you will take, here are some of the advantages and disadvantages of taking the CAT versus the paper test:

Advantages of Taking the CAT-ASVAB

- The length of time of many of the subtests has been reduced, and the number of questions that you are required to answer has been reduced even more.

- The test can be scored immediately. You will know how well you did as soon as you finish the test.

- Test administration is very flexible, so you don't have to wait for the next scheduled test date to take the test.

- There's no chance of losing points by filling out your answer sheet incorrectly.

Disadvantages of Taking the CAT-ASVAB

- You cannot skip around on this test; you must answer the questions one at a time in the order the computer gives them to you.

- If you realize later that you answered a question incorrectly, you cannot go back and change your answer.

- You can't cross off an answer choice and never look at it again, so you'll have to use your scrap paper to keep track of the answers you've eliminated.

KAPLAN'S CAT STRATEGIES IN A NUTSHELL

If you are taking the CAT-ASVAB, applying certain CAT-specific strategies will have a direct, positive impact on your score:

- At the beginning of the section, each question you get right or wrong will rapidly move the computer's estimate of your score up or down. A key strategy for doing well on the CAT is to get the computer's estimate of your score up to where you are handling the hard questions. Thus it pays to spend more time on those early questions, double-checking each answer before you confirm it. Getting to the hard questions as soon as possible can only help your final score.

- As you progress through the middle part of a section, try to avoid getting several questions in a row wrong, as this can sink your score on the CAT. If you know that the previous question you answered was a blind guess, spend a little extra time trying to get the next one right.

- The CAT does not allow you to skip questions. So if you are given a question you cannot answer, you'll have to guess. Guess intelligently and strategically by eliminating any answer choices that you know are wrong and choosing from those remaining.

- Don't get rattled if you see difficult questions. It just means that you are doing well. Keep it up!

- At the end of the section, you will be penalized more heavily for not getting to a question than for answering it wrong. So if you only have a minute left and several questions remaining, you should guess at random rather than leave anything unanswered.

GENERAL ASVAB TEST-TAKING STRATEGIES

This book is broken into chapters that offer specific test-taking strategies for dealing with each of the subtests, particularly those subtests that constitute the AFQT. But there are some general strategies that will help you no matter what subtest you are taking.

Always Answer Every Question

There is no guessing penalty on the ASVAB. This means that it is absolutely in your interest to guess on every question on every subtest of the ASVAB! Even if you have to make a completely blind guess, you have a 25 percent chance of picking the correct answer.

THE ASVAB IS HIGHLY PREDICTABLE

The key to success on the ASVAB is knowing what to expect. The format—which includes the directions, the types of questions, and even the traps that the test maker places among the answer choices—is remarkably similar from test to test. One of the easiest things you can do to improve your performance on the ASVAB is to understand the test format before you take the test.

Take Advantage of the Multiple-Choice Format

As noted, every ASVAB question comes with four answer choices, so you have a 25 percent chance of getting the correct answer just by guessing blindly. If you know that one of the four answer choices cannot be right and eliminate it accordingly, you now have a 33 percent chance of getting the correct answer. Remove one more wrong answer choice, and your chance of getting the question right is now 50-50. On certain ASVAB questions, you will find that using the process of elimination on wrong answer choices is just as effective a way of getting to the correct answer as spotting the correct answer the straightforward way.

Often, even if you are completely confused by a question, you can still make a solid guess by eliminating any "odd men out." By this we mean that you're probably on solid ground if you eliminate answer choices that run counter to the other three answer choices.

GETTING READY FOR THE ASVAB

You should be ready now to take your first ASVAB practice test. As you take this test, and as you work your way through the rest of this book, pay especially close attention to the questions you get wrong and to the techniques we describe in this book for getting these types of questions right. You've made the right move in deciding to prepare for the ASVAB. It is a highly coachable test, and we aim to give you the tools you need to score high on the ASVAB and qualify for the military career of your dreams.

HOW TO READ YOUR ASVAB SCORES

Your official ASVAB scores will come in a variety of styles and will be fully explained to you by your guidance counselor or recruiter. All of the scores matter, though some matter more than others. Here's a quick breakdown of what you will find.

Standard Scores

All test takers receive a "Standard Score" for each of the subtests. These scores are calculated using a comparison of your raw scores to the raw scores of a standard national sample. According to the Department of Defense, roughly half the population achieves a Standard Score of 50 or above but only about 16 percent scores higher than 59.

Career Exploration Scores

In addition to the Standard Scores, students who take the ASVAB as part of the Career Exploration Program also receive three Career Exploration Scores in the composite areas of Verbal Skills, Math Skills, and Science and Technical Skills, which are all reported as a percentile.

Service Composite Scores

Instead of Career Exploration Scores, enlistees receive Service Composite Scores, which are sometimes called Line Scores. These score combinations are used to determine whether a test taker has the necessary vocational aptitude for different job assignments in all the military branches. For example, an enlistee's Navy "General Technician" composite score (abbreviated "GT") is twice the sum of his or her Paragraph Comprehension and Word Knowledge scores plus the Arithmetic Reasoning score. An enlistee must achieve a minimum composite score for the vocation of interest to be able to qualify for the job.

SCORE TERMINOLOGY

Raw Score: The number of correct versus incorrect responses

Standard Score: A comparison of one test taker's performance on a test to the performance of a group of other test takers on the same test.

Composite Score: Various subtests' raw scores combined into one score

Percentile Score: The percentage of test takers in a group that scored at or below a particular score

AFQT Score

All ASVAB test takers receive an AFQT score. Your AFQT score is, quite simply, the determining factor in your acceptance into any branch of the armed forces.

$$2 \times [\textbf{Word Knowledge} + \textbf{Paragraph Comprehension}]$$

$$+$$

$$[\textbf{Arithmetic Reasoning} + \textbf{Mathematical Knowledge}]$$

$$= \textbf{AFQT RAW SCORE}$$

The AFQT raw score you receive is then translated into a percentile score (see explanation of percentile scores above) to determine your eligibility for the armed forces.

AFQT Percentile	AFQT Category
93–99	I
65–92	II
50–64	III-A
31–49	III-B
21–30	IV-A
16–20	IV-B
10–15	IV-C
1–9	V

So you can see now why it is imperative that ASVAB takers with any interest in military enlistment pay particular attention to the math and verbal sections of the ASVAB, as they help determine eligibility not only for general enlistment, but also for job placement and for overall military branch acceptance.

ASVAB Diagnostic Test: Practice Test I

DIRECTIONS FOR THE ASVAB DIAGNOSTIC TEST

This diagnostic test is intended as a tool to help guide you in your ASVAB preparation. Ideally, you should take this test before you go through the review lessons in this book. This test will give you a good idea of the kind of questions you can expect, and can help you identify your areas of strength and weakness. Take the test under timed conditions. If you run out of time before you finish any given section, be sure to fill in all the blanks on your answer sheet, as there's no guessing penalty on the ASVAB. Good luck!

ANSWER SHEET

Part 1: General Science (GS)

1 (A)(B)(C)(D)	6 (A)(B)(C)(D)	11 (A)(B)(C)(D)	16 (A)(B)(C)(D)	21 (A)(B)(C)(D)
2 (A)(B)(C)(D)	7 (A)(B)(C)(D)	12 (A)(B)(C)(D)	17 (A)(B)(C)(D)	22 (A)(B)(C)(D)
3 (A)(B)(C)(D)	8 (A)(B)(C)(D)	13 (A)(B)(C)(D)	18 (A)(B)(C)(D)	23 (A)(B)(C)(D)
4 (A)(B)(C)(D)	9 (A)(B)(C)(D)	14 (A)(B)(C)(D)	19 (A)(B)(C)(D)	24 (A)(B)(C)(D)
5 (A)(B)(C)(D)	10 (A)(B)(C)(D)	15 (A)(B)(C)(D)	20 (A)(B)(C)(D)	25 (A)(B)(C)(D)

Part 2: Arithmetic Reasoning (AR)

1 (A)(B)(C)(D)	7 (A)(B)(C)(D)	13 (A)(B)(C)(D)	19 (A)(B)(C)(D)	25 (A)(B)(C)(D)
2 (A)(B)(C)(D)	8 (A)(B)(C)(D)	14 (A)(B)(C)(D)	20 (A)(B)(C)(D)	26 (A)(B)(C)(D)
3 (A)(B)(C)(D)	9 (A)(B)(C)(D)	15 (A)(B)(C)(D)	21 (A)(B)(C)(D)	27 (A)(B)(C)(D)
4 (A)(B)(C)(D)	10 (A)(B)(C)(D)	16 (A)(B)(C)(D)	22 (A)(B)(C)(D)	28 (A)(B)(C)(D)
5 (A)(B)(C)(D)	11 (A)(B)(C)(D)	17 (A)(B)(C)(D)	23 (A)(B)(C)(D)	29 (A)(B)(C)(D)
6 (A)(B)(C)(D)	12 (A)(B)(C)(D)	18 (A)(B)(C)(D)	24 (A)(B)(C)(D)	30 (A)(B)(C)(D)

Part 3: Word Knowledge (WK)

1 (A)(B)(C)(D)	8 (A)(B)(C)(D)	15 (A)(B)(C)(D)	22 (A)(B)(C)(D)	29 (A)(B)(C)(D)
2 (A)(B)(C)(D)	9 (A)(B)(C)(D)	16 (A)(B)(C)(D)	23 (A)(B)(C)(D)	30 (A)(B)(C)(D)
3 (A)(B)(C)(D)	10 (A)(B)(C)(D)	17 (A)(B)(C)(D)	24 (A)(B)(C)(D)	31 (A)(B)(C)(D)
4 (A)(B)(C)(D)	11 (A)(B)(C)(D)	18 (A)(B)(C)(D)	25 (A)(B)(C)(D)	32 (A)(B)(C)(D)
5 (A)(B)(C)(D)	12 (A)(B)(C)(D)	19 (A)(B)(C)(D)	26 (A)(B)(C)(D)	33 (A)(B)(C)(D)
6 (A)(B)(C)(D)	13 (A)(B)(C)(D)	20 (A)(B)(C)(D)	27 (A)(B)(C)(D)	34 (A)(B)(C)(D)
7 (A)(B)(C)(D)	14 (A)(B)(C)(D)	21 (A)(B)(C)(D)	28 (A)(B)(C)(D)	35 (A)(B)(C)(D)

Part 4: Paragraph Comprehension (PC)

1 (A)(B)(C)(D)	4 (A)(B)(C)(D)	7 (A)(B)(C)(D)	10 (A)(B)(C)(D)	13 (A)(B)(C)(D)
2 (A)(B)(C)(D)	5 (A)(B)(C)(D)	8 (A)(B)(C)(D)	11 (A)(B)(C)(D)	14 (A)(B)(C)(D)
3 (A)(B)(C)(D)	6 (A)(B)(C)(D)	9 (A)(B)(C)(D)	12 (A)(B)(C)(D)	15 (A)(B)(C)(D)

Part 5: Mathematics Knowledge (MK)

1 (A)(B)(C)(D)	6 (A)(B)(C)(D)	11 (A)(B)(C)(D)	16 (A)(B)(C)(D)	21 (A)(B)(C)(D)
2 (A)(B)(C)(D)	7 (A)(B)(C)(D)	12 (A)(B)(C)(D)	17 (A)(B)(C)(D)	22 (A)(B)(C)(D)
3 (A)(B)(C)(D)	8 (A)(B)(C)(D)	13 (A)(B)(C)(D)	18 (A)(B)(C)(D)	23 (A)(B)(C)(D)
4 (A)(B)(C)(D)	9 (A)(B)(C)(D)	14 (A)(B)(C)(D)	19 (A)(B)(C)(D)	24 (A)(B)(C)(D)
5 (A)(B)(C)(D)	10 (A)(B)(C)(D)	15 (A)(B)(C)(D)	20 (A)(B)(C)(D)	25 (A)(B)(C)(D)

ANSWER SHEET

Part 6: Electronics Information (EI)

1 Ⓐ Ⓑ Ⓒ Ⓓ	5 Ⓐ Ⓑ Ⓒ Ⓓ	9 Ⓐ Ⓑ Ⓒ Ⓓ	13 Ⓐ Ⓑ Ⓒ Ⓓ	17 Ⓐ Ⓑ Ⓒ Ⓓ
2 Ⓐ Ⓑ Ⓒ Ⓓ	6 Ⓐ Ⓑ Ⓒ Ⓓ	10 Ⓐ Ⓑ Ⓒ Ⓓ	14 Ⓐ Ⓑ Ⓒ Ⓓ	18 Ⓐ Ⓑ Ⓒ Ⓓ
3 Ⓐ Ⓑ Ⓒ Ⓓ	7 Ⓐ Ⓑ Ⓒ Ⓓ	11 Ⓐ Ⓑ Ⓒ Ⓓ	15 Ⓐ Ⓑ Ⓒ Ⓓ	19 Ⓐ Ⓑ Ⓒ Ⓓ
4 Ⓐ Ⓑ Ⓒ Ⓓ	8 Ⓐ Ⓑ Ⓒ Ⓓ	12 Ⓐ Ⓑ Ⓒ Ⓓ	16 Ⓐ Ⓑ Ⓒ Ⓓ	20 Ⓐ Ⓑ Ⓒ Ⓓ

Part 7: Automotive and Shop Information (AS)

1 Ⓐ Ⓑ Ⓒ Ⓓ	6 Ⓐ Ⓑ Ⓒ Ⓓ	11 Ⓐ Ⓑ Ⓒ Ⓓ	16 Ⓐ Ⓑ Ⓒ Ⓓ	21 Ⓐ Ⓑ Ⓒ Ⓓ
2 Ⓐ Ⓑ Ⓒ Ⓓ	7 Ⓐ Ⓑ Ⓒ Ⓓ	12 Ⓐ Ⓑ Ⓒ Ⓓ	17 Ⓐ Ⓑ Ⓒ Ⓓ	22 Ⓐ Ⓑ Ⓒ Ⓓ
3 Ⓐ Ⓑ Ⓒ Ⓓ	8 Ⓐ Ⓑ Ⓒ Ⓓ	13 Ⓐ Ⓑ Ⓒ Ⓓ	18 Ⓐ Ⓑ Ⓒ Ⓓ	23 Ⓐ Ⓑ Ⓒ Ⓓ
4 Ⓐ Ⓑ Ⓒ Ⓓ	9 Ⓐ Ⓑ Ⓒ Ⓓ	14 Ⓐ Ⓑ Ⓒ Ⓓ	19 Ⓐ Ⓑ Ⓒ Ⓓ	24 Ⓐ Ⓑ Ⓒ Ⓓ
5 Ⓐ Ⓑ Ⓒ Ⓓ	10 Ⓐ Ⓑ Ⓒ Ⓓ	15 Ⓐ Ⓑ Ⓒ Ⓓ	20 Ⓐ Ⓑ Ⓒ Ⓓ	25 Ⓐ Ⓑ Ⓒ Ⓓ

Part 8: Mechanical Comprehension (MC)

1 Ⓐ Ⓑ Ⓒ Ⓓ	6 Ⓐ Ⓑ Ⓒ Ⓓ	11 Ⓐ Ⓑ Ⓒ Ⓓ	16 Ⓐ Ⓑ Ⓒ Ⓓ	21 Ⓐ Ⓑ Ⓒ Ⓓ
2 Ⓐ Ⓑ Ⓒ Ⓓ	7 Ⓐ Ⓑ Ⓒ Ⓓ	12 Ⓐ Ⓑ Ⓒ Ⓓ	17 Ⓐ Ⓑ Ⓒ Ⓓ	22 Ⓐ Ⓑ Ⓒ Ⓓ
3 Ⓐ Ⓑ Ⓒ Ⓓ	8 Ⓐ Ⓑ Ⓒ Ⓓ	13 Ⓐ Ⓑ Ⓒ Ⓓ	18 Ⓐ Ⓑ Ⓒ Ⓓ	23 Ⓐ Ⓑ Ⓒ Ⓓ
4 Ⓐ Ⓑ Ⓒ Ⓓ	9 Ⓐ Ⓑ Ⓒ Ⓓ	14 Ⓐ Ⓑ Ⓒ Ⓓ	19 Ⓐ Ⓑ Ⓒ Ⓓ	24 Ⓐ Ⓑ Ⓒ Ⓓ
5 Ⓐ Ⓑ Ⓒ Ⓓ	10 Ⓐ Ⓑ Ⓒ Ⓓ	15 Ⓐ Ⓑ Ⓒ Ⓓ	20 Ⓐ Ⓑ Ⓒ Ⓓ	25 Ⓐ Ⓑ Ⓒ Ⓓ

Part 9: Assembling Objects (AO)

1 Ⓐ Ⓑ Ⓒ Ⓓ	6 Ⓐ Ⓑ Ⓒ Ⓓ	11 Ⓐ Ⓑ Ⓒ Ⓓ	16 Ⓐ Ⓑ Ⓒ Ⓓ	21 Ⓐ Ⓑ Ⓒ Ⓓ
2 Ⓐ Ⓑ Ⓒ Ⓓ	7 Ⓐ Ⓑ Ⓒ Ⓓ	12 Ⓐ Ⓑ Ⓒ Ⓓ	17 Ⓐ Ⓑ Ⓒ Ⓓ	22 Ⓐ Ⓑ Ⓒ Ⓓ
3 Ⓐ Ⓑ Ⓒ Ⓓ	8 Ⓐ Ⓑ Ⓒ Ⓓ	13 Ⓐ Ⓑ Ⓒ Ⓓ	18 Ⓐ Ⓑ Ⓒ Ⓓ	23 Ⓐ Ⓑ Ⓒ Ⓓ
4 Ⓐ Ⓑ Ⓒ Ⓓ	9 Ⓐ Ⓑ Ⓒ Ⓓ	14 Ⓐ Ⓑ Ⓒ Ⓓ	19 Ⓐ Ⓑ Ⓒ Ⓓ	24 Ⓐ Ⓑ Ⓒ Ⓓ
5 Ⓐ Ⓑ Ⓒ Ⓓ	10 Ⓐ Ⓑ Ⓒ Ⓓ	15 Ⓐ Ⓑ Ⓒ Ⓓ	20 Ⓐ Ⓑ Ⓒ Ⓓ	25 Ⓐ Ⓑ Ⓒ Ⓓ

PART 1: GENERAL SCIENCE (GS)

Time: 11 minutes; 25 questions

<u>Directions</u>: In this section, you will be tested on your knowledge of concepts in science generally reviewed in high school. For each question, select the best answer and mark the corresponding oval on your answer sheet.

1. _____ are necessary for the body's maintenance, growth, and repair.

   (A) Proteins
   (B) Carbohydrates
   (C) Fats
   (D) Vitamins

2. On a Fahrenheit thermometer the boiling point of water at sea level is

   (A) 100°
   (B) 180°
   (C) 212°
   (D) 373°

3. The process by which blood cells absorb oxygen and eliminate carbon dioxide and water vapor is called

   (A) decomposition
   (B) photosynthesis
   (C) oxidation
   (D) respiration

4. _____ carry blood back to the heart from the capillaries.

   (A) Arteries
   (B) Veins
   (C) Ventricles
   (D) Red blood cells

5. Which of the following depicts a chemical process?

   (A) Helium is combined with neon.
   (B) Iron forms rust.
   (C) Sugar dissolves in water.
   (D) Ice melts.

6. What blood type is a universal donor?

   (A) O
   (B) A
   (C) AB
   (D) B

7. Blood enters the right atrium of the heart from the

   (A) aorta
   (B) left ventricle
   (C) pulmonary vein
   (D) vena cava

8. Which of the following substances has the highest pH?

   (A) ammonia
   (B) battery acid
   (C) isopropyl alcohol
   (D) water

9. The bulk of digestion takes place in the

   (A) pancreas
   (B) stomach
   (C) small intestine
   (D) large intestine

GO ON TO THE NEXT PAGE

10. Which of the following is NOT part of a female reproductive system?

    (A) oviduct
    (B) uterus
    (C) ovary
    (D) testes

11. A _____ is a unit of inheritance.

    (A) phenotype
    (B) genotype
    (C) allele
    (D) gene

12. Which of the following is a sedimentary rock?

    (A) granite
    (B) marble
    (C) shale
    (D) slate

13. This is the collection of all ecologically connected species in an area.

    (A) community
    (B) population
    (C) ecosystem
    (D) biome

14. A vulture would be considered a

    (A) producer
    (B) decomposer
    (C) scavenger
    (D) parasite

15. What type of rock is obsidian?

    (A) sedimentary
    (B) igneous
    (C) metamorphic
    (D) none of the above

16. During a lunar eclipse

    (A) the Moon lies between the Earth and Sun
    (B) the Sun lies between the Moon and Earth
    (C) the Earth lies between the Moon and Sun
    (D) none of the above

17. A centimeter is

    (A) one one-hundredth of a meter
    (B) one one-thousandth of a meter
    (C) one-tenth of a meter
    (D) none of the above

18. Momentum is

    (A) the push or pull that forces an object to change its speed or direction
    (B) the rate of change of velocity
    (C) the rate at which an object changes position
    (D) the tendency of an object to continue moving in the same direction

19. What color light has the highest frequency?

    (A) yellow
    (B) green
    (C) red
    (D) violet

20. The major portion of an atom's mass consists of

    (A) neutrons and protons
    (B) electrons and protons
    (C) electrons and neutrons
    (D) neutrons and positrons

GO ON TO THE NEXT PAGE

21. Which of the following is NOT an example of an arthropod?

    (A) crab
    (B) centipede
    (C) sea urchin
    (D) spider

22. Table salt is considered an

    (A) ionic compound
    (B) ion
    (C) covalent compound
    (D) none of the above

23. Over the course of 24 hours

    (A) the Earth rotates 360 degrees around the Sun
    (B) the Moon rotates 360 degrees around the Earth
    (C) the Earth rotates 360 degrees about its axis
    (D) the Moon rotates 360 degrees about its axis

24. Which of the following kingdoms is considered the most primitive?

    (A) Fungi
    (B) Protista
    (C) Monera
    (D) Plantae

25. Which of the following is the phylum that includes man?

    (A) Animalia
    (B) Chordata
    (C) Mammalia
    (D) Primata

STOP. IF YOU FINISH BEFORE THE TIME IS UP, YOU MAY CHECK OVER YOUR WORK ON THIS PART ONLY.

PART 2: ARITHMETIC REASONING (AR)

Time: 36 minutes; 30 questions

<u>Directions:</u> In this section, you are tested on your ability to use arithmetic. For each question, select the best answer and mark the corresponding oval on your answer sheet.

1. John bought a camera on sale that normally costs $160. If the price was reduced 20 percent during the sale, what was the sale price of the camera?

   (A) $120
   (B) $124
   (C) $128
   (D) $140

2. A subway car passes 3 stations every 10 minutes. At this rate, how many stations will it pass in one hour?

   (A) 15
   (B) 18
   (C) 20
   (D) 30

3. On a certain map, $\frac{3}{4}$ inch represents one mile. What distance, in miles, is represented by $1\frac{3}{4}$ inches?

   (A) $1\frac{1}{2}$
   (B) $2\frac{1}{3}$
   (C) $2\frac{1}{2}$
   (D) $5\frac{1}{4}$

4. A certain box contains baseballs and golf balls. If the ratio of baseballs to golf balls is 2:3 and there are 30 baseballs in the box, how many golf balls are in the box?

   (A) 18
   (B) 20
   (C) 36
   (D) 45

5. Four people shared a taxi to the airport. The fare was $36.00, and they gave the driver a tip equal to 25 percent of the fare. If they equally shared the cost of the fare and tip, how much did each person pay?

   (A) $9.75
   (B) $10.25
   (C) $10.75
   (D) $11.25

6. If a car travels $\frac{1}{100}$ of a kilometer each second, how many kilometers does it travel in an hour?

   (A) 36
   (B) 60
   (C) 72
   (D) 100

GO ON TO THE NEXT PAGE

7. $20 - (-5) =$

   (A) -25
   (B) 25
   (C) 15
   (D) -15

8. Ms. Smith drove a total of 700 miles on a business trip. If her car averaged 35 miles per gallon of gasoline and gasoline cost $1.25 per gallon, what was the cost in dollars of the gasoline for the trip?

   (A) $20.00
   (B) $24.00
   (C) $25.00
   (D) $40.00

9. After eating 25 percent of the jelly beans, Brett had 72 left. How many jelly beans did Brett have originally?

   (A) 90
   (B) 94
   (C) 95
   (D) 96

10. A student finishes the first half of an exam in $\frac{2}{3}$ the time it takes him to finish the second half. If the entire exam takes him an hour, how many minutes does he spend on the first half of the exam?

    (A) 20
    (B) 24
    (C) 27
    (D) 36

11. A 25-ounce solution is 20 percent alcohol. If 50 ounces of water are added to it, what percent of the new solution is alcohol?

    (A) $6\frac{2}{3}\%$
    (B) $7\frac{1}{2}\%$
    (C) 10%
    (D) $13\frac{1}{3}\%$

12. Marty has exactly 5 blue pens, 6 black pens, and 4 red pens in his knapsack. If he pulls out one pen at random from his knapsack, what is the probability that the pen is either red or black?

    (A) $\frac{2}{3}$
    (B) $\frac{3}{5}$
    (C) $\frac{2}{5}$
    (D) $\frac{1}{3}$

13. From 1980 through 1990, the population of Country *X* increased by 100 percent. From 1990 to 2000, the population increased by 50 percent. What was the combined increase for the period 1980–2000?

    (A) 150%
    (B) $166\frac{2}{3}\%$
    (C) 175%
    (D) 200%

GO ON TO THE NEXT PAGE

14. If a man earns $200 for his first 40 hours of work in a week and then is paid one-and-one-half times his regular rate for any additional hours, how many hours must he work to make $230 in a week?

    (A) 43
    (B) 44
    (C) 45
    (D) 46

15. If 50 percent of x is 150, what is 75 percent of x?

    (A) 225
    (B) 250
    (C) 275
    (D) 300

16. The total fare for two adults and three children on an excursion boat is $14. If each child's fare is one half of each adult's fare, what is the adult fare?

    (A) $2.00
    (B) $3.00
    (C) $3.50
    (D) $4.00

17. What is the prime factorization of 140?

    (A) 2×70
    (B) 14×10
    (C) $2 \times 2 \times 5 \times 7$
    (D) $2 \times 2 \times 7 \times 10$

18. A painter charges $12 an hour while his son charges $6 an hour. If the father and son worked the same amount of time together on a job, how many hours did each of them work if their combined charge for their labor was $108?

    (A) 6
    (B) 9
    (C) 12
    (D) 18

19. $4! =$

    (A) 24
    (B) 4
    (C) 256
    (D) 16

20. At garage *A*, it costs $8.75 to park a car for the first hour and $1.25 for each additional hour. At garage *B*, it costs $5.50 to park a car for the first hour and $2.50 for each additional hour. What is the difference between the cost of parking a car for 5 hours at garage *A* and parking it for the same length of time at garage *B*?

    (A) $2.25
    (B) $1.75
    (C) $1.50
    (D) $1.25

21. Jan types at an average rate of 12 pages per hour. At that rate, how long will it take Jan to type 100 pages?

    (A) 8 hours and 10 minutes
    (B) 8 hours and 15 minutes
    (C) 8 hours and 20 minutes
    (D) 8 hours and 30 minutes

GO ON TO THE NEXT PAGE

22. Two large sodas contain the same amount as three medium sodas. Two medium sodas contain the same amount as three small sodas. How many small sodas contain the same amount as eight large sodas?

    (A) 24
    (B) 18
    (C) 16
    (D) 12

23. If each digit 5 in the number 258,546 is replaced with the digit 7, how much will it be increased?

    (A) 2,020
    (B) 2,200
    (C) 20,020
    (D) 20,200

24. Michael bought $2\frac{1}{4}$ pounds of lumber at $4.00 per pound. If a 7 percent sales tax was added, how much did Michael pay?

    (A) $9.63
    (B) $9.98
    (C) $10.70
    (D) $11.77

25. The ratio of $3\frac{1}{4}$ to $5\frac{1}{4}$ is equivalent to the ratio of

    (A) 3 to 5
    (B) 4 to 7
    (C) 8 to 13
    (D) 13 to 21

26. A cat is fed $\frac{3}{8}$ of a pound of cat food every day. For how many days will 72 pounds of this cat food feed the cat?

    (A) 160
    (B) 172
    (C) 180
    (D) 192

27. After spending $\frac{5}{12}$ of his salary, a man has $420 left. What is his salary?

    (A) $175
    (B) $245
    (C) $720
    (D) $1,008

28. A stock decreases in value by 20 percent. By what percent must the stock price increase to reach its former value?

    (A) 15%
    (B) 20%
    (C) 25%
    (D) 40%

29. Joan can shovel a certain driveway in 50 minutes. If Mary can shovel the same driveway in 20 minutes, how long will it take them, to the nearest minute, to shovel the driveway if they work together?

    (A) 12
    (B) 13
    (C) 14
    (D) 15

GO ON TO THE NEXT PAGE

30. June's weekly salary is $70 less than Kelly's, which is $50 more than Eileen's. If Eileen earns $280 per week, how much does June earn per week?

    (A) $160
    (B) $260
    (C) $280
    (D) $300

STOP. IF YOU FINISH BEFORE THE TIME IS UP, YOU MAY CHECK OVER YOUR WORK ON THIS PART ONLY.

PART 3: WORD KNOWLEDGE (WK)

Time: 11 minutes; 35 questions

<u>Directions</u>: In this section, you are tested on the meaning of words. Each of the following questions has an underlined word. Select the answer that most nearly means the same as the underlined word and mark the corresponding oval on your answer sheet.

1. <u>Noble</u> most nearly means

   (A) comely
   (B) loose
   (C) majestic
   (D) lackadaisical

2. Couples often have to <u>concede</u> to survive.

   (A) leave
   (B) compromise
   (C) yell
   (D) create

3. <u>Goad</u> most nearly means

   (A) listen
   (B) taunt
   (C) pacify
   (D) ignore

4. Teenagers at the mall love to roam in a <u>herd</u>.

   (A) jacket
   (B) line
   (C) pack
   (D) ratio

5. Panicking in an emergency is not a <u>viable</u> response for an EMT.

   (A) total
   (B) collective
   (C) lucid
   (D) reasonable

6. <u>Judicious</u> most nearly means

   (A) accessible
   (B) cold
   (C) fair
   (D) talkative

7. <u>Hesitating</u> in a time of crisis can often lead to failure.

   (A) broadening
   (B) creating
   (C) leaving
   (D) pausing

8. Applicants who insist on <u>falsifying</u> information ruin the process for everyone.

   (A) fabricating
   (B) listing
   (C) furthering
   (D) taking on

9. <u>Hollow</u> most nearly means

   (A) dangerous
   (B) potent
   (C) empty
   (D) superb

10. <u>Coax</u> most nearly means

   (A) advise
   (B) trade
   (C) plead
   (D) grace

GO ON TO THE NEXT PAGE

11. The <u>monotonous</u> speech left them all feeling sleepy.

    (A) telling
    (B) boring
    (C) caustic
    (D) hilarious

12. A student's <u>consternation</u> may be due to bad teachers.

    (A) desires
    (B) inability
    (C) confusion
    (D) behavior

13. With the holidays approaching, Dave looked forward to a <u>savory</u> feast or two.

    (A) tasty
    (B) guilty
    (C) heroic
    (D) skimpy

14. A man of some <u>renown</u>, the mayor walked with his chest puffed out.

    (A) size
    (B) fame
    (C) confusion
    (D) toil

15. <u>Raconteur</u> most nearly means

    (A) believer
    (B) storyteller
    (C) standout
    (D) pedant

16. She felt that nothing could really <u>quench</u> her curiosity.

    (A) justify
    (B) break
    (C) illuminate
    (D) satisfy

17. The committee was <u>polarized</u> on the issue.

    (A) split
    (B) disgusted
    (C) grateful
    (D) cold

18. The need to be <u>precise</u> was clear to everyone.

    (A) after the fact
    (B) cautious
    (C) exact
    (D) barren

19. Drucker surveyed the <u>terrain</u> before him for water.

    (A) oversight
    (B) landscape
    (C) river
    (D) goal

20. <u>Terminal</u> most nearly means

    (A) easy
    (B) glittering
    (C) busy
    (D) final

GO ON TO THE NEXT PAGE

21. <u>Augment</u> most nearly means

    (A) craft
    (B) end
    (C) throw away
    (D) enhance

22. Her <u>involuntary</u> spasm knocked over a lamp.

    (A) accidental
    (B) basic
    (C) listless
    (D) helpful

23. The other owners accused the brothers of <u>collusion</u>.

    (A) coalition
    (B) secret agreement
    (C) hoping
    (D) pretending

24. The mongoose shows great <u>tenacity</u> in the face of danger.

    (A) fear
    (B) candor
    (C) determination
    (D) speed

25. <u>Tactile</u> most nearly means

    (A) ghastly
    (B) easy
    (C) patient
    (D) tangible

26. No one could <u>portend</u> where they would all end up in five years.

    (A) fake
    (B) lose
    (C) predict
    (D) edit

27. <u>Germinate</u> most nearly means

    (A) seed
    (B) oppress
    (C) adulate
    (D) foster

28. <u>Restore</u> most nearly means

    (A) trip up
    (B) invigorate
    (C) care for
    (D) toughen

29. <u>Filament</u> most nearly means

    (A) horse
    (B) triage
    (C) nightmare
    (D) thread

30. Whatever the original intent, the focus has clearly <u>mutated</u> at this point.

    (A) disappeared
    (B) reiterated
    (C) altered
    (D) intensified

GO ON TO THE NEXT PAGE

31. To be elected president, one must be a calm yet still <u>dynamic</u> figure.

    (A) reassuring
    (B) exciting
    (C) manic
    (D) terrible

32. <u>Congeal</u> most nearly means

    (A) fade
    (B) swirl
    (C) harden
    (D) undulate

33. <u>Reconnoiter</u> most nearly means

    (A) advance
    (B) posit
    (C) grade
    (D) scout

34. Whether one can <u>accrue</u> enough money to live on is always the question.

    (A) accumulate
    (B) acquiesce
    (C) trap
    (D) magnify

35. His <u>innate</u> ability to make the correct turn was amazing.

    (A) unsure
    (B) discussed
    (C) creative
    (D) natural

STOP. IF YOU FINISH BEFORE THE TIME IS UP, YOU MAY CHECK OVER YOUR WORK ON THIS PART ONLY.

PART 4: PARAGRAPH COMPREHENSION (PC)

Time: 13 minutes; 15 questions

<u>Directions</u>: This section contains paragraphs followed by incomplete statements or questions. Read the paragraph and select the answer that best completes the statements or answers the questions that follow, and mark the corresponding oval on your answer sheet.

The first detective stories, written by Edgar Allan Poe and Arthur Conan Doyle, emerged in the mid-nineteenth century, at a time when there was enormous public interest in science. The newspapers of the day continually publicized the latest scientific discoveries, and scientists were acclaimed as the heroes of the age. Poe and Conan Doyle shared this fascination with the methodical, logical approach used by scientists in their experiments, and instilled their detective heroes with outstanding powers of scientific reasoning.

1. The main idea of this passage is

    (A) science fiction was not popular among nineteenth-century readers

    (B) scientific progress made its way into the fiction of the time

    (C) newspapers detailed detective work each day

    (D) the first detective stories were written by scientists

Children have an amazing talent for learning vocabulary. Between the ages of one and seventeen, the average child learns the meaning of about 80,000 words—about 14 per day. Dictionaries and traditional classroom vocabulary lessons only account for part of this knowledge growth. More important are individuals' reading habits and their dialogues with people whose vocabularies are larger than their own. Reading shows students how words are used in sentences. Conversation offers students the chance to ask questions about the language.

2. According to the passage, reading is valuable to students because

    (A) children learn differently than adults

    (B) words used in stories are generally harder

    (C) reading provides vocabulary clues within sentences

    (D) vocabulary is learned mostly through conversation

GO ON TO THE NEXT PAGE

The first truly American art movement was formed by a group of landscape painters that emerged in the early nineteenth century called the Hudson River School. The first works in this style were created by Thomas Cole, Thomas Doughty, and Asher Durand, a trio of painters who worked during the 1820s in the Hudson River Valley and surrounding locations. Heavily influenced by European artists, these painters set out to convey the remoteness and splendor of the American wilderness. The strongly patriotic tone of their paintings caught the spirit of the times, and within a generation the movement had grown to include landscape painters from all over the United States.

3. Which of the following best tells what this passage is about?

    (A) the history of the Hudson River School of painters

    (B) American art movements of the nineteenth century

    (C) how American landscape painters were influenced by European painters

    (D) the artistic origins of nationalism in the United States

The question of whether a child's personality is the result of genetic material inherited from the parents or the nurturing and environment provided by the parents is a perennial subject of debate. While no one would deny that environment and upbringing play a limited role, the genetic traits that a child inherits provide some sort of basic blueprint for who, and what, that child becomes. After all, if one plants tomatoes, _____.

4. Which of the following best completes this passage?

    (A) one must tend them carefully, in order to gather good vegetables

    (B) one had better choose the variety and location with equal care

    (C) one will eventually get tomatoes, but probably not good tomatoes

    (D) one must expect tomatoes to grow, not cucumbers or daffodils

GO ON TO THE NEXT PAGE

5 and 6 refer to the following passage.

The painter Georgia O'Keeffe was born in Wisconsin in 1887, and grew up on her family's farm. At seventeen she decided she wanted to be an artist and left the farm for schools in Chicago and New York, but she never lost her bond with the land. Like most painters, O'Keeffe painted the things that were most important to her, and nearly all her works are portrayals of nature. O'Keeffe became famous when her paintings were discovered in New York by the photographer Alfred Stieglitz, whom she married in 1924. During a visit to New Mexico in 1929, O'Keeffe was so moved by the bleak landscape and broad skies of the Western desert that she began to paint its images.

5. In this context, the word *bleak* most nearly means

    (A) empty
    (B) moody
    (C) cold
    (D) vivid

6. Georgia O'Keeffe's work generally shows

    (A) an ability to paint something complex accurately
    (B) her love for Alfred Stieglitz
    (C) her desire for fame
    (D) her love of the natural land

The four brightest moons of Jupiter were the first objects in the solar system discovered with the use of the telescope. This proof played a central role in Galileo's famous argument in support of the Copernican model of the solar system, in which the planets are described as revolving around the Sun. For several hundred years, scientific understanding of these moons was slow to develop. But spectacular close-up photographs sent back by the 1979 Voyager missions forever changed our perception of these moons.

7. Which best describes the Copernican model of the solar system?

    (A) Planets move counterclockwise as they rotate.
    (B) The Sun and other planets revolve around the Earth.
    (C) The planets move in orbit around the Sun.
    (D) The four brightest moons of Jupiter used to be planets.

GO ON TO THE NEXT PAGE

As the sky opened up and sun at last rushed into the room, Toby smiled knowing that the game would proceed as planned. It had to, if only because his father would be there and it might be the last opportunity he would have to see Toby play. Now the birds began to appear here and there. Toby got out his baseball glove and ball and waited for his dad to arrive to take him to the game.

8. The mood of the character in the passage is

    (A) sad
    (B) careless
    (C) uneasy
    (D) eager

A human body can survive without water for several days and without food for as many as several weeks. If breathing stops for as little as three to six minutes, however, death is likely. All animals require a constant supply of oxygen to the body tissues, and especially to the heart or brain. In the human body, the respiratory and circulatory systems perform this function by delivering oxygen to the blood, which then transports it to tissues throughout the body. Respiration in large animals involves more than just breathing in oxygen. It is a complex process that delivers oxygen while eliminating carbon dioxide produced by cells.

9. Which bodily function, according to the passage, is least essential to the immediate survival of the average human being?

    (A) eating
    (B) drinking
    (C) breathing
    (D) excretion

The media is really out of control. When the press gets a story, it seems that within minutes they have produced flashy moving graphics and sound effects to entice viewers and garner ratings. Real facts and unbiased coverage of an issue are totally abandoned in exchange for an overly sentimental or one-sided story that too often distorts the truth. Viewers need to learn to recognize real reporting from the junk on nearly every television channel these days.

10. The author would be most likely to agree with which of the following?

    (A) Newspapers should have more editorials.
    (B) Flashy graphics add substance to television news reporting.
    (C) Objective news reporting is a dying art.
    (D) Television news anchors are valuable sources of information.

The poems of the earliest Greeks, like those of other ancient societies, consisted of magical charms, mysterious predictions, prayers, and traditional songs of work and war. These poems were intended to be sung or recited, not written down, since they were created before the Greeks began to use writing for literary purposes. The different forms of early Greek poetry all had something in common: They described the way of life of the Greek people. Poetry expressed ideas and feelings that were shared by everyone in a community—their folktales, their memories of historical events, and their religious speculation.

11. Early Greek poetry was which of the following?

    (A) mainly an oral form
    (B) a departure from poetic traditions in other societies
    (C) widely thought to be an act of the gods
    (D) usually about lost love and sadness

GO ON TO THE NEXT PAGE

In computer design, the effectiveness of a program generally depends on the ability of the programmer. Still, remarkable progress has been made in the development of artificial intelligence. This progress has scientists wondering whether it will eventually be possible to develop a computer capable of intelligent thought. When a computer defeated Garry Kasparov, considered by many the greatest chess player of all time, it was taken to be a vindication of the claims of the strongest supporters of artificial intelligence. Despite this accomplishment, others argue that while computers may imitate the human mind, they will never possess the capacity for true intelligence.

12. The main idea of this passage is

   (A) computers can never learn to think
   (B) chess is a game in which computers are superior
   (C) great strides have been made in artificial intelligence
   (D) artificial intelligence is a scientific miracle

13 and 14 refer to the following passage.

Coral reefs are created over the course of hundreds or even thousands of years. The main architect in coral reef formation is the stony coral, a relative of the sea anemone that lives in tropical climates and secretes a skeleton of almost pure calcium carbonate. Its partner is the green alga, a tiny unicellular plant that lives within the tissues of the coral. The two organisms form a mutually beneficial relationship, with the algae consuming carbon dioxide given off by the corals, and the corals thriving on the abundant oxygen produced photosynthetically by the algae.

When the coral dies, its skeleton is left, and other organisms grow on top of it. Over the years the shear mass of coral skeletons together with those of associated organisms combines to form the petrified underwater forest that divers find so fascinating.

13. Which of the following best describes what this passage is about?

   (A) the varieties of animal life that live in coral reefs
   (B) the formation of coral reefs
   (C) the life and death cycles of coral reefs
   (D) the physical beauty of coral reefs

14. The relationship between the coral and the algae is best described as

   (A) parasitic
   (B) competitive
   (C) predatory
   (D) cooperative

GO ON TO THE NEXT PAGE

For do-it-yourself types, the cost of getting regular oil changes seems unnecessary. After all, the steps are fairly easy as long as you are safe. First, make sure that the car is stationary and on a level surface. Always use the emergency brake to ensure that the car does not roll on top of you. Next, locate the drain plug for the oil under the engine. Remember to place the oil drain pan under the plug before you start. When it is drained fully, wipe off the drain plug and the plug opening and then replace the drain plug. Next, simply place your funnel in the engine and pour in new oil. Be sure to return the oil cap when you're done. Finally, run the engine for a minute, and then check the dipstick to see if you need more oil in your engine.

15. After draining the old oil from the engine, you should

    (A) replace the oil cap
    (B) run the engine for a moment and check the dipstick
    (C) wipe off and replace the drain plug
    (D) engage the emergency brake

STOP. IF YOU FINISH BEFORE THE TIME IS UP, YOU MAY CHECK OVER YOUR WORK ON THIS PART ONLY.

PART 5: MATHEMATICS KNOWLEDGE (MK)

Time: 24 minutes; 25 questions

Directions: In this section, you will be tested on your knowledge of basic mathematics. For each question, select the best answer and mark the corresponding oval on your answer sheet.

1. If 48 is divided by 0.08, the result is

   (A) 0.06
   (B) 0.6
   (C) 60
   (D) 600

2. If the number 9,899,399 is increased by 2,082, the result will be

   (A) 9,901,481
   (B) 9,901,471
   (C) 9,902,481
   (D) 9,902,471

3. The cube of 9 is

   (A) 27
   (B) 81
   (C) 243
   (D) 729

4. What is the value of $(-ab)(a)$ when $a = -2$ and $b = 3$?

   (A) −12
   (B) −6
   (C) 6
   (D) 12

5. $(x - 4)(x - 4) =$

   (A) $x^2 + 8x - 16$
   (B) $x^2 - 8x - 16$
   (C) $x^2 - 8x + 16$
   (D) $x^2 - 16x + 8$

6. $0.123 \times 10^4 =$

   (A) 12.3
   (B) 123
   (C) 1,234
   (D) 1,230

7. $\sqrt{100} - \sqrt{64} =$

   (A) 2
   (B) 4
   (C) 6
   (D) 8

8. A circle has a diameter of 6, an area of b square units, and a circumference of c units. What is the value of $b + c$?

   (A) 9π
   (B) 15π
   (C) 18π
   (D) 42π

9. A bag contains 8 white, 4 red, 7 green, and 5 blue marbles. Eight marbles are withdrawn at random. How many of the withdrawn marbles are white if the chance of drawing a white marble is now 1 in 4?

   (A) 3
   (B) 4
   (C) 5
   (D) 6

GO ON TO THE NEXT PAGE

10. Liza has 40 less than 3 times the number of books that Janice has. If B is equal to the number of books that Janice has, which of the following expressions shows the number of books that Liza and Janice have together?

    (A) $3B - 40$
    (B) $3B + 40$
    (C) $4B - 40$
    (D) $4B + 40$

11. If the perimeter of a square is 32 meters, then what is the area of the square, in square meters?

    (A) 16
    (B) 32
    (C) 48
    (D) 64

12. If $x \neq 0$, then $\dfrac{6x^6}{2x^2} =$

    (A) $4x^4$
    (B) $4x^3$
    (C) $3x^4$
    (D) $3x^3$

13. A number is considered "blue" if the sum of its digits is equal to the product of its digits. Which of the following is "blue"?

    (A) 111
    (B) 220
    (C) 321
    (D) 422

14. If $x = \dfrac{1}{8}$, what is the value of y when $\dfrac{2}{x} = \dfrac{y}{4}$?

    (A) $\dfrac{1}{4}$
    (B) 4
    (C) 16
    (D) 64

15. If line p above is parallel to line q, what is the value of $x + y$?

    (A) 90
    (B) 110
    (C) 125
    (D) 180

16. If $3ab = 6$, what is the value of a in terms of b?

    (A) $\dfrac{2}{b}$
    (B) $\dfrac{2}{b^2}$
    (C) $2b$
    (D) $2b^2$

17. For what value of y is $4(y - 1) = 2(y + 2)$?

    (A) 0
    (B) 2
    (C) 4
    (D) 6

GO ON TO THE NEXT PAGE

PLAN

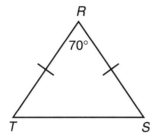

18. In triangle *RST* above, if *RS = RT*, what is the degree measure of angle *S*?

    (A) 40
    (B) 55
    (C) 70
    (D) cannot be determined from the information given

19. When *D* is divided by 15, the result is 6 with a remainder of 2. What is the remainder when *D* is divided by 6?

    (A) 0
    (B) 2
    (C) 3
    (D) 4

20. If the average of 7 consecutive even numbers is 24, then the largest number is

    (A) 26
    (B) 28
    (C) 30
    (D) 34

21. A box that has dimensions of 2 inches by 3 inches by 4 inches has a total surface area of

    (A) 24 square inches
    (B) 26 square inches
    (C) 48 square inches
    (D) 52 square inches

22. If $100 \div x = 10n$, then which of the following is equal to nx?

    (A) 10
    (B) $10x$
    (C) 100
    (D) $10xn$

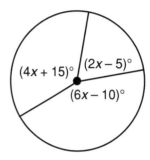

23. In the figure above, what is the value of *x*?

    (A) 15
    (B) 30
    (C) 55
    (D) 70

24. If $7! = 7 \times 6 \times 5 \times 4 \times 3 \times 2 \times 1$, then $5! =$

    (A) 15
    (B) 75
    (C) 120
    (D) 125

25. Melissa took $5n$ photographs on a certain trip. If she gives *n* photographs to each of her 3 friends, how many photographs will she have left?

    (A) $2n$
    (B) $3n$
    (C) $4n - 3$
    (D) $4n + 3$

STOP. IF YOU FINISH BEFORE THE TIME IS UP, YOU MAY CHECK OVER YOUR WORK ON THIS PART ONLY.

PART 6: ELECTRONICS INFORMATION (EI)

Time: 9 minutes; 20 questions

<u>Directions</u>: In this section, you will be tested on your knowledge of electronics basics. For each question, select the best answer and mark the corresponding oval on your answer sheet.

1. A load

    (A) has very low resistance and conducts current throughout the circuit
    (B) is a device that converts electrical energy into heat, light, or motion
    (C) is a voltage source
    (D) switches electrical current off and on

2. Which of the following symbols represents a photosensitive diode?

    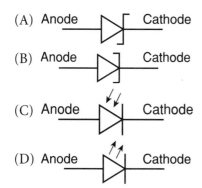

    (A) Anode ────▷│─── Cathode

    (B) Anode ────◁│─── Cathode

    (C) Anode ────▷│─── Cathode

    (D) Anode ────▷│─── Cathode

3. Hertz is a unit of measurement that describes

    (A) frequency
    (B) the number of cycles per second of alternating current
    (C) the cost per day for a rental car
    (D) Both A and B are correct.

4. A(n) _____ is an element that freely conducts electricity.

    (A) insulator
    (B) conductor
    (C) semiconductor
    (D) none of the above

5. An "earth ground" in residential wiring is

    (A) buried conduit
    (B) a copper rod driven into the ground
    (C) made to protect occupants from electrical shock
    (D) All of the above are correct.

6. In _____ electrons flow away from areas of excess negative charge, to those with a deficiency of negative charge.

    (A) electromotive force
    (B) electron flow theory
    (C) Ohm's law
    (D) none of the above

7. Electrical pressure is known as _____.

    (A) voltage
    (B) electrical potential
    (C) ampere
    (D) current

8. This is the symbol for which type of meter?

    (A) Voltmeter
    (B) Ammeter
    (C) ohmmeter
    (D) Galvanometer

GO ON TO THE NEXT PAGE

9. What type of circuit does this symbol represent?

(A) parallel circuit
(B) series-parallel circuit
(C) series circuit
(D) short circuit

10. When resistance in a circuit goes up, current flow

(A) drops
(B) rises
(C) stays the same
(D) none of the above

11. Increasing the voltage in a circuit and keeping resistance the same will result in

(A) increased current flow
(B) decreased current flow
(C) current flow staying the same
(D) zero current flow

12. As resistance in a conductor increases, current flow _____.

(A) stays the same
(B) increases
(C) decreases
(D) none of the above

13. Capacitive reactance decreases as electrical frequency

(A) decreases
(B) increases
(C) varies
(D) gets closer to DC

14. Which is the emitter in the transistor symbol below?

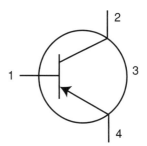

(A) 1
(B) 2
(C) 3
(D) 4

15. The magnetic field in a coil of wire can be made stronger by

(A) increasing the number of turns of wire in the coil
(B) increasing the current flowing through the coil
(C) inserting an iron core into the middle of the coil
(D) all of the above

16. Whenever current passes through a resistance, _____ is generated.

(A) voltage
(B) capacitance
(C) heat
(D) light

17. The formula for Ohm's Law is

(A) $E = I \times R$
(B) $E = I - R$
(C) $E = I + R$
(D) $E = I \div R$

GO ON TO THE NEXT PAGE

18. When current passes through a diode, the diode is

    (A) reverse-biased
    (B) forward-biased
    (C) open
    (D) grounded

19. Transistors are turned on and off by voltages applied to their

    (A) collector
    (B) emitter
    (C) base
    (D) cathode

20. If each resistor in this circuit equals 1,000 ohms, what is the total resistance in this circuit?

    (A) 250 ohms
    (B) 500 ohms
    (C) 1,000 ohms
    (D) 4,000 ohms

STOP. IF YOU FINISH BEFORE THE TIME IS UP, YOU MAY CHECK OVER YOUR WORK ON THIS PART ONLY.

PART 7: AUTO AND SHOP INFORMATION (AS)

Time: 11 minutes; 25 questions

Directions: In this section, you will be tested on your knowledge of automotive and shop basics. For each question, select the best answer and mark the corresponding oval on your answer sheet.

1. High-intensity ultraviolet light is generated during _____.

   (A) stick welding
   (B) MIG welding
   (C) soldering
   (D) A and B

2. Most drill bits are made to cut when

   (A) rotated to the right when looking from the top
   (B) rotated to the left when looking from the top
   (C) rotated to the right when looking from the bottom
   (D) none of the above

3. A motor oil with a ____ prefix for its quality rating would be suited for a diesel engine.

   (A) CD
   (B) SA
   (C) SJ
   (D) none of the above

4. The oil pump

   (A) forms the reservoir for the engine oil at the bottom of the engine
   (B) "screens out" large solids and directs oil into the oil pump
   (C) filters oil from the oil pump before it is sent to the various parts of the engine
   (D) is responsible for pumping the oil through the engine oil galleries

5. A DOHC V-8 engine would have a total of _____ camshafts.

   (A) two
   (B) three
   (C) four
   (D) eight

6. What type of file is depicted below?

   (A) smoothing file
   (B) bastard file
   (C) round rasp
   (D) flat rasp

7. Cutting torches use a mixture of _____ and _____ to produce a high-temperature flame.

   (A) nitrogen : acetylene
   (B) nitrogen : oxygen
   (C) acetylene : helium
   (D) acetylene : oxygen

8. All cars are currently being built with _____ electrical systems.

   (A) direct current
   (B) alternating current
   (C) negative ground
   (D) both A and C are correct

GO ON TO THE NEXT PAGE

9. As lead-acid batteries discharge, their electrolyte gradually turns to

    (A) sulphuric acid
    (B) water
    (C) lead peroxide
    (D) none of the above

10. The camshaft turns at _____ the speed of the engine's crankshaft.

    (A) one-half
    (B) one-fourth
    (C) twice
    (D) triple

11. The outside micrometer is made to measure the

    (A) distance between two parallel surfaces
    (B) thickness of flat objects
    (C) outside diameter of cylindrically shaped objects
    (D) both B and C

12. Which of the following is the most common type of pliers?

    (A)

    (B)

    (C)

    (D)

13. What type of saw is depicted below?

    (A) rip saw
    (B) crosscut saw
    (C) coping saw
    (D) back saw

14. Engine temperature is controlled by the

    (A) electrical system
    (B) water pump
    (C) radiator
    (D) thermostat

15. This image depicts what stroke in the four-stroke cycle?

    (A) intake stroke
    (B) compression stroke
    (C) power stroke
    (D) exhaust stroke

GO ON TO THE NEXT PAGE

16. The three elements needed to initiate combustion are

    (A) air, light, and fuel
    (B) air, fuel, and an ignition source
    (C) air, compression, and an ignition source
    (D) air, heat, and compression

17. A four-cylinder engine's firing order always starts with cylinder number

    (A) 1
    (B) 2
    (C) 4
    (D) 8

18. _____ cylinders will fire in one revolution of a six-cylinder engine.

    (A) two
    (B) three
    (C) four
    (D) eight

19. Which of the following is the LEAST likely to be found in a mechanic's toolbox?

    (A)

    (B)

    (C)

    (D)

20. Most solders are an alloy of _____ and _____.

    (A) tin : copper
    (B) tin : lead
    (C) copper : lead
    (D) brass : copper

21. A lead-acid battery has lead plates immersed in electrolyte composed of _____ and water.

    (A) citric acid
    (B) hydrochloric acid
    (C) carbolic acid
    (D) sulphuric acid

22. The starter motor's drive gear engages with the engine's

    (A) flywheel ring gear
    (B) crankshaft
    (C) vibration damper
    (D) timing chain

23. Sockets come in both _____ and _____ point designs

    (A) 6 and 12
    (B) 7 and 13
    (C) 5 and 10
    (D) 1 and 2

24. The stoichiometric, or ideal, air-fuel ratio is

    (A) 10:1
    (B) 17:1
    (C) 14.7:1
    (D) none of the above

25. With disc brakes, the _____ rotates with the vehicle's wheels.

    (A) brake rotor
    (B) brake caliper
    (C) brake drum
    (D) wheel cylinder

STOP. IF YOU FINISH BEFORE THE TIME IS UP, YOU MAY CHECK OVER YOUR WORK ON THIS PART ONLY.

PART 8: MECHANICAL COMPREHENSION (MC)

Time: 19 minutes; 25 questions

<u>Directions</u>: In this section, you will be tested on your knowledge of mechanics and basic physics. Select the best answer for each question and mark the corresponding oval on your answer sheet.

1. Torque is

   (A) a twisting force
   (B) the same as horsepower
   (C) a push or pull
   (D) Both B and C are correct.

2. Speed is different from velocity because

   (A) speed is a scalar quantity, and velocity is a vector quantity
   (B) velocity involves speed and direction
   (C) speed only expresses a magnitude
   (D) All of the above are correct.

3. A larger mass requires _____ force to achieve the same acceleration rate.

   (A) less
   (B) more
   (C) the same
   (D) none of the above

4. All of the following statements about force are true *EXCEPT*:

   (A) force is a scalar quantity
   (B) force is a push or pull
   (C) greater force results in greater acceleration
   (D) smaller masses require less force to achieve the same acceleration as larger masses

5. In the circuit, how many bulbs will light up when the switch is closed?

   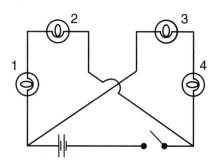

   (A) all bulbs
   (B) two bulbs
   (C) one bulbs
   (D) none

6. A hockey puck sliding on the ice

   (A) has no net force acting on it
   (B) would slide forever if the rink was long enough
   (C) has speed, but not velocity
   (D) has a coefficient of kinetic friction

7. If gear A turns in a counterclockwise direction, how does gear B turn?

   (A) in a counterclockwise direction
   (B) in a clockwise direction
   (C) remains stationary
   (D) turns more slowly than gear A

GO ON TO THE NEXT PAGE

8. All of the following statements about weight are true *EXCEPT*:

    (A) weight increases closer to earth's surface
    (B) weight is not dependent on mass
    (C) weight is greater on planets with greater mass
    (D) weight varies from location to location

9. While attempting to push a heavy box across the floor

    (A) the amount of force required to start the box sliding is more than that required to keep it sliding
    (B) pushing on the box without moving it results in no work being done
    (C) the coefficient of static friction is dependent on the nature of the surface the box is resting on
    (D) all of the above

10. To move the weight at point B, how much effort is required on point A?

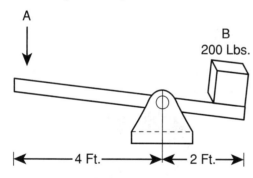

    (A) 100 pounds
    (B) 400 pounds
    (C) 200 pounds
    (D) 800 pounds

11. If it takes a force of 20 pounds to stretch the spring one inch, how much force must be applied to stretch the spring three inches?

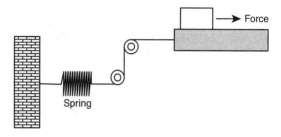

    (A) 60 pounds
    (B) 26 pounds
    (C) 20 pounds
    (D) 30 pounds

12. In order to apply more torque to a bolt, a mechanic would

    (A) use a longer wrench
    (B) apply more force to the wrench
    (C) Both A and B are correct.
    (D) Neither A nor B is correct.

13. A vehicle travels at a constant speed on the highway. It can be said that

    (A) its acceleration rate is zero
    (B) the net forces acting on the vehicle are zero
    (C) the force applied by the vehicle's drive wheels is equal and opposite to the forces that act to slow the vehicle
    (D) All of the above are correct.

GO ON TO THE NEXT PAGE

14. The two water towers below are of equal size and height above the ground. Which of the following statements is true?

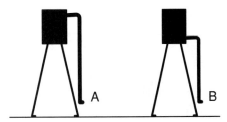

(A) The two towers will release the same amount of water.

(B) Tower B will release more water than tower A.

(C) Tower A will release water three times as fast as tower B.

(D) Tower A will release more water than tower B.

15. Two signs of equal weight are attached to a beam, using cords of equal length. Which of the following statements is true?

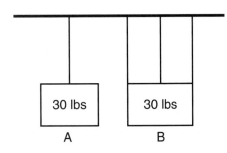

(A) All cords have the same amount of tension because the signs are of equal weight.

(B) The cord holding sign A is under twice the tension of the cords holding sign B.

(C) The cords holding sign B are under 1/3 the tension of the cord holding sign A.

(D) The cords holding sign B are under 1/9 the tension of the cord holding sign A.

16. The illustration is an example of which kind of lever?

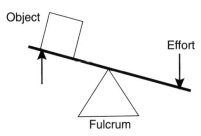

(A) first-class lever

(B) second-class lever

(C) third-class lever

(D) this is not a lever

17. If a vehicle accelerates from a standstill at a rate of $1\frac{m}{s^2}$, its velocity after 10 seconds will be

(A) $0.10\frac{m}{s}$

(B) $0.10\frac{m}{s^2}$

(C) $10\frac{m}{s}$

(D) $10\frac{m}{s^2}$

18. A wheelbarrow, as pictured below, is an example of

(A) a second-class lever

(B) a pulley system

(C) a third-class lever

(D) a crank

GO ON TO THE NEXT PAGE

19. The gears in the illustration all have the same number of teeth. If gear X moves clockwise, which statement about gear Y is true?

    (A) gear Y moves counterclockwise
    (B) gear Y moves twice as fast as gear X
    (C) gear Y moves 1/3 slower than gear X
    (D) gear Y moves clockwise

20. One pound of force is applied to move an object a distance of one foot. _____ of work has been done.

    (A) 1 foot-pound
    (B) 1 watt
    (C) 1 joule
    (D) Both B and C are correct.

21. All of the following statements about energy are true *EXCEPT*:

    (A) energy cannot be created
    (B) the amount of energy in the universe is slowly diminishing
    (C) energy cannot be destroyed
    (D) energy can be converted from one form into another

22. The two pulleys shown have equal weight to move. Which of the following statements is true?

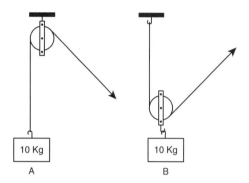

    (A) The pulleys require the same force to move the weight.
    (B) Pulley B will not move the weight.
    (C) Pulley A requires less force to move the weight.
    (D) Pulley B requires less force to move the weight.

23. Which principle of hydraulics states that liquids conform themselves to the shape of their container?

    (A) fourth
    (B) first
    (C) third
    (D) second

GO ON TO THE NEXT PAGE

24. Efficiency of a machine is determined by

    (A) how much horsepower it can produce
    (B) how much energy it consumes
    (C) how much of the source energy is converted into usable energy
    (D) how long the machine can operate at full output

25. In order to hit a baseball farther, the player must

    (A) hit the ball with more force
    (B) make contact with the ball for a longer period of time
    (C) Both A and B are correct.
    (D) Neither A nor B is correct.

STOP. IF YOU FINISH BEFORE THE TIME IS UP, YOU MAY CHECK OVER YOUR WORK ON THIS PART ONLY.

PART 9: ASSEMBLING OBJECTS (AO)

Time: 15 minutes; 25 questions

<u>Directions</u>: In this section, you will be tested on your ability to determine how an object will look when its parts are put together. For each question, select the best answer and mark the corresponding oval on your answer sheet.

For questions 1–12:
Which figure best shows how the objects in the left box will appear if they are fit together?

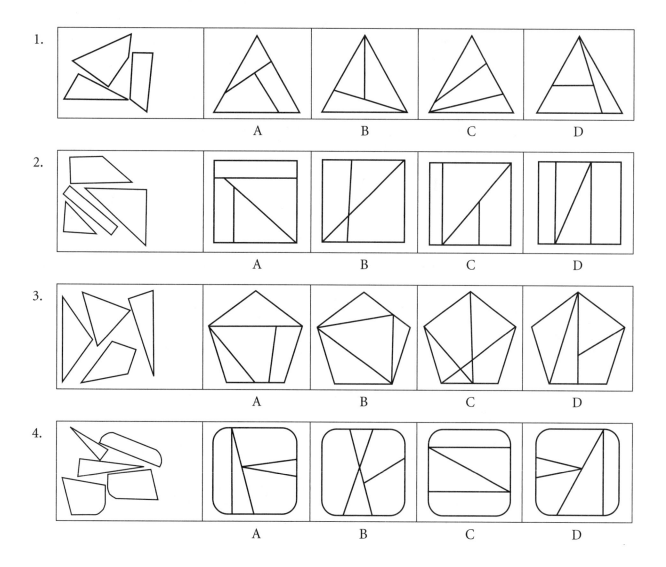

GO ON TO THE NEXT PAGE

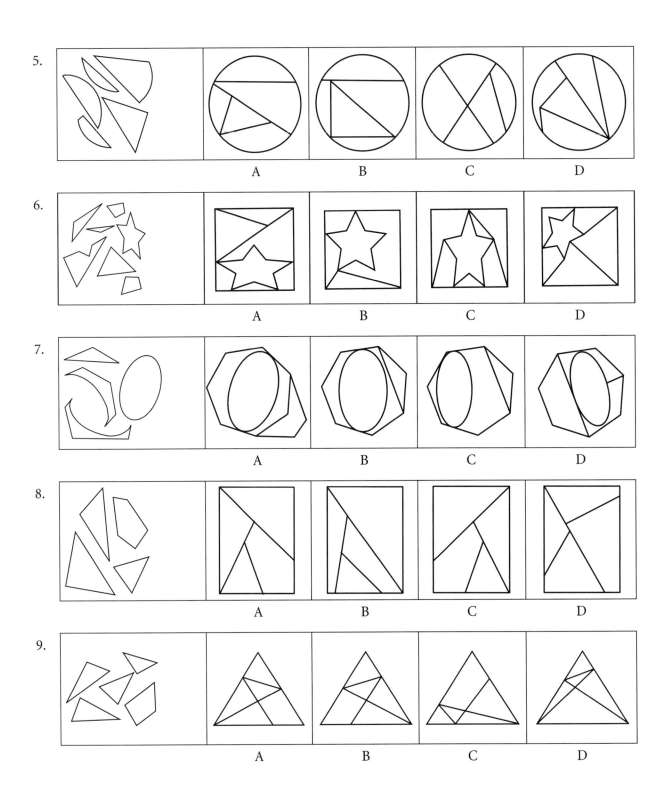

GO ON TO THE NEXT PAGE

KAPLAN

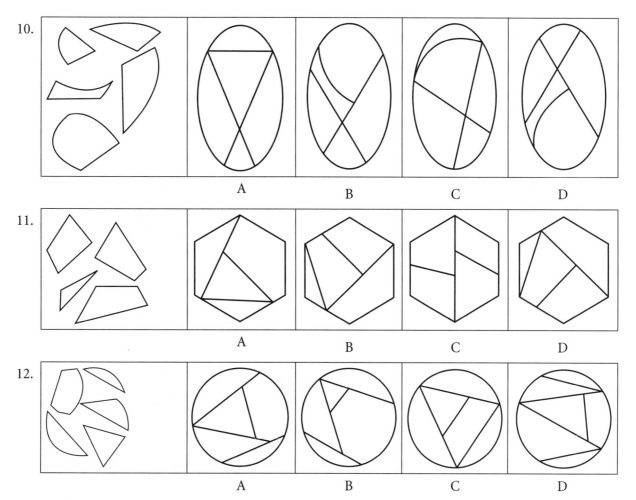

10.

11.

12.

For questions 13–25:

Which figure best shows how the objects in the left box will touch if the letters for each object are matched?

13.

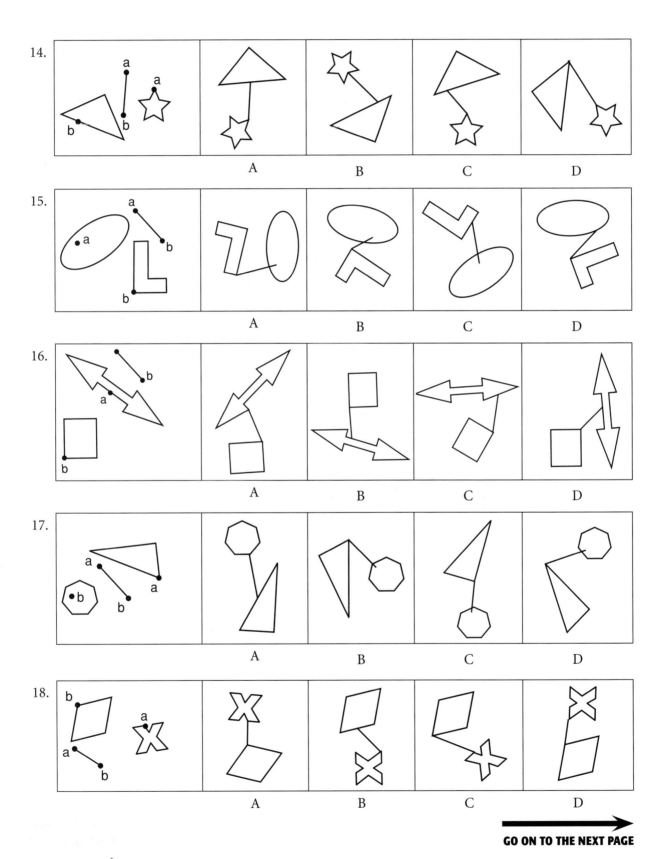

14. A   B   C   D

15. A   B   C   D

16. A   B   C   D

17. A   B   C   D

18. A   B   C   D

GO ON TO THE NEXT PAGE

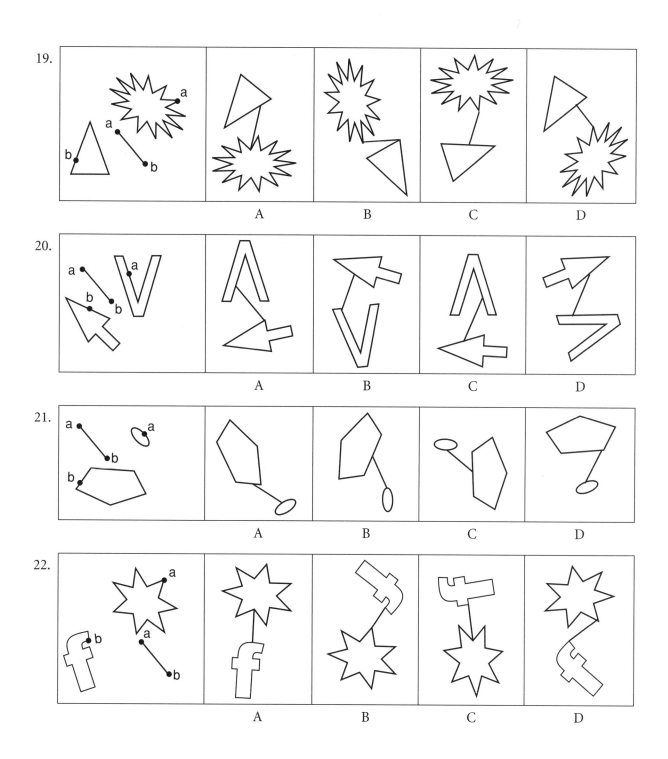

19. A B C D

20. A B C D

21. A B C D

22. A B C D

GO ON TO THE NEXT PAGE

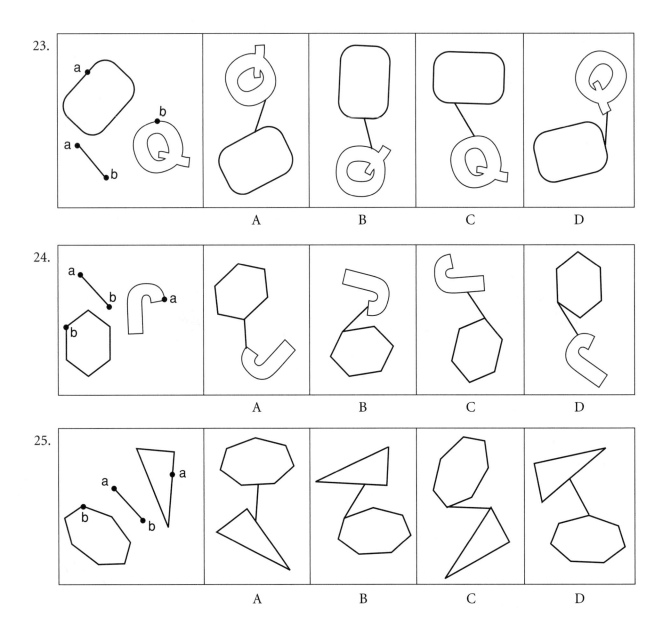

STOP. IF YOU FINISH BEFORE THE TIME IS UP, YOU MAY
CHECK OVER YOUR WORK ON THIS PART ONLY.

STOP! END OF TEST.

ASVAB Practice Test I Answers and Explanations

ANSWER KEY

PART 1: General Science	PART 2: Arithmetic Reasoning	PART 3: Word Knowledge	PART 4: Paragraph Comprehension	PART 5: Mathematics Knowledge
1. A	1. C	1. C	1. B	1. D
2. C	2. B	2. B	2. C	2. A
3. D	3. B	3. B	3. A	3. D
4. B	4. D	4. C	4. D	4. A
5. B	5. D	5. D	5. A	5. C
6. A	6. A	6. C	6. D	6. D
7. D	7. B	7. D	7. C	7. A
8. A	8. C	8. A	8. D	8. B
9. C	9. D	9. C	9. A	9. B
10. D	10. B	10. C	10. C	10. C
11. D	11. A	11. B	11. A	11. D
12. C	12. A	12. C	12. C	12. C
13. A	13. D	13. A	13. B	13. C
14. C	14. B	14. B	14. D	14. D
15. B	15. A	15. B	15. C	15. D
16. C	16. D	16. D		16. A
17. A	17. C	17. A		17. C
18. D	18. A	18. C		18. B
19. D	19. A	19. B		19. B
20. A	20. B	20. D		20. C
21. C	21. C	21. D		21. D
22. A	22. B	22. A		22. A
23. C	23. D	23. B		23. B
24. C	24. A	24. C		24. C
25. B	25. D	25. D		25. A
	26. D	26. C		
	27. C	27. A		
	28. C	28. B		
	29. C	29. D		
	30. B	30. C		
		31. B		
		32. C		
		33. D		
		34. A		
		35. D		

ANSWER KEY

PART 6: Electronics Information	PART 7: Auto and Shop Information	PART 8: Mechanical Comprehension	PART 9: Assembling Objects
1. B	1. D	1. A	1. A
2. C	2. A	2. D	2. C
3. D	3. A	3. B	3. D
4. B	4. D	4. A	4. A
5. D	5. C	5. A	5. B
6. B	6. C	6. D	6. A
7. A	7. D	7. B	7. B
8. C	8. A	8. B	8. C
9. B	9. B	9. D	9. A
10. A	10. A	10. A	10. D
11. A	11. D	11. A	11. B
12. C	12. D	12. C	12. A
13. B	13. C	13. D	13. C
14. D	14. D	14. B	14. C
15. D	15. A	15. C	15. B
16. C	16. B	16. A	16. D
17. A	17. A	17. C	17. B
18. B	18. B	18. A	18. A
19. C	19. C	19. A	19. D
20. A	20. B	20. A	20. C
	21. D	21. B	21. A
	22. A	22. A	22. B
	23. A	23. D	23. C
	24. C	24. C	24. A
	25. A	25. C	25. B

PART 1: GENERAL SCIENCE ANSWERS AND EXPLANATIONS

1. A

Proteins are necessary for the body's maintenance, growth, and repair.

2. C

On a Fahrenheit thermometer the boiling point of water at sea level is 212°. 100° is the degrees Celsius boiling point, and 373° is the degrees Kelvin boiling point.

3. D

The process by which animals convert oxygen and sugars into carbon dioxide and water is called respiration. The reverse process, by which plants convert carbon dioxide and water into sugar and oxygen, is called photosynthesis.

4. B

Veins carry blood back to the heart from the capillaries.

5. B

Iron forms rust when water (or an even better electrolyte) turns iron and oxygen into iron oxide (Fe_2O_3); this is a chemical process. Helium and neon are both inert, so they do not react chemically. Sugar dissolving into water breaks down into particles that are too small to see, which slide between the molecules of water, but neither the sugar nor the water are changed chemically. Ice melting does not alter the chemistry of H_2O.

6. A

Type O is the universal donor, which means that type O blood can be given to anybody without an adverse reaction.

7. D

Blood enters the right atrium of the heart from the vena cava.

8. A

For a substance to have a high pH, it should be basic, or alkaline. A pH of 7 is neutral, like pure water; a pH of less than 7 is acidic; and a pH of greater than 7 is basic. Of the substances listed, only ammonia is a base.

9. C

The bulk of digestion takes place in the small intestine. Food is broken down completely by enzymes produced in the walls of the small intestine, in the pancreas, and in the liver.

10. D

During human reproduction the male organ, or penis, ejaculates more than 250 million sperm, which is produced in the testes. In the female reproductive system, during ovulation, an egg, or ovum, is released from the ovary and begins to travel through the oviduct (fallopian tube) and into the uterus.

11. D

A gene is defined as a unit of inheritance.

12. C

Shale, which derives from clay sediments, is an example of a sedimentary rock.

13. A

A community is the collection of all ecologically connected species in an area. For example, all the different species of birds in a forest might make up a community; however, the fish in the forest ponds are not part of the same community, as they are ecologically separate from the birds.

14. C

A vulture is considered a scavenger. These animals mostly consume refuse and decaying organic matter, especially carrion, which is decaying flesh.

15. **B**

Obsidian is a type of igneous rock.

16. **C**

A lunar eclipse happens when the Moon passes through the Earth's shadow. During a lunar eclipse, the Earth lies between the Moon and Sun.

17. **A**

One one-hundredth of a meter is called a centimeter, and one one-thousandth of a meter is called a millimeter.

18. **D**

Momentum is the tendency of an object to continue moving in the same direction. Velocity is the rate at which an object changes position. Acceleration is the rate of change of velocity. Force is the push or pull that forces an object to change its speed or direction.

19. **D**

Visible light breaks down into different colors, based upon the frequency of the waves. Red has the lowest frequency, which is why wavelengths just below the frequency of visible light are called infrared; likewise, violet has the highest frequency, so wavelengths just above the frequency of visible light are called ultraviolet.

20. **A**

The major portion of an atom's mass consists of neutrons and protons. Electrons, positrons, neutrinos, and other subatomic particles have practically negligible masses.

21. **C**

Arthropods represent a large phylum of the animal kingdom characterized by chitinous exoskeletons, segmented bodies, and jointed legs. Examples include crabs, centipedes, and spiders, but not the sea urchin, which belongs to the phylum Echinodermata.

22. **A**

Table salt is called an ionic compound because each chlorine atom borrows an electron from each sodium atom and the atoms stick closely together to form a very tightly bound crystalline structure when salt is in solid form. When it is placed in solution, however (such as when table salt is poured in water), the atoms dissociate into sodium ions and chloride ions.

23. **C**

Over the course of 24 hours the Earth rotates 360 degrees, or one complete rotation, about its axis.

24. **C**

The Monera kingdom is considered the most primitive kingdom because its organisms are prokaryotic—that is, their cells lack nuclei.

25. **B**

The phylum that includes man is called Chordata, meaning vertebrate animals.

PART 2: ARITHMETIC REASONING ANSWERS AND EXPLANATIONS

1. C

This question asks you to determine the sale price of a camera that normally sells at $160 and is discounted 20%. To solve, determine what 20% of $160 equals. Rewrite 20% as a decimal. 20% = 0.20. So 20% of $160 = 0.20 × $160 = $32. The sale price of the camera would be $160 − $32 = $128, choice (C).

2. B

Since there are 60 minutes in an hour, the subway will pass $\frac{60}{10}$ or 6 times as many stations in 1 hour as it passes in 10 minutes. In 10 minutes it passes 3 stations, so in 60 minutes it must pass 6 × 3 or 18 stations.

3. B

In this question, the ratio is implied: for every $\frac{3}{4}$ inch of map there is 1 real mile, so the ratio of inches to the miles they represent is always $\frac{3}{4}$ to 1. Therefore, we can set up the proportion:

$$\frac{\text{Number of inches}}{\text{Number of miles}} = \frac{\frac{3}{4}}{1} = \frac{3}{4}$$

Now $1\frac{3}{4}$ inches = $\frac{7}{4}$ inches.

Set up a proportion:

$$\frac{\frac{7}{4} \text{ inches}}{\text{Number of miles}} = \frac{3}{4}$$

Cross-multiply:

$$\frac{7}{4}(4) = 3 \text{ (Number of miles)}$$

$$7 = 3 \text{ (Number of miles)}$$

$$\frac{7}{3} = \text{Number of miles}$$

or $2\frac{1}{3}$ = Number of miles

4. D

We can express the ratio of baseballs to golf balls as $\frac{2}{3}$. Since we know the number of baseballs, we can set up a proportion: $\frac{2}{3} = \frac{30}{x}$ where x is the number of golf balls. To solve, we cross multiply to get $2x = 90$, or $x = 45$.

5. D

The total cost of the taxi ride equals $36 + (25% of $36), or $36 + ($\frac{1}{4}$ × $36) = $36 + $9 = $45. If four people split the cost equally, then each person paid $\frac{$45}{4}$, or $11.25 each.

6. A

Find the number of seconds in an hour and then multiply this by the distance the car is traveling each second. There are 60 seconds in a minute and 60 minutes in one hour; therefore, there are 60 × 60, or 3,600, seconds in an hour. In one second the car travels $\frac{1}{100}$ kilometers; in one hour the car will travel 3,600 × $\frac{1}{100}$, or 36 kilometers.

7. B

Subtracting a negative number is basically addition, so 20 − (−5) is really 20 + 5 = 25.

8. C

If Ms. Smith's car averages 35 miles per gallon, she can go 35 miles on 1 gallon. To go 700 miles she will need $\frac{700}{35}$, or 20 gallons of gasoline. The price of gasoline was $1.25 per gallon, so she spent 20 × $1.25, or $25, for her trip.

9. D

Be careful with a question like this one. You're given the percent decrease (25%) and the *new* number (72), and you're asked to reconstruct the original number. Don't just take 25% of 72 and add it on. That 25% is based not on the new number, 72, but on the original number—the number you're looking for. The best way to do a problem like this is to set up an equation:

(Original number) – (25% of Original number) = New number

$$x - 0.25x = 72$$
$$0.75x = 72$$
$$x = 96$$

10. B

The time it takes to complete the entire exam is the sum of the time spent on the first half of the exam and the time spent on the second half. We know the time spent on the first half is $\frac{2}{3}$ of the time spent on the second half. If S represents the time spent on the second half, then the total time spent is $\frac{2}{3}S + S$ or $\frac{5}{3}S$. We know this total time is one hour, or 60 minutes. So we can set up a simple equation and solve for S.

$$\frac{5}{3}S = 60$$
$$\frac{3}{5} \times \frac{5}{3}S = \frac{3}{5} \times 60$$
$$S = 36$$

So the second half takes 36 minutes. The first half takes $\frac{2}{3}$ of this, or 24 minutes. You could also find the first half by subtracting 36 minutes from the total time, 60 minutes.

11. A

You're asked what percent of the new solution is alcohol. The *part* is the number of ounces of alcohol; the *whole* is the total number of ounces of the new solution. There were 25 ounces originally. Then 50 ounces were added, so there are 75 ounces of new solution. How many ounces are alcohol? 20% of the original 25-ounce solution was alcohol. 20% is $\frac{1}{5}$, so $\frac{1}{5}$ of 25, or 5 ounces are alcohol. Now you can find the percent of alcohol in the new solution:

$$\% \text{ alcohol} = \frac{\text{alcohol}}{\text{total solution}} \times 100\%$$
$$= \frac{5}{75} \times 100\%$$
$$= \frac{20}{3}\% = 6\frac{2}{3}\%$$

12. A

To find probability, determine the number of desired outcomes and divide that by the number of possible outcomes. The probability formula looks like this:

$$\text{Probability} = \frac{\#\text{ of desired outcomes}}{\#\text{ of possible outcomes}}$$

In this case, Marty is pulling one pen at random from his knapsack, and we want to determine the probability that the pen is either red or black. There are 5 blue pens, 6 black pens, and 4 red pens in the knapsack. Let's return to the probability formula:

$$\text{Probability} = \frac{\#\text{ of desired outcomes}}{\#\text{ of possible outcomes}}$$

$$= \frac{\text{Number of red + black pens}}{\text{Number of red + black + blue pens}}$$

$$= \frac{4 + 6}{4 + 6 + 5} = \frac{10}{15} = \frac{2}{3}.$$

13. D

Be careful with combined percent increase. You generally cannot just add the two percents, because they're generally percents of different bases. In this instance, the 100% increase is based on the 1980 population, but the 50% increase is based on the larger 1990 population. If you just added 100% and 50% to get 150%, you fell into the test maker's trap.

The best way to do a problem like this one is to pick a number for the original whole and just see what happens. And, as usual, the best number to pick here is 100. (That may be a small number for the population of a city, but reality is not important—all that matters is the math.)

If the 1980 population was 100, then a 100% increase would put the 1990 population at 200. And a 50% increase over 200 would be 200 + 100 = 300.

Since the population went from 100 to 300, that's a percent increase of 200%.

$$\frac{300 - 100}{100} \times 100\% = \frac{200}{100} \times 100\%$$

14. B

To learn the man's overtime rate of pay, we have to figure out his regular rate of pay. Divide the amount of money made, $200, by the time it took to make it, 40 hours. $200 ÷ 40 hours = $5 per hour. That is the normal rate. The man is paid $1\frac{1}{2}$ times his regular rate during overtime, so when working more than 40 hours he makes $\frac{3}{2} \times$ $5 per hour = $7.50 per hour. Now we can figure out how long it takes the man to make $230. It takes him 40 hours to make the first $200. The last $30 are made at the overtime rate. Since it takes the man one hour to make $7.50 at this rate, we can figure out the number of extra hours by dividing $30 by $7.50 per hour. $30 ÷ $7.50 per hour = 4 hours. The total time needed is 40 hours plus 4 hours, or 44 hours.

15. A

The calculations aren't too bad on this one. The most important thing to keep in mind is that you're solving for 75% of x and not for x. First, we are told that 50% of x is 150. That means that half of x is 150, and that x is 300. So 75% of $x = 0.75 \times 300 = 225$. (A) is correct.

16. D

This is a question where backsolving (working with your answer choices) can save you a lot of time. Let's start with choice (B) and see if it works. If (B) is correct, an adult's ticket would cost $3.00, and a child's ticket would cost $1.50. The total fare we are looking for was for two adults and three children. If an adult's fare was $3.00, that total fare would be 2($3.00) + 3($1.50) = $6.00 + $4.50 = $10.50. That's too low since the question states that the total fare is $14.00.

Now see what happens if an adult fare was more expensive. If (D) was correct, an adult's ticket would cost $4.00 and a child's ticket would cost $2.00. The total fare would equal 2($4.00) + 3($2.00) = $8.00 + $6.00 = $14.00. That's the total fare we're looking for, so (D) is correct.

17. C

To find the prime factorization of a number, keep breaking it down until you are left with only prime numbers.

$$140 = 4 \times 35$$
$$= 4 \times 5 \times 7$$
$$= 2 \times 2 \times 5 \times 7$$

18. A

When the painter and his son work together, they charge the sum of their hourly rates, $12 + $6, or $18 per hour. Their bill equals the product of this combined rate and the number of hours they worked. Therefore $108 must equal $18 per hour times the number of hours they worked. We need to divide $108 by $18 per hour to find the number of hours. $108 ÷ $18 = 6.

19. A

$4! = 4 \times 3 \times 2 \times 1 = 24$

20. B

We need to compute the cost of parking a car for 5 hours at each garage. Since the two garages have a split-rate system of charging, the cost for the first hour is different from the cost of each remaining hour.

The first hour at garage *A* costs $8.75

The next 4 hours cost $4 \times \$1.25 = \$5.00$

The total cost for parking at garage *A* = $8.75 + 5.00 = \$13.75$

The first hour at garage *B* costs $5.50

The next 4 hours cost $4 \times \$2.50 = \$10.00$

The total cost for parking at garage *B* = $5.50 + \$10.00 = \$15.50$

So the difference in cost = $15.50 - \$13.75 = \$1.75$, (B).

21. C

Set up a proportion:

$$\frac{12 \text{ pages}}{1 \text{ hour}} = \frac{100 \text{ pages}}{x \text{ hours}}$$

$$12x = 100$$

$$x = \frac{100}{12} = 8\frac{1}{3}$$

One-third of an hour is $\frac{1}{3}$ of 60 minutes, or 20 minutes. So $8\frac{1}{3}$ hours is 8 hours and 20 minutes.

22. B

This problem sets up relationships between large, medium, and small sodas—2 large sodas are equal to 3 medium sodas, and 2 medium sodas are equal to 3 small sodas. How many small sodas equal 8 large sodas? Well, 2 larges equal 3 mediums, so 12 mediums must equal 4×2 or 8 large sodas. You now can find how many small sodas represent 12 mediums. Since 2 mediums are the same as 3 small sodas, 12 mediums must equal 6×3 or 18 small sodas.

23. D

If you change each digit 5 into a 7 in the number 258,546, the new number would be 278,746. The difference between these two numbers would be $278,746 - 258,546 = 20,200$. Choice (D) is correct.

24. A

Since 1 pound of lumber costs $4.00, $2\frac{1}{4}$ pounds of lumber cost $2.25 \times \$4.00 = \$9.00$. Then you need to add 7% sales tax to $9.00. Find 7% of $9.00 by multiplying $0.07 \times \$9.00 = \$0.63$. Add $0.63 to $9.00 to get $9.63, choice (A).

25. D

We are asked which of five ratios is equivalent to the ratio of $3\frac{1}{4}$ to $5\frac{1}{4}$. Since the ratios in the answer choices are expressed in whole numbers, turn this ratio into whole numbers:

$$3\frac{1}{4} : 5\frac{1}{4} = \frac{13}{4} : \frac{21}{4} = \frac{\frac{13}{4}}{\frac{21}{4}} = \frac{13}{4} \times \frac{4}{21} \text{ or } 13 : 21.$$

26. D

This is just another disguised division problem. Divide 72 by $\frac{3}{8}$ and you get:

$$72 \div \frac{3}{8} = 72 \times \frac{8}{3} = 24 \times 8 = 192.$$

27. C

You can save valuable time by estimating on this one. Pay special attention to how much you have left and how much you've already spent. If a man spent $\frac{5}{12}$ of his salary and was left with $420, that means that he had $\frac{7}{12}$ left, and if the man's salary is x dollars, then $\frac{7}{12}x = \$420$. That means that $420 is a little more than half of his salary. So his salary would be a little less than 2($420) = $840. Choice (C), $720 is a little less than $840. So (C) works perfectly, and it's the correct answer here.

28. C

The key to this question is that while the value of the stock decreases and increases by the same *amount*, it doesn't decrease and increase by the same *percent*. When the stock first decreases, that amount of change is part of a larger whole. If the stock were to increase to its former value, that same amount of change would be a larger percent of a smaller whole.

Pick a number for the original value of the stock, such as $100. (Since it's easy to take percents of 100, it's usually best to choose 100.) The 20% decrease represents $20, so the stock decreases to a value of $80. Now in order for the stock to reach the value of $100 again, there must be a $20 increase. What percent of $80 is $20? It's $\frac{\$20}{\$80} \times 100\%$, or $\frac{1}{4} \times 100\%$, or 25%.

29. C

Joan can shovel the whole driveway in 50 minutes, so each minute she does $\frac{1}{50}$ of the driveway. Mary can shovel the whole driveway in 20 minutes; in each minute she does $\frac{1}{20}$ of the driveway. In one minute they do:

$$\frac{1}{50} + \frac{1}{20} = \frac{2}{100} + \frac{5}{100} = \frac{7}{100}$$

If they do $\frac{7}{100}$ of the driveway in one minute, they do the entire driveway in $\frac{100}{7}$ minutes. (If you do $\frac{1}{2}$ of a job in 1 minute, you do the whole job in the reciprocal of $\frac{1}{2}$, or 2 minutes.) So all that remains is to round $\frac{100}{7}$ off to the nearest integer. Since $\frac{100}{7} = 14\frac{2}{7}$, $\frac{100}{7}$ is approximately 14. It takes about 14 minutes for both of them to shovel the driveway.

30. B

Pay attention to your calculations on this one. Proceed carefully, one step at a time, and you're sure to get to the answer they're asking for. We're told that Eileen earns $280 per week. Kelly earns $50 more than Eileen, so Kelly earns $280 + $50 = $330 per week. June's salary is $70 less than Kelly's, so June earns $330 – $70 = $260 per week, and (B) is correct.

PART 3: WORD KNOWLEDGE ANSWERS AND EXPLANATIONS

1. C

Noble means *appearing in a majestic or royal fashion*, therefore choice (C) is correct.

2. B

In this sentence, *concede* refers to a couple's relationship. The intimation is that to succeed, couples need to work together. Of the answer choices, only (B), *compromise*, is a way of working together. By using the context of the given sentence, you could have gotten this answer without knowing the exact meaning of the original word.

3. B

The verb form of *goad* means to *provoke* or *coerce*. Of the answer choices, only (B), *taunt*, is a word that means provoke.

4. C

Using the word *herd* to mean a group being referred to as *a conforming mass*, the correct answer choice is (C), *pack*.

5. D

If you know that an EMT is a rescue technician, then you may grasp the idea that panic is not allowed. *Viable* then can be said to mean rendering something *capable of survival or success*. Of the answer choices given, (C) may seem acceptable. But *lucid* means clear. What we're looking for is a word meaning *acceptable*. Only (D), *reasonable*, works.

6. C

Judicious means *possessing or displaying good judgment*, or in other words, being *fair*.

7. D

Hesitating is a word you probably have seen many times. It can mean different things in different situations. Here it means *to be reluctant or indecisive*. But among the answer choices available, the only possible correct answer is (D), *pausing*.

8. A

You probably know the root word *false* as meaning *wrong*, or in reference to a lie. The textbook definition is to *misrepresent*. Looking at the possible answer choices, choice (A), *fabricating*, which means *making up*, is the best possible answer.

9. C

The word *hollow* means *lacking a center* or *empty*.

10. C

The verb *to coax* means *to try to persuade*. Of the answer choices, only (C), *plead*, approaches being correct.

11. B

The root of the word given, *monotonous*, is "mono" meaning "one." Something *monotone* is in one flat speed and is completely lacking in variety. *Boring* would be another way to say this.

12. C

The big word *consternation* means *unthinkable dismay or frustration*. Of the answer choices, only (C), *confusion*, has this same meaning.

13. A

Savory in reference to food means *appetizing to taste*. Choice (A), tasty, is the best answer.

14. B

Renown means *a person or thing that is wildly famous*. In the case of the mayor, *fame* is the word we are looking for.

15. B

A *raconteur* is someone who tells stories. The word even sounds a little like "recount." Choice (B) is correct.

16. D

To *quench* something is to *sate* or *satisfy* it.

17. A

The word *polarized* has the same root as "polar." Think of "polar opposites" and you will be on the right track. In this case, choice (A), *split*, is closest in meaning to *polarized*.

18. C

Precise means *exact* or *specific*. Choice (C) is the correct answer.

19. B

Terrain comes from the root "terra-" or "earth." So of the answer choices, only river and *landscape* would be appropriate. *Landscape* is the ground in view. Thus, choice (B) is correct.

20. D

Terminal means *relating to an end, limit, or boundary*. Choice (D), *final*, is most similar in meaning.

21. D

Augment means to *enhance something already developed*.

22. A

Something *involuntary* is something done *without plan or accidentally*. Answer choice (A) is correct.

23. B

The noun *collusion* refers to *an agreement of an illicit or secret nature*.

24. C

Tenacity means showing *persistence and determination*. A mongoose is a fierce animal whose ability to stay aggressive even against bigger foes is legendary. Of the answer choices, (C), *determination*, is the best answer.

25. D

Tactile means *relating to the sense of touch*. Of the answer choices, (D), *tangible*, is the most similar in meaning to the original word.

26. C

To *portend* is to make a *prediction*.

27. A

To *germinate* means to *sprout, seed, or bud*. Choice (A) is correct.

28. B

Restore has the prefix "re-", meaning *again*. Thus, *restore* means *bring back something that had been lost*. Of the choices given, both (B) and (D) refer to affecting change on something. But of the two, only (B), *invigorate*, means to renew.

29. D

A *filament* is any *thread or string that is very thin*.

30. C

Mutate is a word you've probably seen before. Comic books often have mutated characters (like the Hulk or Godzilla). The word means *something that has changed from its original state*. Of the choices given, (C), *altered*, is the best choice.

31. B

The adjective *dynamic* means *constantly changing* or *exciting*.

32. C

Congeal means to *solidify, coagulate, or harden.* Choice (C) is correct.

33. D

To *reconnoiter* means to *make a preliminary inspection*, or *see before others*. Of the answer choices, only (D), *scout*, really means the same thing as the given word.

34. A

The verb *accrue* means to *accumulate over time as a result of growth.*

35. D

Something referred to as *innate* is something *that is seen as inherent or natural*. The word even somewhat looks like the root of *natural*. Answer choice (D) is the best answer.

PART 4: PARAGRAPH COMPREHENSION ANSWERS AND EXPLANATIONS

1. B

This is a main idea question that can be answered by asking, "Is this what the author believes?" Choice (B) answers this well, whereas choice (C) cites a detail that helps answer the question, "Why does the author believe this?" Choice (A) is not mentioned in the passage. The author states that science was extremely popular in the nineteenth century, which implies that science fiction was as well, but no direct information is given about the popularity of science fiction. Choice (D) is incorrect because there is no mention of Poe and Doyle being scientists.

2. C

The answer to a detail question such as this will be a paraphrase of what you find in the passage. We are told that reading shows students how words are used in sentences, so (C) is correct. (A) is incorrect because adults are never mentioned. (B) also was not stated in the passage. (D) does not answer the question and is not necessarily true based on the information given.

3. A

Wrong answers on main idea questions are often too broad or too specific. (B) is too broad because the passage is not about all American art movements, only the Hudson River School movement. (C) is too specific because the influence of European painters is just one detail mentioned, while (A), the history of the Hudson River School painters, is being described. (D) is incorrect because nationalism is not the focus of the passage.

4. D

Careful tending, discussed in (A), relates to nurture or upbringing, which the author doesn't consider that important. Devoting equal care to variety and location, (B), would illustrate that nature and nurture are equally important. Choice (C), which

discusses getting tomatoes but not necessarily good tomatoes, is close but no cigar. The issue of quality discussed in choice (C) comes out of nowhere, and thus (C) cannot be the correct answer to this inference question. (D) does a much better job of illustrating that certain outcomes are genetically impossible.

5. A

It is important on vocabulary-in-context questions not to rely on your vocabulary knowledge alone for the word in question, but instead to choose an answer that best represents how the word is being used in the paragraph. *Bleak* can be used to mean *cold*, choice (C), or *depressing*, which might make choice (B) seem appealing. But only choice (A) does not alter the meaning of the sentence when plugged in: "the empty landscape and broad skies." Predicting an answer would have eliminated (D).

6. D

Since the answer to a detail question can be found in the text, the clause "nearly all her works are portrayals of nature" would direct you to choice (D). Choices (A), (B), and (C) all state things that were never mentioned in the passage, a characteristic typical of wrong answer choices to detail questions.

7. C

The text states that the Copernican model of the solar system describes that planets are revolving around the Sun, choice (C). This is contradicted by choice (B). (A) and (D) are not mentioned.

8. D

Toby is smiling while he waits for his father, already holding his baseball glove and ball. He is eager, choice (D), to get to the game. Choice (A) is distracting since it is sad that it might be the last game that Toby's father will be able to attend, but the descriptive language of the passage supports eagerness and not sadness: the sun rushes into the room, now the birds are appearing. Toby is smiling, so there is no evidence of him being uneasy, choice (C). He is anxiously waiting for his father, which contradicts his being careless, choice (B).

9. A

Since the body can survive without food longer than it can survive without drinking (B) or breathing (C), eating is the least essential to survival. Choice (A) is correct. (D) is incorrect because excretion is not mentioned in the passage.

10. C

For inference questions you should read the entire passage and it is often best to attack each answer choice and eliminate those that do not follow from the passage. (B) clearly contradicts the author's words. The author is not likely to agree that news anchors are valuable sources of information, choice (D), but that only "real reporters" are. (A) goes beyond the scope of the passage, and may or may not be true based on what you have read. The correct answer will be something that must be true based on what's given, like choice (C).

11. A

This is a detail question, which means that you can look up the answer in the text. The poems "were intended to be sung or recited, not written down," so they were mainly an oral form, choice (A). (B), which states that Greek poetry was like those of other societies, contradicts the passage. (C) and (D) are not mentioned.

12. C

The correct choice for a main idea question will express what the author believes. The passage states that remarkable progress has been made in artificial intelligence, so choice (C) is correct. While the author discusses the difference of opinion between those who believe that there will eventually be a computer capable of intelligent thought and those who do not, he does not assert the truth of either statement, so choice (A) is incorrect. Be wary of answers such as (D) that use extreme language. Chess is not the main focus of the passage, so choice (B) is incorrect.

13. B

This is a main idea question, so either the correct answer will make so much sense you will want to pick it, or you can eliminate wrong answer choices because they are too broad, too specific, or otherwise don't properly describe the passage. Here the correct answer choice does make a lot of sense. The passage describes how coral reefs are created, so choice (B), the formation of coral reefs, describes the passage well. Choice (A) is out because "varieties" of animal life are nowhere described. (C) is wrong because "death cycles" of coral reefs are never touched upon. And (D) is far too narrow; there's only the barest reference in the passage to "the physical beauty" of coral reefs.

14. D

For this detail question, you just want to pick the answer choice that best paraphrases the relationship between the coral and algae as described in the passage. The passage states that the "two organisms form a mutually beneficial relationship"; in other words, the relationship is cooperative, choice (D).

15. C

For correct sequence questions, look up the answer in the text. According to the passage, when the engine is fully drained, you should wipe off the drain plug and replace it, choice (C).

PART 5: MATHEMATICS KNOWLEDGE ANSWERS AND EXPLANATIONS

1. D

A question like this one tests your ability to play with decimals. $\frac{48}{0.08}$ is the same as $\frac{4,800}{8} = 600$. (D) is correct. When dividing by a decimal, be sure to move the decimal place the same number of spaces for both numbers.

2. A

Be careful with your number crunching here. $9,899,399 + 2,082 = 9,901,481$, choice (A).

3. D

The cube of a number is that number multiplied by itself three times. So the cube of 9 would be $9 \times 9 \times 9 = 729$, choice (D).

4. A

Plug in the values for a and b and remember your order of operations when working through your calculations. When $a = -2$ and $b = 3$,

$$(-ab)(a) = [-(-2) \times 3](-2)$$
$$= (2 \times 3)(-2)$$
$$= (6) \times (-2) = -12, \text{ choice (A)}.$$

5. C

This is a classic product of two binomials. Remember to FOIL, and you're good to go.

$$(x - 4)(x - 4)$$
$$= (x)(x) + (x)(-4) + (-4)(x) + (-4)(-4)$$
$$= x^2 - 4x - 4x + 16$$
$$= x^2 - 8x + 16.$$

Choice (C) is correct.

6. D

$10^4 = 10,000$. So $0.123 \times 10^4 = 0.123 \times 10,000 = 1,230$, choice (D).

7. A

Know your perfect squares. $\sqrt{100} = 10$ and $\sqrt{64} = 8$. So $\sqrt{100} - \sqrt{64} = 10 - 8$, choice (A).

8. B

Given a diameter of 6, the radius must equal $\frac{1}{2}$ of 6, or 3. Next, the circumference $= 2\pi r = 2\pi(3) = 6\pi$. The area $= \pi r^2 = \pi(3^2) = 9\pi$. Summing these two we get: $9\pi + 6\pi = 15\pi$.

9. B

To find the probability of something occurring, divide the number of desired outcomes by the number of total outcomes. In the example of the bag of marbles, you begin with $8 + 4 + 7 + 5 = 24$ marbles, and draw out 8, leaving you with 16 marbles. Out of those 16 marbles, 4 must be white since the chance of drawing a white marble is now $\frac{4}{16}$ or $\frac{1}{4}$. If you are left with 4 white marbles, you must have already withdrawn 4 white marbles. (B) is correct.

10. C

If B is equal to the number of books that Janice has, and we know that Liza has 40 less than 3 times the number of books that Janice has, Liza has $3B - 40$ books, and Janice has B books. Together they have $4B - 40$ books, choice (C).

11. D

The perimeter of a square is $4s$ where s is the length of a side. If a square has a perimeter of 32, then it has a side length of 8. The area of the square is $s^2 = 8^2 = 64$, choice (D).

12. C

You can simplify this expression as follows:

$\dfrac{6x^6}{2x^2} = \dfrac{6}{2}\left(\dfrac{x^6}{x^2}\right) = 3x^4$, choice (C).

Remember to subtract exponents when dividing.

13. C

Go through the answer choices one at a time, and select the choice whose digits have a sum and product that are equal.

(A) 111. Product = $(1)(1)(1) = 1$.
        Sum = $1 + 1 + 1 = 3$. Eliminate.

(B) 220. Product = $(2)(2)(0) = 0$.
        Sum = $2 + 2 + 0 = 4$. Eliminate.

(C) 321. Product = $(3)(2)(1) = 6$.
        Sum = $3 + 2 + 1 = 6$.

Bingo! Choice (C) is correct.

14. D

If $x = \dfrac{1}{8}$, and we are asked to solve for y when $\dfrac{2}{x} = \dfrac{y}{4}$, begin by plugging in $\dfrac{1}{8}$ for x. $\dfrac{2}{\frac{1}{8}} = \dfrac{y}{4}$.

Cross-multiply and solve. $\dfrac{1}{8}y = 8$, so $y = 64$, (D).

15. D

When parallel lines are crossed by a transversal, all acute angles formed are equal, and all acute angles are supplementary to all obtuse angles. So in this diagram, obtuse angle y is supplementary to the acute angle of 55°. Angle x is an acute angle, so it is equal to 55°. Therefore, angle x is supplementary to angle y, and the two must sum to 180°.

16. A

If you're looking for a in terms of b, try to isolate the a on one side of the equation.

$$3ab = 6$$
$$ab = 2$$
$$a = \dfrac{2}{b}$$

(A) is correct.

17. C

Distribute the numbers outside the parentheses and solve for y.

$$4(y - 1) = 2(y + 2)$$
$$4y - 4 = 2y + 4$$
$$2y = 8$$
$$y = 4$$

(C) is correct.

18. B

Since RS and RT are equal, the angles opposite them must be equal. Therefore, angle T = angle S. Since the degree measures of the three interior angles of a triangle sum to 180, 70 + angle measure S + angle measure T = 180, and angle measure S + angle measure T = 110. Since the two angles, S and T, are equal, each must have angle measures half of 110, or 55.

19. B

When D is divided by 15, the result is 6 with a remainder of 2. That means that $D = 6(15) + 2$ or 92. When 92 is divided by 6, the remainder is 2. (B) is correct.

20. C

The average of 7 consecutive even numbers is 24. That means that 24 must be smack dab in the middle of the set of numbers. So the set must be {18, 20, 22, 24, 26, 28, 30}. The largest number is 30, choice (C).

21. D

The surface area of a rectangular solid is $2lw + 2lh + 2wh$. In this case that would be $(2 \times 2 \times 3) + (2 \times 2 \times 4) + (2 \times 3 \times 4) = 12 + 16 + 24 = 52$ square inches, choice (D).

22. A

If $100 \div x = 10n$, that can be rewritten as $\dfrac{100}{x} = 10n$. Cross-multiply and you get $100 = 10nx$. $nx = \dfrac{100}{10} = 10$. (A) is correct.

23. B

A circle contains 360°, so

$$(4x + 15) + (2x - 5) + (6x - 10) = 360$$
$$4x + 2x + 6x + 15 - 5 - 10 = 360$$
$$12x = 360$$
$$x = 30$$

24. C

$5! = 5 \times 4 \times 3 \times 2 \times 1 = 120$. Choice (C) is right.

25. A

If Melissa has $5n$ photographs, and she gives n photographs to each of three friends, she would have given away $3n$ photographs. $5n - 3n = 2n$. (A) is correct.

PART 6: ELECTRONICS INFORMATION ANSWERS AND EXPLANATIONS

1. B

Loads convert electrical energy into some other useful form of energy. Examples of loads include heating elements (heat), light bulbs (light), and solenoids (motion).

2. C

The choices represent four different diode symbols: a zener diode (A), tunnel diode (B), photosensitive diode (C), and light-emitting diode (LED) (D).

3. D

Hertz is an expression of the frequency (cycles per second) of alternating current. One hertz (Hz) is the same as one cycle per second.

4. B

A conductor is an element that freely conducts electricity, whereas an insulator does not conduct electricity at all. A semiconductor is neither a good conductor nor insulator, but has some remarkable properties that make it very useful for making electronic components.

5. D

An earth ground is found outside a building, and normally utilizes conductors such as conduit or pipe that is already in the ground. All of the ground connectors in a residential wiring system will be attached to an earth ground, which is used to "funnel" away stray electricity in appliances and prevent it from causing electrical shock.

6. B

In electron flow theory, electrons flow away from areas of excess negative charge, to those with a deficiency of negative charge. When a conductor is connected across the terminals of the battery, the electrons in the conductor will be forced away from the negative terminal of the battery and toward the positive terminal.

7. A

Electrical pressure is known as voltage, and it is measured in volts (symbolized by the letter V).

8. C

This is the circuit symbol for an ohmmeter (C), which is used to measure resistance.

9. B

This symbol represents a series-parallel circuit, which would have some components, such as an on/off switch, wired in series with a number of loads that are connected in parallel.

10. A

Ohm's law tells us that $E = I \times R$. If voltage E stays constant, and resistance R rises, current I would have to drop.

11. A

Ohm's law tells us that $R = E \div I$. If resistance R stays constant, and voltage E rises, current I will also have to increase.

12. C

As resistance in a conductor increases, current flow decreases. This means that current and resistance are inversely proportional.

13. B

A capacitor is made to block DC (direct current), but allow AC (alternating current) to flow. Capacitive reactance is a capacitor's "opposition" to the flow of current, and this tends to diminish as the frequency of alternating current increases.

14. D

The symbol for the transistor has an arrow that identifies the emitter. The direction of the arrow tells us what type of transistor it is; this is a PNP transistor.

15. **D**

An electromagnet's magnetic field becomes stronger when more turns of wire are added to it, more current is passed through the coil, or an iron core is placed in the middle of the coil.

16. **C**

When current passes through a resistance, a voltage drop will take place. This represents an energy loss, and this energy is normally dissipated in the form of heat.

17. **A**

Ohm's law states that voltage in volts is equal to the current in amperes multiplied by the resistance in ohms, or $E = I \times R$. E represents voltage. This is best remembered as *E*lectromotive force, which is another word for voltage. I represents current. Current is the rate of flow of electrons, or the *I*ntensity of the flow. (Specifically, I is the rate of charge flow.) Finally, R represents *R*esistance.

18. **B**

When current flows freely through a diode, this is known as "forward bias." When current reverses its direction, the diode will block this flow and its condition is known as "reverse bias."

19. **C**

A transistor has three connections: the base, the emitter, and the collector. The transistor is switched off and on by voltages applied to their base. When a voltage appears across the base-emitter junction, the transistor switches on and allows current to flow between the collector and emitter.

20. **A**

For a simple parallel circuit with four resistors of equal value, divide the resistance of a single component by the total number of components. For this parallel circuit, we have four 1,000 ohm resistors, so 1,000 ohms ÷ 4 = 250 ohms.

PART 7: AUTO AND SHOP INFORMATION ANSWERS AND EXPLANATIONS

1. D

Soldering does not produce the electric arc that welding does. Welders must cover all exposed skin with protective clothing and wear face shields with light filters for protection.

2. A

The vast majority of drill bits are made to cut while rotating in a clockwise direction (as viewed from above). These are known as *right hand* drill bits.

3. A

A motor oil with a "C" prefix for its quality rating would be suited for diesel engine use (i.e., a CD rating). Motor oil that had both an "S" and a "C" rating would be suited for either gasoline or diesel engine use. An example of this would be motor oil with a rating of SJ/CD.

4. D

The oil pump is responsible for pumping the oil through the engine oil galleries. It is normally driven by the engine's camshaft.

5. C

A double overhead cam arrangement puts two camshafts into each cylinder head, and makes it so one cam operates the exhaust valves in that head, and the other operates all the intake valves. Thus, four camshafts is the correct answer.

6. C

This is a round rasp. Carpenters would use a round rasp for cleaning out holes in wood. Round rasps are useful for cleaning up holes, where as a flat rasp would be used to smooth flat surfaces.

7. D

Using an oxyacetylene cutting torch involves the burning of oxygen and acetylene to produce a flame that is hot enough to melt steel.

8. A

All automotive electrical systems are designed to utilize direct current (DC). Some vehicles may use a negative ground as part of their electrical systems, but not all cars do, so (C) and (D) are not correct.

9. B

As the lead-acid battery discharges, the sulphuric acid in the electrolyte is reduced to water. The lead plates then become lead sulphate. Charging the battery restores the chemical composition of the lead plates and the electrolyte.

10. A

The camshaft is responsible for the opening and closing of the engine's intake and exhaust valves. The camshaft turns at one-half the speed of the engine's crankshaft.

11. D

The outside micrometer is made to measure the outside diameter of cylindrically shaped objects, as well as the thickness of flat objects.

12. D

The most common type of pliers is the combination slip-joint. These are adjustable at the joint of the two handles of the pliers. With two different positions to choose from, these pliers can grip objects in a wide range of sizes.

13. C

A coping saw is used to make fine, curving cuts. This saw uses a thin, flexible blade that is held tight on a wide frame.

14. D

The thermostat controls engine temperature by allowing coolant to flow into the radiator when the coolant temperature rises above a certain level.

15. A

This image depicts the intake stroke, which is the first stroke in the four-stroke cycle.

16. B

A specific mixture of air and fuel plus an ignition source to get the whole thing going is required for combustion.

17. A

The firing order for four-cylinder engines is 1-3-4-2. Therefore, (A) is the answer.

18. B

It takes two full revolutions of the crankshaft to complete one cycle of events in a four-stroke cycle engine. This means that all of the cylinders in the engine must complete a power stroke in two revolutions of the crankshaft. So in *one* revolution, only three cylinders will fire. Thus, the correct answer is (B).

19. C

Claw hammers are a more specialized tool often preferred by carpenters. Their purpose is two-fold. The hammer head has two ends: One drives nails and the other removes them. This is the tool least likely to be found in a mechanic's tool box.

20. B

Most solders are an alloy of lead and tin. The percentages of each metal in the solder will vary depending on the desired properties of the solder, i.e., melting point.

21. D

An automobile battery, or lead-acid battery, is made up of lead plates immersed in an electrolyte made up of sulphuric acid and water.

22. A

Moving the ignition switch to the "start" position sends an electrical current to the starter solenoid. This engages the starter drive gear onto the engine's ring gear, which is located on the flywheel.

23. A

Sockets come in both 6- and 12-point designs. Six-point is a stronger design, and is usually the mechanic's first choice in the smaller socket drive sizes. However, 12-point is definitely the most popular in large drive sizes.

24. C

The stoichiometric, or ideal, air-fuel ratio is 14.7:1. This means that 14.7 pounds of air is combined with 1 pound of fuel to create an ideal air-fuel mix.

25. A

It is the brake rotor attached to the wheel that rotates. Then the brake caliper clamps to slow the car wheels down.

PART 8: MECHANICAL COMPREHENSION ANSWERS AND EXPLANATIONS

1. A

Torque is a twisting force. This is very different from horsepower (the rate that work is done), or force (a push or pull).

2. D

Speed is very different from velocity, in that velocity (a vector quantity) implies both speed and direction.

3. B

The relationship between force, mass, and acceleration is described using the formula $F = ma$. If mass increases, more force is required to achieve the same acceleration rate.

4. A

Force is a vector quantity. This means that it expresses both magnitude and direction.

5. A

All bulbs will light up when the switch is closed because power will flow to all four bulbs.

6. D

A hockey puck has a coefficient of kinetic friction (however small) that causes it to lose velocity.

7. B

This is an example of meshed gears. Meshed gears always revolve in opposite directions.

8. B

Weight is dependent on mass and acceleration due to gravity ($W = mg$).

9. D

The coefficient of static friction is always greater than the coefficient of kinetic friction. If a force is applied, but the box does not move, no work has been done ($W = Fd$). The nature of the surface the box rests on will define the coefficient of friction between the box and that surface.

10. A

The formula for finding effort required is effort $\times$ effort arm = load $\times$ load arm. In this case, effort $\times$ 4 = 200 $\times$ 2; effort $\times$ 4 = 400; effort = 100.

11. A

Three inches of movement multiplied by 20 pounds per inch is 60 pounds of force.

12. C

Torque (twisting force) can be increased by increasing the length of the wrench, or by increasing the force applied to the wrench.

13. D

A vehicle traveling at a constant speed has no net forces acting on it, so its acceleration rate is zero.

14. B

The outlet pipe on tower B is nearer to the bottom of the cistern than the outlet pipe for tower A. Therefore, it will release more water than tower A.

15. C

Because there are three cords holding sign B, they are under 1/3 the tension of the cord holding sign A.

16. A

The illustration shows a first-class lever, which is used to increase force or distance.

17. C

Accelerating at the rate of $1\frac{m}{s^2}$ will result in a velocity of $10\frac{m}{s}$ at the end of ten seconds. The quantity $1\frac{m}{s^2}$ implies that acceleration is taking place at $1\frac{m}{s}$ each second.

18. A

A wheelbarrow is an example of a second-class lever because the fulcrum is at one end, the effort is at the other, and the load is in between.

19. A

Gears an odd number away from the indicated gear move in the opposite direction, while gears an even number away move in the same direction as the indicated gear. In this case, gear Y is three gears away from gear X, which means it will move in the opposite direction as gear X. Gear X is moving clockwise, so gear Y must move counterclockwise.

20. A

Using the formula $W = F \times d$, it can be seen that 1 pound of force applied through a distance of 1 foot will result in 1 foot-pound of work being done.

21. B

The principle of conservation of energy tells us that the amount of energy in the universe is constant.

22. A

Using the formula $PE = mgh$, the potential energy (PE) of an object is determined by the mass of the object (m), acceleration due to gravity (g), and the height that the object is raised (h).

23. D

The second principle of hydraulics is that liquids conform themselves to the shape of their container. Whether in a pipe or a pump, liquids will always change their shape to fill the space completely.

24. C

A machine's efficiency is expressed as the percentage of the source energy that it converts into usable energy.

25. C

The distance the ball travels will depend upon the impulse that was applied to it. Impulse is determined by multiplying the force by the amount of time that the force was applied.

PART 9: ASSEMBLING OBJECTS ANSWERS AND EXPLANATIONS

For answers 1–12:
Start by numbering the unassembled pieces. Then try to match each piece to parts in each choice.

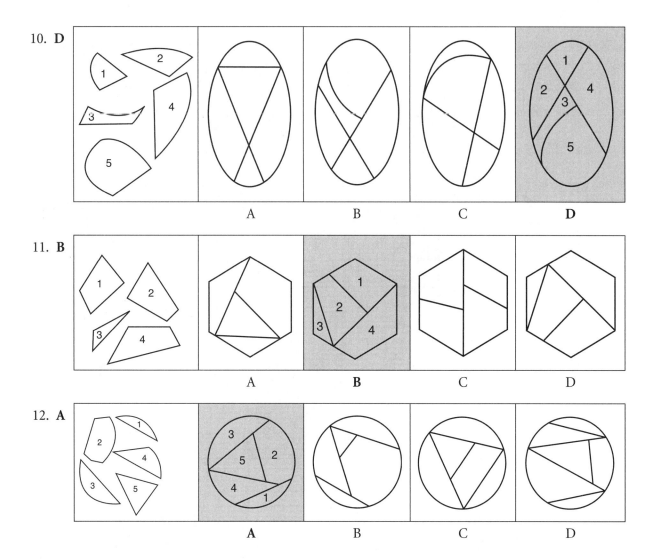

10. **D**

11. **B**

12. **A**

For questions 13–25:

In each choice, place dots where they should be according to the unassembled pieces.

13. **C**

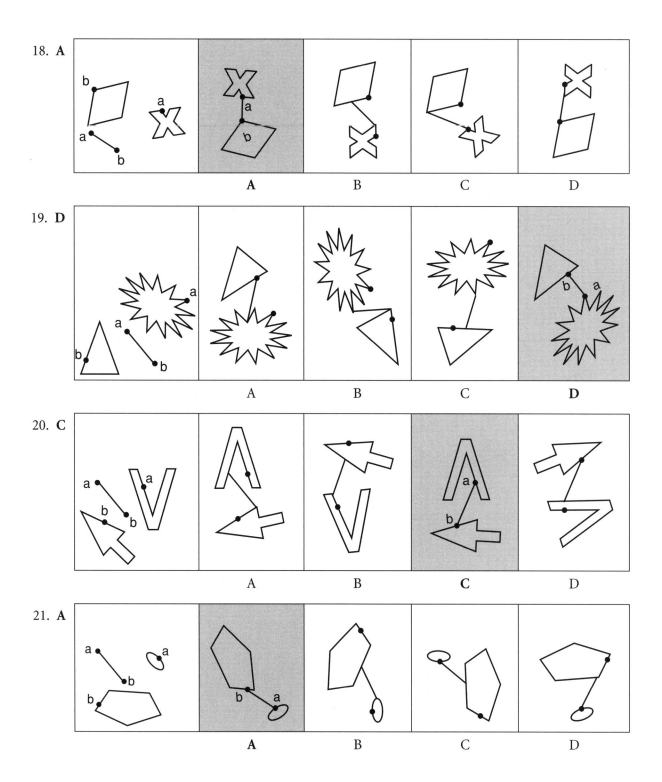

18. **A**

    A   B   C   D

19. **D**

    A   B   C   **D**

20. **C**

    A   B   **C**   D

21. **A**

    A   B   C   D

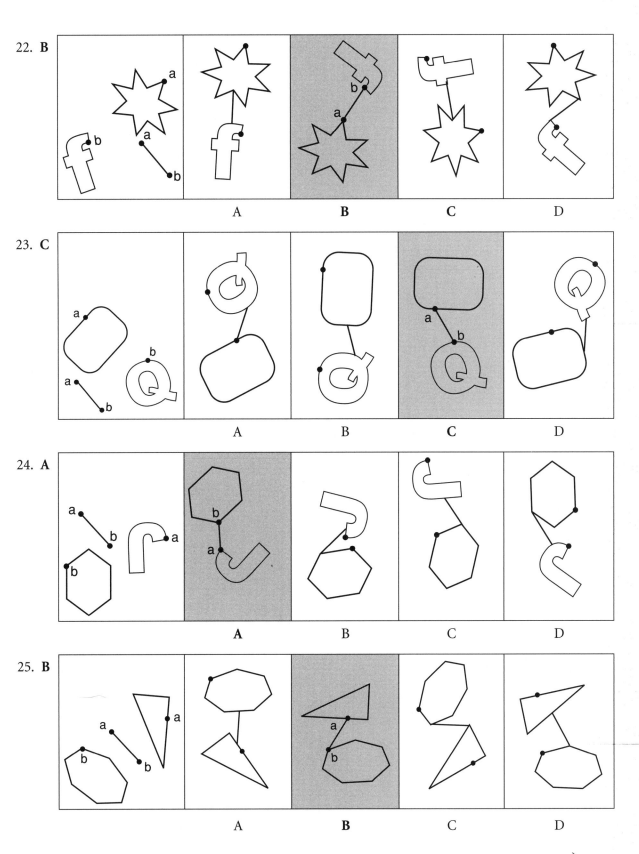

Part Two

AFQT REVIEW

CHAPTER TWO

Word Knowledge

KNOW WHAT TO EXPECT

On the Word Knowledge section of the Paper and Pencil ASVAB, you will be given 11 minutes to complete a total of 35 questions (and 8 minutes for 16 questions on the CAT-ASVAB). Because the questions are short and generally fall into the either-you-know-it-or-you-don't category, most people don't have too much trouble finishing this section.

A little more than half the questions will be straight synonym questions. That's what we call the questions where you are simply given a word and asked to choose the answer choice closest to it in meaning. Here's an example of this type of question.

EXAMPLE 1

1. Gregarious most nearly means

   (A) conspicuous
   (B) twisting
   (C) outgoing
   (D) deep

Unfortunately, these questions don't provide much in the way of context clues. But there are still techniques that can help you find the answer when you aren't sure of the definition. If you were able to come up with (C), *outgoing*, as the closest synonym of gregarious, you may not have to rely on our techniques all that often. But it's still good to learn them for the occasional curve ball that gets thrown on this section.

IT'S NOT JUST A VOCABULARY TEST

Some Word Knowledge questions will provide you with context clues. Make sure to use those clues!

On the remaining questions, the word in question will appear in the context of a sentence. For that reason, we refer to these as in-context questions. Here's an example of this question type.

EXAMPLE 2

2. <u>Nomadic</u> tribes often move their villages when the seasons change.

(A) warlike
(B) wandering
(C) exclusive
(D) hasty

On these questions, you almost always can use the clues in the sentence to help find the answer, even if you aren't familiar with the underlined word. Here, for instance, the sentence describes tribes that move around when the seasons change. What would you call such tribes? Warlike? Not necessarily. Exclusive? Probably not. Hasty? That doesn't quite follow. Oh wait, we skipped one. Wandering? Oh yes, that makes sense! They would be called wandering tribes if they move around with the change of seasons. Surprisingly often, only one answer choice will make sense in the context of the sentence on this question type. The correct answer here has to be (B), and nomadic does in fact mean *wandering* or *migrant*.

IMPROVING AND BUILDING YOUR VOCABULARY

To get a sense of your vocabulary strength, take a few minutes to go through the following list of typical ASVAB vocabulary words and see how many you know. Write your definition and then score yourself. Give yourself one point for every word you know. Answers and study advice based on your score follow the quiz.

resolute _____

terse _____

vanquish _____

cautious _____

lethargic _____

sullen _____

distraught _____

legible _____

fawn (v.) _____

jeer _____

adrift _____

query _____

impure _____

disinterested _____

pathetic _____

Here are the definitions:

resolute	determined
terse	short, abrupt
vanquish	to defeat or conquer in battle
cautious	careful in actions and behaviors
lethargic	sluggish, inactive, apathetic
sullen	depressed, gloomy
distraught	extremely troubled; agitated with anxiety
legible	possible to read or decipher
fawn (v.)	to brown-nose or act in a servile manner
jeer	taunt, ridicule
adrift	wandering aimlessly, afloat without direction

query	a question; to call into question
impure	lacking in purity, containing something unclean
disinterested	impartial; unbiased
pathetic	sad, pitiful, tending to arouse sympathy

If you got six definitions or fewer right, you should start working on building your vocabulary as soon as possible. The techniques and tools in this chapter will teach you ways to improve your vocabulary and help you to make the most out of what you already know about words.

If you got between seven and eleven definitions right, your vocabulary is about average. It's important for you to do well on ASVAB verbal questions in order to ensure your AFQT score is on the level. We recommend using the techniques and tools discussed in this chapter to help you out.

If you got more than eleven definitions right, your vocabulary is above average. You can always polish it further, though. Even if your time is short, you should learn the strategies in this chapter and concentrate on getting the best Word Knowledge score possible.

A Vocabulary-Building Plan

A great vocabulary can't be built overnight, but you can begin building a good ASVAB vocabulary with a little bit of time and effort. Here's our best advice on how to do that.

Learn Words Strategically

The best words to learn are those that often appear on tests like the ASVAB. We recommend that you begin your studies with a vocabulary-building book like Kaplan's *Word Power*. Try to learn ten new words a day by using the following techniques. Keep reviewing those words until you're sure you've committed them to memory.

Study Word Roots and Prefixes

Many tricky vocabulary words are made up of prefixes and suffixes that can get you at least partway to the definition. For instance, if you know that the prefix "bio" means "life," you might be able to decode the definition of *biography*, which means a life story or the history of an individual. Fortunately, many ASVAB word roots may already be familiar if you've studied a foreign language, particularly French, Spanish, or Latin.

Think Like a Thesaurus

On the ASVAB it's better to know a little bit about a lot of words than to know a lot about a few words. For instance, instead of studying the dictionary definition of *lackluster*, you can study *lackluster* in a thesaurus along with words like the following: *drab, dull, flat, lifeless, lethargic,* etc. Instead of just learning one word, learn them together and you'll get 12 words for the price of one definition.

Personalize Your Vocabulary Study

Figure out a study method that works for you and stick to it. Here are some of our studying suggestions:

Use flashcards. Write down new words or word groups and run through them whenever you have some spare time. Write the word or word group on one side of a 3×5 index card and a short definition on the other side.

Create a vocabulary notebook. List words in the left-hand column and their meanings in the right-hand column. Cover up or fold over the page to test yourself. See how many words you can define from memory.

Try to come up with "mnemonics." That is, try to come up with hooks to lodge new words into your head. Create visual images, silly sentences, rhymes, whatever, to build associations between words and their definitions.

PERSONALIZE YOUR HOME STUDY

• Use flashcards.

• Make a vocabulary notebook.

• Look for hooks or phrases that will lodge a new word in your mind.

KAPLAN'S 3-STEP METHOD FOR WORD KNOWLEDGE QUESTIONS

1. Predict a synonym for the underlined word.

On in-context questions, you can usually make a prediction based on the clues in the sentence, even if you are unfamiliar with the word. On synonym questions, you'll have to rely on word knowledge alone. In either case, if you can make an exact prediction, that's excellent. You may proceed to step 2. If not, skip ahead to step 3.

2. Scan the answer choices and pick the closest match.

You may find the very word you predicted among the answer choices, but if not, you should be able to find the closest match. Be somewhat careful here, because sometimes there are close seconds among the answer choices.

3. If you can't come up with an exact prediction, use decoding strategies on the word, and eliminate answer choices accordingly.

If you cannot predict the meaning of the word, try using decoding strategies. Does the word contain word roots that can help you to ascertain the meaning? Have you heard the word used before in a phrase or sentence? Does the word have a positive or a negative charge?

You probably won't see too many words that are totally foreign to you on this test. So use whatever you can dredge up to get a sense of the word and eliminate answer choices that cannot be right. Then guess from the remaining answer choices. Never leave a question blank!

WORD KNOWLEDGE PRACTICE SET

1. <u>Ghastly</u> most nearly means

   (A) fun
   (B) lazy
   (C) torrid
   (D) awful

2. The brothers ran away in <u>cowardice</u>.

   (A) pain
   (B) fear
   (C) hopelessness
   (D) temperance

3. <u>Resignation</u> most nearly means

   (A) losing
   (B) waste
   (C) acceptance
   (D) pride

4. He promised to <u>cooperate</u> with the authorities.

   (A) fight
   (B) talk
   (C) work with
   (D) placate

5. It is <u>imperative</u> that you go to college to get a good job these days.

   (A) sad
   (B) timely
   (C) open
   (D) crucial

6. Everyone says he lost the election due to lack of <u>initiative</u>.

   (A) satisfaction
   (B) irritation
   (C) money
   (D) ambition

7. The city council sought <u>reparations</u> for the oil spill.

   (A) compensation
   (B) sadness
   (C) thanks
   (D) antipathy

8. Many times, the older sibling holds <u>dominion</u> over his younger siblings.

   (A) authority
   (B) safety
   (C) ability
   (D) guilt

9. His professors made a point of acting <u>erudite</u>.

   (A) civil
   (B) progressive
   (C) scholarly
   (D) amoral

10. <u>Tangible</u> most nearly means

    (A) real
    (B) open
    (C) graphic
    (D) costly

ANSWERS AND EXPLANATIONS

1. D

Even if you didn't know that *ghastly* means "awful," if you had a sense that ghastly has a negative charge, you could have gotten the correct answer that way. *Torrid*, by the way, means hot or passionate, as in a "torrid love affair."

2. B

Most people know that *cowardice* means lack of courage, with the closest match here being *fear* (B), but the careless test taker might have chosen a "close second" answer choice from among the other negative words, such as *pain* or *hopelessness*. Don't be in that much of a rush!

3. C

Sometimes, if you are having trouble with a word, such as *resignation* here, try coming up with a different part of speech, and then working on a synonym from the related word. For instance, if you come up with *resigned*, you might be able to make an easier sentence, such as: He was *resigned* to defeat. And from this you figure out that resignation most nearly means *acceptance*.

4. C

Even if you weren't positive of the meaning of *cooperate* here, you could have gotten rid of *fight* (A) and *placate* (D), because these words make no sense in the context of the sentence. And you could also have used word roots to break the underlined word down: *co-* means "with" and *operate* means "work."

5. D

Here's another case where you could get the correct answer just by the context of the sentence (unless you really do think that it is sad that you have to go to college to get a good job these days). *Imperative*, like *crucial*, means very important or essential.

6. D

Choices (A) and (B) clearly make no sense in the context of this sentence. And (C) is a distracter: while he could lose an election because of a lack of *money*, that's not what initiative means. A lack of *ambition* could plausibly explain why he lost the election. *Initiative* more precisely means "resourcefulness," but *ambition* is the closest match here.

7. A

Here none of the answer choices make sense in the context of the sentence except for the correct choice, (A), *compensation*. *Reparations*, like *compensation*, means damages, or repayment for loss suffered.

8. **A**

Here again, you should be able to get the correct answer just from the context of the sentence. Choices (B), (C), and (D) simply make no sense when read into the sentence. *Dominion* means "control," "sway," or "authority."

9. **C**

Choice (C) makes the most sense in the context of the sentence. How would you expect professors to behave. *Civil*? Possibly, but it's not part of the job description. *Progressive*? That describes some professors, but certainly not all of them. *Scholarly*? Why yes! Professors are expected to act like scholars! And as for choice (D), *amoral*, meaning unprincipled or lacking in ethics—let's not even bother going there.

10. **A**

Even if you only "sort of" know the meaning of *tangible*, you might have a sense that something *tangible* can be felt or seen, as oppose to intangible objects that cannot. From that, you should be able to pick *real* (A) as the closest match.

CHAPTER THREE

Paragraph Comprehension

KNOW WHAT TO EXPECT

The ASVAB, like almost every other test of general knowledge, has included a reading section among its several subtests. The Paragraph Comprehension section provides passages for you to read and then asks questions for you to answer based solely on your reading of the passage. But because on the Paper and Pencil version you are given only 13 minutes to read approximately 13 or 14 passages and answer 15 questions—that's 51 seconds per question, including the time it takes to read the passage (and 22 minutes for 11 questions on the CAT-ASVAB)—the ASVAB requires you to read differently from the way you are used to in your everyday life.

The Passages

Compared to typical reading material, Paragraph Comprehension passages are extremely dense with information. Not only is it useless to try to absorb everything you read when you read a Paragraph Comprehension passage, but doing so is likely to slow you down and hurt your score. You need to learn to spend less time reading the passages so that you can spend more time understanding the questions and finding the correct answers.

HOW *NOT* TO READ

- Don't try to understand the passage thoroughly. It's a waste of time.

- Don't get caught up in the details.

- Don't treat every part of the passage the same. Search for the answer you are looking for.

PREPHRASE

To approximate an answer to a question before looking at the answer choices

KAPLAN'S 4-STEP METHOD FOR PARAGRAPH COMPREHENSION

1. Read the question first.

You should always read the question before you look at the passage, because *how* you read and attack the stimulus will vary depending upon the task. If you know what you're supposed to do to the passage, you'll be able to focus your reading on the task ahead.

2. Read the passage.

Once you know your task, read as much of the passage as necessary to answer the question, paraphrasing as you go. Many, but not all, Paragraph Comprehension questions will require you to understand the gist or main idea of the passage. The key is to read actively and skim past unessential information.

3. Try to predict an answer.

Sometimes, depending upon the question, you'll know the answer without even looking at the answer choices. Other times, you'll just have a general idea of what the answer may say. Either way, you'll have an easier time finding the correct answer if you have a sense of what you're looking for.

4. Attack the answer choices.

If you were able to prephrase an answer, skim the choices looking for a match. If you couldn't come up with a prephrase, read and evaluate the answer choices. You can always eliminate answer choices that stray beyond the scope of the passage. Once you've settled on an answer, you may want to reread the question quickly to confirm that you've answered the question that was asked.

PARAGRAPH COMPREHENSION QUESTION TYPES

Main Idea Questions

Nearly anyone who has written a paper for class has been told about *thesis statements*. If you recall, these are the main idea or focus of a written piece. One major type of ASVAB Paragraph Comprehension question asks you to glean from the passage what the main idea, or *thesis*, is. Unlike the details within the paragraph, the thesis is generally less specific. For instance, a thesis might be "Gold is one of the most valuable metals in the world." This would most likely be followed by descriptions of why this is so, perhaps because "gold is scarce," or because "gold is the world's monetary standard." But these statements, alone or together, would only explain *why* gold is valuable. *That* gold is valuable is the main idea.

This, in fact, is one way to distinguish between the main idea and the supporting details. One method for separating the main idea from the rest of the passage is to realize that the supporting details and the main idea answer two different types of questions, as you can see:

This:	*Answers the question:*
Main Idea	What does the author believe?
Supporting Details	Why does the author believe this?

So if you're unsure about whether a particular statement is the main idea, ask yourself: Does this sentence express *what* the author believes? Or does it explain *why* the author believes it?

Unfortunately, sometimes the thesis will not be so clearly laid out for the reader, and the shrewd ASVAB test taker must be prepared to dig out the thesis from the paragraph even if it isn't directly stated. Take a look:

> ### EXAMPLE 1
>
> Alchemy is the name given to the attempt to change lead, copper, and other metals into silver or gold. Today alchemy is regarded as a pseudoscience. It is associated with astrology and the occult in the modern mind, and the alchemist is viewed in retrospect as a charlatan obsessed with dreams of impossible wealth. But for many centuries, alchemy was a respected art. In the search for the elusive secret to making gold, alchemists helped to develop many of the apparatuses and procedures used in laboratories today, and the results of their experiments laid the basic conceptual basis for the modern science of chemistry.
>
> 1. The central point of the passage is that
>
>   (A) alchemy is a pseudoscience
>   (B) alchemists tried, but failed, to make gold from other metals
>   (C) many alchemists dreamt of becoming rich
>   (D) modern chemistry evolved out of alchemy

Here, the main idea has not yet been directly stated by the author, but you should be able to see where the passage is leading. Sure, we tend to look upon alchemy today as a pseudoscience, *but* once it was a widely respected art, and its methods and conclusions led directly to the development of the modern science of chemistry. Thus, the main idea, although not yet explicitly stated, is best expressed by (D), modern chemistry evolved out of alchemy.

One of the tricks to zeroing in on the main idea of the passage is to pay attention to structural clues such as the "but" above. Words such as *but, though, however, although, nonetheless,* and *yet* indicate that the passage is changing directions. When a passage contains one of these contrast clues, the main idea almost invariably occurs after the switch in direction.

Finally, on Main Idea questions it is often easy to eliminate a few answer choices immediately. Wrong answers to Main Idea questions usually do one of the following:

- They're too specific, dealing with just one small detail of the passage.
- They're too general, going beyond the scope of the passage.
- They contradict the passage.
- They're too extreme.

Detail Questions

Detail questions ask you to find specific information explicitly stated within the passage. On these questions, you do not have to read for the author's main idea. In fact, it is crucial on this type of question not to overanalyze or read too much into the question. You should also be somewhat suspicious of answer choices that use the same language as the given passage, because the correct answer to a detail question will almost always be a paraphrase of what you find in the passage.

Check out the following example.

EXAMPLE 2

The dancer and choreographer Martha Graham is regarded as one of the outstanding innovators in the history of dance. In a career that lasted over 50 years, Graham created more than 170 works ranging from solos to large-scale pieces, and danced in most of them herself. Trained in a variety of different international styles of dance, she began in the early 1920s to break away from the rigid traditions of classical ballet. She wanted to create a new dance form that would reflect the transformed atmosphere of the postwar period.

2. Martha Graham introduced new dance techniques in order to

(A) break away from the traditions of classical ballet
(B) attract attention to her dance troupe
(C) express the changed mood of her time
(D) emphasize the rigidity of conventional dance movement

This question is asking *why* Martha Graham introduced new dance techniques. The answer is found in the last sentence: "She wanted to create a new dance form that would reflect the changed atmosphere of the postwar period." The only answer choice that paraphrases this idea is (C).

In this case, choice (A) was a tempting distracter, because its wording can be found almost verbatim in the passage. But choice (A) describes *what* Martha Graham did, not *why* she did it. And of course, you know to be suspicious of answer choices that use the exact same wording as the passage.

In fact, you can almost always eliminate wrong answer choices to detail questions for one of the following reasons:

- They don't answer the question that's been asked.
- They use similar wording to the passage, but distort what was said.
- They contradict the passage.
- They go outside the scope of the passage, stating things that weren't said.
- They use extreme wording.

STRATEGY TIP

The correct answer to a detail question will almost always be a paraphrase of information found in the passage.

Inference Questions

Sometimes the ASVAB will ask you questions about the passage that are not directly stated, but are instead implied by the passage. Scanning the passage details that will allow you to prephrase the answer doesn't work so well on these questions. On these questions, it is often best to read through the entire passage, and then attack the answer choices, eliminating those that do not follow from the passage.

Here are just a few of the ways an inference question might be worded. As you can see, the wording doesn't point you to a specific part of the passage:

Which of the following is implied by the passage?

The author apparently feels that

It can be inferred from the passage that

The answers to inference questions may relate to the main idea of the passage, but they may also follow from secondary details found in the passage. The correct answer to an inference question is the one answer that must be true given what's stated in the passage. Consequently, wrong answer choices on inference questions are those that:

- Contradict the passage
- May or may not be true based on the passage
- Are too strongly worded
- Go beyond the scope of the passage, suggesting things that aren't discussed

Let's take a look at an inference question, one that requires you to connect the dots.

EXAMPLE 3

Dan and Sonya are married and have exactly three children—Betty, George, and Tara—and exactly three grandchildren. George sometimes babysits for Betty's twin daughters, but Tara never babysits for George's child.

3. If these statements are true, which of the following must be true?

   (A) All of Dan's grandchildren are female.
   (B) Tara has no children.
   (C) Tara sometimes babysits for Betty's children.
   (D) Sonya has at least one grandson.

DON'T INFER TOO MUCH!

ASVAB writers don't expect you to infer too much when they ask an inference question. While you may have to combine information from two parts of the passage or make a deduction, you don't want to read between the lines too much. In fact, sometimes the ASVAB writers will make a detail question look like an inference question by asking what the passage implies when the answer is, in fact, explicitly stated.

Here's an instance where you actually do have to put together pieces of information from different parts of the passage. You are told, by inference, that Betty, George, and Tara have three children altogether. You are also told the Betty has two children and that George has one child. Therefore, it must be true that Tara has no children, choice (B). Note that all of the wrong answer choices *could* be true, but none of them has to be true based on the information in the passage.

One other type of inference question requires you to take a look at the passage as a whole and then complete the line of thought. It will ask you to take the stated facts into account and to make a conclusion based on them. Here's an example of what we mean.

EXAMPLE 4

In each of the last three years, a court in this country has awarded a settlement in excess of $300 million. This is a travesty of justice, and it unfairly burdens the court system. To alleviate the strain on the nation's court system, _____.

4. Which of the following best completes the above passage?

   (A) there should be fewer lawsuits
   (B) lawsuits should name more than one defendant
   (C) courts should cease awarding excessive settlements
   (D) settlements should be awarded based solely on need

The correct answer here is choice (C). While the merits of answer choice (A) or (B) are debatable, they are not issues discussed in this passage. And choice (D) likewise is not discussed in the passage, and it's too strongly worded as well. The conclusion you are asked to draw is what should be done to alleviate the burden on the court system. If the gist of the argument is that awards are too big, it would seem logical that if courts stopped being excessive in awarding settlements, it would help alleviate the strain on the courts.

Vocabulary-in-Context Questions

One final type of question found in the Paragraph Comprehension section will ask you for the meaning of a word used in the paragraph. The correct answer will be a word that can replace the word in question without altering the meaning of the sentence.

Here's how we suggest you handle this question type:

1. Read the sentence containing the word, looking for context clues.
2. Predict a word that could replace the vocabulary word.
3. Check the answer choices for a word that matches.
4. Plug your selection into the sentence to make sure it makes sense.

Try this method out on the following Vocabulary-in-Context question.

EXAMPLE 5

Sapphira and the Slave Girl was the last novel of Willa Cather's illustrious literary career. Begun in 1937 and finally completed in 1941, it is regarded by critics as one of her most personal works. Although the story takes place in 1856, well before Cather's own birth, she drew heavily on vivid childhood memories as well as tales handed down by older relatives to describe life in rural northern Virginia in the middle of the nineteenth century. She even went on an extended journey to the area to give the story a further ring of authenticity.

5. In this context, the word *extended* means

    (A) enlarged
    (B) postponed
    (C) stretched
    (D) prolonged

If you tried out our method for handling this question type, you might have predicted that *extended* in this context means "extensive" or "lengthy." By predicting a possible answer, you should have been able to zero in quickly on the closest match, which is (D), prolonged. And if you read that choice back into the sentence, it makes sense: "She even went on a *prolonged* journey to the area to give the story a further ring of authenticity."

Otherwise, you could have eliminated wrong-sounding answer choices. (A), enlarged, might seem related to a long trip, but it doesn't sound quite right in context. (B), postponed, is easy to eliminate; Cather's trip was not put off until a future time. (C), stretched, is a definition of *extended*, but not one that works here. Only choice (D) makes sense in this context.

Now that we've shown you the ins and outs of Paragraph Comprehension, you should try out all the strategies we've discussed in this chapter on the practice set that follows.

PARAGRAPH COMPREHENSION PRACTICE SET

The presidential election in November 2000 showed once again how important it is for all Americans to take advantage of their right to vote. The election was so close that it took weeks to finalize the tally, and the controversy surrounding chads, voting machines, and the court system only served to reinforce the sentiment that each vote counts.

1. The main idea of the passage is that

    (A) voting machines are not adequate
    (B) the Supreme Court should decide who will be the president
    (C) voting is a right that can be taken away
    (D) every voter should exercise his or her right and vote

Four years ago, the governor came into office seeking to change the way politics were run in this state. Now, it appears he has been the victim of his own ambitious political philosophy. Trying to do too much has given him a reputation as being pushy, and the backlash in the state has let him accomplish little. He may very well lose in his reelection bid.

2. The governor's approach to politics was

    (A) business as usual
    (B) overly idealistic
    (C) careless and sloppy
    (D) undeterred by critics

Since its first official documentation by Sir George Everest in 1865, Mount Everest in Nepal has been the "Holy Grail" of mountaineers. Sir Edmund Hillary was the first man to successfully complete the ascent to the peak in May 1953. His feat won him international acclaim, not to mention knighthood. But much less celebrated is the first successful ascent of Everest by a woman, which did not take place until May 16, 1975. Junko Tabei of Japan was the first woman to reach the summit of the world's most famous single peak. The first American woman to scale its heights successfully was Stacy Allison of Portland in 1988.

3. Mount Everest was first conquered by

    (A) Sir George Everest
    (B) Junko Tabei
    (C) Sir Edmund Hillary
    (D) Stacy Allison

It is without question a travesty that our children are no longer given healthy, nutritious food options for lunch in our public schools. Hamburgers, pizza, and chocolate are not only giving our kids a bigger waistline, but these junk foods are also helping teach them poor eating habits. It is imperative that we change the mindset that any food is good food and start offering students better meals at the same prices. Otherwise, a new generation of obese Americans is a given.

4. According to the passage, over the past few years, school lunches have gotten

    (A) more expensive
    (B) more exotic
    (C) healthier
    (D) less nutritious

GO ON TO THE NEXT PAGE

Many times families choose to replace old furniture when just a minor amount of maintenance is all that is needed. To fix a wooden chair that is wobbly, follow these easy steps. First, check the joints of the chair to see if the chair is structurally sound. There should be small dowel rods and a corner block to keep the chair together. Next, use a ripping chisel to remove the corner block. Once the block is free from the chair, you should be able to glue the joints back together. Finally, once the glue looks dry, place the corner block back on the chair and gently mallet the block onto the dowels. In no time, you will have saved not only the chair, but also your hard-earned money!

5. After removing the corner block, you should

    (A) mallet the dowels into place
    (B) check the joints for damage
    (C) glue the joints tightly
    (D) replace the corner block

James felt the pulse of the crowd. There was a low murmur just under the house music. Backstage, his bandmates were tuning or drumming lightly on tabletops. In a few moments, the whole country would watch the band play. What a change from those dingy bars and clubs a few years ago. Maybe all the hard work had finally paid off. Looking down at his callused hands, he wondered if maybe this would be the break they had been working so hard for.

6. The tone of this passage is one of

    (A) sadness
    (B) anticipation
    (C) anger
    (D) ambivalence

Packaging on many popular foods is deceiving to consumers. Too often, the print is small and hard to read. And if you can read it, it's often confusing or intentionally vague. This is especially true on the nutrition label. The government really ought to do something about the nutrition labels on food because the existing laws just don't go far enough.

7. The author would probably support which of the following?

    (A) magazine advertisements for cigarettes
    (B) warning labels on compact discs
    (C) fine print on a contract
    (D) food ads in the Sunday paper

In an age where we have pills for depression, dysfunction, and aggression, not to mention headaches, it is important that we not forget that many drugs can have serious side effects. These may range from internal bleeding, vomiting, or soreness in the limbs to, in more extreme cases, loss of consciousness or even coma. If you experience unwanted side effects, it is important to get to a hospital immediately and seek treatment. Drinking alcohol or smoking cigarettes may also contribute to violent side effects.

8. One of the possible side effects of drugs is

    (A) drinking alcohol
    (B) dysfunction
    (C) internal bleeding
    (D) none of the above

GO ON TO THE NEXT PAGE

A character created at the height of atomic postwar paranoia, the Incredible Hulk is a fascinating look at the dual nature of human beings. On the one hand, he is a mild-mannered, bespectacled scientist. On the other, he is a rampaging beast whose strength is surpassed only by his potential for rage. More than a statement about nuclear dangers, the Hulk is a reflection of the two sides in each of us—the calm, logical human and the raging animal.

9. According to the author, the comic book character of the Hulk is

   (A) a reflection of humanity
   (B) really an animal
   (C) mild mannered
   (D) a protest about atomic power

Once considered the best high school player in the country, the onetime prodigy now spends his days working as a bricklayer for a local construction company. Asked if he is bitter about the way his life turned out, he replies, "Not at all." In fact, he says, his only regret is that he didn't study hard enough and go to college. He still gets recognized on occasion, but an extra 80 pounds and bad knees keep him from reliving his former glory on the court.

10. The word *prodigy* in the passage most nearly means

   (A) depressed loner
   (B) shy scientist
   (C) gifted youngster
   (D) bitter malcontent

ANSWERS AND EXPLANATIONS

1. **D**

From the first sentence to the very last, the reader should be able to glean that the author is vehemently in favor of the idea that "each vote counts." Choice (D) most clearly reflects this sentiment. You can also eliminate wrong answer choices (B) and (C) because they are never mentioned in the passage. And "voting machines," (A), are mentioned in the passage, but only to support the conclusion that every vote counts.

2. **B**

From the information given, you should have seen that the governor was very determined to get things done his way. So his approach could hardly be described as business as usual, choice (A). Nowhere in the passage is his approach described as careless and sloppy, choice (C). And given that the backlash has affected his capacity to succeed, his approach was not undeterred by critics, choice (D). Only (B) is addressed in the paragraph. Seeking to change the way politics are run indicates an idealistic approach to politics.

3. **C**

This detail question asks you for the first person to conquer Mount Everest. Researching the passage, you must be careful not to assume that the mountain is named for its conqueror. While Sir George Everest, (A), first documented and recorded the height of Everest in 1865, it was Sir Edmund Hillary who completed the first ascent to the peak in 1953. The question does not ask for the first woman, or the first American woman, to reach the summit, so (B), Junko Tabei, and (D), Stacy Allison, are out. The correct answer is (C).

4. **D**

The author feels strongly that meals in school cafeterias have become more and more similar to the junk food available at fast food joints. Choice (A) is not applicable, regardless of its validity, because it is not the central point of the passage. Choice (B) is nowhere indicated in the passage, and choice (C) is the opposite of what we are asked in the question. Of the answer choices given, only choice (D), less nutritious, correctly answers the question.

5. **C**

This is a "correct sequence" question, so your first task is to locate the step that discusses removing the corner block. Removing the corner block is finally mentioned in the fifth sentence. After using a ripping chisel to remove the block from the chair, the worker is free to glue the joints back together to tighten them, choice (C).

6. **B**

To correctly gauge the tone of a passage, you should pay attention not only to the details, but also to the language and description. In this passage, James is clearly waiting to go onstage. Words like *pulse*, *murmur*, and *maybe* invite the reader to feel excitement and nervousness as James does. Of the answer choices given, (D) is clearly wrong, as James definitely cares about what is going to happen. He seems wistful, but never sad, (A), or angry, (C). The only answer that successfully captures James's mood is choice (B), anticipation.

7. **B**

Judging from the irate tone of the author and the subject matter at hand, one can safely assume that the author is interested in public safety. Clearly small print is not going to be popular with this author, so choice (C) is out. Choice (D) doesn't make sense and choice (A) is not something thought of as good for public safety. Only choice (B), warning labels on compact discs, is likely to be supported by the author given his passion for consumer labels.

8. **C**

According to the details of the passage, one possible side effect from prescription drug usage is internal bleeding. Others may include vomiting, soreness of the limbs, loss of consciousness, or even coma. Drinking alcohol, (A), can exacerbate side effects, but it is not a side effect itself, and dysfunction, (B), is discussed as one of the conditions treated by drugs, not as a side effect of drug use.

9. **A**

From the details of the passage, it is clear that the author sees the character of Hulk as a symbol. Of the answer choices, only (A) and (D) seem appropriate to readers familiar with Incredible Hulk comic books. And while choice (D) may or may not be true, in this passage, the author chooses to focus on the Hulk's reflection of the dual nature of humans.

10. **C**

According to the passage, the onetime star athlete is now a local bricklayer. There is nothing in the passage to indicate that the person in question was ever a depressed loner (A), shy scientist (B), or bitter malcontent (D), but it only makes sense that he was once a gifted youngster (C). The term *prodigy* refers to a person with natural ability, often at a young age.

CHAPTER FOUR

Math on the ASVAB

KNOW WHAT TO EXPECT

On the ASVAB, solving problems the correct way can slow you down and/or get you into trouble. On other math tests, if you do the work but accidentally miss a step you'll still get partial credit. On the ASVAB you will not.

The two math sections on the ASVAB are called "Arithmetic Reasoning" and "Mathematical Knowledge." Because together they form the quantitative half of the Armed Forces Qualifying Test, you'll want to do well on these sections no matter what your ultimate vocational aim in the military is.

The **Arithmetic Reasoning** section is a 36-minute, 30-question test of your ability to handle arithmetic word problems. This test is designed to measure your ability to apply reasoning to solve common problems involving math. Typical Arithmetic Reasoning questions include questions that involve tallying numbers, as well as questions about rates, percents, ratios, proportions, averages, unit conversions, and the like.

The **Mathematics Knowledge** section is a 24-minute, 25-question test of your understanding of a wide range of concepts in arithmetic, algebra, and geometry. This test is designed to measure general mathematical knowledge. You may still see the occasional word problem on the Mathematical Knowledge section of the ASVAB, but in general the questions are more straightforward than the word problems found on the Arithmetic Reasoning section. For this reason, you are given slightly less time per question on this section than on the Arithmetic Reasoning section.

You are given roughly one minute per math question on the paper and pencil version (about 72 seconds per question on the Arithmetic Reasoning section and 58 seconds per question on the Mathematical Knowledge section, but a minute is close enough) on the ASVAB. And to accomplish this we have developed the Kaplan 3-Step Method for ASVAB Math.

KAPLAN'S 3-STEP METHOD FOR ASVAB MATH

1. Read through the question.

Okay, this may seem a little too obvious. Of course, you're going to read through the question. How else can you solve the problem? In reality, this is not quite as obvious as it seems. The point here is that you need to read the entire question carefully *before* you start solving the problem. If you don't read the question carefully, it's incredibly easy to make careless mistakes.

DON'T WORRY ABOUT ONES THAT GOT AWAY

Sure it feels good to try to answer every question on a given ASVAB math section. By spending more time on the questions you *can* answer, you're likely to get a great score even if you have to guess blindly at a few questions.

2. Solve or Skip.

Remember, on the CAT-ASVAB, you cannot skip questions or go back and change your answer. So you should take your best guess. If you know that the previous question you answered was a blind guess, spend a little extra time trying to get the next one right. If you only have a minute left and several questions remaining, you should guess at random rather than leave anything unanswered.

If you are taking the pencil and paper ASVAB, decide first whether you want to solve a problem or skip it. If you have no idea how to solve the problem, or think it will take a long time to solve, skip it for now and circle the question in your test booklet. Spend time on the problems you can solve quickly, and then return to the ones that give you trouble after you've finished the rest of the section.

3. Look for the fastest way to answer the question.

Once you've understood what the question asks and have decided to tackle it now, it's time to look for shortcuts. Sometimes the "obvious" way to solve the problem is the long way. But if you think carefully, there's often an easier approach.

TEXTBOOK APPROACHES VERSUS BACKDOOR APPROACHES

Two methods in particular are extremely useful when you don't see—or would rather not use—the textbook approach to solving the question. We call these strategies *backsolving* and *picking numbers*. These strategies aren't always quicker than more traditional methods, but they're a great way to make confusing problems more concrete. And if you know how to apply these strategies, you're guaranteed to nail the correct answer every time you use them.

Backsolving

Since almost all the Arithmetic Reasoning questions contain numbers in the answer choices, often you can use this to your advantage by "backsolving." What this means is that sometimes it's easiest to work backwards from the answer choices.

Here's how it works. When the answer choices are numbers, you can expect them to be arranged from small to large (or occasionally from large to small). What you want to do is start with either choice (B) or (C). If that number works when you plug it into the problem, that's the answer, so move on. If it doesn't work, you can usually figure out whether to try a larger or smaller answer choice next. By backsolving strategically this way, you usually don't have to try out more than two answer choices before you zero in on the correct answer. If this seems confusing, check out the following problem and explanation.

> EXAMPLE 1

1. In a certain school, the ratio of boys to girls is 3 to 7. If there are 84 more girls than boys, how many boys are there?

    (A) 48
    (B) 63
    (C) 72
    (D) 147

The correct answer should yield a ratio of boys to girls of 3 to 7, so let's try out choice (B).

If there are 63 boys, there are $63 + 84 = 147$ girls, so the ratio of boys to girls is $\frac{63}{147} = \frac{9}{21} = \frac{3}{7}$, which is just what we want. That means we're done.

Sometimes the answer isn't always the first choice you pick. But usually, when you start with (B) or (C) and that answer doesn't work, you'll know which direction to go. Either (B) or (C) will be too big or too small, leaving you with only one or two answers that could possibly be correct.

Now let's look at another backdoor strategy that comes in handy on a lot of Mathematical Knowledge questions, and also occasionally on Arithmetic Reasoning questions that involve fractions or percents.

Picking Numbers

Sometimes a math problem can seem more difficult than it actually is because it's general or abstract. You can make a question like this more concrete and easier by substituting numbers for the variables. Here's what we mean by picking numbers to make an abstract problem concrete.

EXAMPLE 2

2. When n is divided by 14 the remainder is 10. What is the remainder when n is divided by 7?

(A) 2

(B) 3

(C) 4

(D) 5

For starters, you might note that just because the question contains numbers in the answer choices, that doesn't mean that you can always backsolve. Here, backsolving doesn't make any sense. The problem is confusing because the question contains an unknown value, n, rather than an actual number. So to make this abstract question concrete, you should pick a number for n that leaves a remainder of 10 when divided by 14. The easiest strategy is to pick $n = 24$ (because $14 + 10 = 24$). Now try your number out. $24 \div 7 = 3$ remainder 3. Thus, the answer is (B).

SPEED TIP

When picking a number on a remainder problem, add the remainder to the number you're dividing by.

As we've just seen, picking numbers on problems containing variables involves these steps:

1. Pick nice, easy numbers for the variables in your question.

2. Answer the question using the numbers you've picked. This answer is your target number.

3. Now substitute the numbers you picked for the variables in the answer choices. See which answer gives you your target number.

To be safe, you should always try out all the answer choices. If more than one answer choice gives you your target number, pick different numbers to eliminate the remaining wrong answers.

PICKING GOOD NUMBERS

Don't just pull a number out of a hat. Certain numbers work best on certain types of problems.

- *On percent problems, 100 is an easy number to work with.*

- *On fraction problems, pick the largest denominator in the answer choices.*

Not only does picking numbers make the problems such as the above one easier to understand, but when you solve a problem by picking numbers, you can be sure you got the right answer. This is because you've already proven that your answer works with real numbers; thus there's no need to double-check your work.

The rest of the math section of this book will deal with math content review. Take a look at all of it. Even if you feel comfortable with a particular subject, make sure to do the practice sets. There's no harm in practicing extra problems.

CHAPTER FIVE

Arithmetic Reasoning

As you should know by now, on the Arithmetic Reasoning section of the Paper and Pencil ASVAB, you are given 36 minutes to complete 30 arithmetic word problems. On the CAT-ASVAB, you are given 39 minutes to complete 16 problems.

So let's begin our review.

ARITHMETIC REVIEW

First, take a look at a few definitions.

Number Type	Definition	Examples
Integers	Whole numbers, including 0 and negative whole numbers.	−900, −3, 0, 1, 54
Fractions	A **fraction** is a number that is written in the form $\frac{A}{B}$ where A is the numerator and B is the denominator.	$-\frac{5}{6}, -\frac{3}{17}, \frac{1}{2}, \frac{899}{901}$
	An **improper fraction** is a number that is greater than 1 (or less than −1) that is written in the form of a fraction. An improper fraction can be converted to a **mixed number**.	$-\frac{65}{64}, \frac{9}{8}, \frac{57}{10}$ $-1\frac{1}{64}, 1\frac{1}{8}, 5\frac{7}{10}$
Positive/Negative	Numbers greater than 0 are positive numbers; numbers less than 0 are negative. 0 is neither positive nor negative.	Positive: $\frac{7}{8}$, 1, 5, 900 Negative: −64, −40, −11, $-\frac{6}{13}$

Number Type	Definition	Examples
Even/Odd	An even number is an integer that is a multiple of 2. An odd number is an integer that is not a multiple of 2.	Even numbers: –8, –2, 0, 4, 12, 188 Odd numbers: –17, –1, 3, 9, 457
Prime Number	An integer greater than 1 that has no factors other than 1 and itself. 2 is the only even prime number.	2, 3, 5, 7, 11, 59, 83
Consecutive Numbers	Numbers that follow one after another, in order, without skipping any.	Consecutive integers: 3, 4, 5, 6 Consecutive even integers: 2, 4, 6, 8, 10 Consecutive multiples of 9: 9, 18, 27, 36
Factor	A positive integer that divides evenly into a given number with no remainder.	The complete list of factors of 12: 1, 2, 3, 4, 6, 12
Multiple	A number that a given number will divide into with no remainder.	Some multiples of 12: 0, 12, 24, 60

Positives and Negatives

There are few things to remember about positives and negatives.

Adding a negative number is basically subtraction.

$6 + (-4)$ is really $6 - 4$ or 2.
$4 + (-6)$ is really $4 - 6$ or -2.

Subtracting a negative number is basically addition.

$6 - (-4)$ is really $6 + 4$ or 10.
$-6 - (-4)$ is really $-6 + 4$ or -2.

Multiplying and **Dividing** positives and negatives is like all other multiplication and division, with one catch. To figure out whether your product is positive or negative, simply count the number of negatives you had to start. If you had an odd number of negatives, the product is negative. If you had an even number of negatives, the product is positive.

$6 \times (-4) = -24$ (1 negative → negative product)
$(-6) \times (-4) = 24$ (2 negatives → positive product)
$(-1) \times (-6) \times (-4) = -24$ (3 negatives → negative product)

DIVIDING POSITIVES AND NEGATIVES

Negative ÷ negative = positive

Positive ÷ negative = negative

Similarly,

$-24 \div 6 = -4$ (1 negative → negative quotient)
$-24 \div (-4) = 6$ (2 negatives → positive quotient)

Factors and Multiples

To find the **prime factorization** of a number, keep breaking it down until you are left with only prime numbers.

To find the prime factorization of 168:

$$168 = 4 \times 42$$
$$= 4 \times 6 \times 7$$
$$= 2 \times 2 \times 2 \times 3 \times 7$$

To find the **greatest common factor (GCF)** of two integers, break down both integers into their prime factorizations and multiply all prime factors they have in common.

If you're looking for the greatest common factor of 40 and 140, first identify the prime factors of each integer.

$$40 = 4 \times 10$$
$$= 2 \times 2 \times 2 \times 5$$

$$140 = 10 \times 14$$
$$= 2 \times 5 \times 2 \times 7$$
$$= 2 \times 2 \times 5 \times 7$$

Next, see what prime factors the two numbers have in common and then multiply these common factors.

Both integers share two 2s and a 5, so the GCF is $2 \times 2 \times 5$ or 20.

If you need to find a **common multiple** of two integers, you can always multiply them. However, you can use prime factors to find the **least common multiple (LCM)**. To do this, multiply all of the prime factors of each integer as many times as they appear. When a prime factor appears a different number of times in the integers, then that prime factor is to be multiplied the number of times that the prime factor appears in the integer containing the prime factor the greatest number of times. This may sound confusing, but it is pretty clear once it's demonstrated. Take a look at the example to see how it works.

Common multiple of 20 and 16:

$$20 \times 16 = 320$$

320 is a common multiple of 20 and 16, but it is not the least common multiple.

Least common multiple of 20 and 16:

$$20 = 2 \times 2 \times 5$$
$$16 = 2 \times 2 \times 2 \times 2$$

Least common multiple = $2 \times 2 \times 2 \times 2 \times 5 = 80$

Notice that the prime factor 2 occurs 2 times in 20 and 4 times in 16, so when finding the least common multiple, we took 4 factors of the prime number 2.

REMEMBER *PEMDAS*

When performing multiple operations, remember PEMDAS: **P**arentheses, **E**xponents, **M**ultiplication and **D**ivision, **A**ddition and **S**ubtraction. You may find it easier to remember as *Please Excuse My Dear Aunt Sally*.

The Order of Operations

You need to remember the order in which arithmetic operations must be performed. PEMDAS may help you remember the order.

P̲lease = Parentheses
E̲xcuse = Exponents
M̲y D̲ear = Multiplication and Division (from left to right)
A̲unt S̲ally = Addition and Subtraction (from left to right)

For example:

$$3^3 - 8(4 - 2) + 60 \div 4$$
$$= 3^3 - 8(2) + 60 \div 4$$
$$= 27 - 8(2) + 60 \div 4$$
$$= 27 - 16 + 15$$
$$= 11 + 15$$
$$= 26$$

Fractions and Decimals

Generally, it's a good idea to **reduce fractions** when solving math questions. To do this, simply cancel all factors that the numerator and denominator have in common.

$$\frac{28}{36} = \frac{4 \times 7}{4 \times 9} = \frac{7}{9}$$

To **add fractions**, get a common denominator and then add the numerators.

$$\frac{1}{4} + \frac{1}{3} = \frac{3}{12} + \frac{4}{12} = \frac{3+4}{12} = \frac{7}{12}$$

To **subtract fractions**, get a common denominator and then subtract the numerators.

$$\frac{1}{4} - \frac{1}{3} = \frac{3}{12} - \frac{4}{12} = \frac{3-4}{12} = -\frac{1}{12}$$

To **multiply fractions**, multiply the numerators and multiply the denominators.

$$\frac{1}{4} \times \frac{1}{3} = \frac{1 \times 1}{4 \times 3} = \frac{1}{12}$$

DIVISIBILITY BY FRACTIONS

Dividing by a fraction is the same as multiplying by its reciprocal.

To **divide fractions**, invert the second fraction and multiply. In other words, multiply the first fraction by the reciprocal of the second fraction.

$$\frac{1}{4} \div \frac{1}{3} = \frac{1}{4} \times \frac{3}{1} = \frac{1 \times 3}{4 \times 1} = \frac{3}{4}$$

To **compare fractions**, multiply the numerator of the first fraction by the denominator of the second fraction to get a product. Then, multiply the numerator of the second fraction by the denominator of the first fraction to get a second product. If the first product is greater, the first fraction is greater. If the second product is greater, the second fraction is greater.

Compare $\frac{2}{3}$ and $\frac{5}{8}$.

$$2 \times 8 = 16$$
$$5 \times 3 = 15$$

16 is greater than 15, so $\frac{2}{3}$ is greater than $\frac{5}{8}$.

To **convert a fraction to a decimal**, divide the denominator into the numerator.

To convert $\frac{8}{25}$ to a decimal, divide 25 into 8.

$$\frac{8}{25} = 0.32$$

To **convert a decimal to a fraction**, first set the decimal over 1. Then, move the decimal over as many places as it takes until it is immediately to the right of the units digit. Count the number of places that you moved the decimal. Then add that many 0s to the 1 in the denominator.

$$0.3 = \frac{0.3}{1} = \frac{3.0}{10} \text{ or } \frac{3}{10}$$

$$0.32 = \frac{0.32}{1} = \frac{32.0}{100} \text{ or } \frac{8}{25}$$

> **THE DIVISIBILITY TEST**
>
> Don't confuse the divisibility tests. To test for 2, 4, 5, or 10, just look at the last digit or two. To test for 3 or 9, add all the digits.

Decimal Division and Scientific Notation

One common type of arithmetic problem on the ASVAB involves dividing numbers that contain decimals. Take a look at what we mean.

$$7.2 \div 0.004 = ?$$

Having to keep track of all those decimal places complicates what would otherwise be a simple division problem. That's why we recommend that you get rid of the decimal places before you divide. First, turn the division problem into a fraction:

$$7.2 \div 0.004 = \frac{7.2}{0.004}$$

Then move the decimal points in the denominator and the numerator the same number of places to the right, adding zeros as necessary, until you have completely gotten rid of them.

$$\frac{7.2}{0.004} = \frac{7,200}{4}$$

Now you have that simple division problem you were looking for.

$$\frac{7,200}{4} = 1,800$$

There's also a chance you might see **scientific notation** on the ASVAB, a method of writing very large and very small numbers that also involves moving decimal points.

The exponent of a power of 10 indicates how many zeros the number would contain if it were written out. For example, $10^4 = 10,000$ (4 zeros) since the product of four factors of 10 is equal to 10,000.

$$0.0123 \times 10^4 = 123$$

When multiplying a number by a power of 10, move the decimal point to the right the same number of places as the number of zeros in that power of 10.

$$0.0123 \times 10^4 = 123$$

When dividing by a power of 10, move the decimal point to the left.

$$43.21 \div 10^3 = 0.04321$$

Multiplying by a number with a negative exponent is the same as dividing by a positive exponent. Therefore, when you multiply by a number with a positive exponent, move the decimal to the right. When you multiply by a number with a negative exponent, move the decimal to the left.

Exponents and Roots

Exponents are the small raised numbers written to the right of a variable or number. They indicate the number of times that variable or number is to be used as a factor.

To **add** or **subtract** terms consisting of a coefficient (the number in front of the variable) multiplied by a power (a power is a base raised to an exponent), both the base and the exponent must be the same. As long as the base and the exponents are the same, you can add the coefficients.

$$x^2 + x^2 = 2x^2$$
$$3x^4 - 2x^4 = x^4$$
$$x^2 + x^3 \text{ cannot be combined.}$$

MULTIPLYING POWERS

To multiply powers with the same base, add exponents. To raise a power to an exponent, multiply exponents.

To **multiply** terms consisting of coefficients multiplied by powers having the same base, multiply the coefficients and add the exponents.

$$2x^5 \times 8x^7 = (2 \times 8)(x^{5+7}) = 16x^{12}$$

To **divide** terms consisting of coefficients multiplied by powers having the same base, divide the coefficients and subtract the exponents.

$$6x^7 \div 2x^5 = (6 \div 2)(x^{7-5}) = 3x^2$$

To **raise a power to an exponent**, multiply the exponents.

$$(x^2)^4 = x^{2 \times 4} = x^8$$

A **square root** is a number that, when multiplied by itself, produces the given quantity. The radical sign "$\sqrt{}$" is used to represent the positive square root of a number, so $\sqrt{25} = 5$, since $5 \times 5 = 25$.

PERFECT SQUARE

Learn to recognize perfect squares.

To **add** or **subtract** radicals, make sure the numbers under the radical sign are the same. If they are, you can add or subtract the coefficients outside the radical signs.

$$2\sqrt{2} + 3\sqrt{2} = 5\sqrt{2}$$

$\sqrt{2} + \sqrt{3}$ cannot be combined.

To **simplify** radicals, factor out the perfect squares under the radical, unsquare them, and put the result in front of the radical sign.

$$\sqrt{32} = \sqrt{16 \times 2} = 4\sqrt{2}$$

To **multiply** or **divide** radicals, multiply (or divide) the coefficients outside the radical. Multiply (or divide) the numbers inside the radicals.

$$\sqrt{x} \times \sqrt{y} = \sqrt{xy}$$

$$3\sqrt{2} \times 4\sqrt{5} = 12\sqrt{10}$$

$$\frac{\sqrt{x}}{\sqrt{y}} = \sqrt{\frac{x}{y}}$$

$$12\sqrt{10} \div 3\sqrt{2} = 4\sqrt{5}$$

To **take the square root of a fraction**, break the fraction into two separate roots and take the square root of the numerator and the denominator.

$$\sqrt{\frac{16}{25}} = \frac{\sqrt{16}}{\sqrt{25}} = \frac{4}{5}$$

Factorials

On the ASVAB math sections, you may see an occasional "factorial" question. You'll know you're dealing with a factorial when you see an exclamation point (!) in a seemingly inappropriate place. For instance, when you see the following:

$7! = ?$

The above question is actually asking you what "7 factorial" is, and the answer to that question is:

$7! = 7 \times 6 \times 5 \times 4 \times 3 \times 2 \times 1 = 5,040$

So you tell us. 5! = ?

Answer: $5 \times 4 \times 3 \times 2 \times 1 = 120$.

You should also note that if you're ever given a fraction with factorials, there's always a lot of canceling that you can do before you try to multiply out the factorials.

$$\frac{6!}{4!} = \frac{6 \times 5 \times \cancel{4} \times \cancel{3} \times \cancel{2} \times \cancel{1}}{\cancel{4} \times \cancel{3} \times \cancel{2} \times \cancel{1}} = 6 \times 5 = 30$$

APPLIED ARITHMETIC REVIEW

While the arithmetic concepts we've looked at so far could appear on the Arithmetic Reasoning section of the ASVAB, it's worth noting that due to the very nature of word problems, most of the questions in this section will involve some form of "applied arithmetic"—in other words, the arithmetic used to solve practical problems. Applied arithmetic includes subjects like percent problems, rates, averages, and probability.

FROM FRACTION TO PERCENT

To change a fraction to a percent, multiply by 100%.

Percent Problems

Remember this formula $Percent = \dfrac{Part}{Whole}$, which can also be written as $Part = Percent \times Whole$.

To find **part**, **percent**, or **whole**, plug the values you have into the equation and solve.

To convert the **English into math on a percent problem**, use the following conversion table.

English	Math Translation
%	/100 (or use decimal or fractional equivalent)
of	× (times)
what	*x* (or *n*, or any variable you like)
is	= (equals)

44% of 25 = $0.44 \times 25 = 11$

42 is what percent of 70?

$$42 = \frac{n}{100} \times 70$$

$$\frac{42}{70} = \frac{n}{100}$$

$$n = \frac{4,200}{70}$$

$$n = 60\%$$

To **increase or decrease a number by a given percent**, take that percent of the original number and add it to or subtract it from the original number.

To increase 25 by 60%, first find 60% of 25.

$$25 \times 0.6 = 15.$$

Then add the result to the original number.

$$25 + 15 = 40.$$

To decrease 25 by the same percent, subtract the 15.

$$25 - 15 = 10.$$

The following formulas may also come in handy:

$$\text{Percent increase/greater} = \frac{\text{change}}{\text{original (smaller) number}}$$

$$\text{Percent decrease/less} = \frac{\text{change}}{\text{original (larger) number}}$$

A camera that originally cost $125 was sold on sale for $100. The sale price was what percent less than the original price?

Answer: Percent decrease $= \dfrac{\$25}{\$125} = \dfrac{1}{5} = 20\%$

Ratios, Proportions, and Rates

Ratios, like fractions, are another way of expressing **Part/Whole** relationships, although ratios often refer to **Part/Part** relationships as well. In either case, the setup remains the same:

Classic Ratio Setup: What is the ratio of $\dfrac{\text{(Part)}}{\text{to (Part or Whole)}}$

Look at the following example:

A class contains 12 male students and 21 female students.

The ratio of male students to female students $= \dfrac{12}{21} = \dfrac{4}{7}$.

The ratio of male students to all the students in the class $= \dfrac{12}{12 + 21} = \dfrac{12}{33} = \dfrac{4}{11}$.

By the way, you always want to simplify ratios to their lowest terms.

A **proportion** is just a type of a ratio, one that shows the comparative relation between parts, things, or elements with respect to size, amount, or degree. Here's an example of a proportion question:

A picture that is 4 inches wide and 6 inches long is enlarged so that it is $7\frac{1}{2}$ inches long. What is the width of the enlarged picture?

To handle a proportion such as the one above, set it up as an equation of fractions (in this case, of width/length), and then cross-multiply to solve for the unknown value:

$$\frac{4}{6} = \frac{n}{7.5}$$

$$4 \times 7.5 = 6n$$

$$\frac{30}{6} = n$$

$$n = 5$$

So the enlarged picture is 5 inches wide.

Finally, a **rate** is simply a ratio that compares distance over time, or amount over time, or cost over units.

In other words: $\text{Rate} = \dfrac{\text{Distance}}{\text{Time}}$ or $\text{Rate} = \dfrac{\text{Amount}}{\text{Time}}$ or $\text{Rate} = \dfrac{\text{Cost}}{\text{Units}}$

Take a look at the following rate question.

A waitress serves 3 diners every 5 minutes. At this rate, how many customers will she serve in one hour?

The key to solving rate problems is to set them up as proportions, convert the units if necessary, and solve for the unknown value.

$$\frac{3 \text{ diners}}{5 \text{ minutes}} = \frac{x \text{ diners}}{1 \text{ hour}} \qquad \text{Set up a proportion.}$$

$$\frac{3 \text{ diners}}{5 \text{ minutes}} = \frac{x \text{ diners}}{60 \text{ minutes}} \qquad \text{Convert units.}$$

$$5x = 180 \qquad \text{Cross-multiply and solve.}$$

$$x = 36$$

Averages and Probability

Averages, like ratios, proportions, and rates, are variations of fractions. Here is the Average Formula:

$$\text{Average} = \frac{\text{Sum of the terms}}{\text{Number of terms}}$$

Whenever you are given two of the above pieces of information in an average question, you should go ahead and calculate the third. Take the following, for example:

What is the average of 3, 4, and 8?

Answer: The average is 5, because $\text{Average} = \dfrac{\text{Sum of the terms}}{\text{Number of terms}} = \dfrac{3 + 4 + 8}{3} = \dfrac{15}{3} = 5.$

Finally, a **probability** is the likelihood that a desired outcome will occur, which is once again expressed as a fraction between 0 and 1. The more likely it is that something is going to happen, the closer the probability is to 1.

To find the probability that something is going to happen:

$$\text{Probability} = \frac{\text{Number of favorable outcomes}}{\text{Number of possible outcomes}}$$

If there are 12 books on a shelf and 9 of them are mysteries, what is the probability of picking a mystery?

$\dfrac{9}{12} = \dfrac{3}{4}.$ This probability can also be expressed as 0.75 or 75%.

To find the probability that **two events** will occur, find the probability that the first event occurs and multiply this by the probability that the second event occurs given that the first event occurs.

PROBABILITY IS UNDER ONE

Probability is a part-to-whole ratio and can therefore never be greater than one.

If there are 12 books on a shelf and 9 of them are mysteries, what is the probability of picking a mystery first and a non-mystery second if exactly two books are selected?

Probability of picking a mystery: $\dfrac{9}{12} = \dfrac{3}{4}.$

Probability of picking a nonmystery: $\dfrac{3}{11}.$ (Originally there were 9 mysteries and 3 nonmysteries. After the mystery is selected, there are 8 mysteries and 3 non-mysteries, i.e., 11 books remaining.)

Probability of picking both books: $\dfrac{3}{4} \times \dfrac{3}{11} = \dfrac{9}{44}.$

ARITHMETIC WORD PROBLEMS

As you may have noticed, we already started sneaking word problems into the arithmetic review section you just completed. You should find that ASVAB Arithmetic Reasoning words are pretty straightforward. Generally, all you have to do is translate the text into math and solve. So let's take a look at how to do that.

SIFT THROUGH THE FICTION– FIND THE MATH!

In some questions, the translation will be embedded within a "story." Don't be put off by the details of the scenario– it's the numbers that matter. Focus on the math and translate.

Translation

Often, word problems seem tricky because it's hard to figure out precisely what they're asking. The following table lists some common words and phrases that turn up in word problems, along with their mathematical translations.

When you see:	Think:
sum, plus, more than, added to, combined, total	+
minus, less than, difference between, decreased by	−
is, was, equals, is equivalent to, is the same as, adds up to	=
times, product, multiplied by, of, twice, double, triple	×
divided by, over, quotient, per, out of, into	÷
what, how much, how many, a number	x, n, etc.

Word Problems with Formulas

Some of the more difficult word problems may involve translations with mathematical formulas. Since the ASVAB test does not provide formulas for you, you have to know these going in.

If a truck travels at 50 miles per hour for $6\frac{1}{2}$ hours, how far will the truck travel?

To answer this question, you need to remember the Distance Formula:

$$\text{Rate} = \frac{\text{Distance}}{\text{Time}} \text{ or Distance} = \text{Rate} \times \text{Time}$$

Once you note the formula, you can just plug in the numbers.

$D = 50 \times 6.5$
$D = 325$ miles

ARITHMETIC REASONING PRACTICE SET

1. Professor Jones bought a large carton of books. She gave 3 books to each student in her class and there were no books left over. Which of the following could be the number of books she distributed?

   (A) 133
   (B) 143
   (C) 252
   (D) 271

2. Two teams are having a contest, in which the prize is a box of candy that the members of the winning team will divide evenly. If team A wins, each player will get exactly 3 pieces of candy and if team B wins, each player will get exactly 5 pieces of candy. Which of the following could be the number of pieces of candy in the box?

   (A) 325
   (B) 353
   (C) 425
   (D) 555

3. Barry is four years older than his brother Cole, who is four years older than their sister Darcy. If the sum of their three ages is 60, how old is Barry?

   (A) 16
   (B) 20
   (C) 24
   (D) 28

4. Sheila cuts a 60-foot wire cable in equal strips of $\frac{4}{5}$ of a foot in length each. How many strips does she make?

   (A) 48
   (B) 60
   (C) 70
   (D) 75

5. Susie and Dennis are training for a marathon. On Monday, they both run 3.2 miles. On Tuesday, Susie runs $5\frac{1}{5}$ miles and Dennis runs 3.6 miles. On Wednesday, Susie runs 4.8 miles and Dennis runs $2\frac{2}{5}$ miles. During those 3 days, how many more miles does Susie run than Dennis?

   (A) 4.8
   (B) 4.0
   (C) 3.2
   (D) 3.0

6. A copier can make 150 copies per minute. At this rate, how many minutes would it take to make 4,500 copies?

   (A) 20
   (B) 25
   (C) 30
   (D) 35

GO ON TO THE NEXT PAGE

7. The average (arithmetic mean) age of the members in a five-person choir is 34. If the ages of four of the members are 47, 31, 27, and 36, what is the fifth member's age?

   (A) 29
   (B) 32
   (C) 34
   (D) 37

8. Brad bought a radio on sale at a 20% discount from its regular price of $118. If there is an 8% sales tax that is calculated on the sale price, how much did Brad pay for the radio?

   (A) $86.85
   (B) $94.40
   (C) $101.95
   (D) $127.44

9. Sheila charges $5.00 per haircut during the weekdays. On Saturday, she charges $7.50 per haircut. If Sheila has 6 customers each day of the week except Sunday, how much money does she earn in the five weekdays and Saturday?

   (A) $175.00
   (B) $180.00
   (C) $195.00
   (D) $210.00

10. Team A had 4 times as many losses as it had ties in a season. If Team A won none of its games, which could be the total number of games it played that season?

   (A) 15
   (B) 18
   (C) 21
   (D) 24

ANSWERS AND EXPLANATIONS

1. **C**

If Professor Jones was able to distribute all the books in groups of 3 without any left over, the number of books she started with was divisible by 3. Whichever choice is divisible by 3 must therefore be correct. For a number to be divisible by 3, the sum of its digits must also be divisible by 3. Only 252 (C) fits this requirement: $2 + 5 + 2 = 9$.

2. **D**

This problem tells you that the number of pieces of candy in the box can be divided evenly by 3 and 5. So the correct answer is the choice that has a 0 or 5 as its last digit, and the sum of whose digits is divisible by 3. Eliminate (B) because it doesn't end in either 0 or 5. Of the remaining choices, only 555 (D) is also divisible by 3, since $5 + 5 + 5 = 15$.

3. **C**

Use the answer choices to help find the solution. When backsolving you want to start with one of the middle numbers. We'll start here with (C), 24, for Barry's age. If Barry is 24, then his brother Cole is 20, and his sister is 16. Thus, the sum of their ages is $24 + 20 + 16 = 60$, which is the sum we want. Choice (C) is it.

4. **D**

When you're asked how many strips $\frac{4}{5}$ of a foot in length can be cut from a 60-foot piece of wire, you are really being asked how many times $\frac{4}{5}$ goes into 60, or what is $60 \div \frac{4}{5}$. Before you even do the division, you can eliminate choices (A) and (B). This is because you know the answer has to be greater than 60, since $\frac{4}{5}$ is less than 1, which means it has to go into 60 more than 60 times. Now do the division. Dividing by a fraction is the same as multiplying by its inverse, so $60 \div \frac{4}{5} = 60 \times \frac{5}{4} = 15 \times 5 = 75$.

5. **B**

The simplest way to solve this problem is to convert the numbers so that they are all decimals. $5\frac{1}{5} = 5\frac{2}{10} = 5.2$. $2\frac{2}{5} = 2\frac{4}{10} = 2.4$. Now you can more easily compare the distances. On Monday, they ran the same number of miles. On Tuesday, Susie ran 5.2 miles and Dennis ran 3.6 miles. The difference between the two amounts is $5.2 - 3.6 = 1.6$, so on Tuesday Susie ran 1.6 more miles the Dennis did. On Wednesday, Susie ran 4.8 miles and Dennis ran 2.4 miles, so Susie ran $4.8 - 2.4 = 2.4$ more miles than Dennis did. The total difference for the three days is $1.6 + 2.4 = 4.0$ miles.

6. **C**

St up a proportion: $\dfrac{150 \text{ copies}}{1 \text{ minute}} = \dfrac{4{,}500}{x \text{ minutes}}$

Now cross-multiply and solve: $150x = 4{,}500$, so $x = \dfrac{4{,}500}{150} = 30$.

7. **A**

$\text{Average} = \dfrac{\text{Sum of the terms}}{\text{Number of terms}}$, so here the average is $\dfrac{47 + 31 + 27 + 36 + n}{5}$.

Thus $34 = \dfrac{141 + n}{5}$, so by cross-multiplying you get $170 = 141 + n$.

So $n = 29$ and the answer is (A).

8. **C**

This problem needs to be done in several steps. First find out what the sale price of the radio was. The discount was 20%, so the sale price was 80% of the original price.

   Percent $\times$ Whole = Part

   .80 $\times$ \$118 = sale price

   \$94.40 = sale price

Now figure out how much tax Brad paid. The tax was 8% of the sale price.

   Percent $\times$ Whole = Part

   .08 $\times$ \$94.40 = tax

   \$7.5520 = tax

   \$7.55 = tax

Now just add the tax to the sale price.

   \$94.40 + \$7.55 = \$101.95.

9. **C**

Each weekday Sheila earns:

   \$5.00 $\times$ 6 haircuts = \$30 per weekday

Each Saturday Sheila earns:

   \$7.50 $\times$ 6 haircuts = \$45 per Saturday

   In 5 weekdays she earns 5 $\times$ \$30 = \$150.

   In 1 Saturday she earns \$45.

So in 5 weekdays plus 1 Saturday Sheila earns \$150 + \$45, or \$195.

10. **A**

Let the number of ties Team A had equal x. It lost 4 times as many games as it tied, or $4x$ games. It had no wins, so the total number of games played by Team A is $x + 4x = 5x$. So the number of games played must be a multiple of 5; the only choice that is a multiple of 5 is (A), 15.

CHAPTER SIX

Mathematics Knowledge

The questions on the Mathematics Knowledge section usually take less time to answer than their Arithmetic Reasoning counterparts, about a minute each.

ALGEBRA REVIEW

The difference between algebra and arithmetic is simply that algebra uses symbols called **variables**, such as x and y, to generalize arithmetic relationships.

Algebra problems on the ASVAB can appear in two forms: as straightforward math problems or as word problems. You will likewise find that algebra problems on the Mathematics Knowledge section are highly susceptible to these backsolving approaches. Nonetheless, on algebra questions on the ASVAB, the textbook approach is often the quicker approach.

Expressions

An algebraic **expression** on the ASVAB test is likely to look something like this:

$$(11 + 3x) - (5 - 2x) =$$

The main thing that you need to remember about **expressions** on the ASVAB is that you can combine only "like terms."

For example, to combine monomials or polynomials, simply add or subtract the coefficients (the numbers that come before the variables) of terms that have the exact same variable. When completing the addition or subtraction, do not change the variables.

$6a + 5a = 11a$

$8b - 2b = 6b$

$3a + 2b - 8a = 3a - 8a + 2b = -5a + 2b$ or $2b - 5a$

Remember, you cannot combine:

$6a + 5a^2$

OR

$3a + 2b$

Multiplying and dividing monomials is a little different. In addition and subtraction, you can combine only like terms. With multiplication and division, you can multiply and divide terms that are different. When you multiply monomials, multiply the coefficients of each term. Add the exponents of like variables. Multiply different variables together.

$(6a)(4b) =$

$$= (6 \times 4)(a \times b)$$

$$= 24ab$$

$(6a)(4ab) =$

$$= (6 \times 4)(a \times a \times b)$$

$$= (6 \times 4)(a^{1+1} \times b)$$

$$= 24\,a^2b$$

Use the FOIL method to multiply and divide binomials. FOIL stands for **First, Outer, Inner, Last**.

$(y + 1)(y + 2) =$

$$= (y \times y) + (y \times 2) + (1 \times y) + (1 \times 2)$$

$$= y^2 + 2y + y + 2$$

$$= y^2 + 3y + 2$$

The final expression above, $y^2 + 3y + 2$, is known as a **quadratic**. A quadratic expression or equation is one that is written in the form $ax^2 + bx + c$ or $ax^2 + bx + c = 0$ where $a \neq 0$ (of course, the x can be another variable, such as y in the expression above). Don't be scared here by the terminology. Just realize that you may occasionally be called upon to **factor** a quadratic expression or equation on the ASVAB. This simply involves being able to reverse-FOIL. Take a look.

Factor $x^2 - 4x - 21$

> To begin, build parentheses: $(x\ \ )(x\ \ )$

> Now think . . .
> What **Last** terms will produce **−21**?
> What **Outer** & **Inner** terms will produce **−4x**?
> Consequently: $x - 4x - 21 = (x - 7)(x + 3)$

MEMORIZE THE FOLLOWING

$(x + y)(x - y) = x^2 - y^2$

$(x + y)^2 = x^2 + 2xy + y^2$

$(x - y)^2 = x^2 - 2xy + y^2$

If you see one side of any of the above equations on the ASVAB, rewrite it as the other side of the equation. This should make answering the question very easy.

Equations

The key to **solving equations** is to do the same thing to both sides of the equation until you have your variable isolated on one side of the equation and all of the numbers on the other side of the equation. For instance, you could be asked for the value of a in the following equation.

> $12a + 8 = 23 - 3a$

First, subtract 8 from each side so that the left side of the equation has only variables.

> $12a + 8 - 8 = 23 - 3a - 8$
> $12a = 15 - 3a$

Then, add $3a$ to each side so that the right side of the equation has only numbers.

> $12a + 3a = 15 - 3a + 3a$
> $15a = 15$

Finally, divide both sides by 15 to isolate the variable.

> $\dfrac{15a}{15} = \dfrac{15}{15}$
> $a = 1$

DON'T FORGET

Always do the same thing to both sides to solve for a variable in an equation.

Sometimes you are given an equation with two variables and asked to **solve for one variable in terms of the other**. This means that you must isolate the variable for which you are solving on one side of the equation and put everything else on the other side. In other words, when you're done, you'll have x (or whatever the variable is) on one side of the equation and an expression on the other side.

> Solve $7x + 2y = 3x + 10y - 16$ for x in terms of y.

Since you want to isolate x on one side of the equation, begin by subtracting $2y$ from both sides.

$$7x + 2y - 2y = 3x + 10y - 16 - 2y$$
$$7x = 3x + 8y - 16$$

Then, subtract $3x$ from both sides to get all the x's on one side of the equation.

$$7x - 3x = 3x + 8y - 16 - 3x$$
$$4x = 8y - 16$$

Finally, divide both sides by 4 to isolate x.

$$\frac{4x}{4} = \frac{8y - 16}{4}$$
$$x = 2y - 4$$

Substitution

If a problem gives you the value for a variable, just plug the value into the equation and solve. Make sure that you follow the rules of PEMDAS and are careful with your calculations.

If $x = 15$ and $y = 10$, what is the value of $4x(x - y)$?

Plug 15 in for x and 10 in for y.
$$4(15)(15 - 10) =$$

Then solve.
$$(60)(5) = 300$$

Inequalities

Solve **inequalities** like you would any other equation. Isolate the variable that you are solving for on one side of the equation and everything else on the other side of the equation.

$$4a + 6 > 2a + 10$$
$$4a - 2a > 10 - 6$$
$$2a > 4$$
$$a > 2$$

The only difference here is that instead of finding a specific value for a, you get a range of values for a. The rest of the math is the same.

There is, however, one <u>crucial</u> difference between solving equations and inequalities. **When you multiply or divide an inequality by a <u>negative</u> number, you must change the direction of the sign.**

$$-5a > 10$$
$$a < -2$$

You know that negative $\times$ positive = negative, and that negative $\times$ negative = positive. Since -5 is negative and 10 is positive, -5 has to be multiplied by something negative to get a positive product. Therefore, a has to be *less* than -2, not *greater* than it. If $a > -2$, then any value for a that is greater than -2 should make $-5a$ less than 10. For example, if $a = 20$, $-5a$ would be -100, which is certainly *not* greater than 10.

ALGEBRA WORD PROBLEMS

We have already covered our basic approach to handling word problems in the last chapter, but here are a few additional pointers that may help you to deal in particular with algebra word problems on the ASVAB:

1. Read through the whole question. Do this to get a sense of what's going on. You want to know the basic situation described, the type of information you've been given, and—most important of all—what exactly you are being asked.

2. Identify the different variables or unknowns and label them. For example, if the problem discusses Charlie's and Veronica's freckles, you may wish to use "c" to represent Charlie's freckles and "v" to represent Veronica's freckles. Notice that we didn't use "x" and "y." If we had, we might later forget whether x represented Charlie's freckles or Veronica's.

3. Translate the problem into math. This usually entails rewriting the English sentences into equations or statements. The sentence "Veronica has four fewer freckles than Charlie has" would become: $v = c - 4$. Notice that the math terms are not in the same order as the English terms in the sentence. When you translate, you are translating the ideas. The idea here is "four fewer freckles than Charlie." That means $c - 4$, not $4 - c$!

4. Tackle the math. Solve the equations. Be careful as you crunch the numbers. Make sure you've determined the value that the question is asking you for.

5. Check your work, if you have time.

GEOMETRY REVIEW

Lines and Angles

Line Segments

A **line segment** is a piece of a line, and it has an exact measurable length. Questions will give you a segment divided into several pieces, give you the measurements of some of these pieces, and ask you for the measurement of a particular piece.

If $PR = 12$ and $QR = 4$, $PQ = ?$

$$PQ = PR - QR$$
$$PQ = 12 - 4$$
$$PQ = 8$$

The point exactly in the middle of a line segment, halfway between the endpoints, is called the **midpoint** of the line segment. To bisect means to cut in half, so the midpoint of a line segment bisects that line segment.

M is the midpoint of AB, so $AM = MB$.

Angles

A **right angle** measures 90 degrees and is usually indicated in a diagram by a little box. The figure above is a right angle. Lines that intersect to form right angles are said to be **perpendicular**.

RULE TO REMEMBER
A straight angle contains 180°.

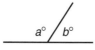

Angles that form a straight line add up to 180 degrees. In the figure above, $a + b = 180$.

When two lines intersect, **adjacent angles are supplementary**, meaning they add up to 180 degrees. In the figure above, $a + b = 180$.

Angles around a point add up to 360 degrees. In the figure above, $a + b + c + d + e = 360$.

When lines intersect, angles across the vertex from each other are called **vertical angles** and **are equal to each other**. Above, $a = c$ and $b = d$.

Parallel Lines

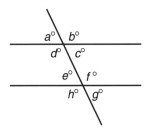

When parallel lines are crossed by another line:
- **Corresponding angles are equal (for example, $a = e$).**
- **Alternate interior angles are equal ($d = f$).**
- **Same side interior angles are supplementary ($c + f = 180$).**
- **All four acute angles are equal, as are all four obtuse angles.**

Triangles

Triangles in General

The three interior angles of any triangle **add up to 180°**. In the figure above, $x + 50 + 100 = 180$, so $x = 30$.

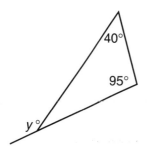

An exterior angle of a triangle is equal to the **sum of the remote interior angles**. In this figure, the exterior angle labeled $y°$ is equal to the sum of the remote angles: $y = 40 + 95 = 135$.

Triangles—Area and Perimeter

The **perimeter** of a triangle is the sum of the lengths of its sides.

The **perimeter** of the triangle in the figure above is: $3 + 4 + 6 = 13$

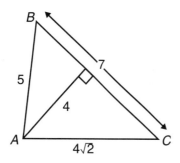

Area of triangle $= \dfrac{1}{2}$(base)(height)

The height is the perpendicular distance between the side that's chosen as the base and the opposite vertex. In this triangle, 4 is the height when the 7 is chosen as the base.

$$\text{Area} = \frac{1}{2}\, bh = \frac{1}{2}(7)(4) = 14$$

Similar Triangles

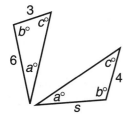

Similar triangles have the same shape: **corresponding angles are equal and corresponding sides are proportional**. These triangles are similar because they have the same angles. The 3 corresponds to the 4 and the 6 corresponds to the *s*.

$$\frac{3}{4} = \frac{6}{s}$$
$$3s = 24$$
$$s = 8$$

Special Triangles

Isosceles Triangles

An **isosceles triangle** is a triangle that has **two equal sides**. Not only are two sides equal, but the angles opposite the equal sides, called **base angles,** are also equal.

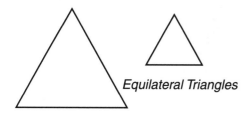

Equilateral Triangles

Equilateral triangles are triangles in which **all three sides are equal**. Since all the sides are equal, all the angles are also equal. All three angles in an equilateral triangle measure 60 degrees, regardless of the lengths of sides.

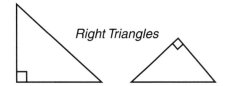

A right triangle is a triangle with a **right angle**. Every right triangle has exactly two acute angles. The sides opposite the acute angles are called the **legs**. The side opposite the right angle is called the **hypotenuse.** Since it's opposite the largest angle, the hypotenuse is the longest side of a right triangle.

The Pythagorean Theorem

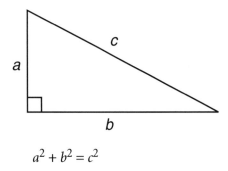

$$a^2 + b^2 = c^2$$

Note: *a* and *b* are the perpendicular sides, or *legs*, of a right triangle, and *c* is the longest side, or *hypotenuse*, of the triangle.

If one leg is 2 and the other leg is 3, then:

$$2^2 + 3^2 = c^2$$
$$c^2 = 4 + 9$$
$$c = \sqrt{13}$$

Quadrilaterals

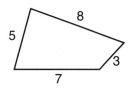

The **perimeter** of a polygon is the sum of the lengths of its sides.

The perimeter of the quadrilateral in the figure above is $5 + 8 + 3 + 7 = 23$.

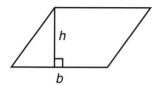

A **parallelogram** is a quadrilateral with two sets of parallel sides. Opposite sides are equal, as are opposite angles. The formula for the area of a parallelogram is:

Area = (base)(height)

In the diagram above, h = height and b = base, so area = bh.

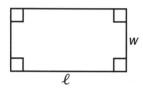

A **rectangle** is a parallelogram containing four right angles. Opposite sides are equal. The formula for the area of a rectangle is:

Area = (length)(width)

In the above diagram above, ℓ = length and w = width, so area = ℓw.

Perimeter = $2(\ell + w)$

A **square** is a rectangle with four equal sides. The formula for the area of a square is:

Area = $(\text{side})^2$

In the diagram above, s = the length of a side, so area = s^2.

Perimeter = $4s$

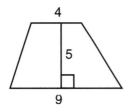

A **trapezoid** is a quadrilateral with one pair of parallel sides. The two parallel sides of a trapezoid are called the **bases.**

The formula for the area of a trapezoid is:

Area $= \frac{1}{2}$ (sum of the lengths of the bases)(height)

In the diagram above, the area of the trapezoid is $\frac{1}{2}$ (4 + 9)(5) = 32.5.

Circles

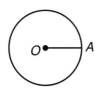

A **circle** is a figure with each point an equal distance from its center. In the diagram, O is the center of the circle.

The **radius** of a circle is the straight line distance from its center to any point on the circle. All radii of one circle have equal lengths. In the figure above, OA is a radius of circle O.

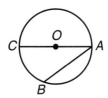

A **chord** is a line segment that connects any two points on a circle. Segments AB and AC are both chords. The largest chord that may be drawn in a circle will be a diameter of that circle.

A **diameter** of a circle is a chord that passes through the circle's center. All diameters are the same length and are equal to twice the radius. In the figure above, AC is a diameter of circle O.

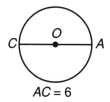

AC = 6

The **circumference** of a circle is the distance around it. It is equal to πd, or $2\pi r$. In this example: Circumference = $\pi d = 6\pi$

The **area** of a circle equals π times the square of the radius, or πr^2. In this example, since *AC* is the diameter, $r = \frac{6}{2} = 3$, and:

Area = $\pi r^2 = \pi(3^2) = 9\pi$

Solid Geometry

The only solid geometry formulas that you are expected to know for the ASVAB concern rectangular solids, or boxes. If you are asked about any other solid on the ASVAB, the question will provide the relevant formula. Here are the two formulas that you may need to know:

Volume of a Rectangular Solid or Box = $\ell \times w \times h$

Surface Area of a Rectangular Solid or Box = $2\ell w + 2wh + 2\ell h$

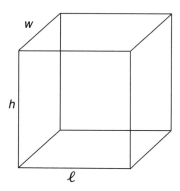

Note: ℓ = length, w = width, h = height

Now you can try these methods out on the practice set that follows.

MATHEMATICS KNOWLEDGE PRACTICE SET

1. If the average of 5 consecutive odd numbers is 11, then the largest number is

   (A) 17
   (B) 15
   (C) 13
   (D) 11

2. If $x = \sqrt{3}$, $y = 2$, and $z = \dfrac{1}{2}$, then $x^2 - 5yz + y^2 =$

   (A) 1
   (B) 2
   (C) 4
   (D) 7

3. $\dfrac{15 \times 7 \times 3}{9 \times 5 \times 2} =$

   (A) $\dfrac{2}{7}$

   (B) $3\dfrac{1}{2}$

   (C) 7

   (D) $7\dfrac{1}{2}$

4. $(3d - 7) - (5 - 2d) =$

   (A) $d - 12$
   (B) $5d - 2$
   (C) $5d + 12$
   (D) $5d - 12$

5. Jim can run at a rate of 1 mile per 5 minutes and Rebecca can run at a rate of 1 mile per 8 minutes. If they both start at point A at the same time and run in the same direction at their respective rates, how far ahead will Jim be from Rebecca in 40 minutes?

   (A) 3 miles
   (B) 5 miles
   (C) 8 miles
   (D) 15 miles

6. If the sales tax on the purchase of a certain item is 8% of the sticker price, and the sales tax comes to $120, what is the sticker price of the item?

   (A) $150.00
   (B) $1,000
   (C) $1,160
   (D) $1,500

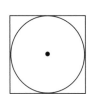

7. If the perimeter of the above square is 36, what is the circumference of the circle?

   (A) 6π
   (B) 9π
   (C) 12π
   (D) 18π

GO ON TO THE NEXT PAGE

8. What is the area of the frame in the above diagram if the inside picture has a length of 8 and a width of 4?

   (A) 16
   (B) 24
   (C) 48
   (D) 56

9. What is the distance from the midpoint of $\overline{PQ}$ to the midpoint of $\overline{RS}$?

   (A) 12
   (B) 14
   (C) 16
   (D) 18

10. If $s - t = 5$ what is the value of $3s - 3t + 3$?

    (A) 11
    (B) 12
    (C) 15
    (D) 18

ANSWERS AND EXPLANATIONS

1. B

One trick for dealing with consecutive numbers is to realize that the middle number in a group of consecutive numbers is equal to the average of the numbers. So of the five consecutive odd numbers, the middle or third number is 11, the fourth number is 13, and the fifth or final number is 15.

2. B

You are given values for all the variables, so just plug those values into the equation you are given. $x^2 - 5yz + y^2 = (\sqrt{3})^2 - 5(2)\left(\dfrac{1}{2}\right) + (2)^2 = 3 - 5 + 4 = 2.$

3. B

$$\frac{15 \times 7 \times 3}{9 \times 5 \times 2} = \frac{\cancel{5} \times \cancel{3} \times 7 \times \cancel{3}}{\cancel{3} \times \cancel{3} \times \cancel{5} \times 2} = \frac{7}{2} = 3\frac{1}{2}$$

4. D

Eliminate the parentheses by distributing the minus operation over the second set of parentheses: $(3d - 7) - (5 - 2d) = 3d - 7 - 5 - (-2d) = 3d - 7 - 5 + 2d$. Now combine like terms and perform the additions and subtractions: $3d + 2d - 7 - 5 = 5d - 12$.

5. A

Jim runs 1 mile per 5 minutes, so in 40 minutes he will run 8 miles. Rebecca runs 1 mile per 8 minutes, so in 40 minutes she will run 5 miles. Thus, if they start out at the same point and run in the same direction, after 40 minutes Jim will be $8 - 5 = 3$ miles ahead of Rebecca.

6. D

The sales tax is 8% of the sticker price, so if the sales tax is $120, and we call the sticker price x, then $\$120 = 0.08x$. So $x = \dfrac{\$120}{0.08} = \dfrac{\$12,000}{8} = \$1,500$.

7. B

If the perimeter of the square is 36, then each of the four sides equals 9. The side of the square is the same length as the diameter of the circle, so if the diameter of the circle is 9, the circumference is 9π.

8. C

The area of the frame is the area of the larger rectangle minus the area of the smaller rectangle, or $(8 \times 10) - (4 \times 8) = 80 - 32 = 48$.

9. **A**

To find the midpoint of a segment on the number line you can add the endpoints and divide the sum by 2. So the midpoint of PQ is $\dfrac{(-12) + (-2)}{2} = \dfrac{-14}{2} = -7$. The midpoint of RS is $\dfrac{1 + 9}{2} = \dfrac{10}{2} = 5$. Thus the distance between the two points is the positive difference between their coordinates, or $5 - (-7) = 12$.

10. **D**

If $s - t = 5$, then if you multiply both sides by 3, you get $3s - 3t = 15$. Thus $3s - 3t + 3 = 15 + 3 = 18$.

Part Three

REVIEW OF TECHNICAL ASVAB SUBTESTS

CHAPTER SEVEN

General Science

The General Science section of the ASVAB covers a grab bag of topics that you may or may not have studied in high school or elsewhere. You'll be answering 25 questions in 11 minutes on the paper and pencil version, and you are given 8 minutes for 16 questions on the CAT-ASVAB.

This review will cover the following broad areas:

- Life Science (health, nutrition, and biology)
- Earth Science (geology, meteorology, and astronomy)
- Physical Science (elementary physics and chemistry)

BREADTH, NOT DEPTH

The General Science section of the ASVAB covers a lot of science topics, but you will never be expected to know too much about any one topic.

LIFE SCIENCE

Health and Nutrition

Although nutritionists themselves don't always agree about what constitutes a healthy diet, certain facts are clear. A healthy diet requires a combination of protein, carbohydrates, fat, minerals, vitamins, and fiber. Proteins, carbohydrates, and fats (macronutrients) are necessary to provide energy. Minerals and vitamins (micronutrients), along with fiber, are necessary to maintain proper bodily functions.

Proteins are necessary for the body's maintenance, growth, and repair. Animal proteins are contained in meat, fish, eggs, and cheese. Vegetable proteins are found in peas, beans, nuts, and some grains.

Carbohydrates include both starches and sugars. They are major sources of energy for the body's metabolism. Starches are found in bread, cereal, rice, potatoes, and pasta. Sugars are found in fruits, cane sugar, and beets, as well as processed foods.

Fats also provide energy for metabolism. There are three types of fats: saturated, monounsaturated, and polyunsaturated. Those wishing to reduce the bad cholesterol levels in their blood should avoid saturated fats, although monounsaturated and polyunsaturated fats can actually decrease levels of bad cholesterol. Sources of saturated fats include meats, shellfish, eggs, milk, and milk products. Sources of monounsaturated fats include olives and olive oil, grape seed oil, almonds, cashews, brazil nuts, and avocados. Sources of polyunsaturated fats include corn oil, flaxseed oil, pumpkinseed oil, safflower oil, soybean oil, and sunflower oil.

Minerals in small quantities are needed for a balanced diet. Some necessary minerals are iron, zinc, calcium, magnesium, and sodium chloride (salt).

Vitamins, such as Vitamin C and D, are necessary for a wide variety of physiological processes from bone hardness to healthy gums. The lack of certain vitamins results in illnesses called deficieny diseases.

Fiber passes through the body unchanged but is part of a healthy diet. Fiber provides bulk, which allows the large intestine to carry away waste matter. Good sources of dietary fiber include leafy green vegetables, carrots, turnips, peas, beans, and potatoes, as well as raw and cooked fruits, cereals, and whole-grain foods.

Water is also essential for survival. The body loses approximately four pints of water each day, which must be replenished. Most foods contain water, facilitating proper water maintenance, although it is still necessary to drink water as well!

The Human Body

The Skeleton and Muscles

The skeleton and muscles are responsible for holding the body together as well as for movement. Without a skeleton you would be just an immobile mass of organs, veins, and skin. Some organisms, namely **arthropods** (a huge animal phylum that includes insects, spiders, and crustaceans), have **exoskeletons**, or external skeletons. **Vertebrate** animals, including man, have internal skeletons, or **endoskeletons**.

The human skeleton contains both **bone** and **cartilage**. Bones provide the primary support, while cartilage, which is more flexible, is found at the end of all bones, at the joints, in the nose, and in the ears. Bones not only provide structural support for the body and protect vital organs, but they also produce blood cells and store minerals such as calcium. Attaching the skeleton to muscles are **tendons**, tough fibrous cords made of connective tissue. And connecting bones to bones at joints such as the elbow, knee, fingers, and vertebral column are **ligaments**, which are also made of connective tissue.

The Respiratory System

Respiration—the process by which blood cells absorb **oxygen** and eliminate **carbon dioxide** and **water vapor**—is performed by the **respiratory system**.

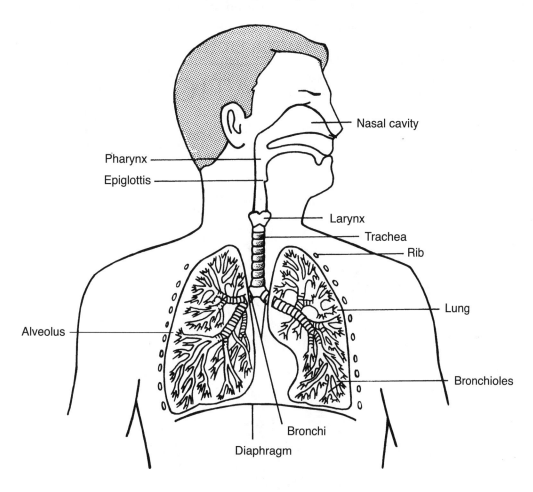

Figure 1. The respiratory system

When air enters through the **nose**, it passes through the **nasal cavity**, which filters, moistens, and warms air, and then through the **pharynx**, which further filters the air and aids in protection against infection. The air then passes through the open **epiglottis**, which closes when swallowing to prevent food from going down the airway, and into the **trachea**, which further cleanses the air. The trachea branches into the **left and right bronchi**, which are two tubes that lead to the **lungs**. There the bronchi further subdivide into smaller tubes called **bronchioles**. Each bronchiole ends in a small sac called an **alveolus**. It is in the alveolus that oxygen from the air enters into the bloodstream via capillaries. The **diaphragm** is a system of muscles that allow the lungs to expand and contract, drawing air in and out.

Circulatory System

In conjunction with the respiratory system, the **circulatory system** functions to transport nutrients throughout the body and get rid of wastes such as carbon dioxide. The main organ that drives the circulatory system is the **heart**. The human heart is a four-chambered pump, with two collecting chambers called **atria**, and two pumping chambers called **ventricles**. The **right atrium** receives deoxygenated blood from the **vena cava**, the two largest veins in the body, and passes it to the **right ventricle**, which pumps the blood through the lungs through the **pulmonary artery**. Oxygenated blood returns through the **pulmonary vein** to the **left atrium**. From there it passes to the **left ventricle** and is pumped through the **aorta** and **arteries** to the rest of the body. The heart's **valves** are essential to efficient pumping of the heart. When blood is pumped out of the ventricles, valves close to prevent the blood from flowing backward into the heart after the contraction of the ventricles is complete.

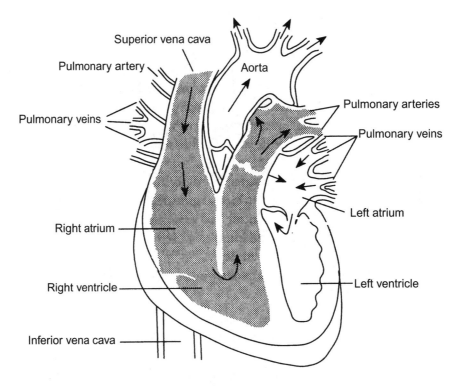

Figure 2. Human heart

The **arteries** carry blood from the heart to the tissues of the body. They repeatedly branch into smaller arteries (**arterioles**), which supply blood to the tissues via the capillaries. Arteries carry blood away from the heart, and for that reason are thick-walled, conducting oxygenated blood at high blood pressure. Only the pulmonary artery does not contain oxygenated blood, as it carries deoxygenated blood into the lungs.

Veins, on the other hand, carry blood back to the heart from the capillaries. Veins are relatively thin-walled, conduct blood at low pressure, and contain many valves to prevent backflow.

Veins have no pulse and carry dark red, deoxygenated blood. The lone exception is the pulmonary vein, which carries freshly oxygenated blood from the lungs back into the heart.

Finally, **capillaries** are thin-walled vessels that are very small in diameter. Capillaries, not arteries or veins, permit exchange of materials between the blood and the body's cells (this is called **diffusion**).

Blood consists of **cells** suspended in **plasma**, the liquid component of blood. There are three types of cells found in blood: **red blood cells**, which are the oxygen-carrying cells; **white blood cells**, which fight infection by destroying foreign organisms; and **platelets**, which are cell fragments that allow blood to clot. All blood cells are created in the **bone marrow**, which is located in the center of bones.

Also note that blood comes in four different types: A, B, AB, and O. Type O is the **universal donor**, which means that type O blood can be given to anybody. Type AB is the **universal recipient**, which means that someone with type AB blood can receive any type of blood.

The Digestive and Excretory Systems

The digestive system is responsible for breaking down foods into material the body can use for energy and bodybuilding. The digestive tract is essentially a long and winding tube that begins at the mouth and ends at the anus.

The process of digestion progresses as follows:

- In the mouth, the teeth and the tongue aid in mechanical digestion, while the enzyme **salivary amylase**, contained in the saliva, begins to break down starch.
- From the mouth, the chewed food moves into the **esophagus**. Contractions push the food down through the esophagus and into the stomach.
- In the **stomach**, food is mixed with **gastric acids** and **pepsin**, which help break down **protein**.
- In the **small intestine**, the bulk of digestion takes place. The small intestine is very long, about 23 feet on average. Food is broken down completely by enzymes produced in the walls of the small intestine, in the pancreas, and in the liver. The acids produced by the **pancreas** contain **lipase**, which changes fat to glycerol and fatty acids; **pancreatic amylase**, which breaks down complex carbohydrates into simple sugars; and **trypsin**, which converts polypeptides into amino acids. **Bile** produced by the **liver** aids in the physical digestion of emulsifying fat. All these digested substances, except for the fatty acids and glycerol, are then absorbed in the small intestine through capillaries that carry the blood into the liver and then throughout the rest of the body.
- In the **large intestine**, water and minerals remaining in the waste matter are absorbed back into the body.

THE SMALL INTESTINE IS NOT THAT SMALL!

In the average adult, the small intestine, if uncoiled, could easily measure 25 feet or longer, making it much larger than the large intestine (although, to be fair, the larger intestine does have a larger diameter). The small intestine is where the great bulk of digestion takes place.

- Chemical waste, such as urea, excess salts, minerals, and water, are filtered from the blood by the **kidney** and secreted into the urine. Urine is transported to the bladder from the kidneys through the **ureters**.

- In the **rectum**, solid waste matter is stored. In the **bladder**, liquid waste (urine) is stored.

- Solid waste matter is periodically released through the **anus**, and urine is released through the **urethra**.

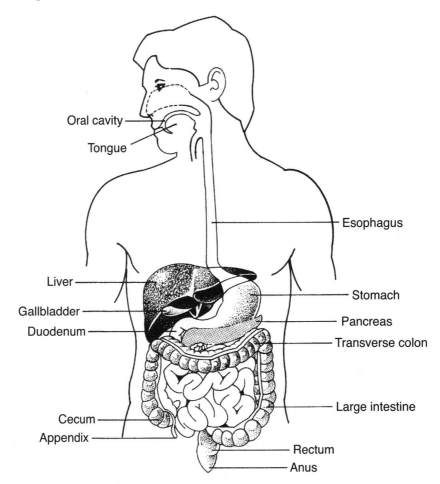

Figure 3. The digestive system

The Nervous System

The nervous system consists of the **brain**, the **spinal cord**, and the network of billions of nerve cells called **neurons**. The nervous system controls the functions of the body and receives stimuli from the environment.

The nervous system consists of the **central nervous system**, which contains the neurons in the brain and spinal cord, and the **peripheral nervous system**, which contains all the other neurons found throughout the body.

The main components of the central nervous system are as follows:

- The **cerebrum** is the major part of the brain. It is thought to be the **center of intelligence**, responsible for hearing, seeing, thinking, etc.

- The **cerebellum** is a big cluster of nerve tissue that forms the basis for the brain. It is concerned with **muscular coordination** and the coordination of impulses sent out from the cerebrum.

- The **medulla** or brain stem, is the connection between the brain and the spinal cord. It controls **involuntary actions** such as breathing, swallowing, and the beating of the heart.

- The **spinal cord** is the major connecting center between the brain and the network of nerves. It **carries impulses** between all organs and the brain and is also the control center for many **simple reflexes**.

- The peripheral nervous system can be subdivided into:

  - The **somatic nervous system**, which consists of peripheral nerve fibers that send sensory information to the central nervous system and control **voluntary actions**.

  - The **autonomic nervous system**, which regulates **involuntary activity** in the heart, stomach, and intestines.

The Reproductive System

The reproductive system involves two sets of organs, male reproductive organs and female reproductive organs. During human reproduction the male organ, or **penis**, ejaculates more than 250 million **sperm**, produced in the **testes**, into the **vagina**, some of which make their way to the uterus. During **ovulation**, which occurs approximately every 28 days, an egg, or **ovum**, is released from the **ovary** and begins to travel through the **oviduct (fallopian tube)** and into the **uterus**. At the same time, the **endometrial lining** of the uterus becomes prepared for implantation. If the sperm unites with the ovum, a fertilized egg, or **zygote**, is formed, which implants in the uterus and eventually develops into a **fetus**. If the ovum fails to become fertilized, the uterine lining sloughs off during **menstruation**. From puberty to menopause, this menstrual cycle repeats monthly except for periods of pregnancy. After childbirth, **prolactin**, a hormone secreted by the pituitary, activates the production of milk.

Genetics

Genetics is the study of heredity, the process by which characteristics are passed from parents to offspring. The basic laws of genetics have been understood since the late eighteenth century, when they were first discovered by Gregor Mendel. What Mendel discovered was that in sexual reproduction, individual heredity traits separate in the reproductive cells, so that reproductive cells, known as **gametes**, have half as many **chromosomes** (large strings of hereditary units) as normal cells (which is why gametes are called **haploid**). Genetic traits are inherited independently of one another, and when different traits are crossed during the fertilization of an egg, often one trait is **dominant** and the other is **recessive**.

In human reproduction, the female gamete (ovum) combines with the male gamete (sperm), each of which contains 23 unpaired chromosomes, to produce a zygote, which contain 23 pairs of chromosomes, or a total of 46. **Meiosis** is the process by which gametes are created. Sexual reproduction by meiosis and fertilization results in a great deal of variation among offspring.

A **gene** is defined as a unit of inheritance. A gene consists of hereditary factors called **alleles**. Each of us has two **alleles** for every gene. These alleles may or may not be alike. If the alleles are alike, that person is **homozygous** for that particular gene. If the alleles are different, he or she is **heterozygous** for that particular gene.

A person's **genotype** is his or her genetic makeup, including both dominant and recessive alleles. A person's **phenotype** is simply how his or her genes express themselves in physical characteristics. Take eye color, for example. If a man has brown eyes, then brown eyes are part of his phenotype.

The sex of babies is determined by the genes contained on the sex chromosome. In females, the two sex chromosomes are alike and are designated as XX. In males, the sex chromosomes are heterozygous and designated as XY.

The Classification of Living Things

All living things fall into a careful classification scheme that goes from the broadest level of similarity—**kingdom**—to the narrowest—**species**. Let's begin by looking at the kingdoms, of which there are five in all.

The Kingdoms	
Monera	Includes bacteria, cyanobacteria (blue green algae), and primitive pathogens. Considered the most primitive kingdom, it represents prokaryotic (as opposed to eukaryotic) life forms—that is, the cells of Moneran organisms do not have distinct nuclei.
Protista	The simplest eukaryotes (cells have nuclei). Includes protozoa, unicellular and multicellular algae, and slime and water slime molds. Ancestor organisms to plants, animals, and fungi; many can move around by means of flagella. Some are also photosynthetic.
Fungi	Includes mushrooms, bread molds, and yeasts. Fungi lack the ability to photosynthesize; they are called decomposers, breaking down and feeding on dead protoplasm (extracellular digestion).
Plantae	Have the ability to photosynthesize, so they are called producers. There are four major phyla, Bryophyta, or mosses, and Tracheophyta, which have vascular systems, gymnosperms, and angiosperms.
Animalia	Produce energy by consuming other organisms, so they are called consumers. Can be either vertebrates, phylum Chordata, or invertebrates such as mollusks, arthropods, sponges, coelenterates, worms, etc.

The classification scheme has seven different levels. They are:

Kingdom—which contains several related *phyla*.

Phylum—which contains several related *classes*.

Class—which contains several related *orders*.

Order—which contains several related *families*.

Family—which contains several related *genera*.

Genus—which contains several related *species*.

Species—which contain organisms so similar that they can only reproduce with one another to create viable fertile offspring.

> **A MUSHROOM IS NOT A PLANT (BUT IT'S SOMEWHAT LIKE AN ANT!)**
>
> Unlike plants, fungi, such as mushrooms, cannot photosynthesize, and instead feed by absorbing nutrients from the organic material in which they live. Most fungi build their cell walls out of chitin. This is the same material as the hard outer shells of insects and other arthropods. Plants do not make chitin.

So you may want to remember: **Kingdom Phylum Class Order Family Genus Species.**

Here's a mnemonic to help you: **King Philip's Class Ordered the Family-sized Gino's Special.**

Ecology

Ecology is the study of the interrelationships between organisms and their physical surroundings. Just as biologists classify organisms according to terminology that goes from the general to the specific, ecologists employ a similar set of terminology:

Biosphere: The zone of planet Earth where life naturally occurs, including land, water, and air, extending from the deep crust to the lower atmosphere.

Biome: A major life zone of interrelated species bound together by similar climate, vegetation, and animal life.

Ecosystem: A system made up of a community of animals, plants, and other organisms as well as the abiotic (non-living) aspects of its environment.

Community: The collection of all ecologically connected species in an area.

Population: A group of organisms of the same species living in the same region.

Ecosystems, Communities, and Populations

The difference between biomes and ecosystems is that biomes need merely to share similar characteristics, whereas ecosystems must be contiguous and contain organisms that actually interact together. An ecosystem can be large or small, and can include both pristine and highly developed areas.

An ecosystem contains a community, and this community may contain many populations of organisms. The various populations within a community fall into one of several roles in the food chain.

Producers (mainly plant life): Also known as **autotrophs**, they make their own food via photosynthesis.

Decomposers (bacteria and fungi): Also known as **saprotrophs**, they break down organic matter and release minerals back into the soil.

Scavengers (many insects and certain vertebrates, such as vultures and jackals): These are animals that function like decomposers, by consuming refuse and decaying organic matter, especially **carrion**, or decaying flesh. Similar organisms called **detritivores** consume the small pieces of decaying organic matter called detritus that are too small for most scavengers to want.

Consumers (most animals): Also known as **heterotrophs**, refers to animals that consume other organisms to survive. Consumers are divided into three types:

Primary consumers: Also known as **herbivores**, they subsist on producers, such as plants. Examples include grasshoppers, deer, cows, squirrels, and rabbits.

Secondary consumers: Also known as **carnivores** or predators, they subsist mainly on primary consumers. Examples include lions, wolves, and sharks. Some secondary consumers are also **omnivores**, meaning they consume producers and consumers as well.

Tertiary consumers: Also known as **top carnivores**, they are capable of eating secondary consumers. Many tertiary consumers are also **omnivores**, meaning they also consume primary consumers and occasionally producers as well.

LIFE SCIENCE PRACTICE SET

1. Which of the following describes the proper pathway of blood through the heart?

   (A) vena cava → right atrium → right ventricle → pulmonary artery → pulmonary vein → left atrium → left ventricle → aorta

   (B) vena cava → right atrium → right ventricle → pulmonary vein → pulmonary artery → left atrium → left ventricle → aorta

   (C) vena cava → right atrium → left atrium → pulmonary artery → pulmonary vein → left atrium → left ventricle → aorta

   (D) vena cava → right atrium → left atrium → pulmonary vein → pulmonary artery → left atrium → left ventricle → aorta

2. Most human digestion takes place in the

   (A) esophagus
   (B) stomach
   (C) small intestine
   (D) large intestine

3. Which blood type can be donated to anyone?

   (A) A
   (B) B
   (C) O
   (D) AB

4. A typical human gamete contains

   (A) 2 chromosomes
   (B) 23 chromosomes
   (C) 46 chromosomes
   (D) 92 chromosomes

5. Which of the following is an example of a primary consumer?

   (A) moss
   (B) mushroom
   (C) jackal
   (D) deer

[Answers found on page 178.]

EARTH SCIENCE

Earth science is the study of the Earth and the universe around it. For purposes of the ASVAB, it's helpful to know a few facts about our planet and the solar system in which it travels. Let's begin with a look at geology.

Geology

Geology is the science that deals with the history and composition of the Earth and its life, especially as recorded in rocks. In part by studying rocks, scientists have been able to determine that the Earth is made up of three layers. The outermost layer, or **crust**, comprises roughly one percent of the total Earth's volume. It varies in thickness from 10 kilometers to as much as 80 kilometers. Beneath the crust lies the **mantle**, which comprises more than 75 percent of the Earth's volume. Roughly 3,500 kilometers thick, the mantle contains mostly iron, magnesium, and calcium, and is much hotter and denser than the Earth's surface because temperature and pressure inside the Earth increase with depth.

At the center of the Earth lies the **core**, which is nearly twice as dense as the mantle because its composition is metallic (iron-nickel alloy) rather than stony. The Earth's core contains two distinct parts: a 2,300-kilometer-thick liquid **outer core** and a 1,200-kilometer-radius solid **inner core**.

Plate Tectonics

As noted, the interior of the Earth is quite hot, somewhere between 3,000° and 4,000° C. This heat is generally prevented from escaping thanks to the solid rock in the Earth's upper mantle and crust. The crust and rigid upper part of the mantle (the lithosphere) consist of approximately 30 separate pieces called **plates**. These plates actually move very slowly upon the more ductile mantle beneath (the asthenosphere), and this has caused the continental landmasses to drift slowly apart over the course of hundreds of millions of years.

Along the edges of these plates are **fault lines**. (Fault lines are simply places where the plates slide relative to each other.) When plates slide relative to each other along fault lines earthquakes can occur. When an earthquake occurs, scientists use the **Richter scale** to measure its intensity. The Richter scale goes from 1 to 10, with each step representing a magnitude that is about 10 times greater than the preceding step.

Types of Rocks

The Earth's rocks fall into three categories, based upon how they are formed.

MYSTERIES OF SCIENCE

About once every million years, the Earth's magnetic poles reverse their polarity (magnetic north becomes magnetic south, and vice versa). The last time they did so was about 700,000 years ago. Within a relatively short period of geologic time–probably less than 10,000 years–the existing magnetic field can reduce to a very small intensity and then reestablish itself with approximately equal intensity in exactly the opposite direction. Scientists still don't know why this happens.

Rock type	How it was formed	Examples
Igneous	Formed from the hardening of molten rock, or magma, which is called lava when it reaches the surface of the Earth.	Granite, pumice, basalt, obsidian
Sedimentary	Formed by the sedimentation, or gradual depositing, of small bits of rock, clay, and other materials. Over time this deposited material becomes cemented together. Most fossils are found in sedimentary rocks.	Shale, sandstone, gypsum, dolomite, coal
Metamorphic	Formed when existing rock material is altered through temperature, pressure, or chemical processes.	Marble, slate, gneiss, quartzite

Geologic Time Scale

Most of what is known about the history of our planet has been learned by studying the fossil record found in sedimentary rock. By studying rocks, we now know that the Earth is approximately 4.6 billion years old, and that for most of that time, very few fossil traces were left. This is why the period from 4.6 billion years to 570 million years ago is called the **Precambrian Eon**, meaning the period before the fossil record began. It turns out, however, that early geologists who studied the Precambrian Eon were unable to recognize early, primitive fossils, and in fact life first appeared on Earth as early as 3.5 billion years ago!

Meteorology

Meteorology is not just the study of weather, but of the atmosphere and atmospheric phenomena in general. The first thing you should know is that there are several layers to the atmosphere, beginning here on the surface of the Earth and continuing up several thousand kilometers above us. Here they are.

Troposphere: The troposphere is the lowest level of the atmosphere where all weather takes place; it is the region of rising and falling packets of air. Depending on the latitude and the season, it can range from 6 to 17 kilometers thick. Most of the air surrounding the Earth, which is roughly 79 percent nitrogen and 21 percent oxygen, is found in the troposphere.

Stratosphere: Above the troposphere is the stratosphere, where airflow is mostly horizontal. The thin **ozone layer** in the upper stratosphere has a high concentration of ozone, a particularly reactive form of oxygen. This layer is primarily responsible for absorbing the ultraviolet radiation from the Sun. As you enter the stratosphere, the temperature is about –60° C.

Mesosphere: Above the stratosphere is the mesosphere, which extends to about 90 kilometers above the Earth. As you enter the mesosphere, the temperature starts to drop again, to as low as –90° C. This is where we see "falling stars," meteors that fall to the Earth and burn up in the atmosphere.

Thermosphere: So called because the temperature continues to increase with the altitude, with recorded temperatures reaching as high as 2,000° C at its upper limits, which extends to several thousand kilometers above the Earth.

Fronts

Differences in air pressure cause wind and the movement of air masses of different temperatures toward each other. When a warm air mass overtakes a cold air mass, you have a **warm front**. As the warm air advances, it rides over the cold air ahead of it, which is heavier. As the warm air rises, the water vapor in it condenses into clouds that can produce rain, snow, sleet, or freezing rain—often all four.

When a cold air mass overtakes a warm air mass, you have a **cold front**. Most cold fronts are preceded by a line of precipitation as they roar across an area. However, some cold fronts produce very little or no precipitation as they move. The only sign that a front has moved through your area is a sudden change in winds and temperature.

Sometimes two air masses meet and neither is displaced. Instead, the two fronts push against each other in a stalemate. This is called a **stationary front**. Stationary fronts often cause cloudy, wet weather that can last a week or more.

Clouds

Clouds come in different varieties based on their shape, size, and altitude. The three main types are:

Stratus clouds, which are low-hanging, broad, flat clouds that blanket the sky. The lowest of low clouds, when they occur on the ground they are called fog. Dark stratus clouds indicate that rain will soon occur.

Cumulus clouds, which are massive clouds that are puffy, like popcorn, with relatively flat bottoms and rounded tops. When cumulus clouds darken you can expect heavy rain.

Cirrus clouds are the thin, wispy clouds that occur much higher in the atmosphere, at elevations of 20,000 feet or more.

Our Solar System

Our solar system consists of one star, which we call the Sun, eight planets and all their moons, several thousand minor planets called asteroids, and an equally large number of comets. The Sun's age is calculated to be around 4.7 billion years, which is only slightly older than the Earth itself.

The Sun

Our **Sun** is classified as a **G2V** star, or **yellow dwarf**. G2 stars are approximately 6,000° C at the surface, are yellow, and contain many neutrally charged metals such as iron, magnesium, and calcium. The "V" indicates that the Sun is a dwarf star, or fairly small by the standards of stars.

Although a dwarf in comparison to other stars, the Sun contains almost 99.9 percent of the mass of our solar system. Like all stars, the Sun is a gigantic ball of superheated gas, kept hot by atomic reactions emanating from its center. The temperature at the core of our Sun is thought to be about 15,000,000° C; temperatures at the surface range between 4,000° and 15,000° C. The diameter of the Sun is about 1.4 million kilometers, or more than 100 times that of Earth, and its surface area is approximately 12,000 times that of Earth.

The Planets and Other Phenomena

The four planets closest to the Sun—**Mercury**, **Venus**, **Earth**, and **Mars**—are called **terrestrial planets**, meaning they are similar to our own planet in composition, with inner metal cores and surfaces of rock. Aside from the Earth, only Mars among the four terrestrial planets has moons of its own, although they are much smaller than our own Moon. Earth is the largest of the terrestrial planets.

The four planets beyond Mars—**Jupiter**, **Saturn**, **Uranus**, and **Neptune**—are referred to as the **outer planets**. They also all have rings, most notably so on Saturn. The rings of Saturn, and most likely the other planets as well, are composed mostly of ice crystals. **Pluto**, once considered the ninth planet, is no longer categorized by scientists as a true planet.

ALL IN A DAY'S WORK

A day is a measure of how long it takes a planet to make one full rotation around its axis. One day on Earth is 23 hours, 56 minutes, and 4.091 seconds.

Other planets have different lengths of day:

- Mercury: 59 days
- Venus: 243 days
- Mars: 24 hours, 37 minutes, 23 seconds
- Jupiter: 9 hours, 55 minutes

In addition, the solar system contains thousands of small bodies such as **asteroids** and **comets**. Asteroids are also known as **meteoroids**, and when they fall into the Earth's gravitational field, they are seen as "falling stars," called **meteors**, as they burn up in the Earth's mesosphere. Those meteors that make it to the Earth's surface are called **meteorites**.

Comets are sometimes called dirty snowballs or icy mudballs. They are a mixture of ices (both water and frozen gases) and dust that for some reason didn't get incorporated into planets when the solar system was formed. Comets are invisible except when they are near the Sun. When they are near the Sun and active, comets have highly visible **tails**, up to several hundred million kilometers long, composed of plasma and laced with rays and streamers caused by interactions with the solar wind.

But by far the most important body in the solar system aside from the Sun, as it relates to life on Earth, is our own **Moon**. Because of the gravitational pull that exists between the Moon and Earth, we have **tides**. High tides occur twice a day, when the Moon is at the points closest to and farthest from the affected mass of water. It is suspected that life would never have evolved on land without the constant ebbing and flowing of the oceanic tides on coastal areas.

EARTH SCIENCE PRACTICE SET

1. The ozone layer is found in the

   (A) troposphere
   (B) stratosphere
   (C) mesosphere
   (D) thermosphere

2. What is the layer that is located beneath the Earth's crust?

   (A) inner core
   (B) plates
   (C) mantle
   (D) outer core

3. The clouds that occur at the highest altitudes are called

   (A) cirrus
   (B) cumulus
   (C) nimbus
   (D) stratus

4. Life on Earth has existed for approximately

   (A) 4.6 billion years
   (B) 3.8 billion years
   (C) 2.5 billion years
   (D) 544 million years

5. Which of the following is most responsible for the oceanic tides?

   (A) the gravitational pull of the Sun on the Earth
   (B) the gravitational pull of the Moon on the Earth
   (C) the heat of the Sun
   (D) the magnetic pull of the poles

[Answers found on page 178.]

PHYSICAL SCIENCE

Scientists would know very little about our solar system without an understanding of physics and chemistry, collectively known as the physical sciences. Scientists don't use British measurements such as miles and gallons; instead, they use the metric system. We've already used the metric system throughout most of this chapter, but let's review it quickly.

Measurement

The standard unit of **length** is the **meter**, which is slightly more than three feet, or about 39.4 inches. One thousand meters is called a **kilometer**, which is approximately three-fifths of a mile. One one-hundredth of a meter is called a **centimeter**, and one one-thousandth of a meter is called a **millimeter**.

Using a similar prefix scheme, **mass** is measured in **grams**, **kilograms** (1000 grams), **milligrams** (one-thousandth of a gram), and so on. There are approximately 28.3 grams in an ounce, and a mass of one kilogram will have a weight of approximately 2.2 pounds (at the surface of the Earth).

Volume is the measurement of three-dimensional space. One **cubic centimeter** can be called just that, or it can be called a **milliliter**. A milliliter is also one one-thousandth of a **liter**. A liter is equal to slightly more than a quart in liquid measure, or about 33.8 ounces, with about 3.79 liters in a gallon.

Finally, the metric system equivalent of temperature is the **Celsius scale**, also known as **degrees centigrade**. According to the **Fahrenheit scale**, which is more familiar to most people in the United States, water freezes at 32° F and boils at 212° F. On the Celsius scale, water freezes at 0° C and boils at 100° C. The general equations for converting from the Fahrenheit scale to the Celsius scale, or vice versa, are as follows:

$$F° = \frac{9}{5}C° + 32$$

$$C° = \frac{5}{9}(F° - 32)$$

Finally, there is one other temperature scale commonly used by scientists, known as the **Kelvin scale**, or the **absolute zero scale**. Absolute zero is the temperature at which matter has no heat and its molecules are completely still; in theory, absolute zero is the lowest temperature possible. On the Kelvin scale, absolute zero is set at 0° K, which is equal to –273° C. Otherwise, degrees Kelvin use the same increments as degrees Celsius, so that water freezes at 273° K and boils at 373° K.

Physics

Physics is the science dealing with the properties, changes, and interactions of matter and energy. There are many branches of physics, including mechanics, thermodynamics, magnetism, optics, and electricity. This review will cover only the physics that might appear on the General Science section of the ASVAB.

Important Formulas and Definitions

In physics, words that are often used imprecisely in common parlance have very strict definitions. For example the words **mass** and **weight** are often used interchangeably, when in fact they have very different meanings. Mass is defined as the amount of matter that something has, whereas weight is defined as the force exerted on an object's mass by gravity.

Velocity, Momentum, and Acceleration

Velocity is the rate at which an object changes position. **Velocity = displacement of an object ÷ time**. In physics, velocity is called a **vector quantity**, meaning it is fully described by both a magnitude and a direction.

Momentum is the tendency of an object to continue moving in the same direction. **Momentum = mass × velocity**.

Acceleration is the rate of change of velocity. **Acceleration = change in velocity ÷ change in time**.

Force, Work, and Power

Force is the push or pull that forces an object to change its speed or direction. **Weight** is just one example of a force, in this case the force of gravity. A unit of force is called a **newton**, which is the force required to impart an acceleration of one meter per second squared to a mass of one kilogram.

Work is defined as the force exerted on an object times the distance moved in the direction of the force. **Work = force × distance**. A unit of work is called a **newton-meter** or **joule**.

Power is the rate at which work is performed. **Power = work ÷ time**, or **Power = (force × distance) ÷ time**. A unit of power is called a **joule per second**, also known as a **watt**.

Newton's Laws

Sir Isaac Newton was an English physicist, mathematician, and certifiable genius. In the seventeenth century he came up with some of our most important formulas for understanding the properties of motion and gravity. Here they are.

1. Newton's first law of motion. *An object at rest tends to stay at rest, and an object in motion tends to stay in motion at a constant speed in a straight line (constant velocity), unless acted upon by an unbalanced force.* An example of an unbalanced force—one that keeps objects in motion from staying in motion on Earth—is friction, the force that resists relative motion between two bodies in contact.

2. Newton's second law of motion. *When dealing with an object for which all existing forces are not balanced, the acceleration of that object, as produced by the net force, is in the same direction as the net force and directly proportional to the magnitude of the net force, and is inversely proportional to the object's mass.* Expressed mathematically, Newton's second law states the following: **Net force = mass × acceleration**. This law is also known as the **law of inertia**, because the greater the mass of an object, the greater the force needed to overcome its inertia (its reluctance to change velocity).

3. Newton's third law of motion. *For every action, there is an equal and opposite reaction.* In other words, when an object exerts a force on another object, the second object exerts a force of the same magnitude but in the opposite direction on the first object. For example, consider what happens when a gun is fired. A bullet fires and the gun recoils. The recoil is the result of action-reaction force pairs. As the gases from the gunpowder explosion expand, the gun pushes the bullet forward and the bullet pushes the gun backward. The acceleration of the recoiling gun is, however, smaller than the acceleration of the bullet, because acceleration is inversely proportional to mass, and the bullet, as a rule, has a smaller mass than the gun.

4. Newton's law of gravitation. *All objects in the universe attract each other with an equal force that varies directly as a product of their masses, and inversely as a square of their distance from each other. This force is known as* **gravity**. Take, for example, the gravitational force between the Sun and the Earth. According to Newton's law of gravitation:

- The force exerted on the Earth by the Sun is equal and opposite to the force exerted on the Sun by the Earth.

- If the mass of the Earth were doubled, the force on the Earth would double.

- If the mass of the Sun were doubled, the force on the Earth would double.

- If the Earth were twice as far away from the Sun, the force on the Earth would be a factor of four smaller.

Energy

Energy can be defined as the **capacity to do work**. It may be either **kinetic** or **potential**. **Kinetic energy** is the energy possessed by a moving object. **Potential energy** is the energy stored in an object as a result of its position, shape, or state.

According to the law of conservation of energy, energy can neither be created nor destroyed. Instead, it changes from one form to another.

Sound and light energy travel in waves (although it gets complicated in the case of light). So let's take a look at the properties of waves.

Sound Waves

Sound waves are produced when an object vibrates, disturbing the medium around it. These waves can travel through air, liquids, and solids, but they cannot be transmitted through a vacuum, or empty space. Sound waves transmitted through air do not travel as fast as those transmitted through water, and those transmitted through water do not travel as fast as those transmitted through metal or wood.

The pitch of sound is directly related to the frequency of the sound waves. Sound waves with a high frequency produce a high pitch. Sound waves with a very high pitch are inaudible to humans, although they can be heard by dogs and other creatures. Sometimes, a human (and probably a dog as well) will perceive a sound as being a different frequency than the actual frequency of the sound. This is due to the **Doppler effect**. The Doppler effect occurs when either the source of the sound waves, the listener, or both, are moving.

Electromagnetic Spectrum

While on the subject of light, you should realize that visible light makes up only one small part—the visible part—of the electromagnetic spectrum. The electromagnetic spectrum covers all the different wavelengths and frequencies of photon energy, radiant energy such as the energy we receive from the Sun. Visible light waves fall in the middle of the electromagnetic spectrum. Starting with lowest frequency (and therefore the longest wavelength), the electromagnetic spectrum goes from **radio waves** to **microwaves** to **infrared waves** to **visible light** to **ultraviolet light** to **X-rays** and finally to **gamma rays**, the most active radiant energy known to exist.

Visible light breaks down into different colors as well, based upon the frequency of the waves. Red has the lowest frequency, which is why wavelengths just below the frequency of visible light are called infrared; likewise, violet has the highest frequency, so wavelengths just above the frequency of visible light are called ultraviolet.

Optics

As noted above, light, as well as the entire electromagnetic spectrum, possesses properties of waves. However, unlike sound waves, which are mechanical, light waves are electromagnetic and can travel through empty space. They also travel at much higher speeds than do sound waves. The speed of light traveling through a vacuum is 299,792,458 meters per second (or roughly 300 million meters per second or 186,000 miles per second).

Refraction

It should be noted, however, that the speed of light can slow down, depending on the material through which the waves move; for example, light travels more slowly through water or glass than through a vacuum. The ratio by which light is slowed down is called the **refractive index** of that medium. For instance, the refractive index of a diamond is 2.4, which means that light travels 2.4 times faster when traveling through a vacuum than when traveling through a diamond. Not only does the light change speeds as it travels through different transparent media, but it bends as well.

Reflection

Any wave, including light, that bounces off a flat, smooth barrier follows the **law of reflection**, which states that the **angle of incidence** is equal to the **angle of reflection** as measured from a line normal to the barrier. In the case of light, this barrier is often a mirror.

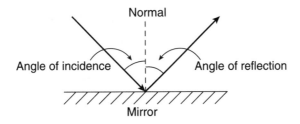

Figure 4. Law of reflection

Concave and Convex Mirrors and Lenses

Mirrors and lenses either can be flat, or they can be concave (curved in, like a cave) or convex (curved out, like a swelling). Because of the law of reflection, a **concave mirror** is also called a **converging mirror**, because the angles of incidence of rays of light parallel to the normal all converge upon a point.

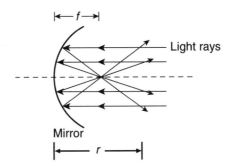

Figure 5. Converging mirror

If you draw the mirror away from the source of the image, the image falls out of focus as the image source nears the mirror's **focal point**, the point where the mirror's angles of incidence converge. As the image source keeps moving beyond the focal point, the image reappears in the mirror, only upside down.

A **convex mirror**, on the other hand, is known as a **diverging mirror** because it diverges the light waves that strike it.

Lenses, unlike mirrors, operate on the principle of refraction. A **concave lens**—one that is thicker on the edges than it is in the middle—is also known as a **diverging lens** because it diverges the light waves that pass through it. In nearsightedness, light waves converge before they meet the retina. A nearsighted person sees objects close up but not far away. A concave lens placed before the eye bends light so that it converges further back in the eye, reaching the retina and correcting nearsightedness.

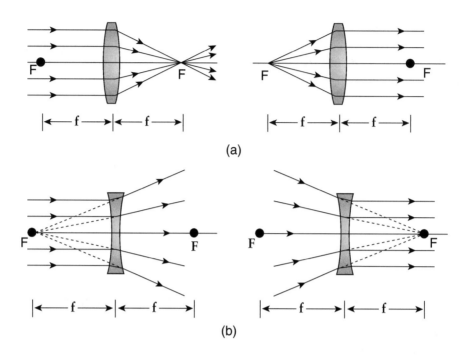

Figure 6. Converging lens (a) and diverging lens (b)

A **convex lens**—one that is thicker in the middle than on the edges—is also called a **converging lens** because it converges parallel waves that pass through it. This type of lens is used in reading glasses to correct farsightedness, as well as in magnifying glasses, cameras, telescopes, and microscopes.

Heat

There are three means by which heat energy may be transferred from one object to another: **conduction**, **convection**, and **radiation**.

Conduction is the simplest method of heat transfer. It is accomplished by direct contact, such as placing your finger on a hot iron, which we recommend you not try at home. Metals are generally good **conductors** of heat. Other materials, such as wood, Styrofoam, and plastic, are poor conductors of heat, which makes them good **insulators**.

Convection is the transfer of heat unevenly in a liquid or gas, lowering the density of the heated liquid or gas, which causes it to rise and the cooler liquid or gas to fall. The resulting circulatory movement is termed convection.

Radiation occurs when electromagnetic waves transmit heat. The heat we get from the Sun is called radiation.

Magnetism

Simple magnets have two poles, a north pole and a south pole. Much like a Hollywood romance, with magnets opposites attract. If you try to bring together two north poles of a magnet—or two south poles for that matter—they will repel one another, and you can feel their repulsive force. If, on the other hand, you move the north pole of one magnet toward the south pole of another magnet, they will attract each other.

Because the Earth itself is magnetized, with a North Pole and a South Pole, a magnetic compass, which contains a small, lightweight magnet balanced on a nearly frictionless, nonmagnetic surface, can be used to tell direction. The magnet, which is generally called a needle, has one end marked with an arrow and often the letter "N." This end of the needle is the magnet's south pole, which constantly orients itself to point toward the Earth's North Pole, allowing the person reading the compass to gain bearings from that direction.

Chemistry

Chemistry is the science dealing with the composition and properties of substances, and with the reactions by which substances are produced from or converted into other substances. Matter is anything that has mass and occupies space, and any form of matter has certain chemical properties based upon its molecular composition. Let's start by going over some basic terms.

Element: A substance that cannot be separated into different substances by ordinary chemical methods. All matter is composed of elements, and all the known elements are listed on the Periodic Table of Elements (see figure 7 on the following page).

Atom: The smallest component of an element that still retains the properties of the element. An atom may combine with similar particles of other elements to produce compounds. Atoms consist of a complex arrangement of electrons in motion about a positively charged nucleus containing protons and (except for hydrogen) neutrons.

Proton: A subatomic particle found in the atom's nucleus that carries a positive electric charge.

Neutron: A subatomic particle found in the atom's nucleus that does not have an electric charge and is therefore neutral.

Electron: A subatomic particle that orbits the nucleus of an atom. An electron carries a negative charge and has a miniscule mass. Ordinarily, an atom has the same number of negative electrons around the nucleus as the number of positive protons in the nucleus.

Molecule: The smallest particle of an element or compound that can exist in the free state and still retain the characteristics of the element or compound. The molecules of elements consist of one atom or two or more similar atoms; the molecules of compounds consist of two or more different atoms.

1 H 1.0																	2 He 4.0
3 Li 6.9	4 Be 9.0											5 B 10.8	6 C 12.0	7 N 14.0	8 O 16.0	9 F 19.0	10 Ne 20.2
11 Na 23.0	12 Mg 24.3											13 Al 27.0	14 Si 28.1	15 P 31.0	16 S 32.1	17 Cl 35.5	18 Ar 39.9
19 K 39.1	20 Ca 40.1	21 Sc 45.0	22 Ti 47.9	23 V 50.9	24 Cr 52.0	25 Mn 54.9	26 Fe 55.8	27 Co 58.9	28 Ni 58.7	29 Cu 63.5	30 Zn 65.4	31 Ga 69.7	32 Ge 72.6	33 As 74.9	34 Se 79.0	35 Br 79.9	36 Kr 83.8
37 Rb 85.5	38 Sr 87.6	39 Y 88.9	40 Zr 91.2	41 Nb 92.9	42 Mo 95.9	43 Tc (98)	44 Ru 101.1	45 Rh 102.9	46 Pd 106.4	47 Ag 107.9	48 Cd 112.4	49 In 114.8	50 Sn 118.7	51 Sb 121.8	52 Te 127.6	53 I 126.9	54 Xe 131.3
55 Cs 132.9	56 Ba 137.3	57 La* 138.9	72 Hf 178.5	73 Ta 180.9	74 W 183.9	75 Re 186.2	76 Os 190.2	77 Ir 192.2	78 Pt 195.1	79 Au 197.0	80 Hg 200.6	81 Tl 204.4	82 Pb 207.2	83 Bi 209.0	84 Po (209)	85 At (210)	86 Rn (222)
87 Fr (223)	88 Ra 226.0	89 Act† 227.0	104 Unq (261)	105 Unp (262)	106 Unh (263)	107 Uns (262)	108 Uno (265)	109 Une (267)									

58 Ce 140.1	59 Pr 140.9	60 Nd 144.2	61 Pm (145)	62 Sm 150.4	63 Eu 152.0	64 Gd 157.3	65 Tb 158.9	66 Dy 162.5	67 Ho 164.9	68 Er 167.3	69 Tm 168.9	70 Yb 173.0	71 Lu 175.0
90 Th 232.0	91 Pa (231)	92 U 238.0	93 Np (237)	94 Pu (244)	95 Am (243)	96 Cm (247)	97 Bk (247)	98 Cf (251)	99 Es (252)	100 Fm (257)	101 Md (258)	102 No (259)	103 Lr (260)

Figure 7. Periodic Table of the Elements

In order to be able to read the Periodic Table of Elements, there are a few things you need to understand. For starters, elements are arranged in order of increasing **atomic number**, from left to right and from top to bottom. The different **rows** of elements are called **periods**. The periods correspond to the **shells**, or the different orbits that electrons occupy around atoms. As a rule, electrons will occupy the lowest shell they can, and move on to higher shells only after lower shells are occupied (although this rule is sometimes violated) so as to minimize the energy of the atom. Every element in the top row (the first period) has one shell for its electrons. Every element in the second row (the second period) has two shells for its electrons, and so on. At this time, the maximum number of shells is seven.

The Periodic Table has a special name for its columns, too. The elements in a column are called a **group**. The elements in a group have the same number of electrons in their outer shell. It is the group that an element occupies, much more than the period, that determines its chemical properties. This is because the number of electrons needed to complete an element's outer shell shapes the way in which it reacts with other elements to form molecules. For instance, every element in the first column (Group I) has one electron in its outer shell. The elements in this group are called **alkali metals**, which describe soft, silvery metals that react strongly with water. The further down the group you go, the more violent this reaction is.

By the same token, every element on the second column (Group II) has two electrons in the outer shell. As you keep counting the columns, you'll know how many electrons are in the outer shell. Note that the far right-hand column is composed of a group called the **noble gases**, sometimes referred to as inert gases, because these elements generally don't react with other elements since their outer shell is completely filled.

Now take a look at an individual element box within the Periodic Table. Here's **chlorine**.

```
17
Cl
35.5
```

Figure 8. Chlorine

Its **atomic number** is 17, which is the number of protons in the nucleus of a chlorine atom, and also the number of electrons orbiting its shells. Its **atomic symbol**, Cl, is fairly close to its name, unlike the symbols of some other common elements, such as **Fe** (iron), **Au** (gold), **Ag** (silver), **W** (tungsten), or **Na** (sodium), symbols that derive from the elements' Latin names, rather than their familiar English names.

Finally, the **atomic weight** of chlorine is listed as **35.45**, which is the weight of one atom of chlorine expressed in atomic mass units.

Compounds

Unstable elements readily form into **compounds** with properties very distinct from the elements from which they are composed. For instance, the aforementioned sodium and chlorine, both of which are extremely unstable and noxious as elements, combine to form the stable and edible compound sodium chloride (NaCl), more commonly known as **table** salt. Table salt is called an **ionic compound** because each chlorine atom borrows an electron from each sodium atom and the atoms stick closely together to form a very tightly bound crystalline structure when salt is in solid form. When it is placed in solution, however, such as when table salt is poured in water, the atoms dissociate into sodium ions and chloride ions.

An **ion** is an electrically charged atom; in this case each of the sodium atoms is positively charged because it has lent an electron to its corresponding chloride atom, and each of the chloride atoms is negatively charged for the same reason.

Table sugar is an example of a **covalent compound**, which means, among other things, that it does not ionize when dissolved in water. In a covalent compound, the atoms in the molecule have covalent bonds; that is, they share electrons in pairs, so that each atom provides half the electrons.

Acids and Bases

An **acid** is a substance that gives up positively charged hydrogen ions (H^+) when dissolved in water. Acids corrode metals and generally have a sour taste (those that are potable, that is). Some common acidic solutions are vinegar (which has acetic acid) and lemon juice (which has citric acid). More potent acids include hydrochloric acid, nitric acid, battery acid, and sulfuric acid, all of which are extremely corrosive and must be handled with the utmost care.

A **base** is a substance that gives up negative charged hydroxyl ions (OH^-) when dissolved in water. Basic substances are also referred to as **alkaline**. Bases typically taste bitter. Some common basic substances found in a kitchen include baking soda and soap. More potent bases include sodium hydroxide (lye) and bleach. When acids and bases react (and they react together rather powerfully), the substances neutralize each other and turn into water and a salt.

The **pH** of a solution is a number from 0 to 14 that indicates how basic or acidic that solution is. According to the pH scale, solutions with a pH less than 7 are acidic, with the degree of acidity increasing tenfold with each declining number. For instance, black coffee has a pH of 5; vinegar, which is 100 times as acidic as coffee, has a pH of 3; and battery acid, which is 100 times as acidic as vinegar, has a pH of 1. A solution with a pH of 7 is neutral. Pure water has a pH of 7. Solutions with a pH greater than 7 are basic, with the degree of alkalinity once again increasing tenfold with each increasing number.

Physical Versus Chemical Reactions

Matter may undergo either a **physical change** or a **chemical change**. The form, size, and shape of matter may be altered in a physical change, but the molecules remain unchanged.

In a chemical change, molecules of new matter are formed that are different from the original molecules of matter. When molecules undergo a chemical change, the process is called a **chemical reaction**. The molecules that enter the reaction are called **reactants** and the molecules that result from the reaction are called **products**. Common examples of chemical reactions include the formation of rust on iron and the conversion of wood to charcoal in a fire.

PHYSICAL SCIENCE PRACTICE SET

1. What is 77° F in degrees Celsius?

   (A) 25°
   (B) 32°
   (C) 37°
   (D) 5°

2. Which of the following best explains the recoil action of a shooting gun?

   (A) Newton's First Law of Motion
   (B) Newton's Second Law of Motion
   (C) Newton's Third Law of Motion
   (D) Newton's Law of Gravitation

3. The most common element in the Earth's atmosphere is

   (A) helium
   (B) hydrogen
   (C) nitrogen
   (D) oxygen

4. Which of the following waves on the electromagnetic spectrum has the highest frequency?

   (A) microwaves
   (B) X-rays
   (C) visible light
   (D) radio waves

5. Pure water has a pH of

   (A) 1
   (B) 7
   (C) 0
   (D) 14

[Answers found on page 179.]

ANSWERS AND EXPLANATIONS

Life Science Practice Set

1. **A**

The proper pathway of blood through the heart is as follows:

vena cava → right atrium → right ventricle → pulmonary artery → pulmonary vein → left atrium → left ventricle → aorta

2. **C**

Most digestion takes place in the small intestine.

3. **C**

Type O blood, also known as the "universal donor" type, can be donated to anyone.

4. **B**

A typical human gamete contains half the number of chromosomes as a normal cell, or 23.

5. **D**

A deer is an example of a primary consumer, that is, an animal that consumes only vegetation.

Earth Science Practice Set

1. **B**

The ozone layer is found in the upper stratosphere.

2. **C**

The mantle lies beneath the Earth's crust.

3. **A**

Cirrus clouds are found at the highest altitudes of all clouds.

4. **B**

Life on Earth has existed for approximately 3.8 billion years.

5. **B**

The oceanic tides are caused by the gravitational pull of the Moon on the Earth.

Physical Science Practice Set

1. **A**

To convert the temperature from degrees Fahrenheit to degrees Celsius, first subtract 32, and then multiply by $\frac{5}{9}$.

$77 - 32 = 45$

$45 \times \frac{5}{9} = 25$

2. **C**

The recoil action of a shooting gun is explained by Newton's Third Law of Motion, that is, for every action there is an equal and opposite reaction.

3. **C**

Nitrogen accounts for about 77 percent of the composition of the atmosphere.

4. **B**

Of the wave states listed, X-rays have the highest frequency in the electromagnetic spectrum (gamma rays have an even higher frequency).

5. **B**

Pure water has a pH of 7, making it a neutral solution.

CHAPTER EIGHT

Electronics Information

Basic electrical and electronics knowledge grows more valuable with each passing day. Many devices that were once controlled by mechanical means have now become part of the electronic domain. Electronics has breathed new life into many machines that have been around for a long time, as well as brought new machines into existence that never would have been possible with older technology.

THE ATOM

A solid understanding of electricity begins at the atomic level. Matter is composed of **atoms**, which are the smallest particles that elements can be broken into and still retain the properties of that element.

Two types of particles are found within the nucleus: **protons** and **neutrons**. Protons have a positive charge, and neutrons are neutrally charged. The nucleus is the heaviest part of the atom and accounts for the majority of the atom's mass. Electrons that are in motion around the nucleus have a negative charge, and there is one electron for each proton that resides in the nucleus.

The various orbits that the electrons occupy around the nucleus are known as **shells**. The shells are thought to be limited in their capacity to hold electrons. The first shell that is closest to the nucleus can hold a maximum of two electrons. If an atom has more than two electrons, this first shell would be filled and then the remaining atoms would occupy the second shell. The second shell can hold a maximum of eight electrons, so an atom with more than ten electrons would fill the first two shells and then any remaining electrons would go into the third shell.

The third shell can hold up to 18 electrons. For example, a copper atom has 29 electrons, so it would fill the first three shells completely and have one electron left to begin a fourth shell. The outer shell of an atom is known as its **valence shell**, and this shell plays a major role in determining the electrical properties of an element.

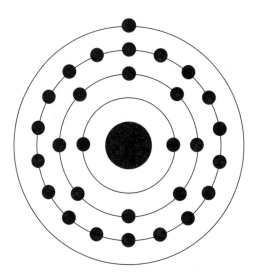

Figure 1. Copper atom (29 electrons)

The number of electrons that reside in the valence shell are what determines whether an element is a **conductor**, a **semiconductor**, or an **insulator**. A conductor is an element that freely conducts electricity, whereas an insulator does not conduct electricity at all. A semiconductor is neither a good conductor nor insulator, but has some remarkable properties that make it very useful for making electronic components.

ELECTRON FLOW THEORY

A convenient way of visualizing how electricity works is to imagine it as electrons flowing through a conductor. The force that inspires this movement is a shortage of electrons at one end of the conductor, and an excess of electrons at the other end. The atoms of the conductor act like a "bucket brigade," sending free electrons down the line as they pick up free electrons from upstream.

In **electron flow theory**, electrons flow away from areas of excess negative charge, to those with a deficiency of negative charge. When a conductor is connected across the terminals of the battery, the electrons in the conductor will be forced away from the negative terminal of the battery and toward the positive terminal.

VOLTAGE

In order to make electrons move through a conductor, there must be a force that causes them to move. Water will move from a high-pressure area in a pipe toward a lower-pressure area, but if the pressure is equal at both ends, no movement takes place. Electricity is no different, as there must be electrical "pressure" applied to a conductor to cause electrons to move.

Electrical pressure is known as **voltage**, and it is measured in volts (symbolized by the letter **V**). The higher the voltage that is applied to a conductor, the greater the electrical pressure. Voltage is also known as **electrical potential**, or **electromotive force**. A technician would measure voltage using a **voltmeter**.

CURRENT

The rate of flow of electrons through a conductor is known as **current**. Current is measured in **amperes**, and an ampere is defined as one **coulomb** of electrical charge flowing past a point in one second. The symbol used for amperes is **A**.

One coulomb is the amount of charge in 6.25×10^{18} electrons. This is the same as 6,250,000,000,000,000,000 electrons. If this many electrons flow past a point in a conductor in one second, one ampere of current is flowing. Current is measured using an **ammeter**.

AC Versus DC

There are two types of electrical current: **direct current** and **alternating current**. Direct current (**DC**) means that current only flows one way in a conductor. This is the type of current that is delivered by a battery. Alternating current (**AC**) is when the current flowing in a conductor changes direction (moves back and forth) many times in a second. Household electrical outlets deliver alternating current.

Here in North America, alternating current is always delivered at **60 cycles per second**. This is also known as **60 hertz** (**Hz**). One cycle would be voltage starting at zero, increasing to a maximum level in one direction, then decreasing to zero, increasing to a maximum level in the reverse direction, then returning to zero again. Sixty hertz means that 60 complete voltage cycles like the one just described take place in one second.

RESISTANCE

Opposition to the flow of current is known as **resistance**. Resistance is measured in **ohms**, and one ohm is the amount of resistance that will allow one ampere of current to flow if one volt of electrical pressure is placed on a conductor. The symbol for the ohm is Ω (omega), and resistance can be measured using an **ohmmeter**.

All conductors have a certain amount of resistance, with some having more than others. Three materials that are most often used as conductors are silver, copper, and aluminum. Of these three, silver is the best conductor as it exhibits the lowest resistance. Unfortunately, silver is relatively expensive, so the next best choice is copper. Copper has only a slightly higher resistance than silver, but is much less expensive. Most cable and wire is currently made from copper. Aluminum has a higher resistance than copper, and exhibits some other characteristics that make it even less than desirable as a conductor. While aluminum was used extensively in residential wiring at one time, it is now used only in a few select applications.

As resistance in a conductor increases, current flow decreases. This means that current and resistance are **inversely proportional**. Voltage and current, on the other hand, are **directly proportional**. Anytime voltage increases, current will also increase.

OHM'S LAW

The relationship between voltage, current, and resistance is summed up in **Ohm's Law**. Ohm's Law states that voltage in volts is equal to the current in amperes multiplied by the resistance in ohms. This is represented by the formula:

$$\textbf{E} = \textbf{I} \times \textbf{R}$$

The letters used in the formula can be confusing, but it's important to be familiar with them since this is the way that Ohm's Law is most often stated. **E** represents voltage. This is best remembered as **Electromotive force**, which is another word for voltage. **I** represents current. Current is the rate of flow of electrons, or the **Intensity** of the flow. (Specifically, **I** is the rate of charge flow.) Finally, **R** represents **Resistance**.

UNITS

When using Ohm's Law, it is important to keep in mind that the quantities used must be expressed in ohms, amperes, and volts. If any of these quantities are given in other units, these should be converted before making calculations with them.

For instance, current is often expressed in **milliamperes**. A milliampere (**mA**) is $\dfrac{1}{1,000}$ of an ampere. Milliamperes can be converted to amperes by moving the decimal point three places to the left. So, 500 mA would be the same as 0.5 A.

Resistance is often expressed as **kilohms** (KΩ) or megohms (MΩ). A KΩ is 1,000 ohms, and a MΩ is 1,000,000 ohms. To convert kilohms to ohms, move the decimal point three places to the right. 6 KΩ would then become 6,000 Ω. Megohms can be converted to ohms by moving the decimal point six places to the right. 10 MΩ would be the same as 10,000,000 Ω.

Voltage can be given in a number of different units. Small voltages are expressed as **millivolts** (**mV**), which are the same as $\frac{1}{1,000}$ of a volt. Converting mV to V requires that the decimal point be moved three places to the left. 1,000 mV would be the same as 1 V.

Large voltages can be given in **kilovolts** (**KV**) or even **megavolts** (**MV**). A KV is 1,000 volts, so converting KV to V requires the decimal point to be moved three places to the right. Therefore, 3 KV equals 3,000 V. Since a MV is 1,000,000 volts, converting to volts requires the decimal point to be moved 6 places to the right. 6 MV then becomes 6,000,000 V.

ELECTRICAL POWER

Electrical power is a term that refers to the actual rate at which energy is provided to and consumed by an electric circuit. Power is expressed in **watts**, and can be calculated by multiplying the voltage (in volts) applied to the circuit by the current (in amperes) that flows in the circuit. This is represented by the formula:

$$\mathbf{P = I \times E}$$

BASIC CIRCUITS

In order for electric current to flow, there must be a **circuit** for it to follow. There are three essential components of an electrical circuit: a voltage **source**, a **load**, and **conductors** to connect the load to the voltage source. When these three components are connected so that current can flow, we have a **closed circuit**.

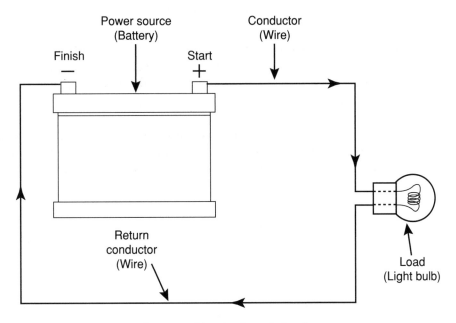

Figure 2. Simple closed circuit

A load is basically a resistance that converts electrical energy into some other energy form. For instance, a light bulb is a load. It is a resistance and it converts electrical energy into light energy and heat. Other examples of loads are electric motors, heating elements, and solenoids.

If a load's resistance were to decrease, the current flowing in the circuit would increase. However, if the circuit were broken, as in a wire (conductor) being disconnected, no current would flow. This would be called an **open circuit**, and the circuit's resistance would be described as infinite. Infinite resistance causes no current flow; low resistance causes high current flow.

Series, Parallel, and Series-Parallel Circuits

An electrical circuit that has only one path for current to flow is known as a **series circuit**. A break (opening) at any point in the circuit will cause current to stop flowing in all parts of the circuit.

Figure 3. Series circuit

In a series circuit, *the current flow will be the same in all parts of the circuit.* Since there is only one path for current to follow in a series circuit, current will be the same throughout the circuit. Voltage measured across each of the components, on the other hand, may be different depending on their resistance.

It is much more common for loads to be wired in **parallel**. With this arrangement, each load is wired "across" the other loads, instead of in-line with them. If any one of the loads were to fail (turn into an open circuit), this would have no impact on the operation of the other loads.

Figure 4. Parallel circuit

Parallel circuits are the exact opposite of series circuits in that *voltage is the same throughout each parallel branch of the circuit,* while current flow varies. All components in a parallel circuit will have the same voltage applied to them, but the current flow through each of these components will vary depending on the resistance of the component.

The most popular arrangement is the **series-parallel circuit**. This would have some components, such as an on/off switch, wired in series with a number of loads that are connected in parallel.

Figure 5. Series-parallel circuit

Most residential wiring circuits are series-parallel. Wall outlets are wired in parallel, but are all fed from a circuit breaker that is wired in series. Switching off the circuit breaker will turn off power to all of the outlets. However, if the circuit breaker is on, voltage is provided to all of the outlets whether there are loads plugged into them or not.

Ground

When electrical circuits are constructed, it is often useful to build them on a chassis that can act as a conductor. This permits common connections in the circuit to be joined at the chassis, which simplifies the wiring immensely. When this common connection represents the zero voltage point of the system, it is known as the circuit's **ground**.

In residential wiring, ground is a common connection throughout the wiring system that protects against electrical shock. All of the wiring grounds are connected to an **earth ground** (such as a copper rod driven into the ground or buried conduit) and this is used to guide electrical current away from panels and equipment should an internal short circuit take place.

The ground wire in an electrical cord is connected to the **chassis** (frame) of the equipment. Since earth ground is a zero voltage point, all "stray" electricity will go to it by following the path of least resistance through the copper ground conductor. This system can only work if the ground prong is intact on the plug of the appliance's electrical cord. Do not use any piece of electrical equipment that does not have an intact ground prong on its plug!

ELECTRICAL COMPONENTS

There are two major types of resistors used today: the **fixed resistor** and the **variable resistor**.

Resistors

Not all components within an electrical circuit require the same voltage. There are also times when it is useful to be able to raise or limit current in a circuit in order to control certain functions (i.e., volume in a stereo). A component that can be utilized to limit current and/or voltage is a **resistor**.

A resistor does what its name suggests: It creates a specific amount of resistance that generates a voltage drop when current passes through it.

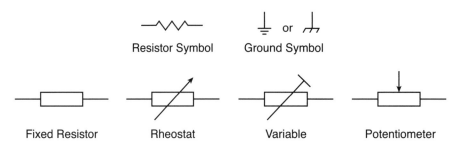

Resistor Symbol   Ground Symbol

Fixed Resistor   Rheostat   Variable   Potentiometer

Figure 6. Resistor symbols

Capacitors

Capacitors (also known as **condensers**) are electrical storage units. They are constructed as two metal foil conducting plates with a very thin insulator (known as a **dielectric**) between them. Because of the very close proximity of the two foil conducting plates, it is possible to connect a DC voltage source across a capacitor and store an electrical charge.

General Capacitor   Fixed Capacitor   Variable Capacitor   Trimmer Capacitor

Figure 7. Capacitor symbols

A capacitor can store an electrical charge because the DC voltage source creates an excess of electrons on the negative plate and a shortage of electrons on the positive plate. The electrostatic attraction between the positive and negative charges keeps the charge intact in the capacitor, even when the voltage source is removed. The capacitor will discharge itself if a conductor is connected across it, as a path is then created for electrons to flow from the negative plate to the positive plate.

Since the capacitor can charge and discharge easily, it will allow AC (alternating current) to flow across it, but will block DC (direct current). As the frequency (cycles per second) of alternating current increases, a capacitor's opposition to the flow of that current decreases.

A capacitor's opposition to the flow of current is known as **capacitive reactance**, and this is measured in ohms.

Figure 8. Simple condenser

Capacitance is represented by the symbol **C**, and its unit of measurement is the **farad**. A farad is sufficient capacitance to store one coulomb of electrons with an electrical potential of one volt applied.

Inductors

As electric current passes through a wire, a magnetic field is generated around the wire. The magnetic field can be made stronger by winding the wire into a coil. This then generates a magnetic field. If the coil is wound onto a ferrous (iron) core, the magnetic field around the coil becomes even stronger. This is because magnetic lines of force travel more easily through iron than through air.

When current first flows through a coil, the magnetic field builds relatively slowly. This is because the expanding magnetic field generates a voltage in the coil that opposes the original current flow. This is known as **counter-emf**, and it is produced by a process known as **self-induction**.

When the current is cut off, the magnetic field then collapses, and this collapsing magnetic field generates a voltage in the coil that keeps the current flowing.

Electrical components that exhibit the property of self-induction are known as **inductors**. Inductors resist change in current flow. If current is increasing, the inductor opposes the increase by generating a voltage that moves against the applied current. If current decreases, the inductor uses the magnetic energy in the coil to oppose the decrease and to keep the current flowing.

Figure 9. Inductor symbol

The symbol used to represent induction is **L**. Induction is measured in **henries**, but since this is a very large unit, it is more common for inductors to be rated in millihenries ($\frac{1}{1,000}$ of a henry) or microhenries ($\frac{1}{1,000,000}$ of a henry).

Inductors work exactly opposite to capacitors, in the sense that they allow DC to pass easily, but resist the flow of AC. This is known as **inductive reactance**, and it will rise in direct proportion to the frequency of the current flowing through the inductor. Higher frequencies mean higher inductive reactance or opposition to the flow of current. Like capacitive reactance, inductive reactance is measured in ohms.

Semiconductors

The term **semiconductor** refers to an element that has four electrons in its valence shell. Since the bonds between these four electrons and the nucleus are somewhat strong, these elements are neither good conductors nor good insulators. Elements that are widely recognized as semiconductors are **silicon** and **germanium**.

In their pure form, silicon and germanium are not particularly useful. However, when impurities are added to their crystalline structure in a process called **doping**, a whole new world of possibilities springs forth.

The crystalline structure of pure silicon is very stable. The four valence electrons in each silicon atom bond with the valence electrons in the atoms around it, so no free electrons exist to allow current flow. This can be changed by "doping" the silicon's crystal structure with either phosphorus, arsenic, or antimony. Since these elements all have five electrons in their valence shell, they will bond themselves to the other silicon atoms, but leave one free electron that is able to migrate throughout the crystal. This changes the silicon crystal into an **N-type** material. This new material is still electrically neutral, but is able to conduct electricity due to the presence of free electrons.

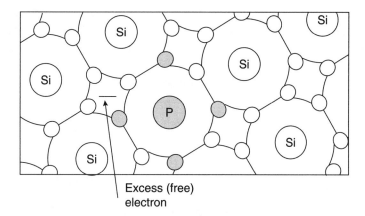

Figure 10. N-type material

If silicon is doped with elements that have three electrons in their valence shells (such as boron or indium), the result is a "**hole**" being left where an electron would normally reside in the crystalline structure. These holes can also migrate throughout the crystal. This takes place as an electron moves into a hole, thus creating a hole in the spot it previously occupied. As electrons flow in one direction, holes will flow in the opposite direction. **P-type** material is thus noted for its ability to conduct current by the movement of holes.

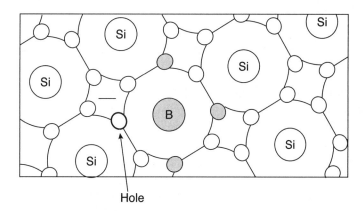

Figure 11. P-type material

Diodes

P-type and N-type materials can do little by themselves. When they are joined together in **junctions**, however, the real magic begins. When a P-type material is joined with an N-type material, a **diode** is created. A diode is an electrical one-way valve. Current can pass easily in one direction, but is blocked in the opposite direction. The reason this happens is because of what takes place at the junction where the P-type and N-type materials are joined.

If a battery is connected to a diode, current may or may not flow, depending on which ends of the diode are connected to the battery's positive and negative terminals. For instance, if the P-type material (also known as the **anode**) is connected to the battery positive and the N-type material (also known as the **cathode**) is connected to the battery negative, current will flow through the diode as it is **forward-biased**.

Figure 12. Current flow through a diode (forward bias)

Since the battery's positive terminal has a shortage of electrons, the holes in the P-type material are repelled toward the junction. The excess of electrons at the battery's negative terminal repels the free electrons in the N-type material and sends them toward the junction as well. The electrons in the N-type material then cross over the junction to fill the holes in the P-type material, and current flows through the diode.

Reversing the diode's connection to the battery creates a new set of conditions. Connecting the P-type material to the battery negative will cause the holes to move away from the junction, as they are attracted to the excess electrons at the negative terminal. The N-type material's free electrons also move away from the junction, since they are attracted to the opposite charge on the battery's positive terminal. Since the holes and electrons have both moved away from the junction, no electron transfer takes place there and current flow stops. The diode is now in a **reverse-bias** condition.

The most common application for diodes is **rectification**. Rectification is the conversion of AC into DC. Four diodes can be connected in a diamond configuration to create a **full-wave rectifier**, which is the foundation for most DC power supplies. Diodes are also used for rectification in automotive alternators, where generated AC is converted into DC to be used in the vehicle electrical system.

Transistors

The transistor is one of the most important inventions of all time. A transistor is versatile, as it can be used as an electrical switch, an amplifier, or a current regulator. Since there are no moving parts in a transistor and it is made from solid silicon, it is known as a **solid state device**, which makes it very reliable. It is also very compact in its design, as thousands of transistors can fit into a single **integrated circuit** (**IC**).

There are two types of transistors: an **NPN transistor** and a **PNP transistor**. An NPN transistor is made up of a thin piece of P-type material sandwiched between two pieces of N-type material. A PNP transistor is the opposite: two pieces of P-type material that have a piece of N-type material between them.

Inside the transistor, wires connect to the three pieces of semiconductor material. Each piece is given a name. The middle piece is always called the **base**; the two outside pieces are called the **collector** and the **emitter**. The symbol for the transistor has an arrow that identifies the emitter. The direction of the arrow tells us what type of transistor it is. The key to remembering which symbol identifies which type of transistor is that the arrow always points in the direction of the N-type material.

FOLLOW THE ARROWS

The key to remembering which symbol identifies which kind of transistor is that the arrow always points to the N-type material.

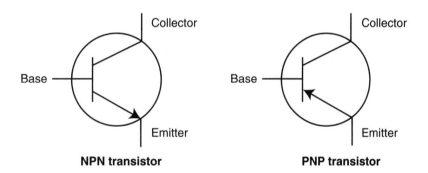

NPN transistor   **PNP transistor**

Figure 13. Symbols for NPN and PNP transistors

The transistor works by using a small amount of current to control a large amount of current. In the case of an NPN transistor, a positive voltage applied to the base will "turn on" the transistor and allow a relatively large current to flow from the collector to the emitter. The moment the positive voltage is removed from the base, the transistor turns off and stops the current flow.

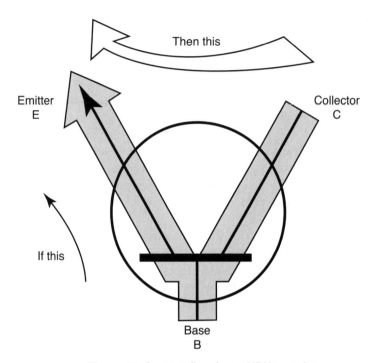

Figure 14. Current flow in an NPN transistor

PNP transistors work in an opposite way than do NPN transistors. A PNP transistor requires a negative voltage at the base to turn it on, and the current then flows from the emitter to the collector (conventional current theory).

Here are additional electronics components symbols that you may come across when you take the ASVAB.

ELECTRONICS INFORMATION PRACTICE SET

1. How much current will flow in a circuit that has 60 mV applied to a 15 KΩ resistance?

    (A) 0.004 mA
    (B) 0.9 A
    (C) 4.0 A
    (D) 900 A

2. What voltage is required for 30 A to flow through a 60 KΩ resistance?

    (A) 1,800 V
    (B) 1.8 KV
    (C) 18 KV
    (D) 1.8 MV

3. What is the current in the 20-ohm resistor?

    (A) 1/2 amp
    (B) 1 amp
    (C) 30 amps
    (D) 100 amps

4. The valence shell is the _____ shell in a copper atom.

    (A) first
    (B) second
    (C) third
    (D) fourth

5. Which is the collector in the transistor symbol below?

    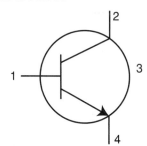

    (A) 1
    (B) 2
    (C) 3
    (D) 4

6. Current is expressed in

    (A) kilohms
    (B) kilovolts
    (C) milliamperes
    (D) millivolts

7. A circuit with flowing current in it is considered

    (A) open
    (B) closed
    (C) short
    (D) dead

GO ON TO THE NEXT PAGE

8. Which of the following symbols represents a polarized capacitor?

(A)

(B)

(C)

(D)

9. When a P-type material is joined with an N-type material, a _____ is created.

(A) resistor
(B) diode
(C) inductor
(D) capacitor

10. Direct current (DC) flows _____ in a conductor.

(A) two ways
(B) backward
(C) one way
(D) answers B and C only

ANSWERS AND EXPLANATIONS

1. **A**

To solve this problem, the first step is to convert 60 mV to V. You can quickly make this conversion by moving the decimal point three places to the left, which yields 0.060 V. Next, convert 15 KΩ to Ω by moving the decimal point three places to the right, which yields 15,000 Ω. Since current is the unknown, the formula needed to finish the calculation is $I = E \div R$. Dividing 0.060 by 15,000 gives 0.000004 amperes. This can be converted to 0.004 mA.

2. **D**

Like the last problem, this one requires you to first convert the given measurements. Take the resistance and move the decimal. 60 KΩ becomes 60,000 Ω. Using our formula for calculating voltage, $E = I \times R$, we get 30 A $\times$ 60,000 Ω = 1,800,000 V, or 1.8 MV.

3. **B**

The resistors in a series circuit add up, so one 40-ohm resistor in series with a 20-ohm resistor is equal to a 60-ohm resistor. To find current flow through a circuit, divide the total circuit resistance (60 ohms) by the voltage across the circuit (60 volts) to get 1 amp.

4. **D**

The valence shell is the outer shell of an atom, which in a copper atom is the fourth shell. A copper atom has 29 electrons, so it would fill the first three shells completely and have one electron left to begin a fourth shell.

5. **B**

In the symbol, the number 2 indicates the collector.

6. **C**

Current is expressed in milliamperes.

7. **B**

A closed circuit has continuity, and will allow current to flow in it.

8. **C**

The choices represent four different capacitor symbols: a fixed capacitor (A), variable capacitor (B), polarized capacitor (C), and trimmer capacitor (D).

9. **B**

When a P-type material is joined with an N-type material, a diode is created.

10. **C**

Direct current (DC) means that current only flows one way in a conductor. This is the type of current in circuits powered by batteries.

CHAPTER NINE

Automotive Information

Take your time with this section, remembering that you can't possibly know everything in this review after one read. You should see it as a learning process whereby you can pick up a little about drive trains one day and a little about exhaust systems the next. We're confident that by the time you're done with this section, the ASVAB's auto questions will seem easier than an oil lube. (Note: You are given 7 minutes to answer 11 questions on the CAT-ASVAB for this section.)

AUTOMOTIVE SYSTEMS

The modern automobile is a technological marvel. Thousands of parts are assembled to form the means that most of us use for our daily transportation. Space-age materials and advanced computer control systems are used extensively in its construction, but in spite of all this, the basic systems within the automobile still function the same as they always have.

Despite its size, any automobile is still only made up of many **parts**. Parts are the smallest pieces that are used in the construction of the automobile. Parts could include such items as bolts and screws, spark plugs, or accessory drive (fan) belts. The parts of the vehicle cannot be disassembled any further, so they form the foundation for the construction of the vehicle.

The major automotive **systems** are:

>   **Engine**: generates power to drive the vehicle's wheels and various accessories.
>
>   **Cooling system**: removes excess heat from the engine.
>
>   **Lubrication system**: circulates motor oil through the engine to reduce friction and make the engine run smoothly.
>
>   **Fuel system**: ensures that correct amounts of air and fuel are available for efficient combustion in the engine.

Ignition system: generates and times the spark that initiates combustion.

Exhaust system: forms a "pipeline" for waste gases to be removed from the engine and then be dissipated to the open atmosphere.

Emission control system: helps limit toxic vehicle emissions.

Electrical system: includes starting, charging, lighting, and accessory systems.

Computer system: controls all aspects of vehicle operation, including engine, drive train, brakes, and suspension.

Drive train: transmits power from the engine to the vehicle's drive wheels.

Suspension and steering: controls the vehicle's ride quality and handling.

Brake system: stops the vehicle safely and predictably.

BASIC ENGINE THEORY

Engines used in most automobiles are known as **internal combustion engines**. Combustion is the rapid burning of an air-fuel mixture. Internal combustion means exactly that: fuel is burned *internally* and the resulting heat is used directly to power an engine.

Internal combustion engines can be fueled with gasoline, diesel fuel, or other petroleum products such as propane or natural gas. Three things must be present before combustion can take place: air, fuel, and a heat source that can be used to ignite the air-fuel mixture. If any one of those three elements is missing, combustion stops and the engine will not run.

There are common components in all internal combustion engines. These components include:

Engine block: forms the framework for the engine cylinders and reciprocating assembly.

Piston: a cylindrically shaped object with a solid crown (top) that moves up and down in the engine's cylinders. Hot gases from the combustion of the air-fuel mixture push on the piston to do the actual work.

Cylinder: forms a guide for the piston to move in; allows the piston to move up and down as the engine completes its cycle.

Piston rings: seal the piston to the cylinder and prevent combustion gases from leaking past. Oil rings prevent oil from the engine crankcase from making its way into the combustion chamber.

Wrist pin: connects the piston to the connecting rod, and forms a pivot point for the small end of the connecting rod to move on.

Connecting rod: connects the piston/wrist pin assembly to the engine's crankshaft. The large end of the connecting rod attaches to the crankshaft on the connecting rod journal.

Crankshaft: converts the linear (straight line) motion of the piston into rotary motion, which can then be used to power a vehicle or drive an accessory.

Cylinder head: located above the piston, it houses the combustion chamber, the intake and exhaust valves, and the intake and exhaust ports.

Combustion chamber: located in the cylinder head directly above the piston, it is where the actual combustion of the air-fuel mixture takes place.

Intake valve: allows air-fuel mixture to be drawn into the combustion chamber. When closed, it must seal the combustion chamber from the intake port.

Exhaust valve: allows waste gases to be removed from the combustion chamber. When closed, it must seal the combustion chamber from the exhaust port.

Camshaft: responsible for the opening and closing of the engine's intake and exhaust valves. The camshaft turns at one-half the speed of the engine's crankshaft.

Figure 1. Basic engine components

The conversion of linear (straight line) motion into rotary motion as achieved by the piston-connecting rod-crankshaft combination is very similar to the leg of a bicycle rider. As the rider's upper leg moves up and down (piston), her lower leg (connecting rod), bicycle pedals, and sprocket (crankshaft) convert that straight line motion into rotary motion that then can be used to drive the wheels of the bicycle.

Most internal combustion engines are built to utilize a **four-stroke cycle**. This means that it takes four strokes of the piston to complete one cycle of events. A stroke of the piston is defined as the piston movement from the top of its travel in the cylinder (**TDC** or **Top Dead Center**) to the bottom of its travel (**BDC** or **Bottom Dead Center**) or vice versa. With the piston connected to the crankshaft through the connecting rod, one stroke of the piston generates one-half turn of the crankshaft. A four-stroke cycle engine thus requires *two complete revolutions* (or turns) of the crankshaft to complete one cycle of events.

The four-stroke cycle begins with the **intake stroke**. The piston is at TDC (Top Dead Center), and the intake valve is beginning to open. As the piston moves downward in the cylinder, a low-pressure area is created above the piston. This low-pressure area can also be described as a vacuum. Since the intake valve is open and is allowing atmospheric air to enter the combustion chamber, higher atmospheric air pressure pushes air through the engine's intake system and toward the low-pressure area above the piston. As the air is traveling through the intake system, fuel is injected into the air stream before it enters the combustion chamber. This allows the cylinder to fill with a fresh charge of air-fuel mixture. Once the piston reaches BDC (Bottom Dead Center), the intake valve is almost closed again and the engine is ready to begin the next phase of the combustion cycle.

The piston now starts on an upward stroke, and both of the engine's valves are closed. With the combustion chamber then sealed, the continued upward motion of the piston will compress the air-fuel mixture in the cylinder as the engine starts its **compression stroke**. The gases in the cylinder are forced into a progressively smaller space as the piston continues toward TDC. These gases become progressively hotter and the air-fuel mixture becomes more easily ignited as the particles of fuel get closer and closer together.

Just before the piston reaches TDC, the spark plug fires and ignites the air-fuel mixture, starting a flame that then travels across the combustion chamber. This flame further heats the gases in the combustion chamber and the resulting rapid expansion of these gases pushes on the piston as it passes TDC and then continues its downward stroke. This is known as the **power stroke** of the engine, and this is where all of the engine's power is generated. The piston continues its descent, with hot gases pushing it downward toward BDC.

| Intake | Compression | Power | Exhaust |

Figure 2. Four-stroke cycle

Just before the piston reaches BDC, the exhaust valve starts to open and the engine begins its fourth and final stroke, the **exhaust stroke**. The gases in the combustion chamber are now spent and must be purged from the engine. As the piston begins its upward movement, it pushes exhaust gases past the open exhaust valve and into the engine's exhaust system where it eventually is sent out to the open atmosphere. The piston continues its travel toward TDC, and at that point will have completed one complete cycle of events. This cycle then starts over as the intake stroke begins again.

Internal combustion engines convert the **chemical energy** in the air-fuel mixture into **heat energy**, and this heat energy is then converted into **mechanical energy**.

CYLINDER ARRANGEMENT

Automotive engines can be built in a number of different configurations, and these can most easily be classified in terms of the engine's **cylinder arrangement**. The most common numbers of cylinders in automobile engines are four, six, and eight, but there are a few designs that utilize three, five, ten, and even twelve cylinders.

The simplest cylinder arrangement is known as the **inline** design, in which all of the engine's cylinders are lined up in a row. This is a practical design for four- and six-cylinder engines. Inline four-cylinder engines are very popular in front-wheel drive cars with transverse (sideways) mounted engines. Inline engines are most often found in small- to medium-sized vehicles.

Another arrangement that has been utilized by engine designers is the **horizontally opposed** or **flat** design. This has all of the cylinders lying on the horizontal plane, with half of the cylinders facing away from the other half and the crankshaft located between them. Some refer to this design as a "boxer" engine because the pistons move back and forth like a boxer throwing punches. The one major advantage to this design is that the engine's center of gravity is much lower so it is easier to build a more stable, better-handling vehicle.

The last and most popular design for 6- and 8-cylinder engines is the V-type engine. These engines have one crankshaft connected to pistons on both sides of the V-shaped engine. The two rows of cylinders are located 60 to 90 degrees away from each other, and each row has one cylinder head, for a total of two heads for the engine. The main advantage of using this type of configuration is the decrease in height and length relative to the in-line engine. The V-type engine improves the aerodynamic flow outside the vehicle because the front of the vehicle can be lower due to the smaller engine size. If an 8-cylinder engine is needed, this type of configuration creates the power required but makes the engine more compact, keeping the vehicle aerodynamic in shape.

CAMSHAFT LOCATION

Another classification used to describe automotive engines is **camshaft location**. The camshaft is responsible for the opening and closing of the engine's valves, and it is driven by the crankshaft through a **timing chain** or **timing belt**. Some modern engines have the camshaft located in the engine block and the intake and exhaust valves located in the cylinder head. Engines built in this manner would be known as **overhead valve** or **OHV** engines.

Engine designers often locate the camshaft above the valves and are then able to eliminate the lifters and pushrods. The mechanism for driving the camshaft becomes somewhat more complex, but the valve operating mechanism itself becomes much simpler and lighter. Less mass in the valve train means that higher engine speeds can be attained. This design is known as **single overhead cam** or **SOHC**. In a V-type engine with two cylinder heads, there would be two camshafts, with one installed above each cylinder head.

One final step to make even higher engine speeds possible is to go to a **double overhead cam** or **DOHC** arrangement. This puts two camshafts into each cylinder head, and makes it so one cam operates the exhaust valves in that head, and the other operates all the intake valves. With this arrangement, it is possible to eliminate the rocker arms that are often used in SOHC engines and have the camshafts operate the valves directly through a follower.

MULTIPLE-VALVE CYLINDER HEADS

Engines may also be classified according to the number of valves used for each cylinder. The least expensive and most common arrangement is to use a **two-valve cylinder head**, with one intake valve and one exhaust valve per cylinder. To improve airflow through the engine and, thus, engine performance, it is possible to design a multiple (more than two) valve cylinder head. Manufacturers have built cars that use three valves per cylinder, but now it is much more common to use a **four-valve** cylinder head in high performance applications. This arrangement has two intake valves and two exhaust valves for each cylinder.

FIRING ORDER

The order that the cylinders fire in is known as the **firing order**. A common firing order for four-cylinder engines is 1-3-4-2. This means that once the first cylinder fires, the crankshaft will make one-half turn, and then the third will fire and so on. Cylinders 1 and 3 will fire on the first turn of the crankshaft, and cylinders 4 and 2 will fire on the second turn of the crankshaft. In the case of a V-8 engine with a firing order of 1-8-4-3-6-5-7-2, cylinders 1, 8, 4, and 3 will fire on the first turn of the crankshaft, and 6, 5, 7, and 2 will fire during the second turn.

Many engines have their firing order cast directly into the intake manifold for easy reference. For those that don't, it is necessary to refer to the engine's service information.

DIESEL ENGINES

Another variation of the internal combustion engine is the diesel. **Diesel engines** are much simpler and more reliable than gasoline engines, mostly because they do not incorporate a spark-ignition system. Instead of using a spark to initiate combustion, diesel engines use a much higher compression ratio to generate sufficient **heat of compression** to ignite the air-fuel mixture. The compression ratio for a diesel engine can range anywhere from 16:1 to 22:1.

Another major difference between a diesel engine and most gasoline engines is that diesels inject their fuel directly into the combustion chamber.

Figure 3. Diesel engine

ENGINE OPERATING CONDITIONS

Air-Fuel Mixture

For an engine to run efficiently, it is necessary to mix air and fuel in the correct amounts. Combustion suffers if there is too much fuel and not enough air, or if there is too much air and not enough fuel. The ideal ratio of air to fuel is known as **stoichiometric**, and it is the responsibility of the engine's fuel system to maintain that balance.

Air-fuel ratio is a comparison of the weight of the air relative to the weight of the fuel that has been mixed with it. The stoichiometric, or ideal, air-fuel ratio is 14.7:1. This means that 14.7 pounds of air is combined with 1 pound of fuel to create an ideal air-fuel mix. When fuel is mixed with air by the fuel system, particles of fuel are **atomized** and directed into the air stream that is entering the engine.

Too much air and not enough fuel would be described as a **lean** mixture. Lean mixtures burn relatively slowly because there is greater space between the fuel molecules and it takes more time for a flame to jump from particle to particle. Lean mixtures also burn much hotter, and thus can cause serious engine damage. A lean air-fuel ratio would be 17:1.

In contrast, a **rich** air-fuel mixture has too much fuel and not enough air. Rich mixtures burn quicker because of the small distances between fuel particles, and they also burn much cooler. A rich air-fuel mixture can cause spark plug fouling and black exhaust smoke, but is certainly less threatening to an engine than lean mixtures. A typical rich air-fuel mixture is 10:1.

Ignition Timing

Another major factor in making an engine run efficiently is **ignition timing**. Ignition timing is the time in the combustion cycle that a spark is generated at the spark plug. This is described relative to the position of the engine's crankshaft. For instance, an ignition timing of five degrees **BTDC** would mean that the spark took place when the crankshaft was five degrees of rotation **before top dead center**.

The spark is most often timed so it will take place before the piston reaches top dead center on the compression stroke, because it takes time for the flame to move across the combustion chamber and to heat the gases in it. Once the heat starts expanding the gases in the combustion chamber, the piston is on its way down again and is ready to make an effective power stroke.

Regardless of how fast the engine is turning, it will take approximately the same amount of time for the flame to travel across the combustion chamber. This means that for higher engine speeds, the flame must be started earlier in order to generate the most effective downward push on the piston. This is known as **advancing the timing**. An example of an advanced timing would be 25 degrees BTDC. In this case, the spark takes place when the crankshaft is 25 degrees of rotation before top dead center.

In contrast, **retarding the timing** means that the spark is adjusted to take place later in the combustion cycle. Certain engine operating conditions might call for a retarded timing as part of normal engine operation. Ignition timing that is unnecessarily retarded, however, will have an adverse effect on engine performance.

Combustion

Gasoline engine combustion is the rapid, thorough burning of a compressed air-fuel mixture, initiated by a spark from the engine's ignition system. It is a flame that starts at the spark plug and then moves rapidly across the combustion chamber, heating the gases and building pressure in an even, controlled manner.

Normal combustion does not involve an explosion, and it is always initiated by an electric arc at the spark plug. If combustion is started by something other than an electric arc at the spark plug, this is an abnormal condition known as **preignition**. Preignition takes place when combustion is started by a hot spot in the combustion chamber, such as a glowing spark plug electrode or a hot piece of carbon.

Detonation is when an air-fuel mixture explodes, rather than burns. It can often take place when an engine's air-fuel mixture is lean. This is because lean mixtures burn very slowly, and as the flame moves across the combustion chamber, the unburned gases become heated due to the advancing flame and the increasing compression in the cylinder. If the temperature of these unburned gases rises sufficiently, they will "auto ignite" and the flame front from this explosion collides with the original flame front. The pressure spike from this abnormal combustion results in a brutal shock to the engine assembly, and can be heard as a "knock." Severe engine damage can result from unchecked detonation.

COOLING SYSTEM

There are two major types of cooling systems in modern automotive engines. The first type is **air-cooling**, where air is circulated over cooling fins on the outside of the engine to remove excess heat. The second type is **water-cooling**. A water-cooled engine uses a liquid coolant to pick up excess heat and then rejects that heat through a radiator.

Coolant

The most critical component of the cooling system is the coolant itself. Engine coolant is normally made up of a 50/50 mix of antifreeze and water. The most common type of antifreeze is ethylene glycol, which has some exceptional properties which make it especially suited to be an automotive engine coolant. A 50/50 mix of ethylene glycol and water will not freeze until its temperature reaches −34° Fahrenheit. This is why it is called **antifreeze**. Frozen coolant can lead to serious engine damage (even a possible cracked block), so it is important that the coolant be freeze-protected. This same 50/50 mix will also raise the boiling point of the coolant. This is important in hot weather, because it makes the coolant that much more efficient at transferring heat.

Components

The major components of a water-cooling system include:

> **Water pump**: responsible for moving coolant through the cooling system in order to transfer and control heat.
>
> **Water jacket**: hollow sections in the engine block and cylinder head that allow coolant to be transferred through them. These are the areas that the coolant must absorb heat from.
>
> **Thermostat**: controls engine temperature by allowing coolant to flow into the radiator when the coolant temperature rises above a certain level.
>
> **Bypass tube**: allows coolant to flow back into the water pump from the cylinder head when the thermostat is closed.
>
> **Radiator hoses**: flexible hoses that allow hot coolant to flow between the engine and the vehicle's radiator.

Radiator: responsible for transferring heat from the coolant to the outside air.

Radiator cap: responsible for maintaining pressure in the system, and allowing coolant to transfer between the coolant reservoir and the radiator.

Coolant recovery bottle: forms a reservoir for coolant to flow in and out of the cooling system as the engine increases and decreases in temperature.

Operation

Coolant is circulated through the engine by a belt- or timing chain-driven water pump. The engine crankshaft drives the belt, so the water pump actually uses engine power to operate it. The water pump takes coolant in and pushes it into the engine block. The coolant then makes its way upward into the cylinder head, and then returns to the inlet of the water pump through the bypass tube. As long as the thermostat is closed (engine is below operating temperature), the coolant will continue to circulate in this manner.

When the thermostat opens, hot coolant moves past the thermostat into the upper radiator hose, and then the coolant enters the radiator itself. One of the methods used to raise the boiling point of the water has already been mentioned: using coolants made up of a 50/50 mix of ethylene glycol and water. The other method that can be utilized is raising the pressure in the cooling system. The **radiator cap** is responsible for this, and most are designed to maintain anywhere from 9 to 16 pounds per square inch (psi) of pressure in the cooling system. For every 1 psi of pressure that is placed on the cooling system, the boiling point of the coolant is raised approximately 3° F. A 15-psi radiator cap would then raise the boiling point of the coolant to 212° F to 260° F.

Radiator caps incorporate two separate valves: a pressure valve and a vacuum valve. As the engine warms up, the coolant in the cooling system will tend to expand. This expansion will raise the pressure in the cooling system, but when the pressure reaches the radiator cap's rating, the pressure valve in the radiator cap will lift and allow some coolant to flow from the radiator into the coolant recovery bottle. This flow will continue as the cooling system pressure exceeds the rating of the radiator cap. The coolant level in the recovery bottle will rise until the engine reaches operating temperature.

When the engine is shut down and begins to cool, the coolant will contract and create a low-pressure area inside the cooling system. If left unchecked, this low-pressure in the cooling system would cause the radiator hoses to collapse and can have an adverse effect on the cooling system at engine startup.

Maintenance

Cooling systems require maintenance in order to keep them operating at peak efficiency. Again, the coolant itself is absolutely critical and making sure to have this replaced every two to three years is a good maintenance practice. The strength of the coolant should be kept at a 50/50 mix of antifreeze and water. This will ensure that the coolant has sufficient freeze protection and corrosion resistance.

Engine cold, thermostat closed

Coolant circulates through bypass to pump and
back to engine but does not go through radiator

Engine warm, thermostat open

Coolant circulates through radiator

Figure 4

Other things to watch for are the condition of the belt driving the water pump, and that there
are no leaks in the system. Most often, a leak will be external and can be observed as it drips
from hose connections or faulty cooling system components.

LUBRICATION SYSTEM

The next most critical system in terms of engine operation is the **lubrication system**. Without lubrication, the internal parts of the engine would develop enough friction to stop (seize) the engine completely. The lubrication system is responsible for the following functions:

Lubricates: puts an oil film between moving parts to reduce friction and smooth engine operation.

Cools: puts motor oil in contact with hot engine parts (such as the underside of the piston) and transfers heat to the oil pan, or the engine oil cooler if applicable.

Seals: motor oil acts as a sealer between the piston, the piston rings, and the engine cylinder walls. This helps seal combustion gases in the combustion chamber and makes the engine run more efficiently.

Cleans: additives in the motor oil cause contaminants to be suspended in the oil, so they can be filtered out by the engine's oil filter.

Quiets: motor oil dampens engine noise and makes the engine run quieter.

Motor Oil

Motor oil is the most critical component of the lubrication system. It is carefully engineered to provide peak performance under the toughest engine operating conditions, so choosing and using high quality motor oil is extremely important for the life of an engine. Motor oil is made up of two main components: **base oil**, and an **additive package**.

One of the most important properties of motor oil is **viscosity**. Viscosity is resistance to flow, and is expressed as a number that is directly proportional to the thickness of the oil. The *Society of Automotive Engineers* (or SAE) is responsible for developing the standards concerning motor oil viscosity. Oil with a viscosity rating of SAE 5 would have a relatively low viscosity (low resistance to flow), whereas SAE 50 oil would have a high viscosity.

Another important motor oil rating system is the API quality rating. API is the *American Petroleum Institute*, and they are responsible for setting standards for motor oil quality. For a gasoline engine, this rating would have a prefix of "S," and then the next letter would identify the specific quality standard that the motor oil meets. The first gasoline motor oils produced had a quality rating of SA, but greater demands on motor oils led to ratings that currently exist at the SJ level. Today's engines would not last very long if they were operated with an SA motor oil.

A motor oil with a "C" prefix for its quality rating would be suited for diesel engine use (i.e., a CD rating). Motor oil that had both an "S" and a "C" rating would be suited for either gasoline or diesel engine use. An example of this would be motor oil with a rating of SJ/CD.

Components

The primary components of the lubrication system are as follows:

Oil pan: forms the reservoir for the engine oil at the bottom of the engine.

Oil pickup tube and screen: immersed in motor oil, this "screens out" large solids and directs oil into the oil pump.

Oil pump: responsible for pumping the oil through the engine oil galleries. It is normally driven by the engine's camshaft.

Pressure relief valve: prevents excessive pressure from building in the lubrication system.

Oil filter: filters oil from the oil pump before it is sent to the various parts of the engine.

Oil galleries: passages or "drillings" in the engine assembly that transport oil to critical components.

Operation

The engine's oil reservoir is at the bottom of the engine, in the oil pan. All oil used in the engine drains to the oil pan, where it has an opportunity to cool. The oil pump draws oil from the oil pan into its inlet through the pickup tube and screen. The motor oil moves through the oil pump, and then is transferred under pressure to the engine's oil filter. The oil filter removes particulates from the oil, and sends the clean oil on to the main oil galleries.

When the engine is cold, the oil has a higher resistance to flow and thus requires a good deal more energy to pump it through the system. This also causes the engine's oil pressure to rise. If the oil pressure rises above the pressure relief valve's setting, the relief valve will open and allow some of the oil to drain back into the oil pan before it is pumped into the oil filter. This prevents engine oil pressure from rising to the point where it can damage components such as the oil filter.

The most critical area in the engine in terms of lubrication requirements is the engine's reciprocating assembly. The pistons, connecting rods, and crankshaft all require motor oil to lower friction and to remove heat. The largest oil galleries in the engine are used to move oil to these areas, and galleries are drilled directly through the crankshaft to provide oil under pressure to the connecting rod bearings. Oil that leaks off the connecting rod bearings is thrown onto the cylinder walls, where it helps lubricate and cool the pistons.

Other oil galleries take oil from the main oil gallery and direct it to the engine's valve train. This is where the camshaft, lifters, push rods, rocker arms, and valve stems get their lubrication. Other parts that may receive lubrication from this oil would be the camshaft drive, or timing chain and associated gear drives for the oil pump, ignition distributor, etc.

Oil that has circulated through the engine eventually drains back into the oil pan. The oil pan is located at the bottom of the engine and thus sits low in the engine compartment where cooler air typically resides. This cool outside air absorbs heat from the oil pan and helps cool the engine oil inside. At this point, the oil is ready to be picked up by the oil pump and to be circulated back into the lubrication system.

Maintenance

The key to lubrication system maintenance is to change the engine oil and filter on a regular basis, and to use top quality motor oil and filters. This is the cheapest and most effective maintenance that can be performed on a vehicle.

FUEL SYSTEM

The **fuel system** is responsible for maintaining the correct air-fuel mixture for efficient engine operation. If the air-fuel mixture is not adjusted correctly, drivability, emission control, fuel economy, and engine service life can suffer.

Up until about 20 years ago, it was most common for air-fuel mixture to be determined through mechanical means. This was accomplished through the use of a **carburetor**, which was very reliable but incapable of providing the precision required in modern fuel systems. Due mostly to the demands of emission control regulations, the carburetor has been made obsolete in favor of **electronic fuel injection**. This system is controlled by an onboard computer and incorporates a feedback function that gives it flexibility to adjust to changing engine conditions very quickly.

Components

The following are the major components of an electronic fuel-injection system:

Electric fuel pump: located in the vehicle's fuel tank, the fuel pump supplies fuel under pressure to the fuel injectors.

Fuel filter: filters contaminants from the fuel before it reaches the fuel rail.

Fuel rail: a manifold that supplies fuel under pressure to the inlets of all the engine's fuel injectors.

Fuel pressure regulator: regulates pressure in the fuel rail according to intake manifold vacuum. Excess fuel is bled to the fuel return line, where it is sent back to the fuel tank.

Fuel injector: sprays fuel into the intake air stream as it receives electrical signals from the Powertrain Control Module (PCM). The location of the injector will determine the specific type of fuel injection system being used on the engine.

Powertrain Control Module (PCM): another name for the vehicle's central computer, it is responsible for control of all functions associated with the engine and transmission.

Intake manifold: distributes air to the intake ports on the cylinder heads.

Intake air filter: all air entering the engine passes through the air filter, which removes airborne contaminants that could damage internal engine parts.

Throttle body/throttle plate: the throttle plate, which is connected to the throttle pedal, controls engine speed and output torque.

Fuel Injection System Designs

When fuel injection systems first came into common use, they were designed to utilize either one or two injectors mounted in a **throttle body** that took the place of the carburetor. This is known as a **throttle body injection system** or **TBI**. While this system proved to be reliable, it was not capable of providing a high enough level of fuel control to meet emission control requirements. Most engines are now built with **multiport fuel injection**, which has an injector for each engine cylinder.

With multiport fuel injection, the injectors are located in the intake manifold, with their spray directed toward the intake valves. As air enters the intake manifold, it will flow all the way to the cylinder head before fuel is injected into it. This allows for much better air-fuel mixing and prevents fuel droplets from falling out on the intake manifold runners.

Throttle body injection

Multiport injection

Figure 5. Fuel injection types

The newest fuel-injection system designs incorporate a fuel injector that sprays fuel directly into the combustion chamber. This is known as **direct injection**. Engineers are working to inject the fuel as close as possible to where the actual combustion takes place, in an effort to increase fuel control and create a cleaner burning, more efficient engine.

Maintenance

The fuel-injection system requires very little maintenance. The filters must be changed occasionally (both air and fuel), and it is a good idea to have a fuel injector cleaning done after an engine has been in service for some time. Aside from that, fuel injection systems are built to give reliable service with a minimum of maintenance.

IGNITION SYSTEM

One of the most critical vehicle systems is the **ignition system**. Without it, combustion cannot take place, so the engine will not run. The ignition system must generate high-voltage sparks at the correct time in order to make the engine run smoothly and efficiently.

Components

The ignition system can be divided into two distinct subsystems: the primary and the secondary. The primary is the low-voltage part of the system, where as the secondary is high voltage.

The following are the major components found in the **primary** of a basic electronic ignition system:

> **Battery**: supplies power to the ignition system for starting the engine.
>
> **Ignition switch**: turns the engine on and off by switching power to the ignition system.
>
> **Primary coil winding**: the low-voltage winding in the ignition coil. This is made up of several hundred turns of relatively heavy wire.
>
> **Ignition module**: a transistorized switch that turns the primary current on and off.
>
> **Reluctor and pickup coil**: responsible for generating a signal that operates the ignition module. The reluctor is mounted on the distributor shaft, and generates a signal in the stationary pickup coil as it rotates with the distributor.
>
> **Distributor**: driven by the engine's camshaft, the distributor is responsible for timing the spark and distributing it to the correct cylinder. Like the camshaft, the distributor turns at one-half the speed of the engine.

The following are the major components found in the **secondary** of a basic electronic ignition system.

> **Secondary coil winding**: the high-voltage winding in the ignition coil. This is made up of several thousand turns of fine wire, wound around the primary coil winding.
>
> **Coil wire**: transmits high voltage from the secondary coil winding to the distributor cap.
>
> **Distributor cap and rotor**: directs high voltage from the coil wire to each cylinder in the firing order. This is a switching mechanism that allows one ignition coil to serve all the engine cylinders.
>
> **Spark plug wires**: transmit high voltage from the distributor cap to each spark plug.
>
> **Spark plugs**: threaded into the cylinder head, the spark plug protrudes into the combustion chamber and generates the spark to initiate combustion.

Figure 6. Electronic ignition systems

Primary Ignition Operation

When the driver turns the ignition switch to the "run" position, current is sent from the battery, through the ignition switch, and on to the primary coil winding. From the coil winding, that same current flows through the ignition module and back to the battery through the vehicle ground circuit. The low-voltage (primary) section of the ignition system is responsible for the control of the secondary, or high-voltage section. Whatever happens in the secondary system is in response to the events in the primary section.

The ignition system works because of a phenomenon known as **electromagnetic induction**. If a magnetic field moves across a stationary wire, voltage is induced in the wire. Another dimension of this principle is that electric current passing through a wire will produce a magnetic field around that wire. This means that electric current can be used to generate a magnetic field, and a magnetic field can be used to generate electric current.

Secondary Ignition Operation

The collapse of the magnetic field in the primary coil winding induces a high voltage in the secondary winding. These secondary system voltages can reach levels of 30,000 volts and higher. This huge increase in voltage in the ignition coil is achieved because of the large number of turns of wire in the secondary winding relative to the primary. The magnetic field in the primary winding cuts across a much larger number of turns of wire in the secondary, creating a **step-up** effect in the coil.

The high-voltage current in the secondary winding must be directed to the correct cylinder in the firing order. This current is directed through the **coil wire** to the center tower of the **distributor cap**. From this point, it flows to the **rotor**, which is mounted on top of the distributor shaft and rotates with the distributor. As the engine turns, the rotor will direct the current to the appropriate cylinder and send it through the **spark plug wire** to the **spark plug**. The electric arc at the spark plug is used to initiate combustion.

Current Ignition System Design

Since engine performance relies heavily on accurate ignition timing, engineers began to look carefully at how to eliminate more moving parts from the ignition system. This led to the elimination of the distributor in a design that was named the **distributorless ignition system** or **DIS**. DIS systems use one ignition coil to operate two spark plugs, so a V-8 engine now required four separate coils instead of one. However, this system still utilized spark plug wires, which are another high-maintenance item.

The most recent ignition system designs have eliminated the spark plug wires, thus requiring an ignition coil for each cylinder. These are known as **coil-on-plug** ignitions. The ignition coils are mounted directly over the spark plugs on this design, and the coils are controlled by the vehicle computer system. While the incorporation of computer control has increased ignition system complexity, the elimination of moving and high-maintenance components has led to an accurate and reliable ignition system design that requires very little maintenance.

EXHAUST SYSTEM

The exhaust system is responsible for removing waste gases from the engine. It must do this so that it allows these gases to flow freely, deadens the sound of the exhaust, and keeps the gases and heat away from the vehicle cabin, and thus, the occupants.

Typical components found in an exhaust system include the following:

Exhaust manifolds: attached directly to the exhaust ports on the cylinder head. The majority of the exhaust heat and noise is focused on the exhaust manifolds. These are often made from cast-iron for durability under high heat conditions.

Catalytic converter: responsible for converting the toxic components of engine exhaust into relatively harmless compounds such as carbon dioxide and water.

Muffler: incorporates an expansion chamber to diminish loud exhaust noises.

Tailpipe: the exit point for exhaust gases as they enter the open atmosphere. The tailpipe normally exits at the rear of the vehicle.

Figure 7. Exhaust system components

Operation

As gases flow from the exhaust ports of the engine, they are collected by the **exhaust manifold**. On a V-type engine there would be two exhaust manifolds, one for each cylinder head. These manifolds would then feed the gases into steel exhaust pipes, which connect the major components of the exhaust system.

The exhaust gases would then be sent into the **catalytic converter**. High heat is developed in the catalytic converter as it reduces the toxic components of the exhaust to less toxic gases. Some vehicles use two, and even three, catalytic converters in an effort to meet emission control regulations.

After leaving the catalytic converter, exhaust gases are directed into the **muffler**. The muffler has expansion chambers built into it that absorb the audio shock waves generated by the engine's exhaust. The muffler is normally located toward the rear of the car, somewhere between the catalytic converter and the tailpipe.

Engine exhaust is highly toxic. The most dangerous of the toxic gases emitted by the engine's exhaust is **carbon monoxide**, an odorless, colorless gas. It is extremely important that these gases be routed in such a way that they do not come into contact with the driver or passengers in the vehicle. This usually involves sending these gases to the rear of the vehicle where they are dissipated to the open air by the **tailpipe**.

Performance enthusiasts often install **header pipes** in the exhaust system. These take the place of the exhaust manifolds that originally came with the engine. The idea is to allow exhaust gases to flow more freely and allow the engine to breathe better. Header pipes are engineered to maximize the flow of exhaust gases from the engine. Increased performance is usually gained at the expense of durability, as header pipes are much more fragile than cast-iron exhaust manifolds.

Maintenance

Inspect the system from time to time for physical damage; there should be no restrictions and no leaks. The system should also be tight in terms of its mounting brackets and clamps. Any damage should be repaired immediately.

The catalytic converter will enjoy a long service life if the vehicle's engine is kept in good running order. An engine that burns oil or has ignition or fuel system problems will damage the catalytic converter.

ELECTRICAL SYSTEM

The vehicle's electrical system is growing in importance with each new vehicle model year. Many systems that were once driven mechanically are now being redesigned to be part of the electrical system.

The major subsystems of the electrical system include the following:

Battery: stores electrical energy in chemical form. Provides direct current (DC) for engine starting and accessory operation.

Starting system: responsible for cranking the engine to get it started. The battery and starter motor are the major components of the starting system.

Charging system: responsible for supplying electrical current to charge the battery, as well as for vehicle operation. The major component of the charging system is the alternator.

Lighting system: headlights, marker lights, brake lights, tail lights, etc.

Accessories: this includes the rear window defogger, windshield wipers, stereo, blower motors, and all other electrically powered accessories.

Battery

The battery is the foundation for the entire electrical system. It produces electrical current for starting the engine, provides current to the electrical system when the load exceeds the output of the alternator, and acts as an electrical "shock absorber," preventing voltage spikes.

An automobile battery is made up of lead plates immersed in an electrolyte made up of sulphuric acid and water. This is why this type of battery is known as a **lead-acid battery**. As the battery discharges, the sulphuric acid in the electrolyte is reduced to water, and the lead plates become lead sulphate. Charging the battery restores the chemical composition of the lead plates and the electrolyte.

Starting System

In order to start the engine, an electrically operated starter motor is utilized. When the ignition switch is moved to the "start" position, an electrical current is sent to the starter solenoid, which engages the starter drive gear onto the engine's ring gear (located on the flywheel). When the drive is engaged, the solenoid connects the battery to the starter motor, which then turns the engine at sufficient speed to start it.

Charging System

Once the engine is running, the charging system provides electrical current to recharge the battery and power the vehicle's electrical system. The main component of the charging system is the **alternator**. The alternator is belt-driven by the engine's crankshaft, and converts mechanical energy into electrical energy. The alternator produces alternating current (AC), which is then **rectified** by an internal set of diodes known as the **rectifier bridge**. The rectifier bridge converts AC to DC, which can be used to power the vehicle's electrical system.

A **voltage regulator** controls the output of the alternator. Normal system voltage during engine operation is around 14.5 volts. Turning on the headlights, heater motor, and other accessories on the vehicle increases the **load** on the electrical system and system voltage drops. The voltage regulator senses this decrease in system voltage and responds by increasing the alternator's output to compensate for it. As long as the alternator's output is able to match the load on the electrical system, the system voltage will remain close to 14.5 volts.

Lighting System

There are many lights built into a vehicle's lighting system. **Headlights** illuminate the road ahead of the car, **tail lights** mark the rear of the car for other drivers, and **interior lights** help the driver see the instrument panel and other areas inside the car when necessary. The various lights are controlled by the driver through **switches** that turn the electrical current to the lighting circuits on and off.

The vehicle's lighting circuits are protected by **fuses** or **circuit breakers**. If, for some reason, the circuit should draw more current than it has been designed for, the fuse will "blow" and cut off current flow. This protects the wires in the circuits from overheating and may even prevent an electrical fire.

COMPUTER SYSTEM

Computer control systems work much like the human nervous system. **Sensors** provide data to the **computer**, which processes this information and sends signals to **actuators** to control vehicle functions. In the case of the human body, the eyes and ears send signals to the brain, which processes this information and sends signals to the various muscles to control body movement.

The major components of the automotive computer system include the following:

> **Sensors**: these generate signals based on rotational speed, temperature, pressure, and relative position. The sensors are the "eyes and ears" of the computer system. An example of a sensor would be an oxygen sensor, which is responsible for sending data to the computer concerning the oxygen content of the exhaust gases. This information is used by the computer to determine whether the engine's air-fuel mixture is rich or lean.

> **Computer**: processes data from the sensors based on a preprogrammed strategy (software) and then generates outputs to control vehicle functions. The computer is the "brain" of the computer system. In today's vehicles, the computer is often referred to as the **Powertrain Control Module** or **PCM**.

> **Actuators**: these receive output signals from the computer and control vehicle functions. An example of an actuator would be a fuel injector, because it responds to signals from the computer to inject a specific amount of fuel into the intake air stream.

Automotive technicians communicate with the PCM using a **scan tool**, which allows them to get information from the computer concerning the operation of the various vehicle systems. The scan tool is connected to the vehicle's computer system through a **diagnostic data link** that is located near the driver's seat.

DRIVE TRAIN SYSTEM

The engine can produce power to move the vehicle, but this energy must be processed and transmitted effectively in order to accelerate the vehicle smoothly and quickly. Transmitting power from the engine to the wheels is the responsibility of the vehicle's drive train.

An important part of any drive train is the **transmission**. The two main types of transmissions are the **automatic** and the **manual**. Drivers who like to have more control over the operation of the vehicle will often choose a manual transmission, because the driver is responsible for shifting the gears up and down. A car with an automatic transmission is much easier to operate because it does not use a **clutch** and does all of the gear shifting automatically.

While rear-wheel drive was the most common design in years past, front-wheel drive has become very popular, especially in small- to medium-sized cars.

The typical components found in a front-wheel drive vehicle with a manual transmission include the following:

Clutch: transmits torque from the engine to the transmission. The clutch can be released and engaged to allow smooth starts and transmission shifting.

Transaxle: has several "gears" that are selected according to the speed of the vehicle and how fast the driver would like to accelerate. The transaxle is a combination of the transmission and the **drive axle**, which are normally two separate components in a rear-wheel drive vehicle.

Half-shaft: a short drive shaft that transmits power from the transaxle to the drive wheels. Used only in front-wheel drive vehicles, the half shafts must be able to apply power to the drive wheels while allowing them to move up and down and turn the vehicle. There are two half shafts, one for each drive wheel.

Constant-velocity (CV) joints: located at each end of a half-shaft, CV joints can transmit power through very steep angles. The inboard CV joint is located at the transaxle, while the outboard CV joint is located behind the vehicle wheel.

 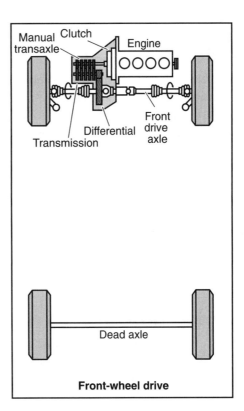

Figure 8. Rear- and front-wheel drive

Other drive train components that may be found in other vehicle designs include the following:

Transmission: used in rear- and four-wheel drive vehicles, the transmission is responsible for matching engine speed to the desired speed of the vehicle.

Drive shaft: a longer version of the half-shaft, the drive shaft transmits torque from the transmission to the drive axle. The drive shaft is also required to allow up and down movement of the vehicle's wheels, but not to the same extent as the half-shaft in a front-wheel drive.

Universal joints: located at each end of the drive shaft, the universal joint allows the shaft to operate at an angle with the component that it is driving. Also known as **U-joints**.

Drive axle: transmits engine power through a 90-degree angle, and splits that power between the two drive wheels. The wheels are attached to the ends of the drive axle. The drive axle incorporates a **differential**, which allows the left and right wheels to turn at different speeds as the vehicle goes around a corner.

Transfer case: located between the transmission and the drive axles on a four-wheel drive vehicle. The transfer case splits the engine's power between the front and rear drive axle.

Gear Selection

Transmissions are built with several forward "speeds" or "gears." For instance, a four-speed transmission would have four forward gears and one reverse. A driver would typically start from a stop using **low (first) gear**. In this gear, the transmission would increase the **torque** from the engine sufficiently to be able to start the vehicle from a standstill. However, this would limit the vehicle's speed once it did start rolling, so the driver would then select **second gear** and so on as the vehicle continued to accelerate.

High (fourth) gear would be used to allow the vehicle to cruise on the highway. Engine speed would be moderate to low in this gear, allowing for maximum fuel economy and quiet running. To accelerate quickly, however, the driver would **downshift** to a lower gear in order to increase engine speed and torque. Proper gear selection is important when operating a vehicle with a manual transmission.

Automatic Transmissions

Automatic transmissions are much more complex than their manual counterparts, yet are much easier to operate. The reason that many drivers prefer them is that automatic transmissions don't use a clutch.

Instead of using a clutch, automatics transmit engine torque from the engine to the transmission through a **torque converter**. The torque converter uses fluid to transmit power, and allows for a certain amount of slippage when the vehicle is stopped.

Automatic transmissions do all of the gear selection for the driver. This is done in the transmission using hydraulics and **planetary gear sets**. The newest automatic transmissions are controlled electronically by the vehicle's powertrain control module.

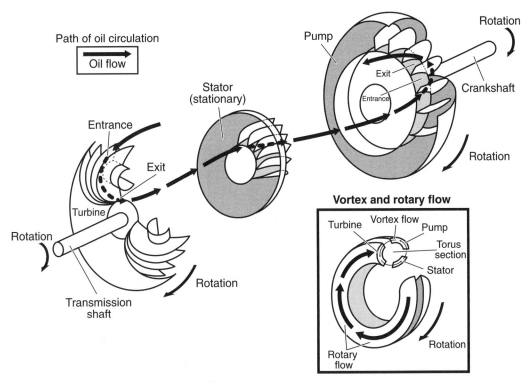

Figure 9. Torque converter

SUSPENSION AND STEERING SYSTEM

The newest suspension and steering systems have incorporated computer control in an effort to achieve these high standards. While the sophistication of computer control has increased the overall complexity of these systems, the basic principles remain the same.

Components

The major components of the long-short arm suspension system include the following:

Springs: hold the vehicle's chassis up and allow the wheels to move up and down in relation to it.

Shock absorbers: absorb the energy released by the up-and-down movement of the vehicle wheels.

Control arms (A-arms): the long-short arm suspension system uses an upper and lower control arm to maintain the vertical orientation of the steering knuckle as the wheel moves up and down.

Steering knuckle: connects to the upper and lower control arms through the use of ball-joints. The wheel hub mounts on the spindle, which is part of the steering knuckle.

Ball joints: "ball and socket" assemblies that allow the steering knuckle to turn and move up and down simultaneously.

Steering linkage: connects the steering wheel to the steering knuckle.

Wheel hub: forms the mounting point for the vehicle's tire assembly.

Tire: makes contact with the road and provides a "footprint" to aid in vehicle stability and handling.

Figure 10. Long-short arm suspension

Construction and Operation

In order to make a vehicle ride smoothly, the wheels must be able to move up and down while the vehicle chassis stays steady. This is the job of the vehicle **springs**; they must be able to allow this movement of the wheels without transmitting road shock. However, the springs absorb energy as this happens and must release this energy without bouncing the vehicle after encountering a bump.

The **shock absorber** is installed between the chassis and a control arm to help absorb some of the energy as the spring is compressed (or **jounced**), and then absorbs energy from the spring as it **rebounds** afterward. This prevents this extra energy from being transmitted to the chassis, and thus, the passengers. The shock absorber uses a piston and hydraulic oil to absorb the excess mechanical energy from the suspension system and then releases that same energy in the form of heat.

The **upper and lower control arms** form the supports for the steering knuckle. The control arms are attached to the chassis through the use of **control arm bushings**. The spring is placed between the chassis and one of the control arms. The spring can be installed on either the upper or lower control arm in a long-short arm suspension. The control arm with the spring on it becomes the load-bearing arm as the vehicle weight is supported through it on the way to the steering knuckle and tire assembly.

An **upper ball joint** and a **lower ball joint** are used to attach the steering knuckle to the control arms. Ball joints are built similar to a human hip joint, with a ball and stud rotating in a socket to allow a wide arc of movement. As the control arms move up and down, the ball joints allow the steering knuckle to move freely with them. They also allow the steering knuckle to turn left and right as it is moved by the steering linkage.

The **steering linkage** forms the connection between the steering wheel and the steering knuckle. There are two main designs in common use, the **linkage steering** and the **rack and pinion**. Long-short arm suspensions most commonly use linkage steering to connect the steering column to the **pitman arm**, **center link**, and **idler arm**. **Tie rods** are then used to make the final connection to the steering knuckles. Smaller vehicles most commonly use the rack-and-pinion steering system because it is the most compact of the two major steering systems.

Tires

Tires are one of the most critical components of the suspension and steering system. They support the weight of the vehicle and make final contact with the road surface. The most common tire design is the **radial tire**, which is known for its stable footprint and low rolling resistance.

Tire construction begins with the **beads**. The bead is a circular piece of steel wire that is encased in rubber. The bead forms the mounting point for the tire on the **rim**. **Body plies** form the main body of the tire and run from bead to bead. All other parts of the tire attach to the body plies, including the **liner** (sealed surface inside the tire), the **sidewalls**, and the **tread**.

Belts are used between the plies and the tread to help stabilize the tire's footprint (where the tire makes contact with the road). A stable footprint means better traction under all road conditions, and makes the vehicle handle and brake better.

Maintenance

The primary maintenance that should be performed on suspension and steering systems is lubrication of the ball joints, tie rod ends, and other components. This should be done with a hand-powered grease gun, and the amount of grease should be metered carefully.

The most important part of tire maintenance is proper inflation. Low inflation pressures increase rolling resistance, and therefore increase fuel consumption.

BRAKE SYSTEMS

Of all the systems on a car, the most important may well be the brake system. It is one thing to not be able to go; it is another thing again to not be able to stop. Anyone who has experienced a brake failure can testify to the helpless feeling inspired by a lack of response from the brake pedal.

The major components found in any brake system include the following:

Brake pedal: the mechanical connection between the driver's foot and the master cylinder.

Master cylinder: located in the engine compartment just in front of the driver, the master cylinder generates the fluid pressure to operate the brake assemblies at the wheels.

Fluid reservoir: provides fluid to the brake circuits. The fluid reservoir is located on top of the master cylinder.

Brake lines: transmit fluid pressure from the master cylinder to the brake assemblies. These can be steel lines that run along the vehicle chassis or flex hoses that are used to connect the steel lines to the brake assemblies.

The two major types of brake assemblies are as follows:

Drum brakes: expanding shoes make contact with a rotating drum to develop friction and slow the vehicle.

Disc brakes: brake pads on either side of a rotating disc are "pinched" together to slow the vehicle.

Brake systems are **hydraulically operated**. A pumping piston, located in the **master cylinder**, is operated by the **brake pedal** and puts pressure on the system's **brake fluid**. Since fluids cannot be compressed, the brake fluid travels through the **brake lines** and moves the pistons in the **brake assemblies** to operate the brakes. The harder the driver presses on the brake pedal, the more fluid pressure is developed and more braking power is generated.

Figure 11. Dual hydraulic brake systems

Drum Brakes

The parts that develop the friction in a drum brake are the **brake shoes**. There are two brake shoes in any drum brake assembly. The brake shoes are operated by a **wheel cylinder** that is located between the brake shoes. As hydraulic pressure is applied to the wheel cylinder, the pistons inside push apart and act against the brake shoes. The brake shoes push outward against the brake drum, and the resulting friction slows the vehicle.

Disc Brakes

Disc brakes are much more powerful than drums. The pistons used to actuate disc brakes are much larger, and can apply more force to the brake pads. Also, brake rotors used in disc brakes are more easily cooled, as they are better exposed to the cool air under the car and are often designed with air passages through them to enhance heat rejection.

The piston that operates a disc brake is housed in a **brake caliper**. This caliper "floats" laterally as the brake is applied and released, and makes it possible for one piston to operate the pads on both sides of the rotor. This makes the caliper operate similar to a "c-clamp." As the screw is tightened on one side, the entire assembly is drawn together and "pinches" tightly on the item being clamped.

Power Brakes

Braking pressure is usually boosted using a **brake booster**. The brake booster is located between the brake pedal and the master cylinder. Engine intake manifold vacuum is utilized to generate greater force on the master cylinder, so higher hydraulic pressures can be generated in the brake system. Some brake booster systems use fluid pressure from the power steering system to increase braking power.

Antilock Brakes

Just like every other vehicle system, computer control is being incorporated into the brake system. Most cars now come equipped with **antilock brakes (ABS)**, which prevent wheel lock under hard braking conditions. This gives more control to the driver in slippery conditions and allows the vehicle to stop more predictably.

AUTOMOTIVE INFORMATION PRACTICE SET

1. How many revolutions of the crankshaft does it take to complete one cycle of events in a four-stroke cycle engine?

   (A) one-half
   (B) one
   (C) two
   (D) four

2. This image depicts what stroke in the four-stroke cycle?

   (A) intake stroke
   (B) compression stroke
   (C) power stroke
   (D) exhaust stroke

3. The engine's crankshaft is connected to the piston through the

   (A) cylinder
   (B) intake valve
   (C) exhaust valve
   (D) connecting rod

4. A 12:1 air-fuel mixture would be a _____ mixture.

   (A) rich
   (B) lean
   (C) stoichiometric
   (D) none of the above

5. Diesel engines utilize a _____.

   (A) high compression ratio
   (B) spark ignition system
   (C) low compression ratio
   (D) carburetor

6. The antifreeze in the engine's coolant will

   (A) lower the boiling point of the coolant
   (B) raise the boiling point of the coolant
   (C) raise the freeze point of the coolant
   (D) lower the corrosion resistance of the coolant

7. Identify this engine component.

   (A) spark plug
   (B) fuel injector
   (C) wrist pin
   (D) valve spring

GO ON TO THE NEXT PAGE

8. Electronic fuel injectors are controlled by the

   (A) powertrain control module
   (B) fuel pressure regulator
   (C) electric fuel pump
   (D) ignition switch

9. Where does combustion take place in the engine?

   (A) 1
   (B) 2
   (C) 3
   (D) 4

10. The PCM receives signals from the vehicle's _____.

   (A) sensors
   (B) diagnostic data link
   (C) actuators
   (D) scan tool

ANSWERS AND EXPLANATIONS

1. **C**

It takes two revolutions of the crankshaft to equal each four-stroke cycle.

2. **C**

This image depicts the power stroke, which is the third stroke in the four-stroke cycle. The power stroke generates the engine's power.

3. **D**

The connecting rod is what links the crankshaft to the piston and helps provide rotary motion, and therefore, power.

4. **A**

A 12:1 ratio of air to fuel would be a rich mixture, fast-burning and possibly producing black smoke.

5. **A**

Diesel engines operate with a high compression ratio. The compression ratio for a diesel engine can range anywhere from 16:1 to 22:1.

6. **B**

Antifreeze raises the boiling point of your coolant, thereby rendering it much more efficient at transferring heat.

7. **A**

This is a spark plug. Spark plugs are threaded into the cylinder head, where they protrude into the combustion chamber and generate the spark to initiate combustion.

8. **A**

Of the items given, only the powertrain control module is in charge of firing and regulating electronic fuel injectors.

9. **B**

The combustion chamber, indicated in the diagram by the number 2, is where the actual combustion of the air-fuel mixture takes place. It is located in the cylinder head directly above the piston (1 in the diagram).

10. **A**

As the "brain" of the car, it is the job of the PCM to gather signals from the car's sensors and generate outputs to control the vehicle's functions. The diagnostic data link, choice (B), connects a scan tool to the PCM; the scan tool, (D), is what technicians use to read the PCM.

CHAPTER TEN

Shop Information

In order to work effectively in any industrial or technical environment, a technician must be able to identify tools correctly and use them safely. Hand tools are the foundation of industry; very little work would get done without them. Even the largest piece of equipment would not run for very long if hand tools were not available for their maintenance and repair. (Note: You are given six minutes to answer 11 questions on the CAT-ASVAB for this section.)

WRENCHES

There are two basic types of wrenches; the **open-end** and the **box-end**. The open-end wrench is made for speed. Since the end is open, it is easy to slide the wrench on and off a fastener, such as a cap screw. To loosen tight fasteners, it is a good idea to use a box-end wrench. The box end wraps completely around the head of a bolt, and therefore makes greater surface contact.

Figure 1a. Open-end wrench

Figure 1b. Box-end wrench

The most common wrench arrangement is the **combination wrench**. This design has an open-end and a box-end built into opposite ends of a wrench. Both ends are made to fit the same size fastener, but the technician can loosen the bolt with the box end, and then finish removing the bolt more quickly using the open end.

When the specific size wrench for a fastener is not available, an **adjustable wrench** (sometimes referred to as a **Crescent® wrench**) can be used.

Figure 2. Adjustable wrench

SOCKETS

An alternative to using wrenches to loosen fasteners is the use of **sockets**. Like wrenches, sockets come in both **6- and 12-point designs**. Six-point is a stronger design, and is usually the mechanic's first choice in the smaller socket drive sizes. However, 12-point is definitely the most popular in large drive sizes, such as $\frac{3"}{4}$ and above.

6-point   12-point

Figure 3. Six-point and twelve-point sockets

To determine the size of a socket required for a job, simply measure the distance between two parallel sides of the bolt head. If the bolt head measures $\frac{9"}{16}$ across two parallel sides, then a $\frac{9"}{16}$ socket is required to loosen it.

Sockets come in a variety of **drive sizes**. The drive size is determined by the size of the opening that attaches to the **drive tool**. For instance, if the square end of a socket measures $\frac{3"}{8}$ across, then that would be a $\frac{3"}{8}$ drive socket. The most popular drive sizes are $\frac{1"}{4}$, $\frac{3"}{8}$, $\frac{1"}{2}$, and $\frac{3"}{4}$.

Larger drive sizes are available for the very large fasteners used in heavy industry. Take a look at the diagram below.

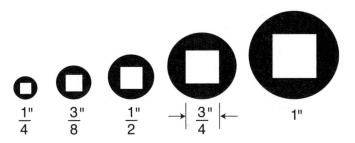

$\frac{1"}{4}$ $\frac{3"}{8}$ $\frac{1"}{2}$ $\rightarrow |\frac{3"}{4}| \leftarrow$ 1"

Figure 4. Common socket drive size range

Sockets are very versatile, because they can be used with a variety of drive tools. The most common drive tool for sockets is the **ratchet**, which turns the fastener in only one direction as the handle is moved back and forth through a narrow arc. Ratchets are reversible, so they can be set to tighten or loosen a fastener.

Figure 5. Ratchet

Sockets can also be used with pneumatic (compressed air) power tools, such as an **air impact wrench**. The air impact wrench can remove fasteners quickly by applying tremendous amounts of torque (twisting force) using a "hammering" action that vibrates fasteners loose. It is important to remember that only **impact sockets** should be used with an air impact wrench.

Figure 6. Air wrench

SCREWDRIVERS

Smaller fasteners (such as machine screws and wood screws) can often be removed and installed using a **screwdriver**. Screwdrivers come in many different sizes and configurations. The oldest screwdriver design is the **flat tip** type, which is basically a flat blade made to turn a screw with a single slot across the top of it.

Figure 7. Flat tip screwdriver

The flat tip screwdriver is far less popular now in light of some newer designs, including the **Phillips**, **Robertson**, and **Torx**. All of these newer designs grip the fastener better so they are much easier to remove and install. Since the screwdriver makes better contact with the fastener, it is also possible to make the fastener tighter.

Figure 8a. Phillips tip screwdriver

Figure 8b. Robertson screwdriver

Figure 8c. Torx screwdriver

HAMMERS

Striking objects in order to remove or install them is the job of the hammer. Almost every technician uses a hammer of some kind, whether it is used to drive a nail or to loosen pieces of an assembly. Hammers come in many designs and sizes according to their intended use.

The type most often used by metal workers and mechanics is known as a **ball-peen hammer**. This hammer is designed with a regular striking face like most hammers, but also has a rounded end that can be used for shaping metal and making gaskets.

Figure 9. Ball-peen hammer

Mechanics will often use a **rubber mallet** to prevent damage to the parts they are striking. Rubber mallets are not made for maximum impact; they are designed to install delicate parts such as hub caps and prevent damage to their surface. A carpenter would use a **wooden mallet** to achieve the same effect.

Figure 10a. Rubber mallet

Figure 10b. Wooden mallet

Carpenters often will use a **claw hammer**, which serves a dual purpose. The hammer head has two ends; one to drive nails and the other to remove nails. Claw hammers come in a variety of sizes, and these are determined by the weight of the hammer head. A general-purpose claw hammer would have a 13 oz. head, while a rough-framing hammer might be anywhere from 16 to 20 oz.

Figure 11. Claw hammer

Heavy jobs require the use of a **sledge hammer**. This is a long-handle hammer with a large steel head that typically requires both hands to operate.

Figure 12. Sledge hammer

CHISELS, PUNCHES, AND DRIFTS

Hammers are often used in conjunction with a **chisel**, a **punch**, or a **drift**. A chisel normally has a long edge and is used for cutting, where as a punch is narrow and is used for driving small fasteners and making layout marks. A drift is used for striking an object where it is important that the hammer itself not come in direct contact with the work.

The most common chisel is the **cold chisel**, which has a straight, sharp edge for cutting off bolt heads or separating two pieces of an assembly. Cold chisels get dull from time to time and must be resharpened on a bench grinder.

Punches are made in a number of different designs, but the most common ones are the **pin punch** and the **center punch**. Pin punches are straight and cylindrical in shape, and are used for driving roll pins. They come in various sizes, normally starting as small as $\frac{1}{16}$" and going up to $\frac{1}{4}$" in diameter. The pin punch is made to drive pins out of holes, and to follow the pin through the hole as it forces it out.

Figure 13. Pin punch

Center punches are used to make small indentations that serve as starting marks for drilling operations. Making a small indentation with a center punch can help the drill bit stay on target long enough to get a hole started. Attempting to drill a hole in metal without first marking it with a center punch can allow the drill bit to "walk" across the work and completely miss the original target.

Figure 14. Center punch

When using a hammer to drive parts in or out of an assembly, it is easy to damage the parts if they are struck directly by the hammer. The head of a ball-peen hammer is made from forged steel, and thus can easily damage parts that are made from softer materials. Placing a **drift** against the object and then striking the drift with a hammer prevents damage to the part that is being driven. Drifts are often made from soft metals such as mild steel, brass, and even aluminum.

Figure 15. Brass drift

SAWS

Cutting a material requires the use of a **saw**. Saws are used in many different trades, but are probably most utilized by carpenters.

The **crosscut saw** is designed to do what its name suggests: cut across the grain of the wood. Crosscut saw teeth are unique in that they cut like a knife. This is in contrast to a **rip saw**, that is made to cut with the grain of the wood and whose teeth are shaped like chisels. A rip saw's teeth are also set (bent) alternately from side to side to cut a relatively wide kerf (slot). This allows the rip saw to move freely as it cuts the wood.

Figure 16. Crosscut saw

Figure 17. Rip saw

A **coping saw** is used to make fine, curving cuts. This saw uses a thin, flexible blade that is held tight on a wide frame. The blade can be rotated in the frame for further flexibility, making it easier to make difficult cuts on larger pieces of material.

Figure 18. Coping saw

The **back saw** is also made from thin material, but has a rigid strip of steel on its top edge for reinforcement. A back saw is normally used for making fine cuts, so it has 14 to 16 teeth per inch. Back saws can be used with a **miter box** for making even cuts at specific angles.

Figure 19. Miter box and back saw

The one saw that can be found in a mechanic's tool box is a **hacksaw**. Hacksaws are used for cutting metals such as steel, aluminum, or copper. The blades in a hacksaw are replaceable, and it is important to choose the right blade for the material that is going to be cut.

Figure 20. Hacksaw

When selecting a hacksaw blade, keep in mind that larger numbers of teeth per inch help when cutting thinner materials. Also, remember that when installing a new blade, orient it so the teeth point away from the handle. This makes the hacksaw cut on the forward stroke, so let up on the downward pressure when pulling the hacksaw back.

DRILLING AND BORING TOOLS

Making small holes in wood or metal is done by **drilling** the material. Large holes can be made in wood or soft metals using a process known as **boring**. The two processes are essentially the same, but they use different tools to get the job done.

Drill bits are used for drilling holes. A carpenter would use drill bits up to $\frac{1}{4}"$ in diameter, but a mechanic would commonly use drill bits as large as $\frac{1}{2}"$. If larger holes than this must be made, special tools would be used to bore the hole.

The vast majority of drill bits are made to cut while rotating in a clockwise direction. These are known as **right-hand** drill bits. **Left-hand** drill bits are made to cut in the opposite direction. The most practical application for a left-hand drill bit is the removal of broken bolts from threaded holes.

Hole saws can also be used for boring large holes. Hole saws are not adjustable, so each one is only capable of drilling one size of a hole.

Figure 21. Hole saw

Today, it is rare for anyone to use hand-operated tools to drive drill bits and other boring tools. Instead, it is common practice to perform these operations using an **electric drill**. Electric drills can be identified by chuck size, reversibility, and whether they are designed to operate at a constant or variable speed.

The **chuck** of an electric drill is the part that holds the drill bit. A chuck is identified by the largest diameter bit that will fit in it. Common chuck sizes include $\frac{1}{4}"$, $\frac{3}{8}"$, and $\frac{1}{2}"$. Regular drill chucks can be tightened and loosened using a **chuck key**. Since it is easy to lose a chuck key, **keyless chucks** are becoming more popular. A keyless chuck makes it possible to tighten and loosen the chuck by hand.

Some drills can operate in both the clockwise and counterclockwise directions. These are known as **reversible drills**. **Variable speed drills** are designed to operate over a range of speeds that can be determined by the position of the trigger.

As battery technology advances, it is getting more common for people to buy **cordless drills**. Longer times between battery recharges are just one of the reasons why these have become so popular.

The most important safety item to remember when using a drill is to use a sharp bit. Dull bits require more time and more pressure placed on the drill to get the job done. With smaller bits, this could result in bit breakage and damage to the surface of the material being drilled. Drill bits can be sharpened on a bench grinder using a special attachment.

PLIERS

Repair operations often call for objects to be gripped, twisted, bent, or cut. Sometimes these objects are irregularly shaped or otherwise difficult to hold. These situations are remedied best through the use of **pliers**.

The most common type of pliers is the **combination slip-joint**. These are adjustable at the joint of the two handles of the pliers. With two different positions to choose from, these pliers can grip objects in a wide range of sizes. Sometimes, this design also incorporates a wire cutter for increased versatility.

Figure 22. Combination slip-joint pliers

When large diameter objects must be gripped or twisted, a technician would use **adjustable joint pliers** to get the job done. These are adjustable over a large range of sizes, as they have multiple "arc-joints" that the pliers can be set into. The handles are also very long, which gives very good leverage and makes for maximum gripping power. These pliers are also commonly known as **water pump pliers** or **Channel-lock® pliers**.

Figure 23. Channel-lock® pliers

Lineman pliers are used for cutting and bending heavy gauge wire. These are not size-adjustable, but are made for maximum leverage at the jaws to make the cutting process easier. This type of pliers would most often be used by electricians, but all trades utilize them at one time or another.

Figure 24. Lineman pliers

Diagonal cutters are pliers that are made exclusively for cutting. The two jaws are set at an angle (diagonally) to make it easier to cut wires straight across. Diagonal cutters are normally used for cutting wire and small cables.

Figure 25. Diagonal cutters

For holding small objects in tight places, a pair of **needle nose pliers** could be used. These have very long, pointed jaws for maximum reach. Needle nose pliers are often used for intricate jobs like soldering circuit boards and small components, and they will most often have a wire cutter built into them at the base of the jaws.

Figure 26. Needle nose pliers

Locking pliers are used by technicians of all trades. Most people know them as **Vise-Grip**® pliers. They are adjustable, made in a large variety of jaw designs, and will lock tightly in place for holding or clamping objects together. Locking pliers often have wire cutters built into them as well for maximum versatility.

Figure 27. Vise-Grip® pliers

PLANING, SMOOTHING, AND SHAPING TOOLS

When working with wood, there are many occasions when it is necessary to remove a small amount of material to make a piece fit properly or to make a surface smooth. One tool that can be used for this purpose is a **plane**.

There are several different types of planes, but the one that would be best-suited for general purpose work is the **jack plane**. The jack plane has a smooth lower surface (plane bottom) and an adjustable-depth blade that protrudes slightly below this surface (through the mouth). This blade is set at an angle, similar to the blade in a disposable razor.

Figure 28. Jack plane

When using a jack plane, the carpenter grasps the plane with both hands and moves it evenly across the surface of the work, "shaving" a thin layer of wood. If a heavier cut is desired, the blade can be adjusted to protrude farther from the lower surface of the plane.

Wood chisels are used to shape wood as well as smooth a wood surface. Wood chisels come in a variety of widths, which can range from $\frac{1}{8}$" to 2". A wood chisel is normally hand-operated, but when making deep cuts, a soft-faced mallet should be used to lightly tap the chisel through the work.

Figure 29. Wood chisels

Rasps are basically very coarse files that are used to trim, shape, and smooth wood. Round rasps are useful for cleaning up holes, whereas a flat rasp would be used to smooth flat surfaces. The cutting teeth on a rasp are coarse enough that it clears sawdust easily and is always ready for the next stroke.

Figure 30. Rasps

Metalworkers use **files** to smooth, polish, and shape metal. Files are made from hardened steel and consist of diagonal rows of teeth. These teeth can be arranged as either a single row of parallel teeth (single-cut) or one row of teeth criss-crossing with another row (double-cut). Files are made in flat, round, half-round, and triangular designs.

DON'T BE SURPRISED

While some of the tools in this chapter are probably more common to you from your own garage or the garage of someone you know, be sure to pay special attention to some of the lesser known items as well, as the ASVAB may surprise you. Welding tools and tips and saws are known to have appeared on recent ASVAB tests.

Most files do not come with handles. It is important to have a handle ready to attach to a file when it is put to use, as this will prevent the end of the file from being driven into the technician's hand. Remember that a file is made to cut only on the forward stroke, so it should be lifted slightly from the work when it is pulled back.

Figure 31. Flat file, half-round file, and triangular files

SOLDERING TOOLS

Soldering is a process that joins metals by bonding a metal alloy to their surfaces. It is a low-temperature process that can be performed with simple tools and inexpensive materials.

Most solder is an alloy of lead and tin. The percentages of each metal in the solder will vary depending on the desired properties of the solder; i.e., melting point, etc. Higher percentages of lead will result in a lower melting point.

The most critical part of soldering is the cleaning of the surfaces to be joined. Any oxides or other contaminants on the surface to be soldered will prevent a solid connection from being made. The best way to prepare a surface for soldering is to use a **flux** that will clean the surfaces with a chemical action. Electrical connections require a **rosin flux**, and solders made for this will have the flux contained in the core of the solder. This is known as **rosin-core solder**.

There are a number of tools that can be used to generate the necessary heat to melt the solder, but in most cases a **soldering iron** will be used. Most soldering irons are electrically powered, and can draw anywhere from 25 to 100 watts. Low-power irons would be used to solder electrical connections, whereas higher powered ones would be used in sheet metal work.

Tip

Power cord

Figure 32. Soldering iron

A tool that is often used for soldering electrical connections is the **soldering gun**. A soldering gun has a two-step trigger that allows the technician to quickly select a low or high heat setting. The main advantage to a soldering gun is the very rapid warm-up cycle. A soldering gun also has a light built into it for illuminating the work.

Figure 33. Soldering Gun

When soldering, start by mechanically cleaning the materials to be joined. This may involve the use of a stainless steel brush or even sandpaper. Heat the surfaces gently while applying flux to them, and then add solder once the flux has thoroughly cleaned the material. Spread the solder thinly over the surface, making sure to heat thoroughly any area that is to be tinned.

Before soldering an electrical connection, it is always a good idea to make a solid mechanical connection first. This will involve stripping insulation from wires and twisting them together. Keep in mind when soldering that the entire connection needs to be heated before applying solder to it. If only the solder is heated and it then is "melted" onto relatively cool wires, a "cold" solder joint is created that can exhibit unusual electrical properties.

MEASURING INSTRUMENTS

A critical skill for any technician is the ability to make accurate measurements.

Automotive technicians will sometimes use a **steel rule** or a **tape measure** to determine distances. These will measure in fractions of an inch as low as $\frac{1}{32}''$, but are ineffective when more accuracy is required. This is because the scale becomes too difficult to read with smaller measurements.

When accuracy down to one-thousandths of an inch is required, a **micrometer** is used. The most common type of micrometer is the **outside micrometer**. The outside micrometer is made to measure the outside diameter of cylindrically shaped objects, as well as the thickness of flat objects. It is built similar to a c-clamp, where the **spindle** of the micrometer is rotated in and out to adjust the distance between it and the **anvil**. All measurements are taken between the spindle and the anvil.

Figure 34. Outside micrometer

The **thimble** of the micrometer is attached directly to the spindle. The **sleeve** of the micrometer is stationary, and has markings on it indicating how far the spindle has been moved. As the thimble moves outward, it uncovers the graduations on the sleeve. The position of the thimble relative to the sleeve is what determines the micrometer reading.

Forty turns of the thimble will move the spindle exactly 1 inch. This means that each turn of the thimble moves the spindle $\frac{1}{40}$" or .025". The graduations on the sleeve are also marked every 0.025" to keep track of how many times the thimble has been turned. Each time the thimble completes one turn, another mark on the sleeve is uncovered. Four complete turns of the thimble move the spindle $\frac{1}{10}$ of an inch or 0.100", so this is marked with a large "1" on the sleeve. The mark at 0.200" is a "2," and so on.

The outside of the thimble has 25 evenly spaced graduations on it. Since a full turn of the thimble moves the spindle 0.025", this means that one of the graduations on the thimble is the equivalent of .001". In order to read a micrometer, it is simply a matter of adding the measurement on the sleeve to the number on the thimble that aligns with the longitudinal line on the sleeve.

Figure 35. Reading a micrometer

FASTENERS

Most man-made assemblies are held together with **fasteners**. Building objects as one piece is often impractical; it is much easier to make a number of pieces and then assemble them. Fasteners hold these pieces together and make it easy to disassemble them for service.

The vast majority of fasteners are **threaded**. A bolt, for instance, has **external threads**, whereas a nut has **internal threads**. A threaded bolt can only be inserted into a nut or hole that has a similar thread. The type of thread that is placed on a fastener will vary according to the diameter of the fastener and the intended strength of the finished product. Threads are identified by their **pitch**, and this is measured using a **thread pitch gauge**.

FASTEN YOUR SEATBELT

Some of the most common types of tools to be tested on the ASVAB are fasteners (screws and bolts). It pays to review this wide range of tools.

Fractional-measurement fasteners (measured in fractions of inches) use threads that are identified by the number of threads per inch. There are two basic thread classifications within this group: **Unified National Coarse (UNC)**, and **Unified National Fine (UNF)**. A UNC or coarse thread would have relatively few threads per inch, where a UNF or fine thread would have a larger number of threads per inch.

A bolt that is $\frac{3}{8}$" in diameter could, therefore, have two possible thread pitches. If it were a UNC bolt, it would have 16 threads per inch, where as if it were a UNF bolt, it would have 24 threads per inch.

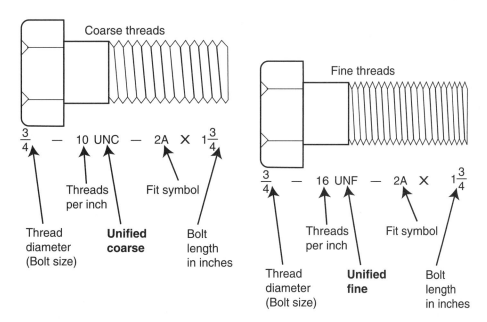

Figure 36. Bolt designation numbers

Two other important measurements of a fastener include the **diameter** and the **length**. The diameter is the distance across the unthreaded portion of the bolt. This would give an indication of the size of hole that the fastener is made to be installed in. The length of the bolt is the distance between the underside of the bolt head and the end of the bolt. Note that the bolt head does not count toward the length of the bolt.

Figure 37. Fastener diameter and length

Generally speaking, threaded fasteners that are $\frac{1}{4}''$ in diameter and larger are known as **bolts**, where as those that are smaller than $\frac{1}{4}''$ are known as **machine screws**.

Nuts thread onto bolts or machine screws to clamp assemblies together. Nuts will have either a square head or a hexagonal head, and can be locked into position using several different methods.

Wing nuts are used when it is necessary to disassemble a component by hand. The two "wings" attached to the nut make it easy to tighten and loosen without the aid of hand tools.

Figure 38. Wing nut

A **castellated nut** uses a **cotter pin** to lock it into place, which must pass through a hole in the bolt or stud that the nut is threaded on.

Figure 39a. Castellated nut

Figure 39b. Cotter pin

Lock nuts have a nylon insert incorporated into its threads that provides enough interference to prevent the nut from loosening.

Figure 40. Lock nuts

Retaining rings (or **snap rings**) are used to prevent end-movement of cylindrical parts in bores or parts mounted on shafts. **External snap rings** are installed in grooves on shafts, whereas **internal snap rings** install in grooves inside a bore. Snap rings are installed and removed using snap ring pliers.

| Internal prong-type | Internal hole-type | External hole-type | External "E"-type |

Figure 41. Internal snap rings, external snap rings

Rivets can also be used to assemble parts. A rivet is simply a pin with a head at one end. A rivet is installed in a hole (the same diameter as the rivet) that is drilled through two pieces that are to be assembled. With the two pieces tightly clamped, the head of the rivet is placed on a hard surface, while the other end is formed into a head using a hammer or special riveting tool. This creates an assembly that is semipermanent, as the rivet must be drilled out to remove it.

A   B   C

Figure 42. Installation of a regular rivet

WELDING TOOLS

The final section of ASVAB shop tool review relates to welding. When joining metals, the best way to achieve a high-strength joint is to use a **welding** process. Welding is very different from soldering in that it involves melting the base metal of the objects to be joined, a process that requires very high temperatures.

There are two major types of welding processes: **oxyacetylene welding** and **electric-arc welding**. Oxyacetylene welding involves the use of a torch that is fueled with oxygen and acetylene. Burning these two gases together creates an extremely hot flame, hot enough to melt steel and other ferrous (iron-based) materials. **Filler rod** is melted along with the base metal to produce a finished weld.

There are many specialized processes that fall under the electric-arc welding classification. The simplest and most easily recognized type is known as **stick welding**. Stick welding involves the use of an electric-arc welding machine and two cables: one that attaches to the work being welded through a ground clamp, and the other going to an electrode that is sometimes referred to as a **stinger**. The stinger is held by the welder and is used to hold the **welding rod**.

240 Volt
Electrical Outlet

ON
OFF
Power Switch

Electrode Holder

Electrode

Arc

Ground

Cables

Ground Clamp

Figure 43. Stick welder

When the welder touches the welding rod on the work, an electric arc is formed. This electric arc generates a tremendous amount of heat and accomplishes three things. First, the heat melts the base metal of the material being welded. Second, the heat melts the electrode and deposits this metal in the weld as filler. Lastly, the **flux** on the outside of the electrodes burns and the generated gases form a "shield" around the weld. This gaseous shield prevents air from reacting with the hot metal and therefore weakening the weld.

As the welder continues the weld, the electrode burns and becomes shorter. The means that the welder must continue moving the stinger closer to the work until the electrode has been consumed. Once the electrode is used up, the welder "breaks off" the arc, and a new electrode is placed in the stinger to continue the weld.

If more heat is needed to perform the weld, the welder can increase the amount of electric current that is supplied by the welding machine. Generally speaking, the larger the pieces that are being welded or the larger the electrode that is being used, the greater the amount of current required to get the weld done.

The electric arc that is generated during this process gives off a very high intensity light. The ultraviolet light is so intense that it can "sunburn" exposed skin and burn the retinas of unprotected eyes. Welders must, therefore, cover all exposed skin with protective clothing (preferably leather) and wear face shields (helmets) with light filters. The filters are usually very dark, so the welder can view the welding process itself but nothing else.

Newer welding helmets have electronic filters that "sense" the ultraviolet light from an electric arc and switch from "clear" to "shaded" in a split second. This allows the welder to leave the helmet down while lining up the next weld, saving the time consumed by flipping the helmet up and down.

Another electric-arc welding process that continues to gain popularity is **MIG welding**. MIG welding is also known as **wire-feed welding** because the electrode used for the weld process is a wire that is automatically fed from a spool. MIG (Metal-Inert Gas) uses a bottled inert gas (such as argon) to shield the weld, and requires a relatively sophisticated welding machine.

Figure 44. MIG Gun

SHOP INFORMATION PRACTICE SET

1. In order to make a bolt tighter, a
   _____ wrench should be used.

   (A) longer
   (B) shorter
   (C) heavier
   (D) shinier

2. A cotter pin is often used in
   conjunction with a _____.

   (A) lock nut
   (B) lock washer
   (C) castellated nut
   (D) machine screw

3. What is the tool shown below known as?

   (A) water pump pliers
   (B) retaining ring pliers
   (C) Channel lock® pliers
   (D) A and C only

4. A $\frac{3}{8}''$ drill bit will fit into an electric
   drill with a _____ chuck.

   (A) $\frac{1}{4}''$

   (B) $\frac{3}{8}''$

   (C) $\frac{1}{2}''$

   (D) B and C only

5. The blade in a hacksaw should be
   installed with its teeth pointed

   (A) toward the handle
   (B) away from the handle
   (C) either A or B
   (D) neither A nor B

6. How is the length of a bolt measured?

   (A) Measure the length from end to end
   (B) Measure the length of the
       threaded portion only
   (C) Measure the length from the
       underside of the head to the end
       of the threads
   (D) None of the above

7. A bolt with a hexagonal head could be
   loosened using a(n)

   (A) open-end wrench
   (B) box-end wrench
   (C) 12-point socket and ratchet
   (D) all of the above

8. The tool shown above is used for

   (A) installing pop rivets
   (B) stapling asphalt shingles
   (C) crimping electrical terminals
   (D) soldering electrical connections

GO ON TO THE NEXT PAGE

9. "Tinning" is a process that is related to

(A) carpentry
(B) roofing
(C) soldering
(D) welding

10. The following screw head would be used with which type of screwdriver?

(A) Flat tip
(B) Phillips
(C) Robertson
(D) Torx

ANSWERS AND EXPLANATIONS

1. **A**

Fasteners can be tightened best with longer wrenches. Adding an extension or using an adjustable wrench (Crescent®) may also improve tightening ability.

2. **C**

A castellated nut uses a cotter pin to lock it into place, which must pass through a hole in the bolt or stud that the nut is threaded on.

3. **D**

When large-diameter objects must be gripped or twisted, a technician would use adjustable joint pliers to get the job done. These are adjustable over a large range of sizes, as they have multiple "arc-joints" that the pliers can be set into. The handles are also very long, which gives very good leverage and makes for maximum gripping power. These pliers are also commonly known as *water pump pliers* or *Channel-lock® pliers*. Since choice (D) allows for both choices (A) and (C), it is the correct answer.

4. **D**

The chuck of an electric drill is the part that holds the drill bit. A chuck is identified by the largest diameter bit that will fit in it. Common chuck sizes include $\frac{1}{4}"$, $\frac{3}{8}"$, and $\frac{1}{2}"$. A $\frac{3}{8}"$ drill bit will fit into a $\frac{3}{8}"$ or $\frac{1}{2}"$ chuck, answers (B) and (C), respectively. The correct answer, therefore, to what a $\frac{3}{8}"$ drill bit will fit into is (D).

5. **B**

When installing a new hacksaw blade, orient it so the teeth point away from the handle. This makes the hacksaw cut on the forward stroke, so let up on the downward pressure when pulling the hacksaw back.

6. **C**

One important measurement of a fastener is the length. The length of the bolt is the distance between the underside of the bolt head and the end of the bolt. Note that the bolt head does not count toward the length of the bolt. Therefore, the best answer is (C).

7. **D**

The two basic types of wrenches—the open end and the box end—are both acceptable for loosening a hexagonal bolt. The open-end wrench is easy to slide on and off a fastener. The downside to the open-end wrench is that it only makes contact with two sides of a six-sided (hex) bolt head. The box-end wraps completely around the head of a bolt, and therefore makes greater surface contact. Box-end wrenches normally come in a 12-point configuration, but some are made as 6-point. Used with a ratchet, the correct size socket is ideal for loosening fasteners such as hexagonal bolts. Thus, because all the choices are acceptable, (D) is the best answer.

8. **D**

The tool shown is a soldering gun. It is used for soldering electrical connections.

9. **C**

If two pieces to be joined by soldering are large, it may pay to tin the surfaces before attempting to join them. Heating the surfaces gently while applying flux to them, and then adding solder once the flux has thoroughly cleaned the material will accomplish this. Since soldering is the process involved, the correct answer is (C).

10. **C**

The Robertson screwdriver is a newer design that grips the fastener better so the screw is much easier to remove and install.

CHAPTER ELEVEN

Mechanical Comprehension

In order to understand how machines work, it is important to have a good grasp of **applied physics**.

Applied physics is the practical application of the laws of physics. In other words, it is the practice of making things work. The purpose of this chapter is to give you a greater understanding of basic mechanics, simple machines, and fluid power.

FORCE

Force is a push or a pull. Forces are acting all around us, whether we know it or not. Some are fairly obvious, such as a tractor pulling a plow, or a baseball being hit into the stands. Other invisible forces are often taken for granted, such as gravity. Gravity is a force that keeps us standing on the ground instead of floating around in midair. Since force has a magnitude and a direction that it is applied in, it is known as a **vector quantity**.

Without force being applied to them, objects would not move (or, if they were already in motion, they would remain in motion). Objects with a great deal of **mass** (such as a freight train) require a large force to move them. Large masses also require large forces to slow them down if they are already moving.

Keep in mind that mass is quite different from **weight**. Weight can vary, as it is related to the force of gravity. If for some reason gravity is diminished, weight will also diminish. Mass, on the other hand, will not vary from location to location. Mass is an amount, with no particular direction related to it, so it is described as a **scalar quantity**.

Isaac Newton (1642–1727) laid the foundation for an area of physics called **mechanics** with his discovery of three laws of motion. These three laws help us understand what causes objects to change their motion.

NEWTON'S FIRST LAW OF MOTION

An object continues in a state of rest or in a state of motion at a constant speed along a straight line, unless compelled to change that state by a net force.

Newton's First Law of Motion

An object continues in a state of rest or in a state of motion at a constant speed along a straight line, unless compelled to change that state by a net force.

An object at rest has no **net** force acting on it. There are forces acting on it, but they are equal and opposite in direction, so they effectively "cancel" each other. Likewise, an object that is in motion will continue in a straight line at a constant speed if no net force acts on it. A bullet flying through the air would continue in a straight line at a constant speed forever, if forces such as gravity or wind resistance did not act on it. Gravity generates a force that causes the bullet to move toward the Earth, whereas wind resistance creates a **drag** (also a force) that causes the bullet to slow down.

Newton's first law of motion is also referred to as the **law of inertia**. Inertia is directly related to the mass of an object, and it is described as "the natural tendency of an object to remain at rest or in motion at a constant speed over a straight line." Objects with greater mass are much harder to get moving, or slow down once they are moving, so they have greater inertia.

Newton's Second Law of Motion

When a net force F acts on an object of mass m, the acceleration a that results is directly proportional to the net force and has a magnitude that is inversely proportional to the mass. The direction of the acceleration is the same as the direction of the net force.

Newton's second law can be summarized by the formula

$$F = ma$$

where m is measured in kilograms (kg), a is in meters per second^2 $\left(\frac{m}{s^2}\right)$, and F is in newtons (N). Note that ma actually means mass $\times$ acceleration (mass multiplied by acceleration).

Acceleration occurs when the velocity of an object changes (increases or decreases). An acceleration of $1 \frac{m}{s^2}$ means that the velocity of the object is increasing 1 meter per second each second. Starting from a standstill, an object with an acceleration rate of $1 \frac{m}{s^2}$ will achieve a velocity of $5 \frac{m}{s}$ in a period of 5 seconds.

Velocity is different from **speed**. Speed indicates how fast an object is moving, but gives no indication of the direction of movement. Velocity gives an indication of both speed and direction, so it is known as a vector quantity.

NEWTON'S SECOND LAW OF MOTION

When a net force F acts on an object of mass m, the acceleration a that results is directly proportional to the net force and has a magnitude that is inversely proportional to the mass. The direction of the acceleration is the same as the direction of the net force.

When a net force acts on an object, the object will accelerate in the direction of the net force. However, the acceleration will be less if the mass of the object is greater. For instance, if a net force of 100 N is applied to a 100 kg block, the block will accelerate in the direction of the force at a rate of $1\,\frac{m}{s^2}$. However, if the size of the block is increased to 200 kg, the acceleration rate will be only $0.5\,\frac{m}{s^2}$. Either increasing the force or decreasing the mass will cause the acceleration rate to increase.

Newton's Third Law of Motion

Whenever one body exerts a force on a second body, the second body exerts an oppositely directed force of equal magnitude on the first body.

Newton's third law is summarized by the oft-used phrase, "for every action (force), there is an equal and opposite reaction." An illustration of this is a handgun being fired. The bullet will exert an equal force on the gun to the one the gun exerts on the bullet. The force on the bullet causes it to accelerate rapidly, as it has very little mass. The gun and the shooter, however, have a great deal more mass than the bullet, so they will accelerate (recoil) at a much slower rate in the opposite direction.

NEWTON'S THIRD LAW OF MOTION

Whenever one body exerts a force on a second body, the second body exerts an oppositely directed force of equal magnitude on the first body.

WEIGHT

As seen previously, weight is different from mass. Mass is an intrinsic property of matter, whereas weight is dependent on the force of gravity. Gravity is the downward pull that the Earth exerts on bodies outside of itself.

Isaac Newton discovered that every particle in the universe is attracted to every other particle. This concept became a physical law known as **Newton's Law of Universal Gravitation**. The gravitational force that each body exerts on the other grows stronger as the bodies get closer. The force also increases as the mass of the bodies increase.

This explains why a man standing on the Moon weighs $\frac{1}{6}$ of what he would weigh on the surface of the Earth. While the radius of the Moon is smaller than the Earth, the mass of the Moon is a fraction of the Earth's mass. Since the mass of the Moon is so much less than that of the Earth, it exerts significantly less gravitational pull on other bodies around it.

Since gravity exerts a force on bodies that pulls them together, this force causes an **acceleration due to gravity**, which is represented by the symbol **g**. For bodies near the Earth's surface, g is calculated to be $9.80\,\frac{m}{s^2}$. This can be used to find the weight of an object using the formula

$$W = mg$$

where W is weight in newtons (N), m is mass in kilograms (kg), and g is acceleration due to gravity.

FRICTION

When moving an object across a surface, **friction** will oppose the movement. An example of this would be a hockey puck sliding along an ice surface. While ice has much less friction than most surfaces, it will still exert a **sliding frictional force** on the puck that eventually causes it to stop moving.

When an object is not moving, a force that attempts to slide it across a surface will encounter a different type of friction. Attempting to push a stationary box across a concrete floor will require the worker to overcome the **static frictional force** that opposes the movement.

According to Newton's third law, for every action there is an equal but opposite reaction. As an object sits on a table, its weight generates a downward force acting on the table. This force is counteracted by an equal upward force generated by the table back on the object. This upward reactive force is called the **normal force**, and is represented by F_N. Normal force has an impact on the frictional force developed by an object. The higher the normal force of an object, the more friction it will develop with the surface it is resting on. In short, the heavier the object, the more friction it will develop.

TENSION

When cables are used to pull an object, forces exerted through the cable result in a force being applied to the object being pulled. This results in **tension** in the cable (the cable is being pulled from both directions) as an object will exert an opposing force to the force being applied by the cable.

The net force applied to the object will cause it to accelerate, but the object by itself will require less force to accelerate it than the combination of the object and the cable. In other words, more force must be applied to the other end of the cable than what is actually applied to the object. This is why a cable is more likely to break at the end where the force is applied rather than where it connects to the object being moved.

WORK

Work is accomplished when force is applied against an object. This is summarized by the formula

$$W = Fd$$

where F is force in newtons (N), d is distance in meters (m), and W is work in joules (J).

If a force of 100 N is applied to a car, and the car is moved 10 meters, then a total of 1,000 joules of work has been done.

Work is done if force *F* is applied over distance *d*

Figure 1. Force *F* pushing a car over distance *d*

If force is applied to the car, but the car does not move, no work has been done. This can be seen in the formula $W = F \times d$, where zero distance (*d*) results in work (*W*) being zero as well. No matter how much force is applied, no movement results in zero work being accomplished.

KINETIC ENERGY

When work is done to move an object, this work will result in an increase in the **kinetic energy** of the object. Kinetic energy is the energy of movement. When an object is moving, its kinetic energy can be calculated using the formula

$$KE = \frac{1}{2}mv^2$$

where *m* is mass in kilograms (kg), *v* is speed in meters per second $\left(\frac{m}{s}\right)$, and *KE* is kinetic energy in joules (J). Note that work and kinetic energy are both measured in joules. This is not a coincidence, as any work that is done to accelerate an object at rest to speed *v* will be converted into the kinetic energy of that object. This principle is known as the **work-energy theorem**.

GRAVITATIONAL POTENTIAL ENERGY

To raise an object to a certain height *h*, work must be done. This work then becomes the **gravitational potential energy** of the object. An object's potential energy (*PE*) can be calculated using the formula

$$PE = mgh$$

where *m* is mass in kilograms (kg), *g* is acceleration due to gravity $\left(9.8\ \frac{m}{s^2}\right)$, *h* is the height of the object in meters (m), and *PE* is gravitational potential energy measured in joules (J). The higher the object is raised (*h*), the greater the potential energy of the object. Increasing the mass (*m*) of the raised object will also increase its potential energy.

A falling object has its potential energy (*PE*) converted into kinetic energy (*KE*) as it falls. Conversely, an object that is thrown straight up into the air will reach its highest point, and the potential energy it has at this point can be no greater than the kinetic energy it had when it was first thrown.

This effect is explained best by the **principle of conservation of mechanical energy**, which states that the total mechanical energy ($PE + KE$) of an object remains constant as the object moves as long as no external work is done on the object, and the object does no work on its surroundings (in other words, in a closed system).

POWER

Power is the **rate** that work is done. Consider the example of a man pushing a small car over a distance of 100 meters. If the man pushes with a force of 100 N to move the car, then using $W = F \times d$, we see that 100 N × 100 m = 10,000 joules of work has been done. If another man can do the same amount of work in one-half the time, then that man has twice as much power as the first man.

Performing work at the rate of 1 joule per second is the same as expending 1 watt of power. The watt is named in honor of James Watt (1736–1819), the inventor of the steam engine. The unit of power that most people in the United States are familiar with is **horsepower**, as this is the unit that is used to rate internal combustion engines. Horsepower uses a different system of measurement, as it is defined as 550 foot-pounds per second of work being done. One horsepower is the equivalent of 746 watts.

SIMPLE MACHINES

The idea behind the invention of many of the machines we use today is to reduce or manage the work that we do. We have already seen that work is defined as force × distance ($w = fd$), so hard work would involve either large forces or long distances, or both.

Mechanical Advantage

What makes work difficult is often the amount of force that must be applied to get the job done. Heavy objects need to be lifted, parts need to be pushed together or apart, and large machines need to be moved. Often, it is difficult or impossible for a human being to apply enough force to get the job done.

In order to increase the available force to a much larger one, **mechanical advantage** is used. Mechanical advantage is defined as "the advantage gained by the use of a mechanism in transmitting force." Using the proper equipment, it is possible to increase or even multiply force many times over what is initially applied.

It is important to remember that there is no free lunch when it comes to work. While mechanical advantage can be used to amplify force, this is done at the expense of distance. In other words, the work put out can never exceed the work put into one of these machines. The good news, however, is that they make hard work easier by breaking it down into smaller, more manageable pieces.

Inclined Plane

One of the simplest ways of managing lifting tasks is through the use of the **inclined plane**. Imagine attempting to lift a 100 kg (about 220 pound) box from ground level to the bed of a pickup truck. This is a difficult, if not impossible, task for one man. This can go much easier if an inclined plane (or ramp) is placed between the ground and the bed of the truck.

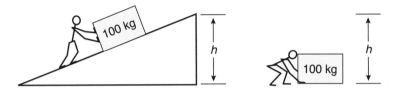

Figure 2. Lifting a box, or pushing up a ramp to height *h*

Remember that the work that is done to lift the box will be the same as the final gravitational potential energy of the box ($PE = mgh$). Therefore, the same amount of work will be done whether the box is pushed up the ramp (assuming no friction), or if it is lifted into the truck directly. The difference with the ramp is that a much smaller force can be applied to load the box into the truck. This force must be applied over a longer distance, but it will give some mechanical advantage to make the task easier.

Wedge

The **wedge** is a variation of the inclined plane, in that it is made to move, whereas the inclined plane stays stationary. It can be used for many purposes, including lifting, splitting, and tightening. The mechanical advantage that can be gained with a wedge is determined by the ratio of its length to its height.

A wedge that is constructed with the same length and height will offer no mechanical advantage. This is because it will lift the same distance as it is pushed horizontally. When the distance of the lift is the same as the distance the initial force travels, the force in will equal the force out.

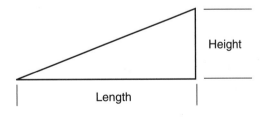

Figure 3. Wedge

Making the wedge longer relative to its height (less slope) will change this by decreasing the amount of lift that takes place as the wedge is moved horizontally. This increases the amount of force that can be generated by the wedge and makes it easier to lift heavy objects. Remember that if force is increased by the wedge, then the distance it will lift will be less than the distance it moved horizontally.

Common applications of the wedge include knives, chisels, log splitters, and securing hammer heads on their handles.

Levers

Another simple machine that can be used to amplify force or distance, as well as change direction, is the **lever**. There are three basic types of levers, so this machine lends itself to many different applications.

The **first-class lever** is used to increase force or distance, and to change the direction of the force. An example of a first-class lever is a child's teeter-totter.

Figure 4. First-class lever

The **fulcrum** is the point that the lever pivots on. When effort is applied to one end of the lever, it changes direction at the other end. The position of the fulcrum will define whether any mechanical advantage is gained. If the fulcrum is closer to the object being lifted, less effort is required to do the work. However, the end that the effort is applied to must move farther to get the job done.

The opposite effect takes place when the fulcrum is moved closer to where the effort is applied. Now the distance the object can be moved is amplified, but the force is diminished.

A **second-class lever** is used to increase force only. An excellent example of a second-class lever is a wheelbarrow.

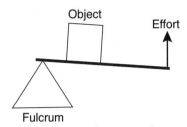

Figure 5. Second-class lever

The mechanical advantage of the second-class lever increases as the object is moved closer to the fulcrum. This can also be accomplished by increasing the length of the lever. As the lever is lifted, the distance that the object is lifted is always less, so lifting force increases.

The **third-class lever** is used to increase distance. It is similar to the second-class lever in that the fulcrum is at one end. The object, however, is at the other end of the lever, with the effort being applied somewhere in between. Examples of third-class levers would be a fishing pole and a catapult.

Figure 6. Third-class lever

Since distance moved is increased with a third-class lever, force is therefore diminished. This effect magnifies as the effort is applied closer to the fulcrum.

Pulleys

Applying force to an object is sometimes best accomplished through the use of a **pulley**. A pulley is a wheel that carries a flexible rope, belt, or chain.

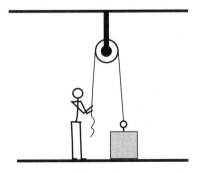

Figure 7. Person pulling a rope through a pulley to lift an object

Block and Tackle

It is relatively uncommon for one pulley to be used by itself. More often, two or more pulleys will be used in an arrangement known as a **block and tackle** to increase lifting force.

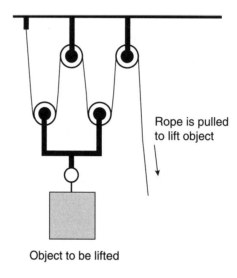

Rope is pulled
to lift object

Object to be lifted

Figure 8. Block and tackle

The block and tackle shown here has four pulleys; two are attached to a stationary object (such as the ceiling or wall of a building) and the other two are attached to the lower block (connected to the load). As the rope is pulled, the lower block moves toward the stationary pulleys. Note that in order to lift the load 1 foot, it is necessary to pull the rope a total of 4 feet. This is because each of the four rope links must shorten by 1 foot to get the lower block to move 1 foot. Neglecting friction, this gives a total mechanical advantage of 4:1, so if 4 pounds of force are required to lift a load, only 1 pound needs to be applied to the rope.

Wheel and Axle

Another variation of the pulley concept is the **wheel and axle**. Like the block and tackle, the wheel and axle can be used to increase mechanical advantage. It uses two wheels mounted on a shaft, with one wheel having a larger diameter than the other. An example of a wheel and axle is the steering wheel of a car.

The large-diameter wheel will usually be the one that has the effort applied to it. Large movements of the large wheel result in small movements of the small wheel. Since a large movement (or distance) is being translated into a small movement, the force is then being increased.

The exact amount of mechanical advantage is determined by the ratio of the radius of the wheels. If the large wheel is 20 inches in diameter, and the small wheel is 10 inches in diameter, the total mechanical advantage is 2:1. This means that force can be doubled across this assembly, but distance at the small wheel will be one-half of the movement of the large wheel.

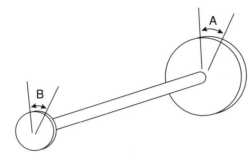

Movement at A becomes smaller than movement at B—force is increased at B

Figure 9. Wheel and axle

Gears and Gear Ratios

While **gears** are not included in the list of classic simple machines, they are of fundamental importance to an understanding of how machines work. Gears can be used anywhere that force is being transmitted between two points, and are excellent for gaining mechanical advantage. In order to understand how gears work, however, a technician must have a thorough understanding of **torque** and its relationship with speed.

Torque is **twisting force**. When a bolt is being tightened, torque is being applied to the bolt. When tightening a fastener, if one uses a wrench that is 1 foot long, and applies a force of 100 pounds to the end of the wrench, 100 foot-pounds (ft-lb) of torque is being applied. Simply multiply the applied force by the length of the wrench to determine the torque.

As an engine moves a vehicle, its crankshaft applies torque to the power train of the vehicle. If an engine can generate a great deal of torque while turning at high RPMs (revolutions per minute), it can do work quickly, and therefore is very powerful.

Gears can be used to change the speed and torque of an engine. The gears are located in the vehicle's power train (transmission and drive axle) and the **overall gear ratio** will determine how fast the vehicle can go and how much torque is applied to the drive wheels.

If a small gear drives a large gear, a **speed reduction** takes place. The large gear will turn slower than the small gear and the speed of the output will be slower. However, there will also be an associated **torque multiplication** (increase) that takes place and now the torque output of the large gear will be greater than what was applied to the small gear. A speed decrease means that torque will increase.

Consider "Torque" and "Speed" to be two boys on a teeter-totter. Whenever "Torque" goes up, "Speed" goes down, and vice versa. A mathematician would describe these two quantities to be **inversely proportional**.

FLUID POWER: HYDRAULICS

Fluid power can also be used to gain mechanical advantage. While the classic simple machines are effective and reliable, they are limited in the sense that force only can be amplified in their immediate area. When more versatility is required, **hydraulics** can be used. Hydraulics is the transmission of force through the use of liquids.

In order to understand how hydraulics works, it is first necessary to have a grasp of the concept of **pressure**. If force is applied evenly over a certain area, then pressure is applied to that area. Pressure is calculated using the formula

$$P = \frac{F}{A}$$

where F is force in pounds (lb), A is area in square inches (in^2), and P is pressure in pounds per square inch (psi). Keep in mind that $\frac{F}{A}$ means that F is divided by A. A force of 100 pounds applied over an area of 10 square inches results in a pressure of 10 pounds per square inch (psi) being developed.

Using the formula for pressure, we can derive $F = PA$, which is useful for calculating the amount of force that is developed when pressure P is applied to area A.

There are three major principles that make hydraulics work:

1. The **first principle** is that **liquids are effectively incompressible**. Even when extremely high pressure is applied to a liquid, the volume of the liquid will decrease only a very small amount. This property makes liquids very effective for transmitting force.

2. The **second principle** of hydraulics is that **liquids conform themselves to the shape of their container**. Whether in a pipe or a pump, liquids will always change their shape to fill the space completely.

3. The **third principle** was discovered in 1650 by a French scientist named Blaise Pascal. Pascal observed that **when pressure is applied to a completely enclosed fluid, this pressure is transmitted undiminished to all parts of the fluid and the enclosing walls**. This observation became **Pascal's Law**, which can be used to explain how force can be amplified in a hydraulic system.

MECHANICAL COMPREHENSION PRACTICE SET

1. Pipe A has a 3-inch diameter and pipe B has a 1-inch diameter. If water is flowing from pipe A to pipe B, which statement is true?

    (A) water pressure in pipe A is greater than in pipe B
    (B) water pressure in pipe B is one-third greater than in pipe A
    (C) water is flowing faster in pipe A than in pipe B
    (D) water pressure is equal in both pipes

2. Which principle of hydraulics states that liquids conform themselves to the shape of their container?

    (A) first
    (B) second
    (C) third
    (D) none of the above

3. Approximately how much force is needed to lift the weight?

    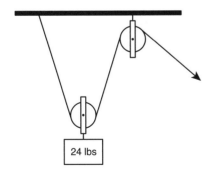

    (A) 48 lbs
    (B) 12 lbs
    (C) 24 lbs
    (D) 6 lbs

4. Which type of lever is used to increase distance?

    (A) first-class lever
    (B) second-class lever
    (C) third-class lever
    (D) fulcrum

5. Which bracket provides the most secure amount of support for the shelf?

    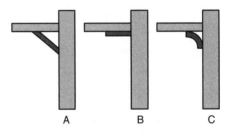

    (A) bracket A
    (B) bracket B
    (C) bracket C
    (D) they are equally secure

6. One foot-pound of torque is equivalent to

    (A) 12 inch-pounds
    (B) 10 inch-pounds
    (C) 1 newton-meter
    (D) 12 newton-meters

7. When using a wrench to loosen a bolt, to apply the maximum possible torque, a force should be applied

    (A) perpendicular to the wrench, halfway up the handle
    (B) parallel to the wrench, at the end of the handle
    (C) perpendicular to the wrench, at the end of the handle
    (D) at an angle between parallel and perpendicular, at the end of the handle

GO ON TO THE NEXT PAGE

8. Gear A has 15 teeth and gear B has 10. If gear A makes 14 revolutions, gear B will make

(A) 14
(B) 21
(C) 7
(D) 28

9. Which one of Newton's laws can be summarized by the formula $F = ma$?

(A) Newton's First Law of Motion
(B) Newton's Second Law of Motion
(C) Newton's Third Law of Motion
(D) Newton's Law of Universal Gravitation

10. A basic kitchen knife, like the one below, is based on which of the following simple machines?

(A) first-class lever
(B) inclined plane
(C) pulley
(D) wedge

ANSWERS AND EXPLANATIONS

1. A

This is an example of Bernoulli's Principle. Water cannot be compressed so the same amount of water must be flowing through both pipes. This means that the water will be flowing faster in the pipe with the smaller diameter (pipe B), decreasing the pressure in pipe B as compared to pipe A.

2. B

The second principle of hydraulics states that liquids conform themselves to the shape of their container. Liquids will always change their shape to fill the space completely.

3. B

With a double pulley system, the weight is divided by two to determine the amount of force needed. Twenty-four divided by two is 12, making the amount of force needed 12 pounds.

4. C

A third-class lever is used to increase distance.

5. A

Bracket A provides more secure support than either bracket B or C.

6. A

One foot-pound is directly equal to twelve inch-pounds.

7. C

Torque is maximized the farther away the force is applied from the axis of rotation, and when force is applied perpendicular to the line of the wrench.

8. B

The gear ratio is 3:2, which means that for every two turns that gear A makes, gear B makes three. If gear A makes 14 turns, divide that by two to get seven and then multiply that by three to get 21.

9. B

The formula $F = ma$ summarizes Newton's Second Law of Motion where a net force F acts on an object of mass m; the acceleration a that results is directly proportional to the net force and has a magnitude that is inversely proportional to the mass.

10. D

A kitchen knife is a simple machine whose design is based on the physics of a wedge.

CHAPTER TWELVE

Assembling Objects

The ASVAB analyzes both abilities and aptitude to discover what jobs you will best be suited for in your military career. For example, pilots, mechanics, machine operators, and engineers need to have or to develop good *spatial relationship* skills. The Assembling Objects subtest examines your spatial relationship skills, to see if you would do well at tasks that involve depth perception and putting things together—whether with your hands or in your mind.

KNOW WHAT TO EXPECT

The **Assembling Objects** (AO) section measures how you visualize relationships of given shapes—in other words, how parts will look when assembled into a whole or when connected. You may claim that some people are naturally gifted at visualizing or seeing patterns. Yes, that's true. Yet for those of us who may not be "naturals," studies show that we can all improve our spatial relationship skills with certain strategies and practice. In this chapter, you'll have the opportunity to both learn and practice.

The CAT-ASVAB test includes 16 AO questions, with a time limit of 16 minutes. While there are time limits imposed on each subtest in the CAT-ASVAB, most examinees complete the individual subtests before the time expires. Remember, unlike the Paper and Pencil ASVAB, you will not be able to review or change an answer once you submit it.

The Paper and Pencil ASVAB includes 25 AO questions, with a 15-minute time limit. We recommend checking with your career counselor or recruiter to see what subtests you will be facing on your specific ASVAB test.

ASSEMBLING OBJECTS QUESTION TYPES

The Assembling Objects subtest contains two types of test items that we are calling

- **Jigsaw Puzzle Assembly Problems,** which test your ability to choose how an object will look when its parts are put together into a larger shape.
- **Connector Assembly Problems,** which test your ability to correctly connect two objects with a line at the indicated points.

In both types of AO items, you are offered five boxes. The left-most or first box contains drawings of unconnected parts. The remaining four answer-choice boxes hold drawings of possible ways to assemble or connect those parts—but only one is exactly right.

KAPLAN'S 3-STEP METHOD FOR ASSEMBLING OBJECTS PROBLEMS

1. Get comfortable with the directions.

Be familiar with the directions for both types of AO problems. In the jigsaw puzzle type, you're looking for the answer that best shows how the objects in the left-most box appear when fit together. In the connector type, you're looking for the answer that best shows how the objects in the left-most box appear when they are connected to the indicated points.

2. Scan the "instructions" box.

In this subtest the left-most box—the instructions box—contains the blueprints or visual instructions that will lead you to the correct answer. Take a quick mental snapshot of the number, size, and shape of the objects before you move on to compare them to the answer choices.

3. Eliminate the losers.

Probably more than one of the answer choices will be believable at first look. Rather than trying to put together the original parts in your mind's eye, use the techniques described in this chapter to eliminate as many of the potential answers as you can.

Jigsaw Puzzle Assembly Problems

Let's explore how to solve the jigsaw puzzle items, which test your ability to choose how an object will look when its parts are put together into a larger shape. In other words, your goal is to make a whole object out of the exact parts in the instructions box. While there may be several ways to combine these parts, *only one* is the right answer that matches *only one* of the answer choices.

EXAMPLE 1

Which figure best shows how the objects in the left box will appear if they are fit together?

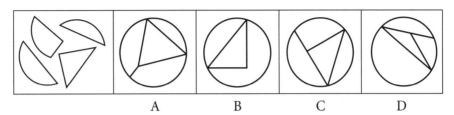

| | A | B | C | D |

In this example, the correct answer is (C).

Do you have to assemble the parts in your head first? Not really. After *scanning* the left-most box, check which of the four answer choices you can eliminate. You may be able to disqualify one, two, or three of the possible solutions and then verify which remaining choice is the only way to assemble the pieces you began with.

Another key tip: You can count on some or all of the pieces in

STRATEGY TIP

On the paper and pencil test, you could number each of the objects in the left-most box and renumber corresponding parts in the answer choices that you have not yet eliminated. If you try this strategy, work quickly, but efficiently.

the problem box to be turned around (rotated) to fit with the other pieces. In the example above, three of the original four parts were rotated in the correct answer (C). However—and this is very important!—don't be tricked by pieces that have been reversed, or flipped over, to their mirror image—they don't count as the same shape as the original piece.

Now we come to some strategies for eliminating wrong answers. If you practice them here, at the end of the chapter, and in the ASVAB Practice Tests, you will discover which work best for which problems, as well as which work best for your test-taking style.

Count the Number of Parts

Quickly count the number of parts in the left-most box, and then eliminate any choices that have more or fewer parts within their final shapes.

Check out the following example.

EXAMPLE 2

Which figure best shows how the objects in the left box will appear if they are fit together?

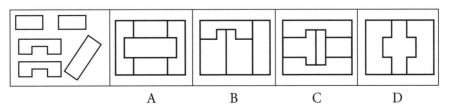

| | A | B | C | D |

The correct solution is (A). How did you do? Did you count five pieces in the instructions box? If you did, you could then eliminate answers (B) and (D) because they had 4 and 3 pieces, respectively. Finally, between (A) and (C), only (A) reflects the exact original shapes.

Find the Biggest or Smallest Part

If there is one especially large or small object in the instructions box, search for the same size or mass within each of the answer choices. Try this strategy on this example:

Which figure best shows how the objects in the left box will appear if they are fit together?

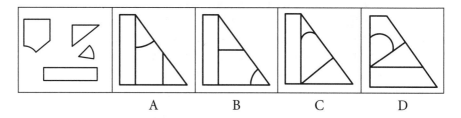

In this example, the correct answer is (B). You will note that one of the original parts is a small pie slice shape. Choice (C) has a similar-sized shape, but one side is concave rather than rounded. Choices (A) and (D) have larger pie slice shapes than the original.

DISQUALIFY FLIPPED SHAPES!

As we've mentioned, do not be fooled by flipped, or mirrored, shapes. In the correct answer, a shape can be rotated (or swiveled on its axis) but not flipped. Consider a jigsaw puzzle piece. You move it around on the table to try to fit it into different openings, but you wouldn't flip it over to the wrong side. Likewise, with these problems, eliminate answers that show the mirror image of a part from the left-most box, rather than its original orientation.

When you get good at this technique, you can spot the largest and the smallest shapes in the left-most box (if they occur) and look for them both among the possible solutions.

Find the Most Unusual Part

Scan quickly to see if there is a uniquely shaped object in the instruction box, and search for that exact object within each of the answer choices. Or look for a distinctive angle or curve on one of the pieces, and eliminate the choices that lack that element.

If this seems confusing, check out the following example and explanation.

EXAMPLE 4

Which figure best shows how the objects in the left box will
appear if they are fit together?

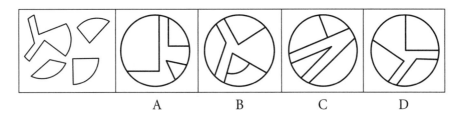

A   B   C   D

In this example, the correct solution is (D). Here's an instance where you have a uniquely
shaped piece in the left-most box:

Eliminate choices (A) and (C), which don't have that piece. You are left with (B) and (D).
Answer (B) has the same shape, but it has been flipped. Remember, in the AO subtest, *you
can rotate shapes, but you cannot flip them (a mirror image)*.

Connector Assembly Problems

The instructions box of connector assembly items shows you two simple geometric shapes
and a connector line. Some problems have familiar shapes such as circles, squares, rectangles,
and triangles. Some have more unusual ones such as letter shapes, clouds, or hearts. The two
shapes and the connector line are labeled with dots and small letters to indicate points where
you are to mentally connect them.

You will see one dot on each shape—one will be labeled with a letter, such as "a." The other
dot will be labeled with a letter such as "b." Dots or points on the ends of the line will
correspond to these letters, here "a" and "b."

You are asked to attach the two shapes to the line at all the right points, based on the
blueprint-type diagram in the problem box. The shapes may be rotated in the solution boxes,
but *the correct solution cannot be flipped*. Try our first example:

EXAMPLE 5

Which figure best shows how the objects in the left box will touch if the letters for each object are matched?

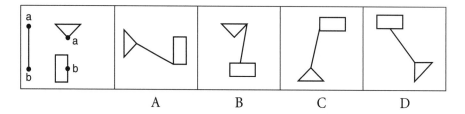

A	B	C	D

SPEED TIP

On the Paper and Pencil test, you can

1. Quickly add dots and letters to the possible solution to verify it.

2. Circle each dot on both shapes in the problem. Then circle the same position on both shapes in each of the remaining answer choices. Where the a-b line intercepts two circles, you have your answer.

You scored if you picked answer (D). This is the only choice where the connected shapes are joined at the right points.

Verify the Placement of the Dots

One efficient strategy is to check the placement of the connector dot on one shape in the problem box; then eliminate the choices that don't have that same placement. Immediately do the same with the second shape. Look at this example:

EXAMPLE 6

Which figure best shows how the objects in the left box will touch if the letters for each object are matched?

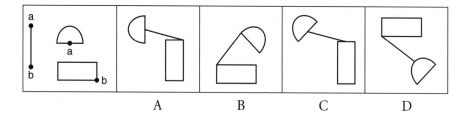

A	B	C	D

Did you pick answer (A)? Good work. In this example, one of the geometric shapes is a half oval with the dot in the center of the flat side. Therefore, you can eliminate choice (B), where the dot is on the corner of the half oval and choice (D), where the dot is in the middle of the curved side of the half oval. Glance at the second shape, a rectangle, and you'll see the connector point is on one corner of the short end. This eliminates choice (C), where the rectangle's point is on the middle of the short end.

Connect a Point That Is Inside a Shape

In the above example, the connection dots are located on the *outline* of each shape, like this:

In some problems, however, one of the lettered dots may be on a line that goes through some part of the shape, like this:

If this is the case, the connecting points *must* exactly match the ones in the instructions box. In other words, if a connection point is on a line that enters a shape, the correct answer must represent this exact same relationship, and must include the line and dot that enters the shape. Try this example:

EXAMPLE 7

Which figure best shows how the objects in the left box will touch if the letters for each object are matched?

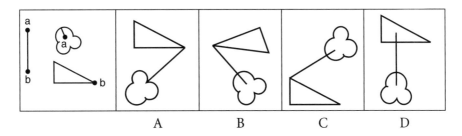

The correct solution is (B). This is the only choice where the connected shapes are joined at the right points and where the indicated point-line relationship within one of the shapes is faithfully reflected.

SPEED TIP

Keep in mind that you have just over half a minute to respond to each problem, so don't spend too much time on any one item!

Look for a Landmark

If you have an *irregular* shape in your problem, find the connecting point's relationship to a "landmark" on that irregular shape. Then check for the same relationship among the possible solutions.

EXAMPLE 8

Which figure best shows how the objects in the left box will touch if the letters for each object are matched?

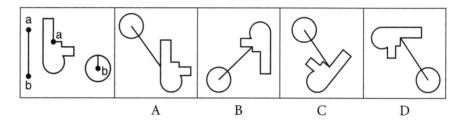

The correct choice is (D). Using the landmark strategy, you might say that the connector dot is placed "inside the elbow" of the "tall step" of this odd shape. Checking for this same placement in the answer choices, you can disqualify (A) and (B). Answer (C) has the correct placement, but the shape has been flipped, so it, too, is eliminated.

ASSEMBLING OBJECTS PRACTICE SET

For questions 1–5:

Which figure best shows how the objects in the left box will appear if they are fit together?

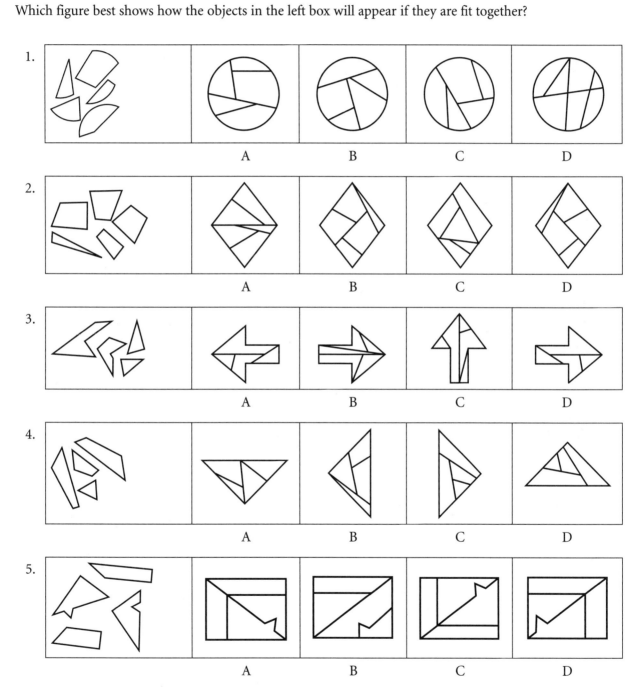

For questions 6–10:

Which figure best shows how the objects in the left box will touch if the letters for each object are matched?

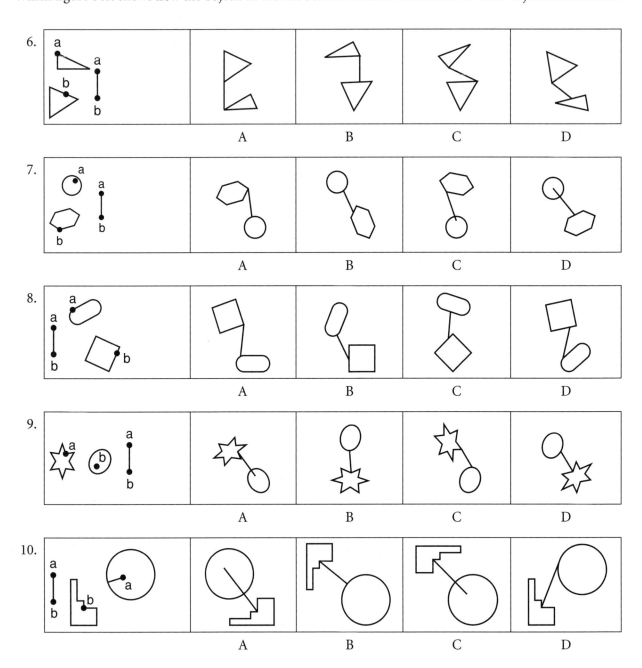

ANSWERS AND EXPLANATIONS

For answers 1–5:

Start by numbering the unassembled pieces. Then try to match each piece to parts in each choice.

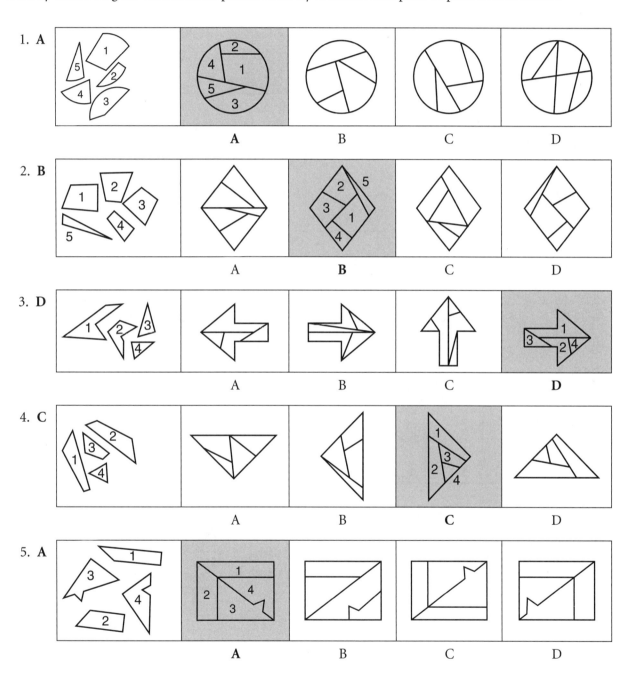

For answers 6–10:

In each choice, place dots where they should be according to the unassembled pieces.

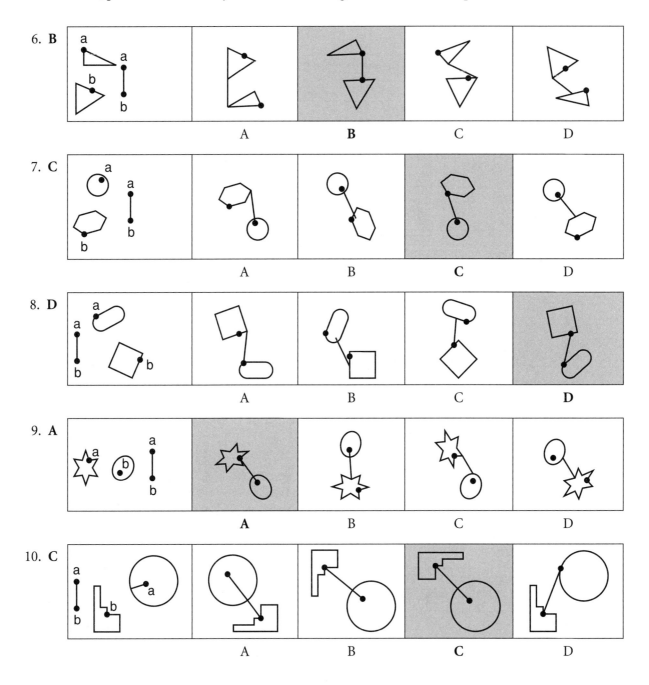

Part Four

ASVAB PRACTICE TESTS

ASVAB Practice Test II

ANSWER SHEET

Part 1: General Science (GS)

1 Ⓐ Ⓑ Ⓒ Ⓓ	6 Ⓐ Ⓑ Ⓒ Ⓓ	11 Ⓐ Ⓑ Ⓒ Ⓓ	16 Ⓐ Ⓑ Ⓒ Ⓓ	21 Ⓐ Ⓑ Ⓒ Ⓓ
2 Ⓐ Ⓑ Ⓒ Ⓓ	7 Ⓐ Ⓑ Ⓒ Ⓓ	12 Ⓐ Ⓑ Ⓒ Ⓓ	17 Ⓐ Ⓑ Ⓒ Ⓓ	22 Ⓐ Ⓑ Ⓒ Ⓓ
3 Ⓐ Ⓑ Ⓒ Ⓓ	8 Ⓐ Ⓑ Ⓒ Ⓓ	13 Ⓐ Ⓑ Ⓒ Ⓓ	18 Ⓐ Ⓑ Ⓒ Ⓓ	23 Ⓐ Ⓑ Ⓒ Ⓓ
4 Ⓐ Ⓑ Ⓒ Ⓓ	9 Ⓐ Ⓑ Ⓒ Ⓓ	14 Ⓐ Ⓑ Ⓒ Ⓓ	19 Ⓐ Ⓑ Ⓒ Ⓓ	24 Ⓐ Ⓑ Ⓒ Ⓓ
5 Ⓐ Ⓑ Ⓒ Ⓓ	10 Ⓐ Ⓑ Ⓒ Ⓓ	15 Ⓐ Ⓑ Ⓒ Ⓓ	20 Ⓐ Ⓑ Ⓒ Ⓓ	25 Ⓐ Ⓑ Ⓒ Ⓓ

Part 2: Arithmetic Reasoning (AR)

1 Ⓐ Ⓑ Ⓒ Ⓓ	7 Ⓐ Ⓑ Ⓒ Ⓓ	13 Ⓐ Ⓑ Ⓒ Ⓓ	19 Ⓐ Ⓑ Ⓒ Ⓓ	25 Ⓐ Ⓑ Ⓒ Ⓓ
2 Ⓐ Ⓑ Ⓒ Ⓓ	8 Ⓐ Ⓑ Ⓒ Ⓓ	14 Ⓐ Ⓑ Ⓒ Ⓓ	20 Ⓐ Ⓑ Ⓒ Ⓓ	26 Ⓐ Ⓑ Ⓒ Ⓓ
3 Ⓐ Ⓑ Ⓒ Ⓓ	9 Ⓐ Ⓑ Ⓒ Ⓓ	15 Ⓐ Ⓑ Ⓒ Ⓓ	21 Ⓐ Ⓑ Ⓒ Ⓓ	27 Ⓐ Ⓑ Ⓒ Ⓓ
4 Ⓐ Ⓑ Ⓒ Ⓓ	10 Ⓐ Ⓑ Ⓒ Ⓓ	16 Ⓐ Ⓑ Ⓒ Ⓓ	22 Ⓐ Ⓑ Ⓒ Ⓓ	28 Ⓐ Ⓑ Ⓒ Ⓓ
5 Ⓐ Ⓑ Ⓒ Ⓓ	11 Ⓐ Ⓑ Ⓒ Ⓓ	17 Ⓐ Ⓑ Ⓒ Ⓓ	23 Ⓐ Ⓑ Ⓒ Ⓓ	29 Ⓐ Ⓑ Ⓒ Ⓓ
6 Ⓐ Ⓑ Ⓒ Ⓓ	12 Ⓐ Ⓑ Ⓒ Ⓓ	18 Ⓐ Ⓑ Ⓒ Ⓓ	24 Ⓐ Ⓑ Ⓒ Ⓓ	30 Ⓐ Ⓑ Ⓒ Ⓓ

Part 3: Word Knowledge (WK)

1 Ⓐ Ⓑ Ⓒ Ⓓ	8 Ⓐ Ⓑ Ⓒ Ⓓ	15 Ⓐ Ⓑ Ⓒ Ⓓ	22 Ⓐ Ⓑ Ⓒ Ⓓ	29 Ⓐ Ⓑ Ⓒ Ⓓ
2 Ⓐ Ⓑ Ⓒ Ⓓ	9 Ⓐ Ⓑ Ⓒ Ⓓ	16 Ⓐ Ⓑ Ⓒ Ⓓ	23 Ⓐ Ⓑ Ⓒ Ⓓ	30 Ⓐ Ⓑ Ⓒ Ⓓ
3 Ⓐ Ⓑ Ⓒ Ⓓ	10 Ⓐ Ⓑ Ⓒ Ⓓ	17 Ⓐ Ⓑ Ⓒ Ⓓ	24 Ⓐ Ⓑ Ⓒ Ⓓ	31 Ⓐ Ⓑ Ⓒ Ⓓ
4 Ⓐ Ⓑ Ⓒ Ⓓ	11 Ⓐ Ⓑ Ⓒ Ⓓ	18 Ⓐ Ⓑ Ⓒ Ⓓ	25 Ⓐ Ⓑ Ⓒ Ⓓ	32 Ⓐ Ⓑ Ⓒ Ⓓ
5 Ⓐ Ⓑ Ⓒ Ⓓ	12 Ⓐ Ⓑ Ⓒ Ⓓ	19 Ⓐ Ⓑ Ⓒ Ⓓ	26 Ⓐ Ⓑ Ⓒ Ⓓ	33 Ⓐ Ⓑ Ⓒ Ⓓ
6 Ⓐ Ⓑ Ⓒ Ⓓ	13 Ⓐ Ⓑ Ⓒ Ⓓ	20 Ⓐ Ⓑ Ⓒ Ⓓ	27 Ⓐ Ⓑ Ⓒ Ⓓ	34 Ⓐ Ⓑ Ⓒ Ⓓ
7 Ⓐ Ⓑ Ⓒ Ⓓ	14 Ⓐ Ⓑ Ⓒ Ⓓ	21 Ⓐ Ⓑ Ⓒ Ⓓ	28 Ⓐ Ⓑ Ⓒ Ⓓ	35 Ⓐ Ⓑ Ⓒ Ⓓ

Part 4: Paragraph Comprehension (PC)

1 Ⓐ Ⓑ Ⓒ Ⓓ	4 Ⓐ Ⓑ Ⓒ Ⓓ	7 Ⓐ Ⓑ Ⓒ Ⓓ	10 Ⓐ Ⓑ Ⓒ Ⓓ	13 Ⓐ Ⓑ Ⓒ Ⓓ
2 Ⓐ Ⓑ Ⓒ Ⓓ	5 Ⓐ Ⓑ Ⓒ Ⓓ	8 Ⓐ Ⓑ Ⓒ Ⓓ	11 Ⓐ Ⓑ Ⓒ Ⓓ	14 Ⓐ Ⓑ Ⓒ Ⓓ
3 Ⓐ Ⓑ Ⓒ Ⓓ	6 Ⓐ Ⓑ Ⓒ Ⓓ	9 Ⓐ Ⓑ Ⓒ Ⓓ	12 Ⓐ Ⓑ Ⓒ Ⓓ	15 Ⓐ Ⓑ Ⓒ Ⓓ

Part 5: Mathematics Knowledge (MK)

1 Ⓐ Ⓑ Ⓒ Ⓓ	6 Ⓐ Ⓑ Ⓒ Ⓓ	11 Ⓐ Ⓑ Ⓒ Ⓓ	16 Ⓐ Ⓑ Ⓒ Ⓓ	21 Ⓐ Ⓑ Ⓒ Ⓓ
2 Ⓐ Ⓑ Ⓒ Ⓓ	7 Ⓐ Ⓑ Ⓒ Ⓓ	12 Ⓐ Ⓑ Ⓒ Ⓓ	17 Ⓐ Ⓑ Ⓒ Ⓓ	22 Ⓐ Ⓑ Ⓒ Ⓓ
3 Ⓐ Ⓑ Ⓒ Ⓓ	8 Ⓐ Ⓑ Ⓒ Ⓓ	13 Ⓐ Ⓑ Ⓒ Ⓓ	18 Ⓐ Ⓑ Ⓒ Ⓓ	23 Ⓐ Ⓑ Ⓒ Ⓓ
4 Ⓐ Ⓑ Ⓒ Ⓓ	9 Ⓐ Ⓑ Ⓒ Ⓓ	14 Ⓐ Ⓑ Ⓒ Ⓓ	19 Ⓐ Ⓑ Ⓒ Ⓓ	24 Ⓐ Ⓑ Ⓒ Ⓓ
5 Ⓐ Ⓑ Ⓒ Ⓓ	10 Ⓐ Ⓑ Ⓒ Ⓓ	15 Ⓐ Ⓑ Ⓒ Ⓓ	20 Ⓐ Ⓑ Ⓒ Ⓓ	25 Ⓐ Ⓑ Ⓒ Ⓓ

ANSWER SHEET

Part 6: Electronics Information (EI)

1 ABCD	5 ABCD	9 ABCD	13 ABCD	17 ABCD
2 ABCD	6 ABCD	10 ABCD	14 ABCD	18 ABCD
3 ABCD	7 ABCD	11 ABCD	15 ABCD	19 ABCD
4 ABCD	8 ABCD	12 ABCD	16 ABCD	20 ABCD

Part 7: Automotive and Shop Information (AS)

1 ABCD	6 ABCD	11 ABCD	16 ABCD	21 ABCD
2 ABCD	7 ABCD	12 ABCD	17 ABCD	22 ABCD
3 ABCD	8 ABCD	13 ABCD	18 ABCD	23 ABCD
4 ABCD	9 ABCD	14 ABCD	19 ABCD	24 ABCD
5 ABCD	10 ABCD	15 ABCD	20 ABCD	25 ABCD

Part 8: Mechanical Comprehension (MC)

1 ABCD	6 ABCD	11 ABCD	16 ABCD	21 ABCD
2 ABCD	7 ABCD	12 ABCD	17 ABCD	22 ABCD
3 ABCD	8 ABCD	13 ABCD	18 ABCD	23 ABCD
4 ABCD	9 ABCD	14 ABCD	19 ABCD	24 ABCD
5 ABCD	10 ABCD	15 ABCD	20 ABCD	25 ABCD

Part 9: Assembling Objects (AO)

1 ABCD	6 ABCD	11 ABCD	16 ABCD	21 ABCD
2 ABCD	7 ABCD	12 ABCD	17 ABCD	22 ABCD
3 ABCD	8 ABCD	13 ABCD	18 ABCD	23 ABCD
4 ABCD	9 ABCD	14 ABCD	19 ABCD	24 ABCD
5 ABCD	10 ABCD	15 ABCD	20 ABCD	25 ABCD

PART 1: GENERAL SCIENCE (GS)

Time: 11 minutes; 25 questions

Directions: In this section, you will be tested on your knowledge of concepts in science generally reviewed in high school. For each question, select the best answer and mark the corresponding oval on your answer sheet.

1. The Genus level contains several related

   (A) species
   (B) families
   (C) orders
   (D) phyla

2. Orbiting around the nucleus of an atom are

   (A) anions
   (B) electrons
   (C) positrons
   (D) photons

3. Air is warmed and filtered first in the

   (A) trachea
   (B) pharynx
   (C) oral cavity
   (D) nasal cavity

4. Which of the following is an example of a tertiary consumer?

   (A) antelope
   (B) house cat
   (C) polar bear
   (D) vulture

5. Which of the following is a substance?

   (A) air
   (B) water
   (C) fire
   (D) earth

6. The Moon's mass is about one-sixth of the Earth's mass. Compared to the gravitational force the Earth exerts on the Moon, the gravitational force the Moon exerts on the Earth is

   (A) one-sixth as much
   (B) one-half as much
   (C) the same
   (D) six times as much

7. Fungi are organisms that break down dead matter and return the organic material back into the environment for reuse. They are examples of

   (A) producers
   (B) decomposers
   (C) consumers
   (D) mutualism

8. In degrees Kelvin, the freezing pointing of water is

   (A) −273°
   (B) 0°
   (C) 100°
   (D) 273°

9. Tough elastic tissues found in the joints that connect bones to bones are called

   (A) ligaments
   (B) tendons
   (C) cartilage
   (D) muscles

GO ON TO THE NEXT PAGE

10. Stress, a poor diet, cigarette smoking, and heredity factors all contribute to individuals developing

    (A) diarrhea
    (B) high blood pressure
    (C) gall stones
    (D) anemia

11. These clouds are thin and wispy clouds that occur high in the atmosphere.

    (A) cirrus
    (B) cumulus
    (C) stratus
    (D) none of the above

12. Fossils are most likely to be found in which of the following types of rock?

    (A) igneous
    (B) metamorphic
    (C) sedimentary
    (D) volcanic

13. Animals that consume plants only are called

    (A) saprophytes
    (B) herbivores
    (C) carnivores
    (D) omnivores

14. The temperature at the core of the sun is thought to be

    (A) 15,000,000° C
    (B) 20,000,000° C
    (C) 25,000,000° C
    (D) 30,000,000° C

15. A _____ is a group of organisms of the same species living in the same region.

    (A) biome
    (B) ecosystem
    (C) community
    (D) population

16. Which one of these planets is NOT an outer planet?

    (A) Jupiter
    (B) Saturn
    (C) Uranus
    (D) Earth

17. A boulder that begins to roll down a hill is an example of an energy conversion from

    (A) potential to thermal
    (B) potential to kinetic
    (C) kinetic to thermal
    (D) kinetic to potential

18. The lowest layer of the Earth's atmosphere is called the

    (A) ionosphere
    (B) mesosphere
    (C) stratosphere
    (D) troposphere

19. Acccording to the law of conservation of energy

    (A) energy is the capacity to do work
    (B) energy can neither be created nor destroyed
    (C) energy is possessed by a moving object
    (D) energy is stored in an object as a result of its position, shape, or state

GO ON TO THE NEXT PAGE

20. As an ambulance passes, its pitch seems to change. This perception is best explained by

    (A) convection
    (B) refraction
    (C) the Doppler effect
    (D) momentum

21. A concave lens is also known as a

    (A) focal point
    (B) converging lens
    (C) convex lens
    (D) diverging lens

22. A molecule is

    (A) a subatomic particle that orbits the nucleus of an atom
    (B) the smallest particle of an element or compound that can exist in the free state and still retain the characteristics of the element or compound
    (C) the smallest component of an element that still retains the properties of the element
    (D) none of the above

23. Which of the following is most responsible for oceanic tides?

    (A) the orbit of the Earth around its own axis
    (B) the magnetic polarity of the Earth
    (C) the orbit of the Moon around the Earth
    (D) the orbit of the Earth around the Sun

24. The elements in a column are called a _____.

    (A) period
    (B) group
    (C) row
    (D) none of the above

25. In a chemical change, the molecules that enter the reaction are called

    (A) reactants
    (B) products
    (C) compounds
    (D) elements

STOP. IF YOU FINISH BEFORE THE TIME IS UP, YOU MAY CHECK OVER YOUR WORK ON THIS PART ONLY.

PART 2: ARITHMETIC REASONING (AR)

Time: 36 minutes; 30 questions

<u>Directions</u>: In this section, you are tested on your ability to use arithmetic. For each question, select the best answer and mark the corresponding oval on your answer sheet.

1. Three apples cost as much as 4 pears. Three pears cost as much as 2 oranges. How many apples cost as much as 72 oranges?

   (A) 36
   (B) 48
   (C) 64
   (D) 81

2. If 48 of the 60 seats on a bus were occupied, what percent of the seats were not occupied?

   (A) 12%
   (B) 15%
   (C) 20%
   (D) 25%

3. Effin sings for $1,000 an hour. Her rate increases by 50 percent after midnight. If she sings one night from 8:30 P.M. until 1:00 A.M., how much should she be paid?

   (A) $4,500
   (B) $5,000
   (C) $5,500
   (D) $6,000

4. Fran has a drawer containing 4 black t-shirts, 3 orange t-shirts, and 5 blue t-shirts. If she picks one t-shirt at random from the drawer, what are the chances that it will *NOT* be orange?

   (A) $\frac{1}{4}$

   (B) $\frac{1}{3}$

   (C) $\frac{2}{3}$

   (D) $\frac{3}{4}$

5. After a 5-hour flight from Newark, Harry arrives in Denver at 2:30 P.M. If the time in Newark is 2 hours later than the time in Denver, what was the time in Newark when Harry began the flight?

   (A) 10:30 A.M.
   (B) 11:30 A.M.
   (C) 3:30 P.M.
   (D) 5:30 P.M.

6. A full box of chocolate contains 24 pieces. If Doris starts out with 198 pieces of chocolate, how many pieces will she have left over if she fills as many boxes as she can?

   (A) 3
   (B) 6
   (C) 8
   (D) 10

7. If 75 percent of x is 150, what is the value of x?

   (A) 150
   (B) 175
   (C) 200
   (D) 250

8. Rachel's average score after 6 tests is 83. If Rachel earns a score of 97 on the 7th test, what is her new average?

   (A) 85
   (B) 86
   (C) 87
   (D) 88

GO ON TO THE NEXT PAGE

9. A delivery service charges $25.00 per pound for making a delivery. If there is an additional 8 percent sales tax, what is the cost of delivering an item that weighs $\frac{4}{5}$ of a pound?

   (A) $20.00
   (B) $21.60
   (C) $22.60
   (D) $24.00

10. A cake recipe requires $\frac{3}{5}$ of an ounce of vanilla extract. How many cakes can be made using a package containing 60 ounces of vanilla extract?

    (A) 48
    (B) 80
    (C) 96
    (D) 100

11. Ed has 100 more dollars than Robert. After Ed spends 20 dollars on groceries, he now has 5 times as much money as Robert. How much money does Robert have?

    (A) $16
    (B) $20
    (C) $24
    (D) $30

12. 587 people are traveling by bus for a field trip. If each bus seats 48 people and all of the buses but one are filled to capacity, how many people sit in the unfilled bus?

    (A) 37
    (B) 36
    (C) 12
    (D) 11

13. Riley brings 100 cookies to school for her class party. If there are 15 students in the class, including Riley, and there are 25 cookies left after the party, what is the average number of cookies that Riley and her classmates ate?

    (A) 1
    (B) 4
    (C) 5
    (D) 6

14. A person 4 feet tall casts a 9-foot shadow at the same time that a nearby tree casts a 21-foot shadow. What is the height of this tree?

    (A) 7
    (B) $8\frac{1}{2}$
    (C) $9\frac{1}{3}$
    (D) 10

15. In a group of 25 students, 16 are female. What percent of the group is female?

    (A) 16%
    (B) 40%
    (C) 60%
    (D) 64%

16. Phil is making a 40-kilometer canoe trip. If he travels at 30 kilometers per hour for the first 10 kilometers, and then at 15 kilometers per hour for the rest of the trip, how many minutes more will it take him than if he travels the entire trip at 20 kilometers per hour?

    (A) 20
    (B) 24
    (C) 30
    (D) 40

GO ON TO THE NEXT PAGE

17. In a certain class, 3 out of 24 students are in student organizations. What is the ratio of students in student organizations to students not in student organizations?

    (A) $\frac{1}{8}$

    (B) $\frac{1}{7}$

    (C) $\frac{1}{6}$

    (D) $\frac{1}{4}$

18. In a certain baseball league, each team plays 160 games. After playing half of their games, team A has won 60 games and team B has won 49 games. If team A wins half of its remaining games, how many of its remaining games must team B win to have the same number of wins as team A at the end of the season?

    (A) 51
    (B) 59
    (C) 60
    (D) 61

19. A vendor bought 10 crates of oranges for a total cost of $80. If he lost 2 of the crates, at what price would he have to sell the remaining crates in order to earn a total profit of 25 percent of the total cost?

    (A) $8.00
    (B) $10.00
    (C) $12.50
    (D) $15.00

20. A machine labels 150 bottles in 20 minutes. At this rate, how many minutes does it take to label 60 bottles?

    (A) 2
    (B) 4
    (C) 6
    (D) 8

21. $15 \times (-5) =$

    (A) 10
    (B) 75
    (C) −75
    (D) none of the above

22. Mike has a collection of baseball cards and baseball figurines. If the ratio of cards to figurines is 5:7 and there are 25 cards in his collection, how many figurines does he have?

    (A) 20
    (B) 35
    (C) 40
    (D) 45

23. Two hot dogs and a soda cost $3.25. If three hot dogs and a soda cost $4.50, what is the cost of two sodas?

    (A) $0.75
    (B) $1.25
    (C) $1.50
    (D) $2.50

GO ON TO THE NEXT PAGE

24. Danielle drives from her home to the store at an average speed of 40 miles per hour. She returns home along the same route at an average speed of 60 miles per hour. What is her average speed, in miles per hour, for the entire trip?

    (A) 48
    (B) 50
    (C) 52
    (D) 55

25. At a certain school the ratio of teachers to students is 1 to 10. Which of the following could be the total number of teachers and students?

    (A) 100
    (B) 121
    (C) 222
    (D) 1,011

26. The average of two numbers is equal to twice the positive difference between the two numbers. If the larger number is 35, what is the smaller number?

    (A) 9
    (B) 15
    (C) 21
    (D) 27

27. Each of seven runners on a relay team must run a distance of 1.27 kilometers. Approximately what is the total combined number of kilometers run by the team in the race?

    (A) 11
    (B) 10
    (C) 9
    (D) 8

28. A scanner can scan 12 photos per minute. At this rate, how many minutes would it take to scan 60 photos?

    (A) 2
    (B) 3
    (C) 5
    (D) 7

29. An employee's net pay is equal to gross pay minus total deductions. A certain employee's gross pay is $1,769.23 and his deductions are as follows: FICA, $218.99; Social Security, $107.05; Medicare, $25.03; state tax, $68.65; municipal tax, $42.75. What is the employee's net pay?

    (A) $1,306.76
    (B) $1,306.66
    (C) $1,305.76
    (D) $1,305.66

30. A student takes four tests. His grades are 95, 72, 84, and 98. What is this student's average test grade?

    (A) 92
    (B) 65
    (C) 87
    (D) 88

STOP. IF YOU FINISH BEFORE THE TIME IS UP, YOU MAY CHECK OVER YOUR WORK ON THIS PART ONLY.

PART 3: WORD KNOWLEDGE (WK)

Time: 11 minutes; 35 questions

<u>Directions</u>: In this section, you are tested on the meaning of words. Each of the following questions has an underlined word. Select the answer that most nearly means the same as the underlined word and mark the corresponding oval on your answer sheet.

1. <u>Impose</u> most nearly means

   (A) create
   (B) force
   (C) damage
   (D) trade

2. <u>Stunted</u> most nearly means

   (A) halted
   (B) daring
   (C) loose
   (D) blatant

3. A <u>sturdy</u> home can withstand nearly any disaster.

   (A) huge
   (B) strong
   (C) cold
   (D) cautious

4. He was <u>undeterred</u> in his quest to find her.

   (A) surprised
   (B) determined
   (C) careless
   (D) brazen

5. <u>Ennui</u> most nearly means

   (A) patient
   (B) gloating
   (C) annoyance
   (D) tasteful

6. <u>Mutable</u> most nearly means

   (A) changing
   (B) silent
   (C) big-hearted
   (D) calm

7. It was gross how they <u>squandered</u> the money.

   (A) gathered
   (B) presented
   (C) wasted
   (D) owned

8. The handwriting was nearly <u>illegible</u>.

   (A) unreadable
   (B) unethical
   (C) creative
   (D) dangerous

9. <u>Infinite</u> most nearly means

   (A) costly
   (B) unending
   (C) babyish
   (D) daily

10. <u>Longevity</u> most nearly means

    (A) training
    (B) lifetime
    (C) girth
    (D) lifestyle

GO ON TO THE NEXT PAGE

11. Kids always fall for that <u>ruse</u>.

   (A) trick
   (B) joke
   (C) story
   (D) backtalk

12. The president <u>proclaimed</u> it a national holiday.

   (A) suggested
   (B) renamed
   (C) announced
   (D) unmade

13. Even the most <u>rudimentary</u> details are crucial to understanding it.

   (A) basic
   (B) ecstatic
   (C) illogical
   (D) fancy

14. <u>Rout</u> most nearly means

   (A) careful
   (B) defeat
   (C) blatant
   (D) open

15. His <u>rogue</u> attitude didn't fit the "team" concept.

   (A) aggressive
   (B) sad
   (C) maverick
   (D) low-brow

16. Her decision didn't <u>resonate</u> very well with some.

   (A) state
   (B) goad
   (C) harmonize
   (D) condone

17. Duplicating steps is far too <u>redundant</u> at this late stage.

   (A) repetitive
   (B) upsetting
   (C) colorful
   (D) wishy-washy

18. Far be it from me to <u>prescribe</u> how to raise one's own children.

   (A) predict
   (B) dictate
   (C) expect
   (D) decide

19. <u>Logical</u> most nearly means

   (A) cognizant
   (B) easy
   (C) rowdy
   (D) sensible

20. <u>Prerequisite</u> most nearly means

   (A) required
   (B) tiny
   (C) gleeful
   (D) tasteful

21. It seems like loud people tend to <u>gravitate</u> toward other loud people.

   (A) stay away
   (B) break
   (C) move toward
   (D) close in on

22. The police felt it was best to be <u>cautious</u> when approaching the house.

   (A) excited
   (B) apathetic
   (C) dodgy
   (D) careful

GO ON TO THE NEXT PAGE

23. <u>Braggart</u> most nearly means

    (A) clown
    (B) leader
    (C) showoff
    (D) deputy

24. Basing his opinions on <u>hearsay</u> doomed the case.

    (A) rumor
    (B) samples
    (C) truth
    (D) belief

25. <u>Taunt</u> most nearly means

    (A) grade
    (B) relate
    (C) ridicule
    (D) party

26. Most respond well to <u>constructive</u> criticism.

    (A) damaging
    (B) productive
    (C) lost
    (D) flattering

27. <u>Quantifiable</u> most nearly means

    (A) laughable
    (B) standard
    (C) countable
    (D) breakable

28. The least <u>effective</u> way of dealing with children is yelling.

    (A) tantalizing
    (B) creative
    (C) useful
    (D) positive

29. <u>Apathy</u> most nearly means

    (A) greatness
    (B) laziness
    (C) boredom
    (D) passion

30. It left a glaring <u>blemish</u> on his permanent record.

    (A) impact
    (B) defect
    (C) hesitancy
    (D) compliment

31. It will take a <u>consensus</u> to get this measure passed.

    (A) agreement
    (B) discussion
    (C) fight
    (D) reprimand

32. No coach can handle <u>dissent</u> from his players for long.

    (A) discussion
    (B) laughter
    (C) thought
    (D) insubordination

GO ON TO THE NEXT PAGE

33. <u>Tempo</u> most nearly means

    (A) hearty
    (B) safety
    (C) modernity
    (D) speed

34. She can take <u>solace</u> in the fact that it couldn't get much worse.

    (A) protection
    (B) comfort
    (C) glee
    (D) depth

35. Many <u>pitfalls</u> await the inexperienced climber.

    (A) joys
    (B) traps
    (C) ropes
    (D) talents

STOP. IF YOU FINISH BEFORE THE TIME IS UP, YOU MAY CHECK OVER YOUR WORK ON THIS PART ONLY.

PART 4: PARAGRAPH COMPREHENSION (PC)

Time: 13 minutes; 15 questions

<u>Directions</u>: This section contains paragraphs followed by incomplete statements or questions. Read the paragraph and select the answer that best completes the statements or answers the questions that follow, and mark the corresponding oval on your answer sheet.

Questions 1 and 2 refer to the following passage.

In modern society, a new form of folktale has emerged: the urban legend. These stories persist both for their entertainment value and for the transmission of popular values and beliefs. Urban legends are stories we all have heard; they are supposed to have really happened, but they cannot be verified. It turns out that the people involved can never be found. Researchers of urban legends call the elusive participant in these supposedly "real-life" events a "FOAF": a friend of a friend.

One classic urban legend involves alligators in the sewer systems of major metropolitan areas. According to the story, before alligators were a protected species, people vacationing in Florida purchased baby alligators to take home as souvenirs. After the novelty of having a pet alligator wore off, people would flush their souvenirs down the toilet. The baby alligators found a perfect growing environment in city sewer systems, where to this day they thrive on an ample supply of rats.

1. The passage suggests the real-life participants of urban legends

   (A) can be difficult to track down
   (B) are usually known, but only barely, by the teller
   (C) seem believable, but do not in fact exist
   (D) are the original tellers of the stories

2. According to the passage, the successful urban legend contains all of the following characteristics *EXCEPT*

   (A) the capacity to entertain
   (B) messages that conform to popular values
   (C) qualities of a folktale
   (D) a basis in reality

For most students of biology, Charles Darwin is considered the father of evolution. But few realize that he is but one of many theorists who noted that genetics and animals showed progression over time. Henri Bergson, for instance, formulated a theory that today is known more commonly as *theistic evolution,* or evolution from God. But Darwin's ability to articulate his theories in writing and to account for many diverse examples of evolutionary biology means that other theories are often seen as little more than offshoots of the original idea of Darwinian evolution.

3. According to the passage, Darwin's theory persists because

   (A) Bergson was right
   (B) Darwin accounted for many variations
   (C) genetics is an inexact science
   (D) evolution is not accepted by the mainstream

GO ON TO THE NEXT PAGE

Local elementary schools have changed considerably over the past 50 years. Where once we had schools in every small town, now students bus for miles to attend larger, more advanced schools. While most parents see this as a positive step for progress and education, some worry about their children losing touch with the simple things around them. A few have even decided to home school their children instead of sending them to nearby towns.

4. The author's tone in this passage is

   (A) embittered
   (B) informative
   (C) biased
   (D) ambivalent

Questions 5 and 6 refer to the following passage.

Most life is fundamentally dependent on photosynthetic organisms that store radiant energy from the Sun. In almost all the world's ecosystems and food chains, photosynthetic organisms such as plants and algae are eaten by other organisms, which are then consumed by still others. The existence of organisms that are not dependent on the Sun's light has long been established, but until recently they were regarded as anomalies.

Over the last 20 years, however, research in deep sea areas has revealed the existence of entire ecosystems in which the primary producers are chemosynthetic bacteria that are dependent on energy from within the Earth itself. Indeed, the growing evidence suggests that these sub-sea ecosystems model the way in which life first came about on this planet.

5. The passage suggests that most life is ultimately dependent on what?

   (A) photosynthetic algae
   (B) the world's oceans
   (C) bacterial microorganisms
   (D) light from the Sun

6. Which of the following conclusions about photosynthetic and chemosynthetic organisms is supported by this passage?

   (A) Both perform similar functions in different food chains.
   (B) Both are known to support communities of higher organisms at great ocean depths.
   (C) Sunlight is the basic source of energy for both.
   (D) Chemosynthetic organisms are less nourishing than photosynthetic organisms.

Halley's Comet has been known since at least 240 BC and possibly since 1059 BC. Its most famous appearance was in 1066 AD when it appeared right before the Battle of Hastings. It was named after the astronomer Edmund Halley, who calculated its orbit. He determined that the comets seen in 1530 and 1606 were the same object following a 76-year orbit. Unfortunately, Halley died in 1742, never living to see his prediction come true when the comet returned on Christmas Eve 1758.

7. It can be inferred from the passage that the last sighting of the Haley's Comet recorded before the death of Edmund Halley took place in

   (A) 1066
   (B) 1530
   (C) 1606
   (D) 1682

Both alligators and crocodiles can be found in southern Florida, particularly in the Everglades National Park. Alligators and crocodiles do look similar but there are several physical characteristics that differentiate the two giant reptiles. The most easily observed difference between alligators and crocodiles is the shape of the head. The crocodile's skull and jaws are longer and narrower than the alligator's. When an alligator closes its mouth, those long teeth slip into sockets in the upper jaw and disappear. When a crocodile closes its mouth, the long teeth remain visible, protruding outside the upper jaw. In general, if you can still see a lot of teeth even when the animal's mouth is closed, you are looking at a crocodile.

8. One can distinguish a crocodile from an alligator

    (A) only when the animal's mouth is closed

    (B) by the location in Florida where the animal is found

    (C) by its thick, heavily armored skin

    (D) by the narrower snout found on a crocodile

A talent agent analyzed her company's records in an attempt to determine why it was placing so few actors in roles. She attributed the company's poor performance to the fact that often the actors sent to an audition were completely inappropriate for the role.

9. It can be inferred from the passage that the agent believes that

    (A) certain actors are inappropriate for certain roles

    (B) the actors her company represents are not very good

    (C) it is difficult to predict how appropriate an actor will be for a role

    (D) her company does not send enough actors to audition for major roles

One of the most commonly used of all meters is iambic pentameter. An iamb is the name for a word or words with two syllables with the stress on the second syllable. Pentameter refers to the number of feet, or groupings of syllables. In this case, the foot is an iamb. William Shakespeare is perhaps the most famous writer of the iambic pentameter, having composed hundred of poems in this meter, popularizing it for the masses.

10. According to the passage, a *foot* is

    (A) a grouping of syllables

    (B) similar to a meter

    (C) named after William Shakespeare

    (D) none of the above

It is often said that American involvement in World War I would not have begun in earnest were it not for the German sinking of the passenger ship the *Lusitania* on February 18th, 1915. Preferring prior to then to stay neutral in the war, America was until that time offering only financial and tactical support for Britain and France against Germany and Austria-Hungary. The sinking of the huge passenger ship, however, altered public opinion about U.S. involvement and subsequently led to military escalation, truly making the war a matter for the whole world.

11. The main idea of the passage is that

    (A) the Germans sank the *Lusitania* because of America's financial and tactical support for Britain and France

    (B) Austria-Hungary and Germany were allies in World War I

    (C) American involvement in World War I was minimal

    (D) the sinking of the *Lusitania* prompted increased American involvement in World War I

GO ON TO THE NEXT PAGE

When a movie panned by most film critics is a popular success, this is often seen as a sign of poor taste on the part of general audiences. But film critics belong to a fairly homogeneous class, and their preferences are often rooted in the prejudices of that class. Their opinions are no more likely to be an unerring guide to quality than those of the average moviegoer.

12. The passage above best supports which of the following conclusions?

    (A) Judgments of film quality by professional film critics are usually wrong.
    (B) Judgments of quality applied to movies are meaningless.
    (C) Film critics usually consider popular movies to be of poor quality.
    (D) When critics and general audiences disagree about a movie's quality, the critics' opinion is not necessarily more accurate.

The tomato originated in the new world. It was first domesticated around 700 AD by the Aztec and Incan civilizations. In the sixteenth century European explorers were so appreciative of the tomato that they introduced it to the rest of Europe. Although the French, Spanish, and Italians quickly began to adapt their recipes to the tomato, the English considered it poisonous. This myth continued into the American colonial period and it wasn't until the middle 1800s that the tomato began to gain acceptance in the U.S.

13. According to the passage, Americans did not start using the tomato until the mid-nineteenth century because

    (A) it was unavailable in the new world
    (B) they lacked recipes for using it
    (C) they believed it to be poisonous
    (D) it was viewed as a Mediterranean food

It was without a sense of humor that the foreign ambassador responded to allegations that his driver had over 2,000 unpaid parking tickets. For a moment it seemed as if he would perhaps go item by item to discount the allegation. Not only did he demand an apology for the way the story had been handled by the press, but he also insinuated that the incident might actually affect the two countries' relations in the future. One thing that was never addressed, however, was the fact that the tickets have still not been paid.

14. The foreign ambassador would be most likely to

    (A) support a resolution to grant diplomats immunity from parking tickets
    (B) support a call for more police on the beat
    (C) admit involvement in parking scams around the city
    (D) return to his country if the tickets were paid

GO ON TO THE NEXT PAGE

Professional basketball will soon overtake Major League Baseball as America's favorite sport. While baseball salaries skyrocket because of owners' willingness to overpay for top players, NBA salaries follow a system of paying players based on the number of years they have been in the league. This system rewards veterans and keeps players happy. And the most recent infusion of international talent to the NBA has only broadened its marketability overseas, opening previously untapped markets in places as far away as China, Japan, Russia, and Australia, thus giving NBA players even more room at the bargaining tables.

15. According to the passage, the NBA's marketability will increase because

   (A) players are getting more money from owners

   (B) Major League Baseball is losing fans

   (C) international markets are opening up to the game

   (D) its system of rewarding veteran players is superior

STOP. IF YOU FINISH BEFORE THE TIME IS UP, YOU MAY CHECK OVER YOUR WORK ON THIS PART ONLY.

PART 5: MATHEMATICS KNOWLEDGE (MK)

Time: 24 minutes; 25 questions

<u>Directions</u>: In this section, you will be tested on your knowledge of basic mathematics. For each question, select the best answer and mark the corresponding oval on your answer sheet.

1. For all x, $(3x + 4)(4x - 3) =$

   (A) $7x - 12$
   (B) $12x^2 - 12$
   (C) $12x^2 - 25x - 12$
   (D) $12x^2 + 7x - 12$

2. If a tree grew 5 feet in n years, what was the average rate at which the tree grew, in inches per year?

   (A) $\dfrac{60}{n}$

   (B) $\dfrac{5}{12n}$

   (C) $\dfrac{12n}{5}$

   (D) $\dfrac{n}{60}$

3. In the figure above, if the perimeter of rectangle $ABCD$ is 56, and the length of AD is 16, what is the area of $ABCD$?

   (A) 40
   (B) 64
   (C) 160
   (D) 192

4. A square is a rectangle with four _____ sides.

   (A) equal
   (B) parallel
   (C) unequal
   (D) none of the above

5. If $a < b$ and $b < c$, which of the following must be true?

   (A) $b + c < 2a$
   (B) $a + b < c$
   (C) $a - b < b - c$
   (D) $a + b < 2c$

6. In the figure above, $x = 2z$ and $y = 3z$. What is the value of z?

   (A) 24
   (B) 30
   (C) 36
   (D) 54

GO ON TO THE NEXT PAGE

7. If the minute hand of a properly functioning clock moves 45 degrees, how many minutes have passed?

   (A) 6
   (B) 7.5
   (C) 12
   (D) 15

8. If $5^n > 10,000$ and n is an integer, what is the smallest possible value of n?

   (A) 8
   (B) 7
   (C) 6
   (D) 5

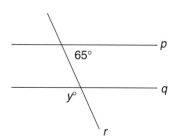

9. In the figure above, if line p is parallel to line q, what is the value of y?

   (A) 65
   (B) 115
   (C) 125
   (D) 130

10. 15 percent of 15 percent of 200 is

    (A) 4.5
    (B) 6
    (C) 45
    (D) 60

11. What is the average (arithmetic mean) of $\frac{1}{20}$ and $\frac{1}{30}$?

    (A) $\frac{1}{25}$

    (B) $\frac{1}{24}$

    (C) $\frac{2}{25}$

    (D) $\frac{1}{12}$

12. If an angle measures $y°$, what will its supplement measure in terms of y?

    (A) $90 - y$
    (B) $90 + y$
    (C) $180 - y$
    (D) $180 + y$

13. Diane painted $\frac{1}{3}$ of her room with $2\frac{1}{2}$ cans of paint. How many more cans of paint will she need to finish painting her room?

    (A) 2
    (B) 5
    (C) $7\frac{1}{2}$
    (D) 10

14. If $13 + a = 25 + b$, then $b - a =$

    (A) 38
    (B) 12
    (C) 8
    (D) −12

GO ON TO THE NEXT PAGE

15. For all x, $3x^2 \times 5x^3 =$

    (A) $8x^5$
    (B) $8x^6$
    (C) $15x^5$
    (D) $15x^6$

16. If the sides of a square increase in length by 10%, the area of the square increases by

    (A) 10%
    (B) 15%
    (C) 20%
    (D) 21%

17. If $\dfrac{m}{2} = 15$, then $\dfrac{m}{3} =$

    (A) 7.5
    (B) 10
    (C) 22.5
    (D) 30

18. Which of the following is a polynomial factor of $6x^2 - 13x + 6$?

    (A) $2x + 2$
    (B) $2x + 3$
    (C) $3x - 2$
    (D) $3x - 3$

19. If the product of 3 and x is equal to 2 less than y, which of the following must be true?

    (A) $\dfrac{3x - 2}{y} = 0$
    (B) $3x - y - 2 = 0$
    (C) $3x + y - 2 = 0$
    (D) $3x - y + 2 = 0$

20. If $x > 1$ and $\dfrac{a}{b} = 1 - \dfrac{1}{x}$, then $\dfrac{b}{a} =$

    (A) $\dfrac{x}{x - 1}$
    (B) $\dfrac{x - 1}{x}$
    (C) $x - 1$
    (D) $\dfrac{1}{x} - 1$

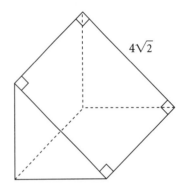

21. If the solid above is half of a cube, then the volume of the solid is

    (A) 16
    (B) $16\sqrt{2}$
    (C) 32
    (D) 64

22. When 7.6 is divided by 0.019, the quotient is

    (A) 4,000
    (B) 400
    (C) 40
    (D) 4

GO ON TO THE NEXT PAGE

23. What is the area of a circle with a circumference of 8?

 (A) $\dfrac{16}{\pi}$

 (B) 4π

 (C) 16

 (D) 16π

24. 36 percent of 18 is 18 percent of what number?

 (A) 9

 (B) 36

 (C) 72

 (D) 200

25. $\sqrt{104{,}906}$ is between

 (A) 100 and 200

 (B) 200 and 300

 (C) 300 and 400

 (D) 400 and 500

STOP. IF YOU FINISH BEFORE THE TIME IS UP, YOU MAY CHECK OVER YOUR WORK ON THIS PART ONLY.

PART 6: ELECTRONICS INFORMATION (EI)

Time: 9 minutes; 20 questions

<u>Directions</u>: In this section, you will be tested on your knowledge of electronics basics. For each question, select the best answer and mark the corresponding oval on your answer sheet.

1. Resistance is measured in

   (A) amperes
   (B) ohms
   (C) V
   (D) B and C are correct.

2. Protons have a _____ charge, and neutrons are _____ charged.

   (A) positive, negatively
   (B) positive, neutrally
   (C) negative, positively
   (D) neutral, negatively

3. _____ is when the current flowing in a conductor changes direction (moves back and forth) many times in a second.

   (A) Alternating current
   (B) Direct current
   (C) Electromotive force
   (D) none of the above

4. What type of circuit does this symbol represent?

   (A) parallel circuit
   (B) series circuit
   (C) series-parallel circuit
   (D) short circuit

5. In the formula for Ohm's Law $E = I \times R$, the I represents

   (A) voltage
   (B) current
   (C) resistance
   (D) none of the above

6. The P-type material in a diode is also known as the

   (A) electrode
   (B) cathode
   (C) base
   (D) anode

7. Introducing impurities into the crystal structure of silicon is also known as

   (A) tinning
   (B) enhancing
   (C) processing
   (D) doping

8. Inductance is measured in

   (A) ohms
   (B) henries
   (C) millihenries
   (D) B and C are correct.

9. Capacitive reactance is measured in

   (A) ohms
   (B) farads
   (C) microfarads
   (D) B and C are correct.

GO ON TO THE NEXT PAGE

10. All of the following statements about transistors are true *EXCEPT*:

    (A) N-type material has free electrons
    (B) NPN transistors require a positive voltage at the base to turn them on
    (C) the arrow in the transistor symbol is always placed on the collector
    (D) P-type material conducts current through the movement of holes

11. This is the symbol for which type of meter?

    (A) Voltmeter
    (B) Ammeter
    (C) Ohmmeter
    (D) Galvanometer

12. Which is *NOT* an essential component of an electrical circuit?

    (A) voltage source
    (B) watt
    (C) load
    (D) conductor

13. What type of switch would be utilized by a doorbell?

    (A) ──o‾‾o──
    (B) ──o⊥o──
    (C) ──o⁄ o──
    (D) ──o⁄
         o──

14. Which of the following is the symbol for an AC voltage source?

    (A) ─|⊦ | ⊢─
            +

    (B) Ⓥ (circle with ∿)
    (C) ──Ⓐ──
    (D) ──Ⓟ──

15. Capacitors are also known as _____.

    (A) capacitance
    (B) dielectric
    (C) condensers
    (D) inductors

16. A material that will not conduct electricity is known as

    (A) a conductor
    (B) a semiconductor
    (C) an insulator
    (D) none of the above

17. All of the following materials are conductors *EXCEPT*:

    (A) rubber
    (B) silver
    (C) copper
    (D) aluminum

18. A circuit with four 6-ohm resistors wired in series has 12 volts applied to it. What current flows through this circuit?

    (A) 5 mA
    (B) 50 mA
    (C) 500 mA
    (D) 5 A

GO ON TO THE NEXT PAGE

19. An element that is widely recognized as a semiconductor is

   (A) silicon
   (B) germanium
   (C) both A and B
   (D) none of the above

20. This is the symbol for which type of meter?

   (A) Voltmeter
   (B) Ammeter
   (C) Ohmmeter
   (D) Galvanometer

STOP. IF YOU FINISH BEFORE THE TIME IS UP, YOU MAY CHECK OVER YOUR WORK ON THIS PART ONLY.

PART 7: AUTOMOTIVE AND SHOP INFORMATION (AS)

Time: 11 minutes; 25 questions

<u>Directions</u>: In this section, you will be tested on your knowledge of automotive and shop basics. For each question, select the best answer and mark the corresponding oval on your answer sheet.

1. Wood can be shaped using all of the following tools *EXCEPT*:

   (A) jack plane
   (B) wood chisel
   (C) flat rasp
   (D) miter box

2. Ride quality is the job of the vehicle's _____ system.

   (A) steering
   (B) suspension
   (C) charging
   (D) brake

3. The cut in the wood left behind by a saw is known as the

   (A) gap
   (B) line
   (C) trace
   (D) kerf

4. A four-wheel drive vehicle uses a _____ to distribute power to the front and rear drive axles.

   (A) transmission
   (B) drive shaft
   (C) torque converter
   (D) transfer case

5. What type of cut is this saw made for?

   (A) cut with the grain of the wood
   (B) cut across the grain of the wood
   (C) cut plywood only
   (D) cut steel only

6. This image depicts what stroke in the four-stroke cycle?

   (A) intake stroke
   (B) power stroke
   (C) compression stroke
   (D) exhaust stroke

7. Thread pitch of a fractional measurement fastener is determined by

   (A) counting the number of threads per inch
   (B) measuring the distance in millimeters between threads
   (C) measuring the distance in inches between threads
   (D) counting the number of threads per millimeter

GO ON TO THE NEXT PAGE

8. Which would be best to use to loosen tight fasteners?

(A)

(B)

(C)

(D) both (B) and (C)

9. All of the following are parts of the vehicle's steering system *EXCEPT*:

(A) coil spring
(B) steering knuckle
(C) tie rod end
(D) idler arm

10. Which engine component is responsible for the opening and closing of the engine's intake and exhaust valves?

(A) 2
(B) 1
(C) 4
(D) 3

11. On a fuel-injected engine, the fuel pump is normally located

(A) on the engine
(B) on the vehicle frame
(C) near the rear bumper
(D) in the fuel tank

12. UNC fasteners have _____ threads per inch when compared to UNF fasteners of the same diameter.

(A) more
(B) less
(C) the same number of
(D) none of the above

13. In power brake systems, braking pressures are increased using

(A) engine intake manifold vacuum
(B) fluid pressure from the power steering system
(C) Both A and B are correct.
(D) Neither A nor B is correct.

14. All of the following are parts of the ignition primary system *EXCEPT*:

(A) battery
(B) ignition switch
(C) reluctor and pickup
(D) rotor

15. "Stoichiometric" is a term that describes

(A) the ideal air-fuel mixture in a gasoline engine
(B) the voltage required to generate a spark
(C) the engine's breathing efficiency
(D) theoretical horsepower

16. An oil's resistance to flow is known as its

(A) quality rating
(B) pumpability
(C) lubricity
(D) viscosity

17. All cars are currently being built with _____ electrical systems.

    (A) direct current
    (B) alternating current
    (C) negative ground
    (D) Both A and C are correct.

18. When arc-welding, the ground clamp should be connected to the

    (A) floor
    (B) welding rod
    (C) electrical outlet
    (D) work

19. What cylinder design is referred to as a "boxer" engine?

    (A) inline
    (B) flat
    (C) horizontally opposed
    (D) both B and C

20. What is this tool used for?

    (A) cutting
    (B) striking an object where it is important that the hammer itself not come in direct contact with the work.
    (C) driving small fasteners and making layout marks
    (D) none of the above.

21. In a V-type engine with two cylinder heads, this design would have two camshafts, with one installed above each cylinder head.

    (A) single overhead cam or SOHC
    (B) double overhead cam or DOHC
    (C) overhead value or OHV
    (D) none of the above

22. Air entering an engine's combustion chamber must pass through the

    (A) air filter
    (B) intake manifold
    (C) intake port in the cylinder head
    (D) all of the above

23. Which tool would be best suited for loosening a very tight nut?

    (A) open-end wrench
    (B) 12-point socket and breaker bar
    (C) 6-point socket and ratchet
    (D) 6-point socket and breaker bar

24. What type of retaining ring is depicted here?

    (A) internal prong-type
    (B) internal hole-type
    (C) external "E"-type
    (D) external hole-type

25. As lead-acid batteries discharge, their electrolyte gradually turns to

    (A) sulphuric acid
    (B) water
    (C) lead peroxide
    (D) none of the above

STOP. IF YOU FINISH BEFORE THE TIME IS UP, YOU MAY CHECK OVER YOUR WORK ON THIS PART ONLY.

PART 8: MECHANICAL COMPREHENSION (MC)

Time: 19 minutes; 25 questions

<u>Directions:</u> In this section, you will be tested on your knowledge of mechanics and basic physics. Select the best answer for each question and mark the corresponding oval on your answer sheet.

1. A car rolls down a hill. It travels progressively faster because

   (A) its potential energy is being converted into kinetic energy
   (B) the car's total mechanical energy remains constant as it moves
   (C) Both A and B are correct.
   (D) Neither A nor B is correct.

2. When a ball is thrown into the air, it has its maximum potential energy when

   (A) it leaves the hand of the person throwing it
   (B) it reaches the highest point in its travel
   (C) its velocity is zero
   (D) Both B and C is correct.

3. Objects that require more force to get them moving have greater

   (A) momentum
   (B) inertia
   (C) Both A and B are correct.
   (D) Neither A nor B is correct.

4. Isaac Newton discovered that every particle in the universe is attracted to every other particle. This law is called

   (A) First Law of Motion
   (B) Third Law of Motion
   (C) Law of Universal Gravitation
   (D) none of the above

5. In the illustration below, piston X is a 1 square inch piston and piston Y is a 200 square inch piston. If there is 20 pounds of force on piston X, the output force on piston Y will be

   (A) 200 pounds
   (B) 20 pounds
   (C) 10 pounds
   (D) 4,000 pounds

6. Lifting a heavy box directly from ground level up to the top of a ramp is doing _____ pushing the box up the ramp (neglecting friction).

   (A) less work than
   (B) more work than
   (C) the same amount of work as
   (D) none of the above

7. All of the following statements about work are true *EXCEPT*

   (A) force is a component of work
   (B) it is possible to get more work out of a machine than what is put in
   (C) to do work, an object must be moved
   (D) work can be measured in foot-pounds

8. A chisel is illustrated below. A chisel is an example of

   (A) wedge
   (B) first-class lever
   (C) inclined plane
   (D) wheel and axle

9. The difference between a wedge and an inclined plane is

   (A) a wedge has a steeper slope than an inclined plane
   (B) a wedge is made to move, whereas an inclined plane stays stationary
   (C) a wedge offers greater mechanical advantage than an inclined plane
   (D) none of the above

10. Which post holds up the greater part of the load?

    (A) post A
    (B) post B
    (C) both are equal
    (D) answer cannot be determined based on information provided

11. Work and kinetic energy are both measured in

    (A) kilograms
    (B) meters per second
    (C) joules
    (D) none of the above

12. The design of a screwdriver is based on which of the following simple machines?

    (A) inclined plane
    (B) wheel and axle
    (C) first-class lever
    (D) pulley

13. An increase in force accomplished through mechanical advantage is always accompanied by _____ in distance moved.

    (A) an increase
    (B) a decrease
    (C) no change
    (D) none of the above

14. The design of a prybar, as illustrated, is based on which of the following simple machines?

    (A) first-class lever
    (B) second-class lever
    (C) third-class lever
    (D) inclined plane

GO ON TO THE NEXT PAGE

15. The shaft in the illustration spins in a clockwise direction. What will happen to balls A and B as the speed of the shaft increases?

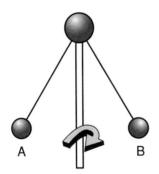

(A) they will move in and down toward the shaft due to coriolis force

(B) they will remain at the same level

(C) they will move in a counterclockwise direction due to coriolis force

(D) they will move out and up due to centrifugal force

16. In order to increase force with a first-class lever, the fulcrum should be

(A) moved toward where the effort is applied

(B) kept in the same position

(C) moved toward where the object is moved

(D) removed altogether

17. In the illustration below, what action is being taken upon the hole?

(A) the hole is being tapped

(B) the hole is being drilled

(C) the hole is being reamed

(D) the hole is being plugged

18. If a small gear drives a large gear, a _____ takes place.

(A) mechanical advantage

(B) block and tackle

(C) torque multiplication

(D) speed reduction

19. A block and tackle, as shown below, utilizes

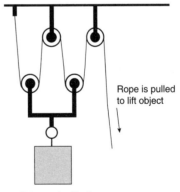

Rope is pulled to lift object

Object to be lifted

(A) one pulley

(B) more than one pulley

(C) a flexible rope, belt, or chain

(D) Both B and C are correct.

GO ON TO THE NEXT PAGE

20. In the arrangement of pulleys shown, which pulley turns fastest?

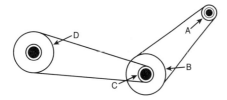

(A) A

(B) B

(C) C

(D) D

21. The design of a doorknob is based on which of the following simple machines?

(A) inclined plane

(B) wheel and axle

(C) first-class lever

(D) pulley

22. An automobile transmission can be used to

(A) increase speed

(B) increase torque

(C) decrease speed

(D) all of the above

23. Torque and speed can be described as

(A) exactly the same

(B) directly proportional

(C) inversely proportional

(D) none of the above

24. An object's potential energy can be calculated using the formula

(A) $PE = m - g - h$

(B) $PE = m + g + h$

(C) $PE = m \times g \times h$

(D) none of the above

25. The gears shown below represent

(A) a hypoid bevel

(B) a rack and pinion

(C) a piston

(D) a spiral bevel

STOP. IF YOU FINISH BEFORE THE TIME IS UP, YOU MAY CHECK OVER YOUR WORK ON THIS PART ONLY.

PART 9: ASSEMBLING OBJECTS (AO)

Time: 15 minutes; 25 questions

<u>Directions</u>: In this section, you will be tested on your ability to determine how an object will look when its parts are put together. For each question, select the best answer and mark the corresponding oval on your answer sheet.

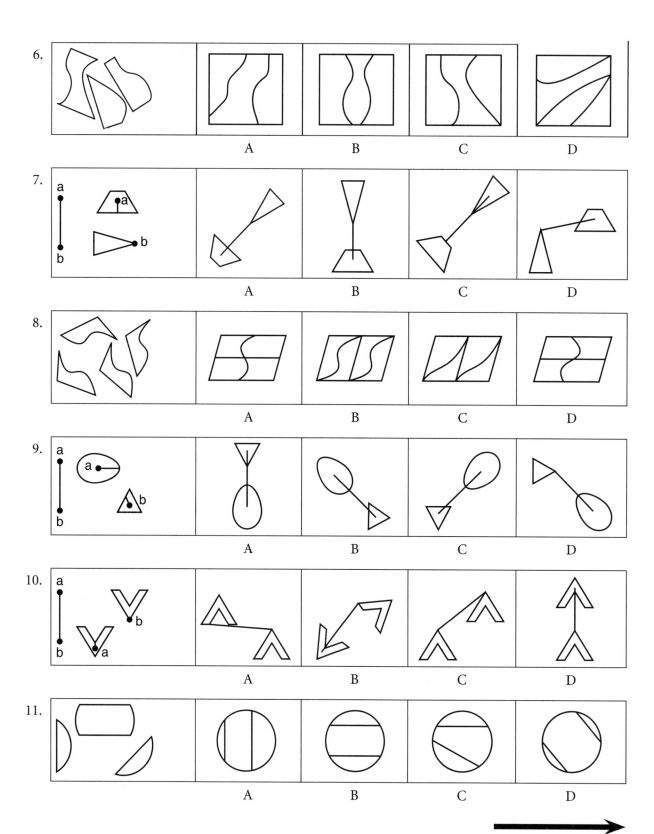

6. A B C D

7. A B C D

8. A B C D

9. A B C D

10. A B C D

11. A B C D

GO ON TO THE NEXT PAGE

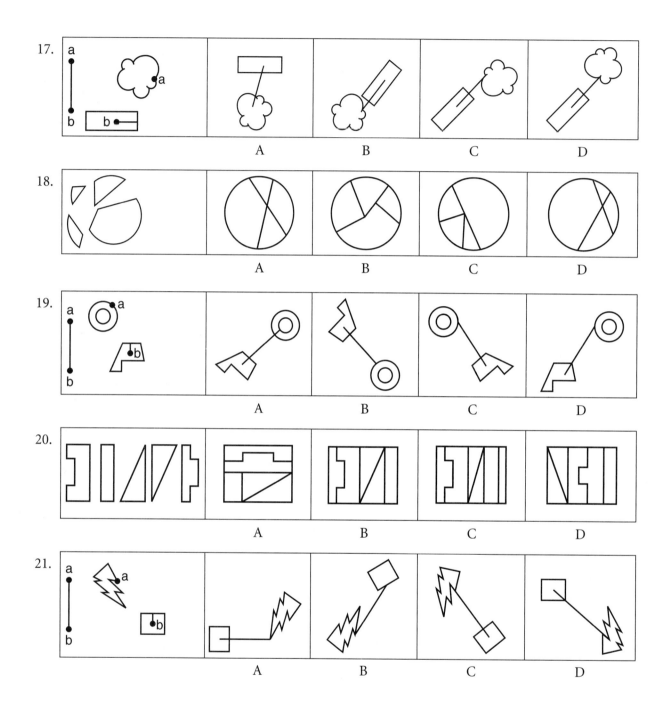

17. A B C D

18. A B C D

19. A B C D

20. A B C D

21. A B C D

GO ON TO THE NEXT PAGE

22.

A B C D

23.

A B C D

24.

A B C D

25.

A B C D

STOP. IF YOU FINISH BEFORE THE TIME IS UP, YOU MAY
CHECK OVER YOUR WORK ON THIS PART ONLY.

STOP! END OF TEST.

ASVAB Practice Test II
Answers and
Explanations

ANSWER KEY

PART 1: General Science	PART 2: Arithmetic Reasoning	PART 3: Word Knowledge	PART 4: Paragraph Comprehension	PART 5: Mathematics Knowledge
1. A	1. D	1. B	1. C	1. D
2. B	2. C	2. A	2. D	2. A
3. D	3. B	3. B	3. B	3. D
4. C	4. D	4. B	4. B	4. A
5. A	5. B	5. C	5. D	5. D
6. C	6. B	6. A	6. A	6. C
7. B	7. C	7. C	7. D	7. B
8. D	8. A	8. A	8. D	8. C
9. A	9. B	9. B	9. A	9. B
10. B	10. D	10. B	10. A	10. A
11. A	11. B	11. A	11. D	11. B
12. C	12. D	12. C	12. D	12. C
13. B	13. C	13. A	13. C	13. B
14. A	14. C	14. B	14. A	14. D
15. D	15. D	15. C	15. C	15. C
16. D	16. A	16. C		16. D
17. B	17. B	17. A		17. B
18. D	18. A	18. B		18. C
19. B	19. C	19. D		19. D
20. C	20. D	20. A		20. A
21. D	21. C	21. C		21. C
22. B	22. B	22. D		22. B
23. C	23. C	23. C		23. A
24. B	24. A	24. A		24. B
25. A	25. B	25. C		25. C
	26. C	26. B		
	27. C	27. C		
	28. C	28. C		
	29. A	29. C		
	30. C	30. B		
		31. A		
		32. D		
		33. D		
		34. B		
		35. B		

ANSWER KEY

PART 6: **Electronics Information**	PART 7: **Auto and Shop Information**	PART 8: **Mechanical Comprehension**	PART 9: **Assembling Objects**
1. B	1. D	1. C	1. C
2. B	2. B	2. D	2. A
3. A	3. D	3. B	3. D
4. D	4. D	4. C	4. B
5. B	5. B	5. D	5. D
6. D	6. C	6. C	6. C
7. D	7. A	7. B	7. A
8. D	8. D	8. A	8. B
9. A	9. A	9. B	9. C
10. C	10. D	10. A	10. D
11. A	11. D	11. C	11. B
12. B	12. B	12. B	12. C
13. A	13. C	13. B	13. A
14. B	14. D	14. A	14. D
15. C	15. A	15. D	15. B
16. C	16. D	16. C	16. A
17. A	17. D	17. A	17. C
18. C	18. D	18. D	18. D
19. C	19. D	19. D	19. B
20. D	20. B	20. A	20. B
	21. A	21. B	21. C
	22. D	22. D	22. A
	23. D	23. C	23. D
	24. D	24. C	24. B
	25. B	25. A	25. C

PART 1: GENERAL SCIENCE ANSWERS AND EXPLANATIONS

1. A

A genus contains several related species.

2. B

Electrons orbit around the nucleus of an atom.

3. D

Air is warmed and filtered first in the nasal cavity.

4. C

A polar bear is an example of a tertiary consumer, which is an animal that consumes secondary consumers, or other carnivores. The polar bear consumes animals, such as walruses, that also consume other animals, such as fish.

5. A

Chemically speaking, a substance is matter of particular or definite chemical composition. Water is considered a substance (H_2O), while air, fire, and earth can have variable chemical composition.

6. C

The gravitational force the Moon exerts on the Earth is the same as the gravitational force the Earth exerts on the Moon. According to Newton's third law, when the Earth exerts its gravitational force on an object, such as the Moon, that object exerts an equal and opposite force on the Earth.

7. B

Fungi are decomposers (also known as saprophytes), returning the organic material from dead matter such as leaves, trees, and animal remains back into the environment. Producers make their own food, consumers must eat to gain energy, and mutualism is the type of symbiosis whereby organisms living together benefit.

8. D

In degrees Kelvin, the freezing point of water is 273°. In the Kelvin temperature scale absolute zero, which is −273° Celsius, is set at 0°, and any temperature in degrees Celsius is 273 degrees less than the same temperature as read in degrees Kelvin. Since the freezing point of water in degrees Celsius is 0°, in degrees Kelvin it is 273°.

9. A

Tough elastic tissues found in the joints that connect bones to bones are called ligaments. Tendons are connective tissue that unite a muscle with some other part, such as a bone. Cartilage is a somewhat elastic tissue (unlike bone) that in adults is found in some joints, respiratory passages, and the external ear. Finally, muscles are body tissue consisting of long cells that contract when stimulated to produce motion.

10. B

Stress, a poor diet, cigarette smoking, and heredity factors all contribute to an individual's developing high blood pressure.

11. A

Cirrus clouds are the thin, wispy clouds that occur very high in the atmosphere, at elevations of 20,000 feet or more.

12. C

Fossils are most likely to be found in sedimentary rock such as shale, which is a fissile rock formed by the sedimentation of clay, mud, or silt, and is composed of minerals and other matter, such as animal remains.

13. B

Animals that consume only plants are called herbivores.

14. A

The temperature at the core of our Sun is thought to be about 15,000,000° C.

15. D

A population is a group of organisms of the same species living in the same region.

16. D

The four planets beyond Mars—Jupiter, Saturn, Uranus, and Neptune, are referred to as the outer planets. Earth is a terrestrial planet.

17. B

A boulder that begins to roll down a hill is an example of an energy conversion from potential energy to kinetic energy.

18. D

The lowest layer of the Earth's atmosphere is called the troposphere. This layer extends from the surface to the bottom of the stratosphere. Most weather changes occur here and the temperature generally decreases rapidly with altitude.

19. B

According to the law of conservation of energy, energy can neither be created nor destroyed. Instead, it changes from one form to another.

20. C

As an ambulance passes, its pitch seems to change. This perception is best explained by the Doppler effect. As the ambulance approaches, the sound waves from its siren are compressed toward the observer. The intervals between waves diminish, which translates into an increase in frequency or pitch. As the ambulance recedes, the sound waves are stretched relative to the observer, causing the siren's pitch to decrease. By the change in pitch of the siren, one can determine if the ambulance is coming nearer or speeding away.

21. D

A concave lens—one that is thicker on the edges than it is in the middle—is also known as a diverging lens because it diverges the light waves that pass through it.

22. B

A molecule is the smallest particle of an element or compound that can exist in the free state and still retain the characteristics of the element or compound. The molecules of elements consist of one atom or two or more similar atoms; those of compounds consist of two or more different atoms.

23. C

The orbit of the Moon around the Earth, which exerts a gravitational pull on the ocean's waters, is the phenomenon most responsible for oceanic tides.

24. B

The elements in a column on the periodic table are referred to as a group; each member of a group has the same number of electrons in its outer shell. Each row on the periodic table is referred to as a period.

25. A

When molecules undergo a chemical change, the process is called a chemical reaction. The molecules that enter the reaction are called reactants and the molecules that result from the reaction are called products.

PART 2: ARITHMETIC REASONING ANSWERS AND EXPLANATIONS

1. **D**

Pick a number for the cost of one apple. Let's say each apple costs 4 cents. Then 3 apples cost 12 cents. The first sentence says that 3 apples cost as much as 4 pears, so 4 pears also cost 12 cents. How much would three pears cost? We know 4 pears cost 12 cents, so 1 pear must cost 3 cents, and 3 pears must cost 9 cents. Since 3 pears cost as much as 2 oranges, 2 oranges must also cost 9 cents. Since $36 \times 2 = 72$, 72 oranges cost the same as $36 \times$ the cost of 2 oranges, or 36×9 cents, which is $3.24. Now we have to figure out how many apples cost $3.24. If one apple costs 4 cents, we just have to figure out how many times 4 cents goes into $3.24. It goes in 81 times, so 81 apples cost as much as 72 oranges, making (D) the correct answer.

2. **C**

If 48 of 60 seats are occupied, then 12 of 60 seats are unoccupied (since $60 - 48 = 12$). What percent of the seats are unoccupied?

$$\text{Percent} = \frac{\text{Part}}{\text{Whole}} \times 100\% = \frac{12}{60} \times 100\% =$$
$$\frac{1}{5} \times 100\% = 20\%, \text{ choice (C)}.$$

3. **B**

Let's break this question down into pieces. Before midnight, Effin gets paid $1,000 an hour. If she starts singing at 8:30 P.M., then she sings for $3\frac{1}{2}$ hours before midnight. Her earnings for that time are $3\frac{1}{2}$ times $1,000, or $3,500. Now let's find out how much she earns after midnight. Her rate increases 50% after midnight, so her hourly rate after midnight is $1,000 + 50% of $1,000. 50% of $1,000 is $500, so her rate per hour after midnight is $1,000 + $500 = $1,500. So she earns $1,500 for the hour she sings after midnight. For the last step, we add that to the amount she earns before midnight, so her total pay is $3,500 + $1,500 = $5,000, answer choice (B).

4. **D**

The probability of an event occurring is a fraction: the number of possible outcomes in which the event can occur divided by the total number of possible outcomes. Fran is going to pick one shirt and we want to figure out the probability that it will not be orange. In other words, what is the probability of picking a non-orange shirt? Aside from the orange shirts, there are 4 black shirts and 5 blue shirts, so altogether there are 9 non-orange shirts. So there are nine possible successful outcomes. The total number of shirts to choose from, including the orange shirts, is 12, so there are 12 possible outcomes. So the probability of Fran picking a non-orange shirt is $\frac{9}{12}$, which can be reduced to $\frac{3}{4}$, answer choice (D).

5. **B**

Draw a chart or table to help organize the information. Newark is two hours later than Denver, so if the time in Denver when Harry arrives is 2:30 P.M., then the time in Newark when he arrives in Denver is 4:30 P.M. The flight takes 5 hours, so the time he began in Newark is 5 hours earlier than 4:30 P.M., or 11:30 A.M., choice (B).

6. **B**

How many times does 24 go into 198? $198 \div 24 = 8$ with a remainder of 6, so Doris will have 6 pieces of chocolate left over.

7. C

If 75% of x is 150, then $0.75(x) = 150$ or $\frac{3}{4}(x) = 150$. Multiply both sides by $\frac{4}{3}$ and you find that $x = 200$, choice (C). You could also work backward from the answer choices. Only choice (C), 200, works. If $x = 200$, then $0.75(x) = 150$ since $0.75(200) = 150$.

8. A

The formula for finding the average is

$$\text{Average} = \frac{\text{Sum of the terms}}{\text{Number of terms}}$$

Don't just average the old average and the last test score—that would give the last score as much weight as all the other scores combined. The best way to deal with changing averages is to use the sums. Use the old average to figure out the total of the first 6 scores:

$$\text{Sum of first 6 scores} = (83)(6) = 498$$

Then add the 7th score and divide:

$$\frac{498 + 97}{7} = \frac{595}{7} = 85.$$

9. B

If the charge for one pound is $25.00, then the charge for $\frac{4}{5}$ of a pound would be $\frac{4}{5} \times \$25.00 = \$20.00$ plus 8% sales tax. 8% of $20.00 = 0.08(\$20.00) = \$1.60$. $\$20.00 + \$1.60 = \$21.60$, choice (B).

10. D

To answer this question we just have to figure out how many times $\frac{3}{5}$ goes into 60. We know that it will be more than 60, so right away we can eliminate (A). $60 \div \frac{3}{5} = \frac{60}{1} \times \frac{5}{3}$. This is easier to multiply if we do some canceling. 3 goes into 60 twenty times, so we can replace the 3 with a 1, and replace the 60 with a 20. So now we have $\frac{20}{1} \times \frac{5}{1}$, which equals 20×5, or 100, choice (D).

11. B

Solve a question like this using algebra if it's a strong area for you. Otherwise, work backward from the answer choices. To solve this question using algebra, we'll need to set up equations and solve for R, which is Robert's money. We're told that Ed has 100 more dollars than Robert.

$$E = R + 100.$$

Ed then spends 20 dollars and has five times as much money as Robert.

$$E - 20 = 5R.$$

Substitute $R + 100$ for E and solve. So:

$$R + 80 = 5R.$$

$$80 = 4R. \ R = \$20, \text{ choice (B)}.$$

If you were to backsolve, choose a value like $20 or $24 for Robert's money. Then see which value would work for all the information we're given in the question. Only choice (B), $20, works.

12. D

This question is actually a remainder question in disguise. If 587 people are to be divided among a number of buses that each seat 48 people, we need to divide 587 by 48 to see how many buses we would fill completely. The remainder would be the number of people in the unfilled bus. $587 \div 48 = 12$ and the remainder is 11, so (D) is correct.

13. C

Riley brought 100 cookies, and 25 are left over. That means that Riley and her classmates ate 75 cookies. So:

$$\text{Average} = \frac{\text{Sum of the terms}}{\text{Number of terms}} = \frac{75 \text{ cookies}}{15 \text{ students}}$$

$$= 5 \text{ cookies for each student.}$$

(C) is correct.

14. C

This is a proportion question.

$$\frac{4 \text{ ft object}}{9 \text{ ft shadow}} = \frac{x \text{ ft object}}{21 \text{ ft shadow}}$$

Cross-multiply to solve.

$$4 \times 21 = 9x$$

$$\frac{84}{9} = \frac{9x}{9}$$

$$x = 9\frac{1}{3}$$

Choice (C) is correct.

15. D

Percent times Whole equals Part:

$$\text{Percent} \times 25 = 16$$

$$\text{Percent} = \frac{16}{25} = \frac{16}{25} \times 100\% = 64\%$$

16. A

First find how long the trip takes him at each of the two different rates, using the formula

$$\text{Time} = \frac{\text{Distance}}{\text{Rate}}$$

He travels the first 10 km at 30 km per hour, so he takes $\frac{10}{30} = \frac{1}{3}$ hour for this portion of the journey.

He travels the remaining 30 km at 15 km per hour, so he takes $\frac{30}{15} = 2$ hours for this portion of the journey.

So the whole journey takes him $2 + \frac{1}{3} = 2\frac{1}{3}$ hours.

Now we need to compare this to the amount of time it would take to make the same trip at a constant rate of 20 km per hour. If he traveled the whole 40 km at 20 km per hour, it would take $\frac{40}{20} = 2$ hours. Now $2\frac{1}{3}$ hours is more than 2 hours by $\frac{1}{3}$ hour, or 20 minutes.

17. B

Since 3 out of 24 students are in student organizations, the remaining $24 - 3$, or 21, students are not in student organizations. Therefore, the ratio of students in organizations to students not in organizations is $\frac{3}{21} = \frac{1}{7}$.

18. A

Begin by determining how many games each team has won and lost by midseason. Team A had won 60 and lost 20 by midseason. Team B had won 49 and lost 31 by midseason. Over the remaining 80 games, team A won 40 and lost 40. That means that team A wound up with 60 + 40 = 100 wins. To win 100 games, team B would have to win 100 − 49 = 51 games over the remainder of the season. (A) is correct.

19. C

A vendor bought 10 crates for a total cost of $80. He wants to make a total profit of 25% over the total cost. So the total sale would have to equal $80 + (0.25)($80) = $80 + $20 = $100. He lost 2 crates, so he would need to sell the remaining 10 − 2 = 8 crates for $100 to make the required profit. $\frac{$100}{8 \text{ crates}}$ = $12.50 per crate; (C) is correct.

20. D

Set up a simple proportion on questions like this one:

$$\frac{150 \text{ bottles}}{20 \text{ minutes}} = \frac{60 \text{ bottles}}{x \text{ minutes}}.$$

$$150x = 1,200$$

Divide both sides by 150:

$$x = \frac{1,200}{150} = 8$$

(D) is correct.

21. C

To figure out whether your product is positive or negative, simply count the number of negatives you had to start. If you had an odd number of negatives, the product is negative. If you had an even number of negatives, the product is positive. $15 \times (-5) = -75$.

22. B

We can express the ratio of baseball cards to baseball figurines as 5/7. Since we know the number of cards, we can set up a proportion: 5/7 = 25/x where x is the number of figurines. To solve, we cross-multiply to get 5x = 175, or x = 35.

23. C

Take your time and work through a problem like this one step at a time. If two hot dogs and a soda cost $3.25 and three hot dogs and a soda cost $4.50, then the difference between the two prices would be the price of a single hot dog. A single hot dog costs $4.50 − $3.25 = $1.25. Now that we know the price of a single hot dog, we can solve for the price of a soda.

$$2($1.25) + a \text{ soda} = $3.25$$
$$$2.50 + a \text{ soda} = $3.25$$
$$a \text{ soda} = $0.75$$

Remember, we're looking for the cost of two sodas, so 2($0.75) = $1.50, choice (C).

24. A

This is a classic trap question. Intuitively, you'd assume that the average of 40 mph and 60 mph would be 50 mph. Unfortunately, your intuition would be wrong here. Keep in mind that you spend more time traveling at a slower speed, so your average for the entire trip will be closer to the slower speed. A quick way to solve a question like this one is to pick a convenient distance for the entire trip. Since we're dealing with 40 and 60 as rates, let's say the trip is 120 miles long because 120 is a multiple of both 40 and 60. The total average for the trip will be the total distance divided by the total time. Carefully line up your distances and times to solve:

$$120 \text{ miles at 40 mph} = 3 \text{ hours}$$
$$120 \text{ miles at 60 mph} = 2 \text{ hours}$$

Total distance = 240 miles. Total time = 5 hours.

$$\text{Average speed} = \frac{\text{Total distance}}{\text{Total time}} = \frac{240 \text{ miles}}{5 \text{ hours}} = 48 \text{ mph}.$$

Choice (A) is correct.

25. B

Call the number of teachers n. Then the number of students is $10n$. The total number of teachers and students is $n + 10n = 11n$.

Since you can't have a fraction of a student, n must be an integer, so that means the total number of teachers and students must be a multiple of 11. Scan the answer choices and locate (B), 11×11, as the correct answer.

26. C

Work backward from your answer choices on this one. Begin with choice (C). If the smaller number is 21 (and the larger number is 35), does the math from the question make sense? If (C) is correct, then the average of 21 and 35 is equal to twice the positive difference between the two numbers. The average of 21 and 35 $= \dfrac{21 + 35}{2} = \dfrac{56}{2} = 28$. The positive difference between 21 and 35 is 14. Twice the positive difference would be 2(14) or 28. As we've already seen, this is also the average of the numbers, so (C) is correct.

We can also solve this question algebraically: Call the smaller number y. The average of the two numbers is $\dfrac{35 + y}{2}$. Twice the positive difference of the two numbers is $2(35 - y)$. The average is equal to twice the positive difference, so $\dfrac{35 + y}{2} = 2(35 - y)$. Solve:

$$\frac{35 + y}{2} = 2(35 - y)$$
$$35 + y = 4(35 - y)$$
$$35 + y = 140 - 4y$$
$$5y = 105$$
$$y = 21$$

27. C

Approximate on questions like this one. If each of seven runners is running a little more than 1.25 kilometers, the total distance run would be a little more than 7(1.25) = 8.75 or close to 9 kilometers. Choice (C) is correct.

28. C

Set up a proportion:

$$\frac{12 \text{ photos}}{1 \text{ minute}} = \frac{60 \text{ photos}}{x \text{ minutes}}$$

Now cross-multiply and solve: $12x = 60$, so $x = \dfrac{60}{12} = 5$.

29. A

This is a pure arithmetic computation question. That means that if you're careful, you should have no problems banking a correct answer here. Your computations should look something like this:

Add up all your deductions:

218.99 + 107.05 + 25.03 + 68.65 + 42.75 = 462.47

Now subtract total deductions from gross pay:

1,729.23 − 462.47 = 1,306.76, choice (A) is correct.

30. C

This is a standard average problem. Take the sum of all the terms and divide by the number of terms. 95 + 72 + 84 + 98 = 349. 349 ÷ 4 = 87.25. Round that off, and you get 87.

PART 3: WORD KNOWLEDGE ANSWERS AND EXPLANATIONS

1. B

Impose as a verb means to *establish by authority*. Of the answer choices given, only one seems to imply one person dictating to another. *Force* as a verb can be construed as *imposing*. Thus, answer choice (B) is correct.

2. A

Stunted means *stopped short* or *cancelled abruptly*. Answer choice (A), *halted*, also means stopped short.

3. B

While a *sturdy* home might be huge, it does not by nature have to be. Something sturdy, however, would be considered *strong*. Choice (B) is the most accurate answer.

4. B

Undeterred uses the prefix "un-," meaning *opposite of*, with the root word "deter." To deter something is to stop or hinder it. So something *undeterred* would be something unhindered or *determined*.

5. C

Ennui is a French word meaning *annoyed, bored*. Choice (C) is correct.

6. A

Mutable means *prone to change*. Choice (A), *changing*, is the best answer.

7. C

To *squander* is to *waste* or *fritter away* something. Of the choices given, only (C), *wasted*, satisfies as an answer.

8. A

Legible means *able to be read*. Here, the word given is *illegible*, or "not readable." Choice (A) is correct.

9. B

The word *infinite* means *lasting forever* or *unending*.

10. B

Longevity means *length of life*, so choice (B), *lifetime*, is correct.

11. A

Kids fall for lots of things, but even the phrasing of the question gives away the answer a little. Try to remember where you have heard "to fall for" used before. One "falls for" a trick. Answer (A) is correct.

12. C

To *proclaim* is to *announce or decree*, especially in regards to a prominent figure like a president. Answer (C), *announced*, is a synonym for the given word.

13. A

Rudimentary means *simple or easy*. Of the answer choices given, only (A), *basic*, applies to something simple or rudimentary.

14. B

The word *rout* means *to defeat soundly* in battle or competition. Answer choice (B) is correct.

15. C

A *rogue* is someone who does not play by the rules. Thus, of the answer choices given, while a rogue may be aggressive or sad or low-brow, he or she is always a *maverick*, which also means someone who ignores the rules. Answer choice (C) is correct.

16. C

To *resonate* means *to sound appropriate* or hit the right note. Knowing a little musical terminology helps here, as *harmonizing* also refers to sounds mixing well together. Choice (C) is the best answer.

17. A

Redundant starts with the prefix "re-," or "again." The first choice you have available is *repetitive*, which means again and again. Answer choice (A) is correct.

18. B

Prescribe looks like a lot of words you know. It means *to lay down a rule or idea as law*. Think of prescriptions that doctors give that tell you what medicines to take and how. Of the words given as choices, (A) and (B) both seem possible. But given the meaning of *prescribe* (*as in prescription*), it is logical that (B), *dictate*, is the correct answer.

19. D

Logical means based on logic or *sensible*. Answer choice (D) is correct.

20. A

Note that choice (A) is the word *required*, which has the same root as the given word. In this case, those roots are the same. Answer choice (A) is correct.

21. C

Gravitate is based on the word it most looks like: gravity. So even if you didn't know that gravitate means *moving towards*, you might be able to make a guess based on your knowledge that the force of gravity pulls things closer together. Choice (C) is correct.

22. D

Cautious means *careful*. Answer choice (D) is correct.

23. C

The meaning of *braggart* is as simple as *someone who brags*. So while many leaders do brag, the correct answer choice here is (C), *showoff*.

24. A

Hearsay is a term often used in law. It means *unfounded stories*. A *rumor* is a story without proof. Choice (A) is correct.

25. C

To *taunt* is to *ridicule* or *tease*. Answer choice (C) is most correct.

26. B

The term *constructive criticism* refers to criticism that constructs or *builds up* the listener rather than destroying him or her. While *flattery* might build some people up, the correct answer here is choice (B), *productive*.

27. C

To *quantify* something is to *be able to count* it. Therefore, (C) is correct.

28. C

Something *effective* is useful, efficient, or productive. *Useful* is an answer choice, so choice (C) is correct.

29. C

Apathy means the state of not caring or *boredom*. Choice (C) is correct.

30. B

A *blemish* is a *glaring problem or defect*.

31. A

Consensus has a root of "con-" meaning *with* (don't confuse this with "con-" meaning *not*). Only answer choice (A) invites togetherness. Another way of tackling this question is to read the sentence carefully and glean that to get a measure passed, one would need *agreement*, not fighting. (A) is the correct answer.

32. **D**

Dissent has a negative connotation due to the root "dis-," meaning *not*. Answer choice (D) is the only negative choice. *Insubordination*, choice (D), is the correct response.

33. **D**

Tempo means *the speed of something*. Choice (D) is the right answer.

34. **B**

Try to fit some of the words into the sentence given to test their context. *Glee* and *protection* are both possible, but neither really seems appropriate to helping her feel better when times are bad. Glee is too happy and protection isn't enough. But *comfort*, (B), would make her feel better.

35. **B**

Pitfalls are *traps and problems that await*. Answer choice (B) is correct.

PART 4: PARAGRAPH COMPREHENSION ANSWERS AND EXPLANATIONS

1. C

This is an inference question, so the correct answer may be implied but not spelled out directly. The first paragraph talks about the participants of urban legends. It turns out that they can never be found. In other words, the elusive participant in these supposedly "real-life" events does not actually exist, choice (C). Once you realize that urban legends are fictional, choices (A), (B), and (D) cannot be correct.

2. D

This is an *EXCEPT* question, so you are looking for the one answer choice that does not characterize successful urban legends. Here again, if you were able to glean that urban legends are fictional, the correct answer choice (D), a basis in reality, is clearly the correct answer. Otherwise, you could use the process of elimination on the wrong answer choices. The passage states that urban legends "persist both for their entertainment value and for the transmission of popular values and beliefs," so choices (A) and (B), which paraphrase this, are wrong. Finally, the very first sentence describes urban legends as a new form of folktale, so (C) is out.

3. B

The author, while maintaining that there were other scientists with competing ideas, notes toward the end that Darwin's eloquence and his ability "to account for many diverse examples" helped him establish his theories as the benchmark by which others stacked up. Thus, choice (B) is correct. None of the other choices are supported by the passage.

4. B

Remember that in tone questions the answers tend to be from the less extreme of the choices. Choice (B) is correct because the passage merely conveys relevant facts about an issue. While the author does describe two opposing reactions that parents have had to the changes that have taken place in elementary schools, no preference is implied. Therefore choices (A) and (C) are incorrect. Be cautious with choices such as these that use extreme language.

5. D

Although the wording of this question indicates that this is an inference question, the correct answer choice (D) can be gleaned directly from the first sentence. If most life is "dependent on organisms that store radiant energy from the Sun," it doesn't take much to infer that most life is ultimately dependent on light from the Sun. Remember that on inference questions you are looking for the one answer that must be true based on what is stated in the passage.

6. A

The first paragraph describes ecosystems that are dependent on photosynthetic organisms, while the second paragraph describes ecosystems that are dependent on chemosynthetic organisms. In both cases, the organisms serve similar functions as primary producers within their different food chains, so choice (A) is correct. Choice (B) is wrong because only chemosynthetic organisms are described in the passage as supporting higher organisms "at great ocean depths." (C) is clearly wrong because chemosynthetic organisms do not rely on sunlight for their basic source of energy. Choice (D) is never discussed in the passage.

7. D

This is a slightly tricky inference question, because a lot of dates are mentioned in the passage. Nonetheless, the passage states that Halley determined that the comet followed a 76-year orbit. He never lived to see the comet that appeared in 1758, so it follows that the last time the comet appeared before his death took place 76 years earlier, or in $1758 - 76 = 1682$, choice (D).

8. D

The passage discusses a few ways to distinguish a crocodile from an alligator. The first and most easily observed of these is the fact that the crocodile's head and jaws are longer and narrower; in other words, it has a narrower snout, choice (D). (A) is out, because the animals' mouths do not necessarily have to be closed to distinguish one from the other. Choice (B) is out because both animals can be found in the Everglades National Park, and (C) is never discussed as one of the ways to distinguish one giant reptile from the other.

9. A

On this question you are asked to infer what the agent believes. Clearly she must assume that certain actors are inappropriate for certain parts, because if she didn't believe this her conclusion would make no sense; it wouldn't be possible for an actor to audition for an inappropriate part. The actors' talent (B) isn't questioned by the agent; she focuses on the types of roles. The possibility that an actor's appropriateness for the part may be difficult to predict (C) is never assumed by the agent; in fact, if anything, such a belief would weaken her conclusion. Major roles (D) are never discussed in the passage.

10. A

To answer this detail question, scan the passage for a reference to foot or feet. The first such mention is in the third sentence, which states: "Pentameter refers to the number of feet, or groupings of syllables." So clearly, a foot is just that, a grouping of syllables, choice (A).

11. D

This is a main idea question, so reading the passage for details is not necessary, although paying attention to the overall effect of those details is. The author notes that public opinion on the war was swayed when the *Lusitania* was attacked, prompting increased military involvement from the U.S. Choice (D) is a paraphrase of this main idea. Of the wrong answer choices, (A) is out because it distorts a detail found in the passage, implying a causal link between America's support for Britain and France and Germany's sinking of the *Lusitania* that is not supported by the passage. Choice (B) refers to a minor detail in the passage, and choice (C) is simply not true according to the passage, particularly after the sinking of the *Lusitania*.

12. D

In this inference question, you are asked to supply a conclusion that is best supported by the passage. The author seems to believe that critics' opinions aren't necessarily more significant than those of the average Joe, so (D), which restates this main idea, is easy to conclude. Though the author says the critics' opinions aren't more correct than those of average moviegoers, he doesn't imply (A), that they are usually incorrect. Choice (B) is out because it's not that judgments are meaningless, but that critics don't always make the right judgments. And we don't know how frequently critics dislike popular movies (C), only that when they do, they may not be right.

13. **C**

This detail question asks why Americans did not start using the tomato until the mid-nineteenth century. So what does the passage say? According to the passage, the English considered the tomato poisonous, and this myth continued to hold sway in America until the mid-nineteenth century; in other words, they, too, believed it to be poisonous, choice (C). None of the other answer choices are supported by the statements in the passage.

14. **A**

This question asks you to infer what the foreign ambassador might do in a given situation. From the details given, one can see the ambassador as a man who expects certain favors and protests loudly when those favors are not granted. Thus, of the choices given, choice (A) makes the most sense, as the ambassador clearly does not feel parking tickets should apply to diplomats.

15. **C**

Don't try to overanalyze a detail question. They are straightforward and to find the answer you need only to check the text, which says that "the recent infusion of international talent has . . . broadened its marketability overseas," paraphrased in choice (C). While (A) and (D) are mentioned in the passage, they are used as evidence for the assertion that basketball will overtake baseball as America's favorite sport. (B) is not mentioned.

PART 5: MATHEMATICS KNOWLEDGE ANSWERS AND EXPLANATIONS

1. D

Use FOIL to solve:

$$(3x + 4)(4x - 3)$$
$$= (3x)(4x) + (3x)(-3) + (4)(4x) + (4)(-3)$$
$$= 12x^2 - 9x + 16x - 12 = 12x^2 + 7x - 12.$$

2. A

Pick numbers to solve this one. Let's say that $n = 2$. That means the tree grew 5 feet, or 60 inches, in 2 years, which means it grew at a rate of 30 inches per year. Plug in 2 for n into the answer choices, and only (A) gives the answer of 30 that you are looking for.

3. D

If the perimeter of $ABCD$ is 56, then half that, or 28, is the sum of the length and the width, since the perimeter of a rectangle = 2(length + width). So if $AD = 16$, then $AB = 28 - 16 = 12$, and the area of $ABCD$ must be $16 \times 12 = 192$.

4. A

A square is a rectangle with four equal sides.

5. D

We're given two inequalities here: $a < b$ and $b < c$, which we can combine into one, $a < b < c$. We need to go through the answer choices to see which *must* be true. Choice (D): $a + b < 2c$. We know that $a < c$ and $b < c$. If we add the corresponding sides of these inequalities we'll get $a + b < c + c$, or $a + b < 2c$. This statement is *always* true, so it must be the correct answer.

6. C

Since the angle marked $x°$ and the angle marked $y°$ together form a straight angle, their measures must sum to 180°. Substitute in $2z$ for x and $3z$ for y, and solve for z.

$$x + y = 180$$
$$2z + 3z = 180$$
$$5z = 180$$
$$z = 36$$

7. B

There are 360 degrees in a circle and 60 minutes in an hour, so you could solve this question by setting up a proportion. $\dfrac{45}{360} = \dfrac{n}{60}$, where n is the number of minutes. $n = \dfrac{45 \times 60}{360} = 7.5$, so the answer is (B).

8. C

$5 \times 5 \times 5 = 125$, and $125 \times 125 = 15{,}675$, which is the smallest power of 5 that's greater than 10,000. So $(5 \times 5 \times 5) \times (5 \times 5 \times 5)$, or $5^6 = 5^n$, and $n = 6$.

9. B

Since lines p and q are parallel, we can use the rule about alternate interior angles. The angle marked $y°$ is adjacent and supplementary to a 65° angle, $y = 180 - 65 = 115$.

10. A

You could either turn the percents into decimals and multiply: $0.15 \times 0.15 \times 200 = 0.15 \times 30 = 4.5$, so the answer is (A), or you could take it one step at a time. 15 percent of 200 is $\frac{15}{100} \times 200 = 15 \times 2 = 30$. 15 percent of 30 is $\frac{15}{100} \times 30 = \frac{3}{20} \times 30 = \frac{3}{2} \times 3 = \frac{9}{2} = 4.5$, so the answer is (A).

11. B

Don't fall for the answer choice trap and assume that the average of $\frac{1}{20}$ and $\frac{1}{30}$ is $\frac{1}{25}$. Instead, use the average formula: Average $= \frac{\text{Sum of the terms}}{\text{Number of terms}}$. So, in this case, Average $= \frac{\frac{1}{20} + \frac{1}{30}}{2} = \frac{\frac{3}{60} + \frac{2}{60}}{2} = \frac{\frac{5}{60}}{2} = \frac{5}{120} = \frac{1}{24}$.

12. C

This question is just testing your knowledge of definitions. The *supplement* of an angle is the angle that when added to the original angle equals 180°. So if an angle measures $y°$, its supplement is $180 - y$.

13. B

If Diane has $\frac{2}{3}$ of her room still to paint, she'll need $2 \times 2\frac{1}{2}$ or 5 more cans to do the job.

14. D

You can't find the value of either variable alone, but you don't need to. Rearranging the equation, you get:

$$13 + a = 25 + b$$
$$13 = 25 + b - a$$
$$13 - 25 = b - a$$
$$b - a = -12$$

15. C

When you multiply terms that have exponents over the same base, you add the exponents and multiply the coefficients, so in this case you get:

$$3x^2 \times 5x^3 = (3 \times 5)x^{2+3} = 15x^5.$$

16. D

You can pick numbers to make sense of this geometry problem. You are asked to increase the sides of a square by 10 percent, so you want to pick a number for the original sides of the square of which it's easy to take 10 percent. For instance, you could say that the original square is 10 by 10. 10 percent of 10 is 1, so the dimensions of the increased square are 11 by 11. In this case, the area of the original square is 100, and the area of the new square is 121, which represents a 21 percent increase, choice (D).

17. B

If $\frac{m}{2} = 15$, then $m = 15 \times 2 = 30$, so $\frac{m}{3} = \frac{30}{3} = 10$.

18. C

To factor $6x^2 - 13x + 6$, you need a pair of binomials whose "first" terms will give you a product of $6x^2$ and whose "last" terms will give you a product of 6. And since the middle term of the result is negative, the two last terms must both be negative. You know that one of the factors is among the answer choices, so you can use them in your trial-and-error effort to factor. You know you're looking for a factor with a minus sign in it, so the answer's either (C) or (D).

Try (C) first: Its first term is $3x$, so the other factor's first term would have to be $2x$ (to get that $6x^2$ in the product). (C)'s last term is -2, so the other factor's last term would have to be -3. Check to see if $(3x - 2)(2x - 3)$ works:

$$(3x - 2)(2x - 3)$$
$$= (3x)(2x) + 3x(-3) + (-2)(2x) + (-2)(-3)$$
$$= 6x^2 - 9x - 4x + 6$$
$$= 6x^2 - 13x + 6$$

It works. There's no need to check (D).

19. D

Just be careful and translate the English into math: "the product of 3 and x is equal to 2 less than y" becomes $3x = y - 2$. But all of the equations in the answer choices set the right side of the equation to zero, so let's do that to our equation:

$$3x = y - 2$$
$$3x - y = -2$$
$$3x - y + 2 = 0.$$

20. A

Since $\dfrac{b}{a}$ is the reciprocal of $\dfrac{a}{b}$, $\dfrac{b}{a}$ must be the reciprocal of $1 - \dfrac{1}{x}$ as well. Combine the terms in $1 - \dfrac{1}{x}$ and then find its reciprocal.

$$\frac{a}{b} = 1 - \frac{1}{x} = \frac{x}{x} - \frac{1}{x} = \frac{x - 1}{x}$$

Therefore, $\dfrac{b}{a} = \dfrac{x}{x - 1}$.

21. C

This figure is an unfamiliar solid, so we shouldn't try to calculate the volume directly. We are told that the solid in question is half of a cube. We can imagine the other half lying on top of the solid, forming a complete cube.

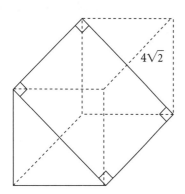

Notice that the diagonal with length $4\sqrt{2}$ and two of the cube's edges form an isosceles right triangle. In an isosceles right triangle, the hypotenuse is $\sqrt{2}$ times the length of a leg. Here the hypotenuse has length $4\sqrt{2}$, so the legs have length 4. Thus, the edges of the cube have a length of 4. The volume of

a cube is the length of an edge cubed. So the volume of the whole cube is $4 \times 4 \times 4$, or 64. The volume of the solid in question is $\dfrac{1}{2}$ of this, or 32.

22. B

Begin by writing the division problem as a fraction: $\dfrac{7.6}{0.019} = x$. Now move the decimal points on the top and the bottom of the fraction the same number of places to the right until you are dealing with whole numbers: $\dfrac{7.6}{0.019} = \dfrac{7,600}{19}$. Now go ahead and divide: $\dfrac{7,600}{19} = 400$.

23. A

The circumference of a circle $= 2\pi(\text{radius})$, so the radius of a circle with a circumference of 8 is $\dfrac{8}{2\pi} = \dfrac{4}{\pi}$. The area of a circle $= \pi(\text{radius})^2$, so the area of a circle with a radius of $\dfrac{4}{\pi}$ is $\pi\left(\dfrac{4}{\pi}\right)^2 = \pi\left(\dfrac{16}{\pi^2}\right) = \dfrac{16}{\pi}$, choice (A).

24. B

You could translate the English into math to get: $.36 \times 18 = .18 \times n$, so $n = \dfrac{.36 \times 18}{.18} = 2 \times 18 = 36$. Of course, you don't have to go through all that work if you realize that x percent of $y = y$ percent of x.

25. C

Here you're looking for an extremely rough approximation (the answer choices all have a range of 100), so you could square the upper bounds of the ranges in the answer choices, until you find the range that encompasses 104,906. For instance, starting with the upper bound of (A), $(200)^2 = 40,000$, which is less than 104,906. Now try (B): $(300)^2 = 90,000$, which is still too low. Now check (C): $(400)^2 = 160,000$. 104,906 is between 90,000 and 160,000, so (C) is the answer.

PART 6: ELECTRONICS INFORMATION ANSWERS AND EXPLANATIONS

1. B

Resistance is measured in ohms, and the symbol for an ohm is Ω (omega).

2. B

Two types of particles are found within the nucleus: protons and neutrons. Protons have a positive charge, and neutrons are neutrally charged.

3. A

Alternating current (AC) is when the current flowing in a conductor changes direction (moves back and forth) many times in a second.

4. D

This symbol represents a short circuit, which is an accidental path of low resistance that passes an irregularly high amount of current.

5. B

I represents current. Current is the rate of flow of electrons, or the *I*ntensity of the flow. (Specifically, I is the rate of charge flow.)

6. D

The P-type material in a diode is the anode, and the N-type material is known as the cathode.

7. D

Pure silicon must be doped in order to generate holes or free electrons. This process creates the P and N materials needed to make diodes and transistors.

8. D

Inductance is measured in henries, but one henry (1 H) represents a very large amount of inductance. It is much more common to rate inductors using millihenries (mH).

9. A

A capacitor's capacitance is measured in farads, or microfarads. Its capacitive reactance, however, is measured in ohms.

10. C

The arrow in a transistor symbol is always placed on the emitter, and the arrow always points toward the N-type material at that junction.

11. A

This is the circuit symbol for a voltmeter, which is used to measure voltage.

12. B

There are three essential components of an electrical circuit: a voltage source, a load, and conductors to connect the load to the voltage source. When these three components are connected so that current can flow, we have a closed circuit.

13. A

A doorbell is typically operated by a push switch, which allows current to flow only when a button is pressed. (A) is the symbol for a push switch.

14. B

This is the schematic symbol for an alternating current (AC) voltage source.

15. C

Capacitors that are electrical storage units are also known as condensers.

16. C

An insulator is a material that does not conduct electricity.

17. A

Rubber is an example of an insulator. All of the other examples in this question are conductors.

18. **C**

Four 6-ohm resistors wired in series will have a total resistance of 24 ohms. Using $I = E \div R$, a total of 0.5 A will flow in this circuit. 0.5 A is the same as 500 mA.

19. **C**

The term semiconductor refers to an element that has four electrons in its valence shell. Since the bonds between these four electrons and the nucleus are somewhat strong, these elements are neither good conductors nor good insulators. Elements that are widely recognized as semiconductors are silicon and germanium.

20. **D**

This is the circuit symbol for a galvanometer, which is used to measure extremely small currents, usually of 1 mA voltage or less.

PART 7: AUTO AND SHOP INFORMATION ANSWERS AND EXPLANATIONS

1. D

A bit of a trick question, because while a *miter box* might be used with a backsaw to make even cuts in wood at specific angles, by itself, it is not capable of shaping wood. All of the other choices are tools capable of making cuts or smoothing edges on wood. The correct answer is (D).

2. B

Of all the aspects of vehicle operation, two that are a high priority for most drivers are ride comfort and handling. The suspension system, choice (B), is responsible for the ride quality of the vehicle.

3. D

The cut or slot left by a saw in a piece of wood is also know as a *kerf*, choice (D).

4. D

The *transfer case* is located between the transmission and the drive axles on a four-wheel drive vehicle and is the piece that splits the engine's power between the front- and rear-drive axle.

5. B

This is a crosscut saw. It is designed to, as its name suggests, cut across the grain of the wood (B). Crosscut saw teeth are unique in that they cut like a knife, in contrast to a ripsaw, which is made to cut with the grain of wood.

6. C

This image depicts the compression stroke, which is the second stroke in the four-stroke cycle.

7. A

Fractional measurement fasteners (measured in fractions of inches) use threads that are identified by the number of threads per inch.

8. D

To loosen tight fasteners, it is good to use a box-end wrench. Choice (B) depicts a combination wrench, which has an open end wrench on one side and a box end on the other. Choice (C) shows a wrench with box ends on both sides. Therefore, both (B) and (C) are suitable for loosening tight fasteners; choice (D) is the correct answer. The box end wraps completely around the head of a bolt, and therefore makes greater surface contact.

9. A

Of the answer choices given, only (A), *coil spring,* is not a part associated with the steering system. Coil springs are what aid the wheels in moving up and down while the vehicle chassis stays steady. The other pieces listed—steering knuckle, tie rod end, and idler arm—are all parts of the steering system.

10. D

The camshaft, indicated in the diagram by the number 3, is responsible for the opening and closing of the engine's intake and exhaust valves. The camshaft turns at one-half the speed of the engine's crankshaft.

11. D

In fuel-injected engines, the electric fuel pump is located in the vehicle's fuel tank and is what supplies fuel under pressure to the fuel injectors.

12. B

The two basic thread classifications—*Unified National Coarse (UNC)*, and *Unified National Fine (UNF)*—have different numbers of threads per inch. A UNC or coarse thread would have relatively few threads per inch, where a UNF or fine thread would have a larger number of threads per inch. Thus, the answer to this question is (B), less.

13. C

Power brake systems use both the engine intake manifold vacuum and fluid pressure from the power steering system to increase pressure. Engine intake manifold vacuum is utilized to generate greater force on the master cylinder, so higher hydraulic pressures can be generated in the brake system. Some brake booster systems use fluid pressure from the power steering system to increase braking power. The answer is (C), both of these.

14. D

The primary is the low-voltage part of the system and contains a battery, an ignition switch, a primary coil winding, an ignition module, a reluctor and pickup coil, and a distributor. A rotor is not a part of the ignition primary system. Thus, the correct answer is (D).

15. A

Stoichiometric is the ideal ratio of air to fuel in the engine and it is the responsibility of the engine's fuel system to maintain this balance.

16. D

Viscosity is resistance to flow, and is expressed as a number that is directly proportional to the thickness of the oil.

17. D

Because they serve different purposes within an automobile, both negative ground current and direct current electrical systems are being built. Alternating current is used primarily for household appliances.

18. D

Stick welding involves the use of an electric arc welding machine and two cables: one that attaches to the work being welded through a *ground clamp*, and the other going to an electrode that is sometimes referred to as a *stinger*. For safety reasons, always clamp to the work.

19. D

The last major cylinder arrangement that has been utilized by engine designers is the horizontally opposed or flat design. This has all of the cylinders lying on the horizontal plane, with half of the cylinders facing away from the other half and the crankshaft located between them. Some refer to this design as a "boxer" engine because the pistons move back and forth like a boxer throwing punches.

20. B

The tool pictured is a drift. It is used for striking an object where it is important that the hammer itself does not come in direct contact with the work. A chisel normally has a long edge and is used for cutting (A), where a punch is narrow and is used for driving small fasteners and making layout marks (C).

21. A

This design is known as single overhead cam or SOHC. In a V-type engine with two cylinder heads, there would be two camshafts, with one installed above each cylinder head.

22. D

Any air passing through to the car's combustion chamber must naturally pass through the intake port in the cylinder head, the intake manifold, and the air filter. All of these are correct. Since the intake valve is open and is allowing atmospheric air to enter the combustion chamber, higher atmospheric air pressure pushes air through the engine's intake system and toward the low-pressure area above the piston. As the air is traveling through the intake system, fuel is injected into the air stream before it enters the combustion chamber.

23. D

Since most nuts are smaller sized, and because the *6-point* is a stronger design, it is usually the mechanic's first choice in the smaller socket drive sizes. And a *breaker bar* attached to a socket can give enough twisting force to loosen very tight fasteners. Thus, the best choice is (D).

24. **D**

This is an external hole-type retaining ring. Retaining rings (or snap rings) are used to prevent end-movement of cylindrical parts in bores or parts mounted on shafts. External snap rings are installed in grooves on shafts, whereas internal snap rings install in grooves inside a bore. Snap rings are installed and removed using snap ring pliers.

25. **B**

As the battery discharges in lead-acid batteries, the sulphuric acid in the electrolyte is reduced to water, and the lead plates become lead sulphate.

PART 8: MECHANICAL COMPREHENSION ANSWERS AND EXPLANATIONS

1. C

The principle of conservation of mechanical energy tells us that the total mechanical energy of an object ($PE + KE$) remains constant as an object moves. As the car rolls down the hill, its speed increases because its potential energy (PE) is being converted into kinetic energy (KE).

2. D

When a ball is thrown straight up, it has its maximum kinetic energy when it leaves the thrower's hand. This kinetic energy is converted into potential energy as it rises. Maximum potential energy (PE) occurs when the ball stops rising, and this is where its velocity is zero.

3. B

Inertia is a function of an object's mass. A large mass will require a large amount of force to cause it to accelerate. The larger the mass, the greater the inertia of the object.

4. C

Isaac Newton discovered that every particle in the universe is attracted to every other particle. This concept became a physical law known as Newton's Law of Universal Gravitation. The gravitational force that each body exerts on the other grows stronger as the bodies get closer. The force also increases as the mass of the bodies increase.

5. D

When a 20 pound force is placed on piston X, measuring 1 square inch, the same force is placed on every square inch of piston Y. To determine the output force, multiply 20 pounds by piston Y's 200 square inches. 20×200 is 4,000.

6. C

Work is defined as force times distance. Lifting a box straight up to the top of a ramp will require the same amount of work as pushing the box up the ramp (neglecting friction). The end result is the same in both cases (the box is at the top of the ramp), so the work done is also the same.

7. B

It is not possible to get more work out of a machine than what is put in. Machines do not reduce the work we do, they simply manage it and make it easier by diminishing the amount of force that is required.

8. A

A chisel is an example of a wedge.

9. B

The wedge is a variation of the inclined plane, but is made to move whereas the inclined plane stays stationary.

10. A

The distance from post A to the load is less than the distance from post B to the load; therefore, it holds the greater part of the load.

11. C

Work and kinetic energy are both measured in joules. This is not a coincidence, as any work that is done to accelerate an object at rest to speed v will be converted into the kinetic energy of that object. This principle is known as the work-energy theorem.

12. B

A screwdriver gains mechanical advantage through the use of a large wheel (screwdriver handle) rotating a small wheel (screwdriver tip), much like a wheel and axle. Large movements converted into small movements will amplify the force applied.

13. B

Any time that force is increased through mechanical advantage, there will always be a proportional decrease in the distance moved.

14. A

A prybar can increase mechanical advantage, and can change the direction of motion, so it is a first-class lever.

15. D

The centrifugal force from the spinning shaft will cause them to move out and up.

16. C

Moving the fulcrum toward the object will increase the force applied to the object, but decrease the distance that the object can be moved.

17. A

The hole is being tapped by a tap.

18. D

If a small gear drives a large gear, a speed reduction takes place. The large gear will turn slower than the small gear and the speed of the output will be slower.

19. D

A block-and-tackle requires a minimum of two pulleys, with a rope, belt, or chain used to operate them.

20. A

Pulley A will turn the fastest because it is the smallest.

21. B

A doorknob is similar to a wheel and axle in that a large wheel (the doorknob or handle) is used to operate a small wheel (the latch mechanism).

22. D

An automobile transmission has multiple speed ranges, which make it capable of increasing torque and decreasing speed (speed reduction), or increasing speed and decreasing torque (overdrive).

23. C

Consider "Torque" and "Speed" to be two boys on a teeter-totter. Whenever "Torque" goes up, "Speed" goes down, and vice versa. A mathematician would describe these two quantities to be inversely proportional.

24. C

An object's potential energy (*PE*) can be calculated using the formula

$$PE = mgh$$

where *m* is mass in kilograms (kg), *g* is acceleration due to gravity (9.8 m/s^2), *h* is the height of the object in meters (m), and *PE* is gravitational potential energy measured in joules (J).

25. A

The illustration is of a hypoid bevel.

PART 9: ASSEMBLING OBJECTS ANSWERS AND EXPLANATIONS

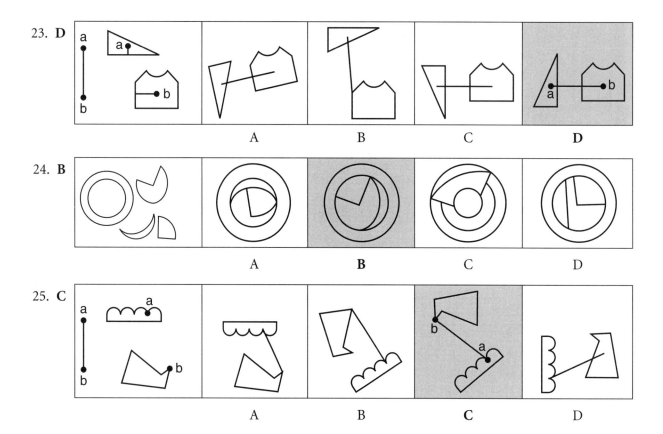

23. **D**

    A   B   C   **D**

24. **B**

    A   **B**   C   D

25. **C**

    A   B   **C**   D

ASVAB Practice Test III

ANSWER SHEET

Part 1: General Science (GS)

1 Ⓐ Ⓑ Ⓒ Ⓓ	6 Ⓐ Ⓑ Ⓒ Ⓓ	11 Ⓐ Ⓑ Ⓒ Ⓓ	16 Ⓐ Ⓑ Ⓒ Ⓓ	21 Ⓐ Ⓑ Ⓒ Ⓓ
2 Ⓐ Ⓑ Ⓒ Ⓓ	7 Ⓐ Ⓑ Ⓒ Ⓓ	12 Ⓐ Ⓑ Ⓒ Ⓓ	17 Ⓐ Ⓑ Ⓒ Ⓓ	22 Ⓐ Ⓑ Ⓒ Ⓓ
3 Ⓐ Ⓑ Ⓒ Ⓓ	8 Ⓐ Ⓑ Ⓒ Ⓓ	13 Ⓐ Ⓑ Ⓒ Ⓓ	18 Ⓐ Ⓑ Ⓒ Ⓓ	23 Ⓐ Ⓑ Ⓒ Ⓓ
4 Ⓐ Ⓑ Ⓒ Ⓓ	9 Ⓐ Ⓑ Ⓒ Ⓓ	14 Ⓐ Ⓑ Ⓒ Ⓓ	19 Ⓐ Ⓑ Ⓒ Ⓓ	24 Ⓐ Ⓑ Ⓒ Ⓓ
5 Ⓐ Ⓑ Ⓒ Ⓓ	10 Ⓐ Ⓑ Ⓒ Ⓓ	15 Ⓐ Ⓑ Ⓒ Ⓓ	20 Ⓐ Ⓑ Ⓒ Ⓓ	25 Ⓐ Ⓑ Ⓒ Ⓓ

Part 2: Arithmetic Reasoning (AR)

1 Ⓐ Ⓑ Ⓒ Ⓓ	7 Ⓐ Ⓑ Ⓒ Ⓓ	13 Ⓐ Ⓑ Ⓒ Ⓓ	19 Ⓐ Ⓑ Ⓒ Ⓓ	25 Ⓐ Ⓑ Ⓒ Ⓓ
2 Ⓐ Ⓑ Ⓒ Ⓓ	8 Ⓐ Ⓑ Ⓒ Ⓓ	14 Ⓐ Ⓑ Ⓒ Ⓓ	20 Ⓐ Ⓑ Ⓒ Ⓓ	26 Ⓐ Ⓑ Ⓒ Ⓓ
3 Ⓐ Ⓑ Ⓒ Ⓓ	9 Ⓐ Ⓑ Ⓒ Ⓓ	15 Ⓐ Ⓑ Ⓒ Ⓓ	21 Ⓐ Ⓑ Ⓒ Ⓓ	27 Ⓐ Ⓑ Ⓒ Ⓓ
4 Ⓐ Ⓑ Ⓒ Ⓓ	10 Ⓐ Ⓑ Ⓒ Ⓓ	16 Ⓐ Ⓑ Ⓒ Ⓓ	22 Ⓐ Ⓑ Ⓒ Ⓓ	28 Ⓐ Ⓑ Ⓒ Ⓓ
5 Ⓐ Ⓑ Ⓒ Ⓓ	11 Ⓐ Ⓑ Ⓒ Ⓓ	17 Ⓐ Ⓑ Ⓒ Ⓓ	23 Ⓐ Ⓑ Ⓒ Ⓓ	29 Ⓐ Ⓑ Ⓒ Ⓓ
6 Ⓐ Ⓑ Ⓒ Ⓓ	12 Ⓐ Ⓑ Ⓒ Ⓓ	18 Ⓐ Ⓑ Ⓒ Ⓓ	24 Ⓐ Ⓑ Ⓒ Ⓓ	30 Ⓐ Ⓑ Ⓒ Ⓓ

Part 3: Word Knowledge (WK)

1 Ⓐ Ⓑ Ⓒ Ⓓ	8 Ⓐ Ⓑ Ⓒ Ⓓ	15 Ⓐ Ⓑ Ⓒ Ⓓ	22 Ⓐ Ⓑ Ⓒ Ⓓ	29 Ⓐ Ⓑ Ⓒ Ⓓ
2 Ⓐ Ⓑ Ⓒ Ⓓ	9 Ⓐ Ⓑ Ⓒ Ⓓ	16 Ⓐ Ⓑ Ⓒ Ⓓ	23 Ⓐ Ⓑ Ⓒ Ⓓ	30 Ⓐ Ⓑ Ⓒ Ⓓ
3 Ⓐ Ⓑ Ⓒ Ⓓ	10 Ⓐ Ⓑ Ⓒ Ⓓ	17 Ⓐ Ⓑ Ⓒ Ⓓ	24 Ⓐ Ⓑ Ⓒ Ⓓ	31 Ⓐ Ⓑ Ⓒ Ⓓ
4 Ⓐ Ⓑ Ⓒ Ⓓ	11 Ⓐ Ⓑ Ⓒ Ⓓ	18 Ⓐ Ⓑ Ⓒ Ⓓ	25 Ⓐ Ⓑ Ⓒ Ⓓ	32 Ⓐ Ⓑ Ⓒ Ⓓ
5 Ⓐ Ⓑ Ⓒ Ⓓ	12 Ⓐ Ⓑ Ⓒ Ⓓ	19 Ⓐ Ⓑ Ⓒ Ⓓ	26 Ⓐ Ⓑ Ⓒ Ⓓ	33 Ⓐ Ⓑ Ⓒ Ⓓ
6 Ⓐ Ⓑ Ⓒ Ⓓ	13 Ⓐ Ⓑ Ⓒ Ⓓ	20 Ⓐ Ⓑ Ⓒ Ⓓ	27 Ⓐ Ⓑ Ⓒ Ⓓ	34 Ⓐ Ⓑ Ⓒ Ⓓ
7 Ⓐ Ⓑ Ⓒ Ⓓ	14 Ⓐ Ⓑ Ⓒ Ⓓ	21 Ⓐ Ⓑ Ⓒ Ⓓ	28 Ⓐ Ⓑ Ⓒ Ⓓ	35 Ⓐ Ⓑ Ⓒ Ⓓ

Part 4: Paragraph Comprehension (PC)

1 Ⓐ Ⓑ Ⓒ Ⓓ	4 Ⓐ Ⓑ Ⓒ Ⓓ	7 Ⓐ Ⓑ Ⓒ Ⓓ	10 Ⓐ Ⓑ Ⓒ Ⓓ	13 Ⓐ Ⓑ Ⓒ Ⓓ
2 Ⓐ Ⓑ Ⓒ Ⓓ	5 Ⓐ Ⓑ Ⓒ Ⓓ	8 Ⓐ Ⓑ Ⓒ Ⓓ	11 Ⓐ Ⓑ Ⓒ Ⓓ	14 Ⓐ Ⓑ Ⓒ Ⓓ
3 Ⓐ Ⓑ Ⓒ Ⓓ	6 Ⓐ Ⓑ Ⓒ Ⓓ	9 Ⓐ Ⓑ Ⓒ Ⓓ	12 Ⓐ Ⓑ Ⓒ Ⓓ	15 Ⓐ Ⓑ Ⓒ Ⓓ

Part 5: Mathematics Knowledge (MK)

1 Ⓐ Ⓑ Ⓒ Ⓓ	6 Ⓐ Ⓑ Ⓒ Ⓓ	11 Ⓐ Ⓑ Ⓒ Ⓓ	16 Ⓐ Ⓑ Ⓒ Ⓓ	21 Ⓐ Ⓑ Ⓒ Ⓓ
2 Ⓐ Ⓑ Ⓒ Ⓓ	7 Ⓐ Ⓑ Ⓒ Ⓓ	12 Ⓐ Ⓑ Ⓒ Ⓓ	17 Ⓐ Ⓑ Ⓒ Ⓓ	22 Ⓐ Ⓑ Ⓒ Ⓓ
3 Ⓐ Ⓑ Ⓒ Ⓓ	8 Ⓐ Ⓑ Ⓒ Ⓓ	13 Ⓐ Ⓑ Ⓒ Ⓓ	18 Ⓐ Ⓑ Ⓒ Ⓓ	23 Ⓐ Ⓑ Ⓒ Ⓓ
4 Ⓐ Ⓑ Ⓒ Ⓓ	9 Ⓐ Ⓑ Ⓒ Ⓓ	14 Ⓐ Ⓑ Ⓒ Ⓓ	19 Ⓐ Ⓑ Ⓒ Ⓓ	24 Ⓐ Ⓑ Ⓒ Ⓓ
5 Ⓐ Ⓑ Ⓒ Ⓓ	10 Ⓐ Ⓑ Ⓒ Ⓓ	15 Ⓐ Ⓑ Ⓒ Ⓓ	20 Ⓐ Ⓑ Ⓒ Ⓓ	25 Ⓐ Ⓑ Ⓒ Ⓓ

ANSWER SHEET

Part 6: Electronics Information (EI)

1 Ⓐ Ⓑ Ⓒ Ⓓ	5 Ⓐ Ⓑ Ⓒ Ⓓ	9 Ⓐ Ⓑ Ⓒ Ⓓ	13 Ⓐ Ⓑ Ⓒ Ⓓ	17 Ⓐ Ⓑ Ⓒ Ⓓ
2 Ⓐ Ⓑ Ⓒ Ⓓ	6 Ⓐ Ⓑ Ⓒ Ⓓ	10 Ⓐ Ⓑ Ⓒ Ⓓ	14 Ⓐ Ⓑ Ⓒ Ⓓ	18 Ⓐ Ⓑ Ⓒ Ⓓ
3 Ⓐ Ⓑ Ⓒ Ⓓ	7 Ⓐ Ⓑ Ⓒ Ⓓ	11 Ⓐ Ⓑ Ⓒ Ⓓ	15 Ⓐ Ⓑ Ⓒ Ⓓ	19 Ⓐ Ⓑ Ⓒ Ⓓ
4 Ⓐ Ⓑ Ⓒ Ⓓ	8 Ⓐ Ⓑ Ⓒ Ⓓ	12 Ⓐ Ⓑ Ⓒ Ⓓ	16 Ⓐ Ⓑ Ⓒ Ⓓ	20 Ⓐ Ⓑ Ⓒ Ⓓ

Part 7: Automotive and Shop Information (AS)

1 Ⓐ Ⓑ Ⓒ Ⓓ	6 Ⓐ Ⓑ Ⓒ Ⓓ	11 Ⓐ Ⓑ Ⓒ Ⓓ	16 Ⓐ Ⓑ Ⓒ Ⓓ	21 Ⓐ Ⓑ Ⓒ Ⓓ
2 Ⓐ Ⓑ Ⓒ Ⓓ	7 Ⓐ Ⓑ Ⓒ Ⓓ	12 Ⓐ Ⓑ Ⓒ Ⓓ	17 Ⓐ Ⓑ Ⓒ Ⓓ	22 Ⓐ Ⓑ Ⓒ Ⓓ
3 Ⓐ Ⓑ Ⓒ Ⓓ	8 Ⓐ Ⓑ Ⓒ Ⓓ	13 Ⓐ Ⓑ Ⓒ Ⓓ	18 Ⓐ Ⓑ Ⓒ Ⓓ	23 Ⓐ Ⓑ Ⓒ Ⓓ
4 Ⓐ Ⓑ Ⓒ Ⓓ	9 Ⓐ Ⓑ Ⓒ Ⓓ	14 Ⓐ Ⓑ Ⓒ Ⓓ	19 Ⓐ Ⓑ Ⓒ Ⓓ	24 Ⓐ Ⓑ Ⓒ Ⓓ
5 Ⓐ Ⓑ Ⓒ Ⓓ	10 Ⓐ Ⓑ Ⓒ Ⓓ	15 Ⓐ Ⓑ Ⓒ Ⓓ	20 Ⓐ Ⓑ Ⓒ Ⓓ	25 Ⓐ Ⓑ Ⓒ Ⓓ

Part 8: Mechanical Comprehension (MC)

1 Ⓐ Ⓑ Ⓒ Ⓓ	6 Ⓐ Ⓑ Ⓒ Ⓓ	11 Ⓐ Ⓑ Ⓒ Ⓓ	16 Ⓐ Ⓑ Ⓒ Ⓓ	21 Ⓐ Ⓑ Ⓒ Ⓓ
2 Ⓐ Ⓑ Ⓒ Ⓓ	7 Ⓐ Ⓑ Ⓒ Ⓓ	12 Ⓐ Ⓑ Ⓒ Ⓓ	17 Ⓐ Ⓑ Ⓒ Ⓓ	22 Ⓐ Ⓑ Ⓒ Ⓓ
3 Ⓐ Ⓑ Ⓒ Ⓓ	8 Ⓐ Ⓑ Ⓒ Ⓓ	13 Ⓐ Ⓑ Ⓒ Ⓓ	18 Ⓐ Ⓑ Ⓒ Ⓓ	23 Ⓐ Ⓑ Ⓒ Ⓓ
4 Ⓐ Ⓑ Ⓒ Ⓓ	9 Ⓐ Ⓑ Ⓒ Ⓓ	14 Ⓐ Ⓑ Ⓒ Ⓓ	19 Ⓐ Ⓑ Ⓒ Ⓓ	24 Ⓐ Ⓑ Ⓒ Ⓓ
5 Ⓐ Ⓑ Ⓒ Ⓓ	10 Ⓐ Ⓑ Ⓒ Ⓓ	15 Ⓐ Ⓑ Ⓒ Ⓓ	20 Ⓐ Ⓑ Ⓒ Ⓓ	25 Ⓐ Ⓑ Ⓒ Ⓓ

Part 9: Assembling Objects (AO)

1 Ⓐ Ⓑ Ⓒ Ⓓ	6 Ⓐ Ⓑ Ⓒ Ⓓ	11 Ⓐ Ⓑ Ⓒ Ⓓ	16 Ⓐ Ⓑ Ⓒ Ⓓ	21 Ⓐ Ⓑ Ⓒ Ⓓ
2 Ⓐ Ⓑ Ⓒ Ⓓ	7 Ⓐ Ⓑ Ⓒ Ⓓ	12 Ⓐ Ⓑ Ⓒ Ⓓ	17 Ⓐ Ⓑ Ⓒ Ⓓ	22 Ⓐ Ⓑ Ⓒ Ⓓ
3 Ⓐ Ⓑ Ⓒ Ⓓ	8 Ⓐ Ⓑ Ⓒ Ⓓ	13 Ⓐ Ⓑ Ⓒ Ⓓ	18 Ⓐ Ⓑ Ⓒ Ⓓ	23 Ⓐ Ⓑ Ⓒ Ⓓ
4 Ⓐ Ⓑ Ⓒ Ⓓ	9 Ⓐ Ⓑ Ⓒ Ⓓ	14 Ⓐ Ⓑ Ⓒ Ⓓ	19 Ⓐ Ⓑ Ⓒ Ⓓ	24 Ⓐ Ⓑ Ⓒ Ⓓ
5 Ⓐ Ⓑ Ⓒ Ⓓ	10 Ⓐ Ⓑ Ⓒ Ⓓ	15 Ⓐ Ⓑ Ⓒ Ⓓ	20 Ⓐ Ⓑ Ⓒ Ⓓ	25 Ⓐ Ⓑ Ⓒ Ⓓ

PART 1: GENERAL SCIENCE (GS)

Time: 11 minutes; 25 questions

<u>Directions</u>: In this section, you will be tested on your knowledge of concepts in science generally reviewed in high school. For each question, select the best answer and mark the corresponding oval on your answer sheet.

1. Those wishing to reduce the bad cholesterol levels in their blood should avoid

   (A) polyunsaturated fats
   (B) carbohydrates
   (C) monounsaturated fats
   (D) saturated fats

2. Water at sea level freezes at what temperature?

   (A) 373° K
   (B) 0° F
   (C) 100° C
   (D) 32° F

3. Which of the following subatomic particles has the largest mass?

   (A) proton
   (B) electron
   (C) positron
   (D) neutrino

4. Which of the following is an example of an autotroph?

   (A) a vulture
   (B) an apple tree
   (C) a toadstool
   (D) a sea anemone

5. The period from 4.6 billion years to 570 million years ago is called

   (A) Phanerozoic Eon
   (B) Mesozoic era
   (C) Paleozoic era
   (D) Precambrian Eon

6. Which of the following planets is larger than Earth?

   (A) Mars
   (B) Mercury
   (C) Uranus
   (D) Venus

7. When these fall into the Earth's gravitational field, they are seen as "falling stars."

   (A) asteroids
   (B) meteors
   (C) comets
   (D) none of the above

8. The study of interactions between organisms and their interrelationships with the physical environment is known as

   (A) cytology
   (B) ecology
   (C) physiology
   (D) embryology

9. Most of the nutrients in food are absorbed in the body's

   (A) stomach
   (B) pylorus
   (C) small intestine
   (D) large intestine

GO ON TO THE NEXT PAGE

10. High tide occurs

    (A) four times a year
    (B) once a day
    (C) once a year
    (D) twice a day

11. Which is *NOT* a fact according to Newton's Law of Gravitation?

    (A) If the mass of the Earth were doubled, the force on the Earth would double.
    (B) The force exerted on the Earth by the Sun is equal and opposite to the force exerted on the Sun by the Earth.
    (C) If the mass of the Earth were doubled, the force on the Earth would quadruple.
    (D) If the mass of the Sun were doubled, the force on the Earth would double.

12. Which of the following states of electromagnetic radiation has the longest wavelength and lowest frequency?

    (A) radio waves
    (B) microwaves
    (C) gamma rays
    (D) visible light

13. The ratio by which light is slowed down by a medium is called the _____ of that medium.

    (A) electromagnetic spectrum
    (B) angle of incidence
    (C) reflection
    (D) refractive index

14. Which of the following has the highest pH?

    (A) vinegar
    (B) water
    (C) baking soda
    (D) cranberry juice

15. Carbohydrates include

    (A) starches
    (B) sugars
    (C) Both A and B are correct.
    (D) Neither A nor B is correct.

16. Members of an order are more alike than members of a

    (A) class
    (B) family
    (C) genus
    (D) species

17. The number of protons in the nucleus of an atom is its

    (A) atomic symbol
    (B) atomic weight
    (C) atomic number
    (D) none of the above

18. The _____ is a system of muscles that allow the lungs to expand and contract, drawing air in and out.

    (A) diaphragm
    (B) pharynx
    (C) trachea
    (D) bronchioles

19. The atom of an element with an atomic number of 17 must have

    (A) 17 electrons
    (B) 17 protons
    (C) 17 neutrons
    (D) an atomic mass of 17

GO ON TO THE NEXT PAGE

20. Because mushrooms absorb nutrients from decaying leaves, they are classified as

    (A) autotrophs
    (B) anaerobes
    (C) saprophytes
    (D) protozoans

21. The blood vessel with the *LEAST* oxygenated blood is the

    (A) pulmonary artery
    (B) aorta
    (C) pulmonary vein
    (D) superior vena cava

22. Saliva in the mouth begins the process of breaking down

    (A) starch
    (B) fat
    (C) protein
    (D) all of the above

23. In which of the following kingdoms do cells lack nuclei?

    (A) Fungi
    (B) Monera
    (C) Plantae
    (D) Protista

24. An atom that is not electrically neutral is called a(n)

    (A) isotope
    (B) positron
    (C) ion
    (D) allotrope

25. Which of the following is an example of a metamorphic rock?

    (A) granite
    (B) marble
    (C) limestone
    (D) shale

STOP. IF YOU FINISH BEFORE THE TIME IS UP, YOU MAY CHECK OVER YOUR WORK ON THIS PART ONLY.

PART 2: ARITHMETIC REASONING (AR)

Time: 36 minutes; 30 questions

<u>Directions:</u> In this section, you are tested on your ability to use arithmetic. For each question, select the best answer and mark the corresponding oval on your answer sheet.

1. A certain machine caps 5 bottles every 2 seconds. At this rate, how many bottles will be capped in 1 minute?

    (A) 75
    (B) 150
    (C) 225
    (D) 300

2. Jonah traveled 650 miles on his most recent trip and averaged 25 miles to the gallon. If gasoline cost $1.30 per gallon, how much did he spend on his trip?

    (A) $26.00
    (B) $27.30
    (C) $32.50
    (D) $33.80

3. If there are approximately 3.86 liters in a gallon, and gasoline costs $1.54 per gallon, to the nearest penny what is the cost of a liter of gasoline?

    (A) $0.35
    (B) $0.40
    (C) $0.44
    (D) $0.47

4. How many minutes are there in one week?

    (A) 3,600
    (B) 7,200
    (C) 10,080
    (D) 86,400

5. Pat deposited 15 percent of last week's take-home pay into a savings account. If she deposited $37.50, what was last week's take-home pay?

    (A) $56.25
    (B) $112.50
    (C) $225.00
    (D) $250.00

6. If the ratio of males to females in a group of students is 3:5, which of the following could be the total number of students in the group?

    (A) 148
    (B) 150
    (C) 152
    (D) 154

7. A car travels 288 miles in 6 hours. At that rate, how many miles will it travel in 8 hours?

    (A) 360
    (B) 368
    (C) 376
    (D) 384

8. Martin's average score after 4 tests is 89. What score on the 5th test would bring Martin's average up to exactly 90?

    (A) 91
    (B) 92
    (C) 93
    (D) 94

GO ON TO THE NEXT PAGE

9. In 2010, the population of town A was 9,400 and the population of town B was 7,600. Since then, each year the population of town A has decreased by 100 and the population of town B has increased by 100. Assuming that in each case the rate continues, in what year will the two populations be equal?

(A) 2019
(B) 2020
(C) 2027
(D) 2028

10. One number is 5 times another number and their sum is –60. What is the lesser of the two numbers?

(A) –10
(B) –12
(C) –48
(D) –50

11. John gets paid $6.00 for each of the first 40 toy cars he makes in a week. For any additional toy cars beyond 40 his pay increases by 50%. How much does John get paid in a week in which he makes 48 toy cars?

(A) $288
(B) $300
(C) $312
(D) $321

12. If a bora = 2 fedis, and a fedi = 3 glecks, how many boras are equal to 48 glecks?

(A) 8
(B) 16
(C) 32
(D) 96

13. Nine temperature readings were taken, one reading every four hours, with the first reading taken at 12 P.M. What will be the time when the final reading is taken?

(A) 4 P.M.
(B) 8 P.M.
(C) 12 A.M.
(D) 4 A.M.

14. A school raised monthly tuition payments from $225.00 per month to $300.00 per month. The percent of the tuition increase is which of the following?

(A) 25 percent
(B) $33\frac{1}{3}$ percent
(C) $66\frac{1}{2}$ percent
(D) 75 percent

15. A truck going at a rate of 20 miles per hour takes 6 hours to complete a trip. How many fewer hours would the trip have taken if the truck were traveling at a rate of 30 miles per hour?

(A) 4
(B) 3
(C) 2
(D) 1

16. If a barrel has the capacity to hold 75 gallons, how many gallons does it contain when it is $\frac{3}{5}$ full?

(A) 45
(B) 48
(C) 54
(D) 60

GO ON TO THE NEXT PAGE

17. If a salary of $45,000 is subject to a 40 percent deduction, the new salary is

    (A) $18,000
    (B) $27,000
    (C) $30,000
    (D) $36,000

18. 8! =

    (A) 64
    (B) 40,320
    (C) 8
    (D) 40,000

19. Fifteen people chip in $40 dollars each to throw a birthday bash for a mutual friend. If 35 percent of the money is spent on a group gift and the rest is spent on the party, how much was spent just on the party?

    (A) $210
    (B) $300
    (C) $350
    (D) $390

20. If an employee worked a total of $33\frac{1}{2}$ hours over five days, what was the average amount of time that the employee worked each day?

    (A) 6 hours, 35 minutes
    (B) 6 hours, 40 minutes
    (C) 6 hours, 42 minutes
    (D) 6 hours, 45 minutes

21. If a train starting out at point A travels 180 miles at a rate of 60 miles per hour and then 150 miles at a rate of 75 miles per hour before arriving at point B, what was the average rate, in miles per hour, for the entire trip?

    (A) 66
    (B) 67.5
    (C) 68.5
    (D) 70

22. After being discounted by 20 percent, a bicycle sells for $140.00. What was the original price of the bicycle?

    (A) $155.00
    (B) $162.00
    (C) $175.00
    (D) $180.00

23. A checking account has a balance of $1,162.76. After a check for $352.68 is deposited into the account and three checks are drawn from the account for the amounts of $152.45, $82.85, and $255.50, what is the new balance for the checking account?

    (A) $1,024.54
    (B) $1,024.64
    (C) $1,025.54
    (D) $1,025.64

24. Harold works 4.5 hours a day, 3 days each week after school. He is paid $4.25 per hour. How much is his weekly pay rounded to the next highest cent?

    (A) $13.50
    (B) $19.13
    (C) $54.00
    (D) $57.38

GO ON TO THE NEXT PAGE

25. Convert $\frac{6}{24}$ into a decimal.

    (A) 0.25
    (B) 4.0
    (C) 0.2
    (D) none of the above

26. What is the total cost of 4 sheets of 23¢ stamps, 2 sheets of 37¢ stamps, and 3 sheets of 60¢ stamps if each sheet has 100 stamps?

    (A) $336
    (B) $346
    (C) $356
    (D) $366

27. The Pacific Standard Time (PST) in Los Angeles is 3 hours earlier than the Eastern Standard Time (EST) in New York. A plane leaves Los Angeles at 5:30 P.M. PST and arrives in New York City at 12:45 A.M. EST. How long did the flight take?

    (A) 4 hours, 15 minutes
    (B) 4 hours, 45 minutes
    (C) 6 hours, 45 minutes
    (D) 7 hours, 15 minutes

28. After the price of a digital camera is discounted 25 percent, the camera sells for $120. What was the original price of the camera?

    (A) $145
    (B) $150
    (C) $160
    (D) $180

29. The square root of 225 is

    (A) 5
    (B) 25
    (C) 112
    (D) 15

30. If it takes 20 minutes to type 5 pages, how long will it take to type a 162-page document?

    (A) 10 hours, 12 minutes
    (B) 10 hours, 36 minutes
    (C) 10 hours, 45 minutes
    (D) 10 hours, 48 minutes

STOP. IF YOU FINISH BEFORE THE TIME IS UP, YOU MAY CHECK OVER YOUR WORK ON THIS PART ONLY.

PART 3: WORD KNOWLEDGE (WK)

Time: 11 minutes; 35 questions

<u>Directions</u>: In this section, you are tested on the meaning of words. Each of the following questions has an underlined word. Select the answer that most nearly means the same as the underlined word and mark the corresponding oval on your answer sheet.

1. <u>Listless</u> most nearly means

   (A) capable
   (B) directionless
   (C) talkative
   (D) bungled

2. His ability to <u>comprehend</u> complex ideas made him a great teacher.

   (A) create
   (B) loosen
   (C) understand
   (D) compute

3. Whichever one shows first will be the <u>victor</u>.

   (A) singer
   (B) manufacturer
   (C) best
   (D) winner

4. <u>Lackadaisical</u> most nearly means

   (A) talented
   (B) relaxed
   (C) actual
   (D) personable

5. It was his <u>contention</u> that more money should be spent on education.

   (A) celebration
   (B) position
   (C) ideal
   (D) sacrifice

6. The arrest wasn't even <u>newsworthy</u>.

   (A) notable
   (B) defaming
   (C) incredulous
   (D) safe

7. His attendance in class was, if anything, <u>sporadic</u>.

   (A) latent
   (B) calming
   (C) irregular
   (D) common

8. <u>Potential</u> most nearly means

   (A) scary
   (B) trustable
   (C) telling
   (D) possible

9. <u>Blacklisted</u> most nearly means

   (A) sacred
   (B) barred
   (C) old-fashioned
   (D) barren

10. It is <u>presumptuous</u> to expect too many volunteers for such a tough task.

    (A) exciting
    (B) predictable
    (C) satisfying
    (D) overly assuming

GO ON TO THE NEXT PAGE

11. A <u>memento</u> can provide a way to remember your vacation once you are home.

    (A) sacrifice
    (B) emblem
    (C) souvenir
    (D) symbol

12. The school's president is far too concerned with his <u>legacy</u> and not the present.

    (A) memory
    (B) salary
    (C) tension
    (D) grace

13. The economy has some parents worried that their children's future is in <u>jeopardy</u>.

    (A) limbo
    (B) danger
    (C) custody
    (D) salvation

14. <u>Integrity</u> most nearly means

    (A) ability
    (B) coercion
    (C) togetherness
    (D) sincerity

15. He was punished harshly for such a minor <u>infraction</u>.

    (A) aptitude
    (B) belief
    (C) gift
    (D) violation

16. <u>Collective</u> most nearly means

    (A) group
    (B) rare
    (C) soft
    (D) free

17. *The War of the Worlds* was early radio's biggest <u>hoax</u>.

    (A) trick
    (B) story
    (C) treat
    (D) complication

18. The <u>genesis</u> of the idea was scribbled on a napkin.

    (A) cancellation
    (B) detail
    (C) origin
    (D) craft

19. The brothers' <u>feud</u> goes back to their childhood days.

    (A) love
    (B) dispute
    (C) sensitivity
    (D) belief

20. <u>Fraud</u> most nearly means

    (A) pretty
    (B) fake
    (C) disgusting
    (D) sanitary

21. <u>Adept</u> most nearly means

    (A) older
    (B) talkative
    (C) cautious
    (D) skilled

22. She is an <u>ardent</u> supporter of families' rights.

    (A) vocal
    (B) testy
    (C) unaffiliated
    (D) tired

GO ON TO THE NEXT PAGE

23. The town suffered from <u>rampant</u> overcrowding and crime.

    (A) overstated
    (B) widespread
    (C) old
    (D) predictable

24. Such a <u>puny</u> fence stands no chance with that big dog.

    (A) satisfying
    (B) colorful
    (C) ghastly
    (D) weak

25. <u>Sinister</u> most nearly means

    (A) brotherhood
    (B) believable
    (C) gaudy
    (D) evil

26. <u>Witty</u> most nearly means

    (A) sulking
    (B) bloody
    (C) clever
    (D) careless

27. The witness's <u>vivid</u> account of the crime certainly opened the jury's eyes.

    (A) clear
    (B) unobstructed
    (C) false
    (D) condescending

28. <u>Relinquish</u> most nearly means

    (A) concede
    (B) color
    (C) trick
    (D) berate

29. I can only hope that these good times <u>recur</u>.

    (A) disappear
    (B) satiate
    (C) return
    (D) let go

30. <u>Incite</u> most nearly means

    (A) induce
    (B) intrigue
    (C) blow
    (D) react

31. It was wise to <u>implement</u> such a bold strategy while his critics were distracted.

    (A) introduce
    (B) suggest
    (C) trivialize
    (D) guess

32. <u>Query</u> most nearly means

    (A) telling
    (B) question
    (C) bogus
    (D) captive

GO ON TO THE NEXT PAGE

33. No one should be in awe of such a <u>timid</u> animal.

    (A) crazy
    (B) fearful
    (C) dangerous
    (D) salty

34. <u>Colleague</u> most nearly means

    (A) enemy
    (B) savior
    (C) peer
    (D) pedant

35. His opponent proved to be a <u>potent</u> mixture of tough and smart.

    (A) costly
    (B) derelict
    (C) sad
    (D) powerful

STOP. IF YOU FINISH BEFORE THE TIME IS UP, YOU MAY CHECK OVER YOUR WORK ON THIS PART ONLY.

PART 4: PARAGRAPH COMPREHENSION (PC)

Time: 13 minutes; 15 questions

<u>Directions</u>: This section contains paragraphs followed by incomplete statements or questions. Read the paragraph and select the answer that best completes the statements or answers the questions that follow, and mark the corresponding oval on your answer sheet.

The character of Sherlock Holmes illustrates author Arthur Conan Doyle's admiration for the logical mind. In each case that Holmes investigates, he is able to use the most seemingly insignificant evidence to track down his opponent. In fact, Holmes's painstaking attention to detail often reminds the reader of Charles Darwin's *On the Origin of the Species*, published some 20 years earlier.

1. The author compares Sherlock Holmes to Charles Darwin to

   (A) show Holmes's educational background
   (B) explain evolution
   (C) show how both were logical and meticulous
   (D) praise Darwin for his research skills

The climate of a major city is often very different from the climate of the surrounding areas. However, the geographic differences between the city and the country do not have to be dramatic to show major climatic differences. Even between the center of a city and its suburbs, there are often differences in air temperature, humidity, wind speed, and direction. Tall buildings, paved streets, and parking lots affect such patterns as wind flow and water runoff.

2. According to the passage, the relationship between cities and climate is

   (A) based on pollution controls
   (B) based on urban structures and the environment
   (C) based on city politics
   (D) drastically different than in rural areas

Marianne had seen it all on television—the Cuban Missile Crisis, man's first steps on the Moon, the fall of the Berlin Wall, even the economic boom of the 1990s. So when she won the lottery and the news vans started gathering outside her house, it didn't yet dawn on her just how much her life would be changed. A little attention doesn't hurt you, she thought. But when she stepped outside to an army of eager young reporters, however, she began to wonder if there weren't bigger events somewhere in need of coverage.

3. The character in the passage would probably do which of the following?

   (A) wear revealing clothing
   (B) donate money anonymously
   (C) dye her hair bright colors
   (D) refuse the money publicly

GO ON TO THE NEXT PAGE

In the "Gunpowder Plot" of 1605, a group of conspirators planned to blow up the English King and Parliament. The conspirators were a group of English Catholics who objected to the government's religious policies and who decided to carry out a daring assassination. They rented a cellar under the Palace of Westminster and hid 20 barrels of gunpowder there, intending to explode the gunpowder when the King and Parliament met. However, the conspirators were unable to keep the plot secret and their infamous plan was foiled.

4. The word *infamous* most nearly means

    (A) heroic
    (B) funny
    (C) obscene
    (D) notorious

Just as Johnny hit yet another red light, his cell phone began to ring. He looked at his watch and saw that he was already 20 minutes late to what might be the most important meeting of his career. Reaching for his phone, he knocked over his drink, spilling piping hot coffee all over his lap. He screamed loudly in his car, and though it looked like no one could hear him, a woman nearby ran away from the edge of the car quickly.

5. The tone of this passage is

    (A) perturbed
    (B) tender
    (C) exciting
    (D) snooty

The presence or absence of water can have a dramatic effect on the plants in a given environment. The desert, for example, is a biologically complex area where rain is often violent and unpredictable. Since desert plants are dependent on the occasional rain for survival, they must act quickly to make the most of it when it appears. Many desert plants, as a result, can complete an entire life cycle in a matter of months or even weeks. The more barren a desert is, and thus the less rain, the more rare and astounding these life cycles and the blooms that accompany them will be.

6. According to the passage, the life cycle of desert plants

    (A) is unrelated to rain levels
    (B) is directly related to their color
    (C) is akin to that of local wildlife
    (D) may be short and dynamic

It is a common belief among writers that great art is born from experience. However, some of the greatest writers in literary history have been people with a very limited knowledge of the world. Novelist Jane Austen, for example, didn't venture far beyond her circle of family and friends. And yet, just by observing the people around her, she was able to write acclaimed comedies about love and marriage. Similarly, Robert Louis Stevenson, the author of classic adventures such as *Treasure Island* and *Kidnapped*, was an invalid who was stuck in his bed for much of his life. Their achievements illustrate that if you have a good imagination, you can write a novel, no matter how unadventurous your life may seem.

7. Based on the information in the passage, a writer should

    (A) always write about people and their social scenes
    (B) write only adventure stories
    (C) rely on imagination and not just experience
    (D) get advice from close family and friends

GO ON TO THE NEXT PAGE

Tania is an extremely versatile actress. In a recent series of plays, she played a schoolteacher, two divorcees, three best friends, and a stepmother. She played a divorcee throughout the first play, but in subsequent plays she often played more than one part. Who would have suspected her acting prowess a few years ago when she ran crying off the stage with a terrible case of stage fright?

8. The word *prowess* most nearly means

    (A) knowledge
    (B) disaster
    (C) talent
    (D) bias

Many people dream about living on a coral island, but probably few of us would be able to describe one with any accuracy. Popular books and films create a romantic image of these islands, and it is not always as nice if seen from the land. Beneath the waves, however, the coral island is a fantastic and very beautiful world, depending entirely upon a complex web of interrelationships between plants and animals. The environment of the coral reef is formed over thousands of years by the life cycle of vast numbers of animals.

9. One logical conclusion to draw from this passage is

    (A) coral animals are more colorful than other animals
    (B) the true beauty of coral islands is underwater
    (C) all coral islands are tropical paradises
    (D) coral islands are formed mostly by volcanos

Questions 10 and 11 both refer to the passage below.

Few of the immigrants of the period just before the turn of the century found life in America easy. Many of those who lacked professional skills and did not speak English found themselves living in slum conditions in the busy cities of the Northeast, exploited by their employers and trapped at poverty level. Around the turn of the century a number of different organizations made efforts to help these newly arrived immigrants adapt to American life. While many groups emerged as leaders in these efforts to aid immigration, one organization preached a much colder answer to adapting to America.

A conservative group called the Daughters of the American Revolution approached immigrants with the expectation that newcomers should completely adopt American customs and culture. Consequently, they supported laws that required immigrants to take oaths of loyalty and to pass English language tests. They also tried to discourage the use of languages other than English in the schools.

10. Which of the following best tells what this passage is about?

    (A) the history of immigration in the United States
    (B) the cultural contributions offered by immigrants
    (C) how some sought to assimilate immigrants into America
    (D) how immigrant life affected U.S. cities

11. The author seems to imply that the Daughters of the American Revolution

    (A) understood the difficulties facing new immigrants
    (B) were ruthless in their intentions toward immigrants
    (C) preached fitting in, not standing out
    (D) believed that immigrants would not survive in America

GO ON TO THE NEXT PAGE

Some animals use coloring to safeguard themselves from predators. In certain cases an animal adapts in color, shape, and behavior in order to blend into its environment. The camouflage of the pale green tree frog is a good example of this. The tree frog blends so perfectly into its surroundings that when it sits motionless it is all but invisible against a background of leaves. Another type of camouflage, shown by zebras and leopards, is a pattern that diverts the eye from the outline of the animal. The chameleon, even more versatile than these, changes color in just a few minutes to match whatever surface it happens to be lying on or clinging to.

12. According to the passage, a reason that animals use camouflage is

    (A) to divert the eye from the animal's outline
    (B) to make nesting more safe
    (C) so that frogs' and chameleons' habitats remain protected
    (D) to ensure predatory dominance

Perhaps the biggest surprise of the Voyager mission was the discovery on the moons of Jupiter of intense volcanic activity. First seen on the moon Io, the eruptions were recognized as plumes of dust and gas and were immediately noticeable on the Voyager photographs. Further inspection revealed at least seven such events occurring all at once on Io's otherwise frigid surface. At other points, scientists detected three hot spots believed to be ponds of molten lava, sulfur, or sodium. The largest of these hot lakes was estimated to have a greater surface area than the state of Hawaii.

13. What was the most unexpected fact to emerge from the Voyager photographs?

    (A) the size of Io's molten lakes
    (B) the disappearance of impact sites on Europa
    (C) the discovery of volcanic activity on Io
    (D) the evidence of asteroid bombardment on all four moons

GO ON TO THE NEXT PAGE

Questions 14 and 15 both refer to the passage below.

Most people think that the Hula Hoop was a fad born in the 1950s, but in fact people were doing much the same thing with circular hoops made from grapevines and stiff grasses all over the ancient world. More than 3,000 years ago, children in Egypt played with large hoops of dried grapevines. The toy was propelled along the ground with a stick or swung around at the waist. During the fourteenth century, a "hooping" craze swept England, and was as popular among adults as kids.

The word *hula* became associated with the toy in the early 1800s when British sailors visited the Hawaiian Islands and noted the similarity between hooping and hula dancing. In 1957, an Australian company began making wood rings for sale in retail stores. The item attracted the attention of Wham-O, a fledgling California toy manufacturer. The plastic Hula Hoop was introduced in 1958 and was an instant hit.

14. According to the passage, all of the following statements are true *EXCEPT*

    (A) most people do not appreciate the origins of the Hula Hoop
    (B) the earliest prototypes of the Hula Hoop were made of grape leaves and stiff grasses
    (C) early precursors to the Hula Hoop were primarily children's toys
    (D) the Hula Hoop was an early success for the toy maker Wham-O

15. The author's primary purpose in this passage is to

    (A) describe the way that fads like the Hula Hoop come and go
    (B) discuss the origins of the Hula Hoop
    (C) explain how the Hula Hoop got its name
    (D) question the reasons for the Hula Hoop's popularity

STOP. IF YOU FINISH BEFORE THE TIME IS UP, YOU MAY CHECK OVER YOUR WORK ON THIS PART ONLY.

PART 5: MATHEMATICS KNOWLEDGE (MK)

Time: 24 minutes; 25 questions

<u>Directions</u>: In this section, you will be tested on your knowledge of basic mathematics. For each question, select the best answer and mark the corresponding oval on your answer sheet.

1. If $\frac{3}{4} + 1\frac{1}{3} = \frac{5}{6} - x$, then $x =$

    (A) $-2\frac{11}{12}$

    (B) $-1\frac{1}{4}$

    (C) $\frac{1}{6}$

    (D) $1\frac{1}{4}$

2. For all a, $(3a + 4)(4a - 3) =$

    (A) $3a^2 - 4$
    (B) $9a^2 - 4$
    (C) $12a^2 + 7a - 12$
    (D) $9a^2 - 16$

3. If $2m > 24$ and $3m < 48$, which of the following could *NOT* be a possible value for m?

    (A) 13
    (B) 14
    (C) 15
    (D) 16

4. $\sqrt{75} + \sqrt{108} =$

    (A) $11\sqrt{3}$
    (B) $6\sqrt{5}$
    (C) $5\sqrt{6}$
    (D) $\sqrt{183}$

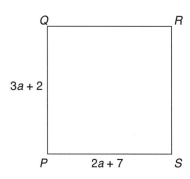

5. In the figure above, if *PQRS* is a square, what is the value of *a*?

    (A) $\frac{9}{2}$

    (B) 5
    (C) 7
    (D) 9

6. In triangle *ABC*, the degree measures of the three interior angles are in the ratio of 1:2:3. What is the difference in the degree measures between the largest and the smallest angles?

    (A) 30
    (B) 60
    (C) 90
    (D) 120

7. What is the perimeter of a right triangle with perpendicular sides of lengths 3 and 6?

    (A) $9 + 3\sqrt{5}$
    (B) $9 + 5\sqrt{3}$
    (C) $12 + 3\sqrt{3}$
    (D) 18

GO ON TO THE NEXT PAGE

A   B C   D   E

8. In the diagram above, if $AD = BE = 6$, $AE = 8$ and $CD = 3(BC)$, then $BC =$

    (A) 4
    (B) 3
    (C) 2
    (D) 1

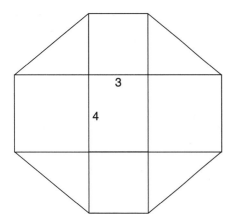

9. The figure above is composed of nine regions: four squares, four triangles, and one rectangle. If the rectangle has sides length 4 and width 3, what is the perimeter of the entire figure?

    (A) 30
    (B) 34
    (C) 40
    (D) 48

10. If $\dfrac{\sqrt{n}}{3}$ is an even integer, which of the following could be the value of n?

    (A) 27
    (B) 48
    (C) 81
    (D) 144

11. Gheri is n years old. Carl is 6 years younger than Gheri and 2 years older than Jean. What is the sum of the ages of all three?

    (A) $3n + 4$
    (B) $3n - 4$
    (C) $3n - 8$
    (D) $3n - 14$

12. Which of the following is *NOT* a prime number?

    (A) 2
    (B) 37
    (C) 51
    (D) 67

13. What is the area of a circle whose circumference is 2π?

    (A) $\dfrac{n}{2}$
    (B) π
    (C) 2π
    (D) 4π

14. A high school band is composed of 13 freshmen, 20 sophomores, 16 juniors, and 15 seniors. What is the probability that a band member chosen at random will be a sophomore?

    (A) $\dfrac{2}{5}$
    (B) $\dfrac{1}{3}$
    (C) $\dfrac{4}{13}$
    (D) $\dfrac{5}{16}$

GO ON TO THE NEXT PAGE

15. If $k - 3 = -\dfrac{5}{3}$, then $3 - k =$

    (A) $-\dfrac{5}{3}$

    (B) $-\dfrac{3}{5}$

    (C) $\dfrac{5}{3}$

    (D) $\dfrac{3}{5}$

16. If $x \neq 0$ and $\dfrac{3x}{5} = 3x^2$, then $x =$

    (A) $\dfrac{1}{5}$

    (B) $\dfrac{3}{5}$

    (C) 3

    (D) 5

17. For all positive values a, b, c, and d, $a = 2b$, $\dfrac{1}{2}b = c$, and $4c = 3d$. What is the value of $\dfrac{d}{a}$?

    (A) $\dfrac{1}{3}$

    (B) $\dfrac{3}{4}$

    (C) $\dfrac{4}{3}$

    (D) 3

18. How many rectangular tiles with dimensions of 3 inches by 4 inches are needed to cover a rectangular area with dimensions of 2 feet and 3 feet?

    (A) 60

    (B) 72

    (C) 120

    (D) 144

19. For how many integer values of x will $\dfrac{7}{x}$ be greater than $\dfrac{1}{4}$ and less than $\dfrac{1}{3}$?

    (A) 6

    (B) 7

    (C) 12

    (D) 28

20. A circular manhole is covered by a circular cover that has a diameter of 14 inches. If the manhole has a diameter of 12 inches, how much greater than the area of the manhole is the area of the cover, in square inches?

    (A) π

    (B) 13π

    (C) 36π

    (D) 52π

21. Which of the following is closest in value to the decimal 0.40?

    (A) $\dfrac{1}{3}$

    (B) $\dfrac{4}{7}$

    (C) $\dfrac{3}{8}$

    (D) $\dfrac{1}{2}$

22. If x oranges cost the same as y peaches, peaches cost 39 cents each, and the cost of each orange is the same, how many dollars does each orange cost?

    (A) $\dfrac{39y}{100x}$

    (B) $\dfrac{39x}{100y}$

    (C) $\dfrac{3,900}{xy}$

    (D) $\dfrac{39x}{y}$

GO ON TO THE NEXT PAGE

23. A class of 40 students is to be divided into smaller groups. If each group is to contain 3, 4, or 5 people, what is the largest number of groups possible?

    (A) 10
    (B) 12
    (C) 13
    (D) 14

24. If the area of a triangle is 36 and its base is 9, what is the length of the altitude to that base?

    (A) 4
    (B) 6
    (C) 8
    (D) 12

25. If $x = -5$, then $2x^2 - 6x + 5 =$

    (A) 15
    (B) 25
    (C) 85
    (D) 135

STOP. IF YOU FINISH BEFORE THE TIME IS UP, YOU MAY CHECK OVER YOUR WORK ON THIS PART ONLY.

PART 6: ELECTRONICS INFORMATION (EI)

Time: 9 minutes; 20 questions

<u>Directions</u>: In this section, you will be tested on your knowledge of electronics basics. For each question, select the best answer and mark the corresponding oval on your answer sheet.

1. Voltage and current are _____.

   (A) inversely proportional
   (B) directly proportional
   (C) both A and B
   (D) none of the above

2. To increase the magnetic field of a current passing through a wire,

   (A) make the wire longer
   (B) place the wire underwater
   (C) wrap the wire around a nail
   (D) wrap the wire into a coil

3. Voltage can be expressed by all of the following units *EXCEPT*

   (A) millivolts
   (B) gigabolts
   (C) megavolts
   (D) kilovolts

4. Which is the base in the transistor symbol below?

   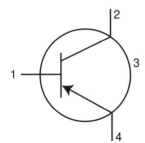

   (A) 1
   (B) 2
   (C) 3
   (D) 4

5. If each resistor in this circuit equals 750 ohms, what is the total resistance in this circuit?

   (A) 250 ohms
   (B) 375 ohms
   (C) 750 ohms
   (D) 1,500 ohms

6. Counter-emf is produced by a process known as _____.

   (A) inductive resistance
   (B) capacitive resistance
   (C) self-induction
   (D) none of the above

7. What resistance will allow 5 mA to flow when 50 volts is applied to it?

   (A) 10 Ω
   (B) 10 KΩ
   (C) 10,500 Ω
   (D) Both A and C are correct.

8. _____ material is noted for its ability to conduct current by the movement of holes.

   (A) Doping
   (B) P-type
   (C) N-type
   (D) Diode

GO ON TO THE NEXT PAGE

9. Diodes are rated based on

   (A) current flow in forward-bias direction
   (B) current flow in reverse-bias direction
   (C) current flow away from the center of the diode
   (D) Both A and B are correct.

10. N-type material can conduct electricity because of

    (A) silicon's unique structure
    (B) a free electron outside the valence shell
    (C) the presence of boron
    (D) none of the above

11. Which is a type of transistor?

    (A) NPN
    (B) PNP
    (C) both A and B
    (D) none of the above

12. Which of the following is *NOT* an antenna symbol?

    (A)
    (B)
    (C)
    (D)

13. Which of the following is the symbol for an earphone?

    (A)
    (B)
    (C)
    (D)

14. An element with an atomic number of 10 will have _____ electrons in its valence shell.

    (A) 0
    (B) 2
    (C) 8
    (D) 10

15. An element with five electrons in its valence shell is a(n)

    (A) conductor
    (B) semiconductor
    (C) insulator
    (D) none of the above

16. An ampere is defined as one _____ of electrical charge flowing past a point in one second.

    (A) hertz
    (B) coulomb
    (C) ohm
    (D) none of the above

GO ON TO THE NEXT PAGE

17. Unlike capacitors, inductors

    (A) allow DC current to pass easily
    (B) resist the flow of AC current
    (C) turn DC power around to increase power
    (D) Both A and B are correct.

18. The ground wire in an electrical cord is connected to the

    (A) steering column
    (B) chassis
    (C) engine block
    (D) crankshaft

19. This is the symbol for which type of meter?

    (A) Voltmeter
    (B) Ammeter
    (C) Ohmmeter
    (D) Galvanometer

20. All of the following statements about series circuits are true, *EXCEPT*:

    (A) current flow is the same throughout
    (B) there is only one path for current to follow
    (C) current flow varies throughout the circuit
    (D) voltage drops across the loads depend on their resistance

STOP. IF YOU FINISH BEFORE THE TIME IS UP, YOU MAY CHECK OVER YOUR WORK ON THIS PART ONLY.

PART 7: AUTOMOTIVE AND SHOP INFORMATION (AS)

Time: 11 minutes; 25 questions

<u>Directions</u>: In this section, you will be tested on your knowledge of automotive and shop basics. For each question, select the best answer and mark the corresponding oval on your answer sheet.

1. What is detonation?

    (A) when an air-fuel mixture explodes, rather than burns
    (B) if combustion is started by something other than electric arc at the spark plug
    (C) rapid, thorough burning of a compressed air-fuel mixture, initiated by a spark from the engine's ignition system
    (D) none of the above

2. The ignition _____ coil generates the high voltage for the spark plugs.

    (A) primary
    (B) preliminary
    (C) secondary
    (D) tertiary

3. Engine coolant is normally made up of a _____ mix of antifreeze and water.

    (A) 60/40
    (B) 75/25
    (C) 50/50
    (D) none of the above

4. A socket can be used with which tool?

    (A) ratchet
    (B) impact wrench
    (C) both A and B
    (D) none of the above

5. Automotive technicians will sometimes use _____ to determine distances.

    (A) outside micrometer
    (B) tape measure
    (C) steel rule
    (D) all of the above

6. This image depicts what stroke in the four-stroke cycle?

    (A) intake stroke
    (B) exhaust stroke
    (C) power stroke
    (D) compression stroke

7. A fuel injector sprays fuel into the intake air stream as it receives electrical signals from the

    (A) fuel rail
    (B) intake manifold
    (C) fuel pressure regulator
    (D) Powertrain Control Module (PCM)

8. A general purpose claw hammer would have a _____ oz. head.

    (A) 7
    (B) 13
    (C) 40
    (D) 212

GO ON TO THE NEXT PAGE

9. What would this tool be used to do?

(A) stop a rotating motor
(B) start a hole for drilling
(C) make a new belt loop on your jeans
(D) stabilize a car jack

10. Spark plugs are threaded into the

(A) battery
(B) distributor
(C) cylinder head
(D) coil wire

11. Automatic transmissions use _____ to create speed ratios and transmit torque.

(A) planetary gear sets
(B) idler gears
(C) spur gears
(D) countershaft gears

12. The brake system is _____ operated.

(A) hydraulically
(B) cable
(C) electrically
(D) none of the above

13. Which of the following saws is designed to cut metal?

A.

B.

C.

D.

14. MIG welding is also known as

(A) Russian welding
(B) coaxle welding
(C) electric-bit welding
(D) wire-feed welding

15. Identify this tool.

(A) Carpenter's level
(B) Machinist's level
(C) Line level
(D) Striding level

16. Contact points would be found in _____ ignition systems.

(A) coil-on-plug
(B) distributorless
(C) electronic
(D) none of the above

17. To remove a small sliver of wood in order to create a better fit, use

(A) a plane
(B) a flat file
(C) needle-nosed pliers
(D) Johnson bars

18. The _____ connects the steering box to the steering linkage.

(A) center link
(B) idler arm
(C) tie rod end
(D) pitman arm

GO ON TO THE NEXT PAGE

19. The catalytic converter is part of the vehicle's _____ system.

    (A) exhaust
    (B) emission control
    (C) Both A and B are correct.
    (D) Neither A nor B is correct.

20. Which of the following additions often increases the versatility of slip-joint pliers?

    (A) ratchet head
    (B) extension capability
    (C) wire cutter
    (D) variable speeds

21. Advancing the ignition timing means that the spark takes place _____ in the combustion cycle.

    (A) earlier
    (B) later
    (C) at the same time
    (D) none of the above

22. Which of the following hammers is used for forming soft metal?

    (A)

    (B)

    (C)

    (D)

23. Long-short arm suspensions use

    (A) ball joints
    (B) upper control arms
    (C) lower control arms
    (D) all of the above

24. To cut off a bolt head, you would most likely use which of the following?

    (A) miter box
    (B) pin punch
    (C) coping saw
    (D) cold chisel

25. A loss of compression in an engine cylinder can be caused by all of the following, *EXCEPT*:

    (A) worn engine bearings
    (B) worn piston rings/cylinder wall
    (C) burned valves
    (D) blown head gasket

STOP. IF YOU FINISH BEFORE THE TIME IS UP, YOU MAY CHECK OVER YOUR WORK ON THIS PART ONLY.

PART 8: MECHANICAL COMPREHENSION (MC)

Time: 19 minutes; 25 questions

<u>Directions</u>: In this section, you will be tested on your knowledge of mechanics and basic physics. Select the best answer for each question and mark the corresponding oval on your answer sheet.

1. The rollers shown are identical and are required to go over a step, from lower to higher. Force is being applied to each roller as shown: Roller A is being pushed and roller B is being pulled. Which roller requires less force to get over the step?

    (A) roller A
    (B) roller B
    (C) The rollers require the same amount of force.
    (D) The answer cannot be determined based on the information provided.

2. The formula for work is

    (A) $W = F \div d$
    (B) $W = F - d$
    (C) $W = F + d$
    (D) $W = F \times d$

3. A small pulley drives a large pulley with a belt. Which of the following statements about this arrangement are true?

    (A) the pulleys turn in opposite directions
    (B) the smaller pulley turns faster
    (C) speed output is greater than the input
    (D) A and C only are correct.

4. Any work that is done to accelerate an object at rest to speed v will be converted into the kinetic energy of that object. This principle is known as

    (A) work-energy theorem
    (B) gravitational potential energy
    (C) principle of conservation of mechanical energy
    (D) none of the above

5. Performing work at the rate of 1 joule per second is the same as expending

    (A) 100 foot-pounds
    (B) 10 psi
    (C) 1 meter per second
    (D) 1 watt of power

6. All of the following statements about liquids are true *EXCEPT*:

    (A) liquids are practically incompressible
    (B) liquids can be used to transmit force
    (C) all liquids are good lubricants
    (D) liquids conform to the shape of their container

GO ON TO THE NEXT PAGE

7. To most effectively cut a branch, how would it be best to hold the handles on pruning shears?

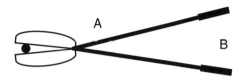

(A) with one hand at point A and one hand at point B
(B) at point A
(C) at point B
(D) halfway between points A and B

8. If 100 pounds of force are applied over an area of 2 square inches, the pressure would be

(A) 50 pounds per square inch
(B) 50 psi
(C) 200 pounds per square inch
(D) Both A and B are correct.

9. _____ is defined as "the advantage gained by the use of a mechanism in transmitting force."

(A) Pressure
(B) Hydraulics
(C) Torque multiplication
(D) Mechanical advantage

10. The _____ is the point that the lever pivots on.

(A) gear
(B) torque
(C) fulcrum
(D) none of the above

11. The identical floats illustrated below are measuring the specific gravity of two different liquids. Which of the two liquids has the higher specific gravity?

(A) A
(B) B
(C) The liquids have the same specific gravity.
(D) The answer cannot be determined from the information provided.

12. When a net force acts on an object,

(A) the object will slow to a stop
(B) the force will give the object a cumulative force
(C) the object will accelerate in the direction of the net force
(D) constant velocity is impossible

13. If pulley X turns in a clockwise direction, in which direction will pulley Y turn?

(A) clockwise
(B) counterclockwise
(C) The direction cannot be determined based on the information provided.

GO ON TO THE NEXT PAGE

14. The illustration below represents

(A) a fixed pulley
(B) a moving pulley
(C) a rear axle
(D) a pendulum

Questions 15 and 16 apply to the following formula for calculating pressure:

$$P = \frac{F}{A}$$

15. A load piston has a total surface area of 10 square inches and wants to raise 100 pounds. How much force will have to be applied?

(A) 1,000 psi
(B) 50.5 psi
(C) 10 psi
(D) cannot calculate with the information given

16. In the equation above, the ratio of the surface area of the pistons to the load piston is

(A) 1:1
(B) 1:10
(C) 1:50
(D) 1:100

17. Given a block and tackle with four ropes to lift a load one foot, barring friction, what is the mechanical advantage gained?

(A) 24:1
(B) 10:1
(C) 8:1
(D) 4:1

18. A child's teeter-totter, of the sort shown below, is an example of which kind of lever?

(A) first-class
(B) second-class
(C) third-class
(D) none of the above

19. A hockey puck slides across frozen ice. The puck will eventually slow to a stop because of

(A) wind drag
(B) gravity
(C) sliding frictional force
(D) inertia

20. What is being applied to the bolt as it is being tightened?

    (A) torque
    (B) friction
    (C) kinetic energy
    (D) gear ratio

21. When tightening a fastener, if one uses a wrench that is 1 foot long, and applies a force of 100 pounds to the end of the wrench, _____ of torque is being applied.

    (A) 1,000 foot-pounds
    (B) 100 foot-pounds
    (C) 10 foot-pounds
    (D) 10,000 foot-pounds

22. Based on the carburetor bore pictured below, which of the statements is true?

    (A) Vacuum gauge Y will indicate the highest vacuum.
    (B) Vacuum gauge Z will indicate a higher vacuum than Y but a lower vacuum than X.
    (C) All gauges will indicate the same level.
    (D) Vacuum gauge X will indicate the highest vacuum.

23. If the box above, weighing 200 kg, will be moved 10 meters with a force of 100 N, assuming no friction, how much work will have been done once the box is moved?

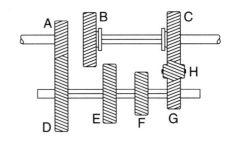

    (A) 10 joules
    (B) 100 joules
    (C) 1,000 joules
    (D) 1 million joules

24. The symbol g in Newton's formula for the Second Law of Motion stands for

    (A) acceleration due to gravity
    (B) mass, in grams
    (C) the Earth's surface
    (D) none of the above

25. Which gear is gear B planned to mesh with?

    (A) gear E
    (B) gear F
    (C) gear A
    (D) gears E and F

STOP. IF YOU FINISH BEFORE THE TIME IS UP, YOU MAY CHECK OVER YOUR WORK ON THIS PART ONLY.

PART 9: ASSEMBLING OBJECTS (AO)

Time: 15 minutes; 25 questions

Directions: In this section, you will be tested on your ability to determine how an object will look when its parts are put together. For each question, select the best answer and mark the corresponding oval on your answer sheet.

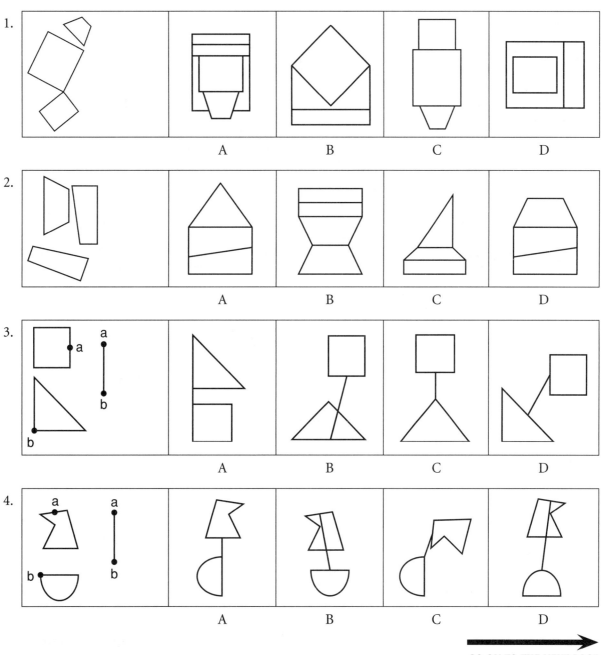

GO ON TO THE NEXT PAGE

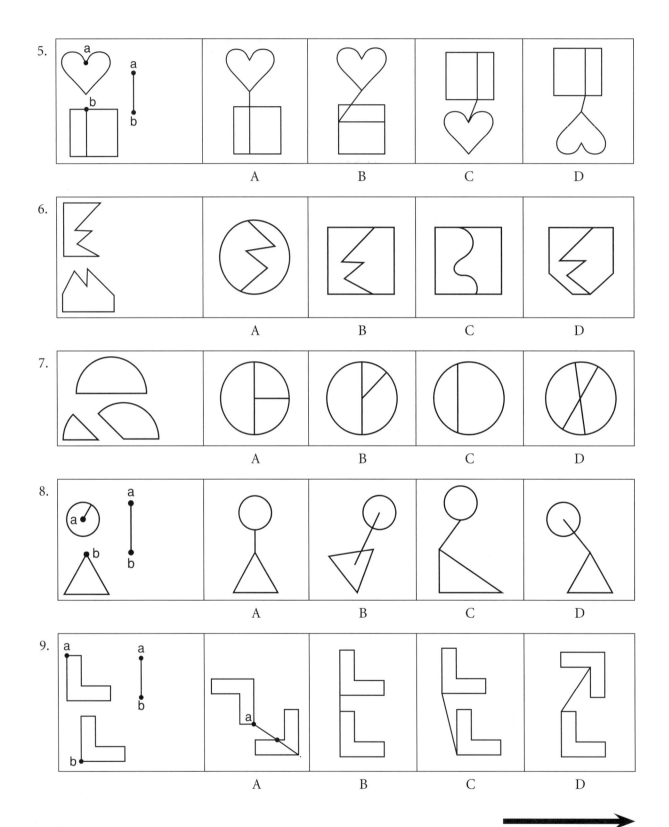

GO ON TO THE NEXT PAGE

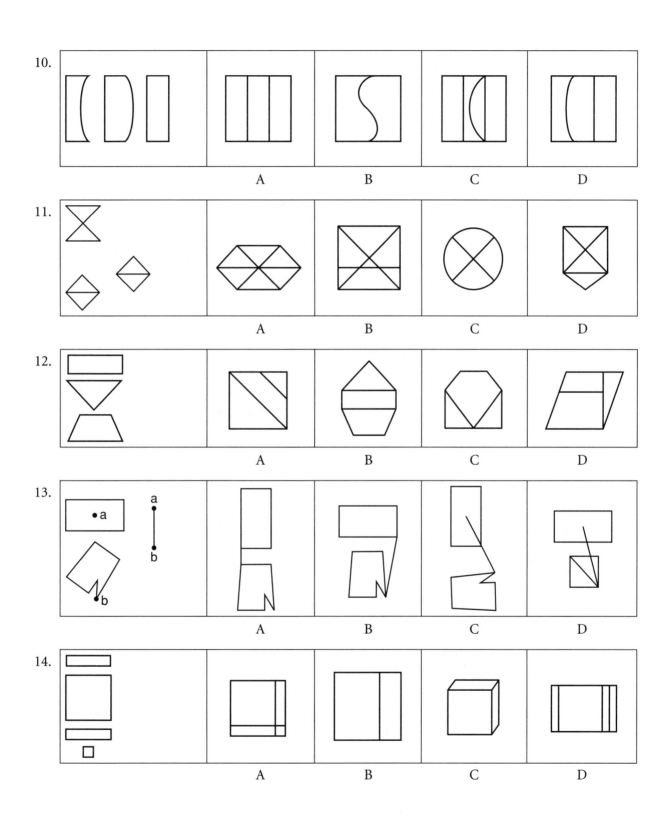

GO ON TO THE NEXT PAGE

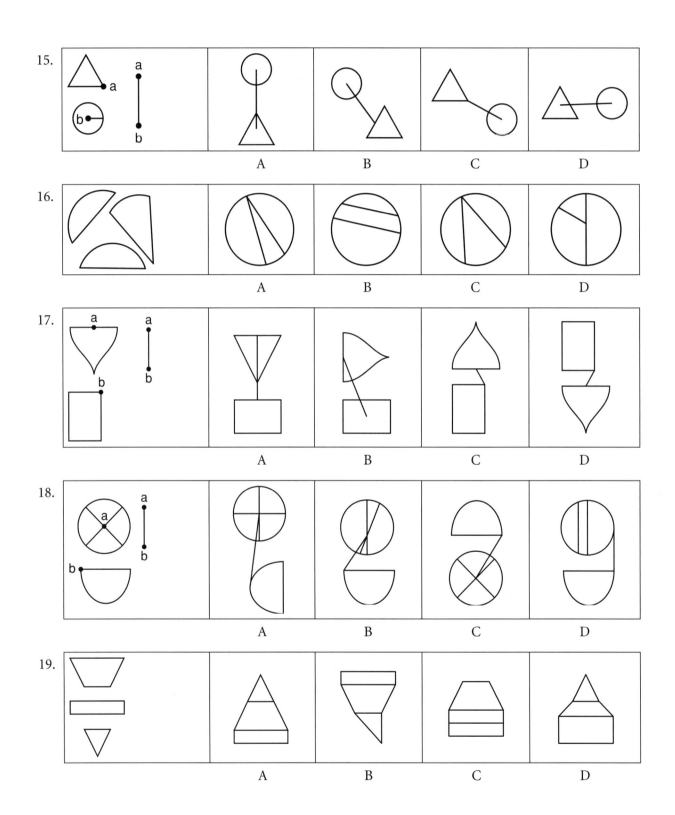

GO ON TO THE NEXT PAGE

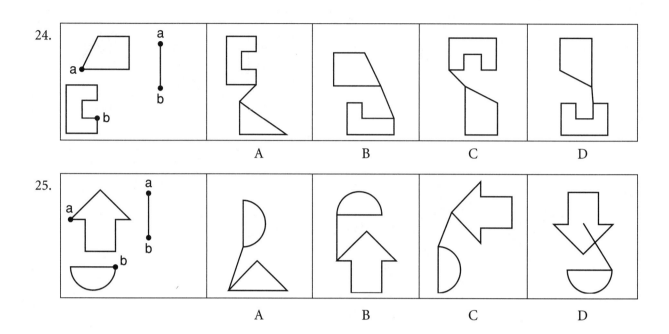

STOP. IF YOU FINISH BEFORE THE TIME IS UP, YOU MAY
CHECK OVER YOUR WORK ON THIS PART ONLY.

STOP! END OF TEST.

400 KAPLAN

ASVAB Practice Test III
Answers and
Explanations

ANSWER KEY

PART 1: **General Science**	PART 2: **Arithmetic Reasoning**	PART 3: **Word Knowledge**	PART 4: **Paragraph Comprehension**	PART 5: **Mathematics Knowledge**
1. D	1. B	1. B	1. C	1. B
2. D	2. D	2. C	2. B	2. C
3. A	3. B	3. D	3. B	3. D
4. B	4. C	4. B	4. D	4. A
5. D	5. D	5. B	5. A	5. B
6. C	6. C	6. A	6. D	6. B
7. B	7. D	7. C	7. C	7. A
8. B	8. D	8. D	8. C	8. D
9. C	9. A	9. B	9. B	9. B
10. D	10. D	10. D	10. C	10. D
11. C	11. C	11. C	11. C	11. D
12. A	12. A	12. A	12. A	12. C
13. D	13. B	13. B	13. C	13. B
14. C	14. B	14. D	14. C	14. D
15. C	15. C	15. D	15. B	15. C
16. A	16. A	16. A		16. A
17. C	17. B	17. A		17. A
18. A	18. B	18. C		18. B
19. B	19. D	19. B		19. A
20. C	20. C	20. B		20. B
21. A	21. A	21. D		21. C
22. A	22. C	22. A		22. A
23. B	23. B	23. B		23. C
24. C	24. D	24. D		24. C
25. B	25. A	25. D		25. C
	26. B	26. C		
	27. A	27. A		
	28. C	28. A		
	29. D	29. C		
	30. D	30. A		
		31. A		
		32. B		
		33. B		
		34. C		
		35. D		

ANSWER KEY

PART 6: **Electronics Information**	PART 7: **Auto and Shop Information**	PART 8: **Mechanical Comprehension**	PART 9: **Assembling Objects**
1. B	1. A	1. B	1. C
2. D	2. C	2. D	2. D
3. B	3. C	3. B	3. C
4. A	4. C	4. A	4. C
5. C	5. D	5. D	5. C
6. C	6. B	6. C	6. B
7. B	7. D	7. C	7. B
8. B	8. B	8. D	8. D
9. D	9. B	9. D	9. A
10. B	10. C	10. C	10. D
11. C	11. A	11. B	11. A
12. D	12. A	12. C	12. B
13. D	13. B	13. A	13. C
14. C	14. D	14. A	14. A
15. C	15. A	15. C	15. C
16. B	16. D	16. B	16. C
17. D	17. A	17. D	17. C
18. B	18. D	18. A	18. C
19. B	19. C	19. C	19. A
20. C	20. C	20. A	20. A
	21. A	21. B	21. B
	22. A	22. A	22. A
	23. D	23. C	23. C
	24. D	24. A	24. D
	25. A	25. A	25. B

PART 1: GENERAL SCIENCE ANSWERS AND EXPLANATIONS

1. D

Those wishing to reduce the bad cholesterol levels in their blood should avoid saturated fats. Sources of saturated fats include meats, shellfish, eggs, milk, and milk products.

2. D

Water at sea level freezes at 32° F, 0° C, and 273° K.

3. A

Of the subatomic particles listed, the proton has the largest mass. Among subatomic particles, protons and neutrons have the most mass. Electrons, positrons, and neutrinos all have negligible masses relative to protons and neutrons.

4. B

An apple tree is an example of an autotroph. An autotroph is an organism capable of synthesizing its own organic substances from inorganic compounds, as through photosynthesis. Another term for an autotroph is a producer.

5. D

By studying rocks, we now know that the Earth is approximately 4.6 billion years old, and that for most of that time, very few fossil traces were left. This is why the period from 4.6 billion years to 570 million years ago is called the Precambrian Eon, meaning the period before the fossil record began.

6. C

Mercury, Venus, and Mars are all smaller than Earth. Of the planets listed, only Uranus is larger than Earth.

7. B

Asteroids are also known as meteoroids, and when they fall into the Earth's gravitational field, they are seen as "falling stars," called meteors, as they burn up in the Earth's mesosphere.

8. B

The study of interactions between organisms and their interrelationships with the physical environment is known as ecology. Cytology is the study of cells, physiology is the study of the organism, and embryology is the study of embryos and their development.

9. C

Most of the nutrients in food are absorbed in the body's small intestine.

10. D

Because of the gravitational pull that exists between the Moon and Earth, we have tides. High tides occur twice a day, when the Moon is at the points closest to and farthest from the affected mass of water.

11. C

According to Newton's Law of Gravitation, if the mass of the Earth were doubled, the force on the Earth would double, not quadruple.

12. A

Of the states of electromagnetic radiation listed, radio waves have the longest wavelength and lowest frequency.

13. D

The speed of light can slow down, depending on the material through which the waves move; for example, light travels more slowly through water or glass than through a vacuum. The ratio by which light is slowed down is called the refractive index of that medium.

14. C

A high pH indicates a substance that is basic rather than acidic. Of the food products listed, baking soda is the most basic and has the highest pH.

15. C

Carbohydrates include both starches and sugars, which makes choice (C), both (A) and (B), correct.

16. A

Members of an order are more alike than members of a class.

17. C

The number of protons in the nucleus of an atom and the number of electrons orbiting its shells equal its atomic number. Atomic symbols are symbols that derive from the elements' Latin names, rather than their familiar English names. Atomic weight is the weight of one atom of chlorine expressed in atomic mass units.

18. A

The diaphragm is a system of muscles that allow the lungs to expand and contract, drawing air in and out.

19. B

The atom of an element with an atomic number of 17 must have 17 protons.

20. C

Because mushrooms absorb nutrients from decaying leaves, they are classified as saprophytes. Another term for a plant living on dead or decaying organic matter is decomposer.

21. A

The vessel with the *LEAST* oxygenated blood is the pulmonary artery, which sends oxygen-depleted blood from the heart into the lungs to be oxygenated.

22. A

Saliva in the mouth often begins the process of breaking down starch. Fats and proteins begin breaking down later in the digestive process.

23. B

The Moneran kingdom is composed of prokaryotic organisms, that is, organisms with cells that lack nuclei.

24. C

An atom that is not electrically neutral is called an ion. An isotope is any of two or more species of atoms of a element that have the same atomic number and nearly identical chemical behavior but differ in atomic mass or mass number and other physical properties. A positron is a positively charged particle having the same mass and magnitude of charge as the electron and constituting the antiparticle of the electron. An allotrope is an element that has two or more different forms (as of crystals) usually in the same phase; an example of allotropy is carbon, which can exist in such different forms as graphite and diamonds.

25. B

A metamorphic rock is a rock that has undergone a pronounced change effected by pressure, heat, and water, resulting in a more compact and more highly crystalline condition. Marble is one example of a metamorphic rock.

PART 2: ARITHMETIC REASONING ANSWERS AND EXPLANATIONS

1. B

If a machine caps 5 bottles every 2 seconds, then it would cap 30 times as many bottles in one minute (since a minute is 60 seconds). $5 \times 30 = 150$ bottles per minute, choice (B).

2. D

Jonah traveled 650 miles at 25 miles per gallon. To determine how many gallons he used, divide 650 by 25. $650 \div 25 = 26$ gallons. Each gallon costs $1.30, so his cost for the trip would be $26 \times \$1.30 = \$33.80$, choice (D).

3. B

On a problem like this, which involves annoying calculations (they can't really expect us to do long division, can they?), often the best way to go is to backsolve from the answer choices. You can start with either (B) or (C). Since (B), $0.40, is the easier number, we'll start there: If there are 3.86 liters in a gallon, and a liter of gasoline costs $0.40, a gallon of gasoline costs $3.86 \times \$0.40 = \$1.544$, or roughly $1.54 a gallon, which is the answer we want.

4. C

To determine the number of minutes in a week, begin with the number of minutes in an hour and work your way up from there. There are 60 minutes per hour and 24 hours per day, so there are $60 \times 24 = 1,440$ minutes per day. There are 7 days per week, so there are $1,440 \times 7 = 10,080$ minutes per week.

5. D

We know that 15% of take home pay = $37.50. So $0.15(x) = \$37.50$. $x = \dfrac{37.5}{0.15} = \dfrac{3,750}{15} = 250$, so choice (D) is correct. You could also work backward from the answer choices. $0.15 \times \$250 = \$37.50$. Either way you solve it, (D) is correct.

6. C

If the ratio of males to females is 3:5, then there are 8 parts total in the ratio. The total number of students must be a multiple of 8. Only choice (C), 152, is a multiple of 8.

7. D

A car travels 288 miles in 6 hours. Divide 288 by 6 to find the rate in miles per hour. $288 \div 6 = 48$ miles per hour. Then (48 miles per hour) $\times$ (8 hours) = 384 miles, choice (D).

8. D

If Martin's average score after 4 tests is 89, then the sum for his 4 tests would be $4 \times 89 = 356$. To average 90 on 5 tests, you would have to reach a sum of 450 for the 5 tests.

$450 - 356 = 94$, choice (D).

9. A

If the first year begins with town A at 9,400 and town B at 7,600, the populations are $9,400 - 7,600 = 1,800$ apart. Each year after 2010 beginning in 2011, the gap will close by 200. So it would take 9 more years for the gap to close entirely. So by 2019, the populations will be equal, choice (A).

10. D

One number is 5 times another number, and their sum is −60. You could rewrite that sentence as two equations and solve:

$$x = 5y$$
$$x + y = -60$$
$$5y + y = -60$$
$$6y = -60, \text{ and } y = -10$$

If $y = -10$, $x = 5y = 5(-10) = -50$. −50 is less than −10, so (D) is correct.

11. C

First, you must see that there are two rates by which John gets paid: one for the first 40 cars ($6 per car) and a different rate for all other cars after those first 40 ($6 per hour plus 50% of $6, which is $6 + $3, or $9 per car). Since he makes 48 cars, he gets paid $6 × 40 cars ($240) plus 8 extra cars at $9 per car ($72), which totals $312, choice (C).

12. A

48 glecks at 3 glecks per fedi would equal $\frac{48}{3} = 16$ fedi. 16 fedi at 2 fedis per bora would equal $\frac{16}{2} = 8$ bora, choice (A).

13. B

Work through the clock systematically: First reading at 12 P.M., second at 4 P.M., third at 8 P.M., fourth at midnight, fifth at 4 A.M., sixth at 8 A.M., seventh at 12 P.M., eighth at 4 P.M., ninth and final reading at 8 P.M., choice (B).

14. B

If monthly tuition payments were raised from $225 to $300, you can use the percent increase formula to determine how much the tuition went up.

$$\text{Percent Increase} = \frac{\text{New} - \text{Old}}{\text{Old}} \times 100\%$$

$$= \frac{300 - 225}{225} \times 100\%$$

$$= \frac{75}{225} \times 100\%$$

$$= 33\frac{1}{3}\%, \text{ choice (B)}.$$

15. C

If a truck takes 6 hours to complete a trip at 20 miles per hour, the total distance for the trip must be 6 × 20 = 120 miles. When traveling 120 miles at a rate of 30 miles per hour, the truck would take $\frac{120}{30} = 4$ hours.

So instead of taking 6 hours, the truck took 4 hours. That saves 2 hours, so choice (C) is correct.

16. A

If a full barrel can hold 75 gallons, when it is $\frac{3}{5}$ full it will hold $\frac{3}{5}$ of 75 gallons. $\frac{3}{5} \times 75 = 3 \times 15$ or 45 gallons, choice (A).

17. B

A salary of $45,000 is reduced by 40 percent; that is like reducing it by $\frac{2}{5}$. $\frac{1}{5}$ of $45,000 is $9,000, so $\frac{2}{5}$ would be $18,000. $45,000 − $18,000 = $27,000 for a new salary, choice (B).

18. B

$8! = 8 \times 7 \times 6 \times 5 \times 4 \times 3 \times 2 \times 1 = 40,320$

19. D

If 15 people contribute $40 each, that would amount to 15 × $40 = $600. Thirty-five percent of the money is spent on a group gift, so the remaining 65% of the money is spent on the party. 0.65($600) = $390, choice (D).

20. C

$\text{Average} = \frac{\text{Sum of the terms}}{\text{Number of terms}}$. In this question, an employee works for a sum total of 33.5 hours over 5 days. The average hours worked per day would be determined as follows:

$$\text{Average} = \frac{\text{Sum of the terms}}{\text{Number of terms}} =$$

$$\frac{33.5}{5} = 6 + \frac{3.5}{5} \text{ hours}.$$

We're not done, though. All the answers appear as minutes, not hours. So we need to convert 0.7 hours into minutes. There are 60 minutes in an hour, so 0.7 hours = 60(0.7) = 42 minutes. So the average amount of time worked on a given day is 6 hours and 42 minutes, choice (C).

21. A

To find the average speed for an entire trip, divide the total distance by the total time. If a train travels 180 miles at an average speed of 60 miles per hour, that leg of the journey must have taken $\frac{180}{60} = 3$ hours. The second leg of 150 miles at an average speed of 75 miles per hour would take $\frac{150}{75} = 2$ hours.

$$\text{Average speed} = \frac{\text{Total distance}}{\text{Total time}}$$

$$= \frac{180 + 150}{3 + 2}$$

$$= \frac{330}{5} = 66 \text{ mph.}$$

So choice (A) is correct.

22. C

Try backsolving on a question like this one. Start with choice (C). If a bicycle sells for $175.00 and is discounted 20%, its price would be reduced by $(0.20)(\$175) = \$35$. So the new price would be $175 − $35 = $140. That's the discount price we're looking for, so (C) is the correct answer.

23. B

This is purely an addition/subtraction question. Be careful, and double check your work, and you should be fine here.

Begin by adding the deposit to the balance:
$$1{,}162.76 + 352.68 = 1{,}515.44.$$

Then sum up the withdrawals:
$$152.45 + 82.85 + 255.50 = 490.80.$$

Then find your answer by subtracting the sum of the withdrawals from the balance:
$$1{,}515.44 - 490.80 = 1{,}024.64.$$

Choice (B) is correct.

24. D

If Harold works 4.5 hours per day for 3 days, then he works $4.5 \times 3 = 13.5$ hours at $4.25 per hour. He earns $13.5 \times \$4.25 = \$57.375$. That rounds up to $57.38, choice (D).

25. A

To convert a fraction to a decimal, divide the denominator into the numerator. $6 \div 24 = 0.25$.

26. B

Once again, you're up against a tricky computation question here. You can save yourself time if you realize that there are 100 stamps per sheet, which means that each sheet of 100 23-cent stamps would cost $23, each sheet of 37-cent stamps would cost $37, and each sheet of 60-cent stamps would cost $60. So your calculations should look something like this:

$$(4 \times \$23) + (2 \times \$37) + (3 \times \$60) =$$
$$\$92 + \$74 + \$180 = \$346, \text{ choice (B).}$$

27. A

Keep in mind that Pacific time is three hours behind Eastern time. So if a plane leaves Los Angeles at 5:30 P.M. PST, it leaves at 8:30 P.M. EST. So if it arrives in New York at 12:45 A.M. EST, the total time of the flight would be 4 hours, 15 minutes, choice (A).

28. C

Try backsolving here. Start with choice (C). If the original cost of the camera was $160, and it was reduced by 25% or $\frac{1}{4}$, the new cost would be $160 $- 0.25(\$160) = \$160 - \$40 = \$120$. That's the value we're looking for, so (C) is the correct answer.

29. D

A square root is a number that, when multiplied by itself, produces the given quantity. $15 \times 15 = 225$.

30. **D**

If it takes 20 minutes to type 5 pages, then we can think of the 162-page document as a group of 5-page chunks, each taking 20 minutes to complete. That means there are $\dfrac{162}{5} = 32.4$ five page chunks to the document. Each chunk takes 20 minutes to type. So the total document takes $32.4(20) = 648$ minutes to type. 600 minutes is 10 hours, so 648 minutes is 10 hours and 48 minutes. (D) is correct.

PART 3: WORD KNOWLEDGE ANSWERS AND EXPLANATIONS

1. **B**

Listless means *without aim or direction*; thus *directionless*, (B), is the correct answer.

2. **C**

Comprehend means *to grasp the nature or meaning of*, and *understand*, (C), is the answer closest to the original word.

3. **D**

A *victor* is defined as *one that defeats or vanquishes a foe*, so (D), *winner*, is the best answer.

4. **B**

Lackadaisical can't be understood from context, but something *lacking* means "missing," so taking a quick look at the other answers, the only answer missing anything is (B), *relaxed*, which is the lack of stress or action. Sure enough, the textbook definition of lackadaisical is *lacking life, spirit, or zest*.

5. **B**

A *contention* is defined as a *point advanced in a debate or argument*, so the answer (B), *position*, is closest in meaning to the given word.

6. **A**

Newsworthy is an adjective meaning *interesting enough to warrant coverage*, so (C) and (D) are out. While the arrest might make the arrested incredulous, answer (A), *notable*, is clearly the closest in meaning.

7. **C**

Something *sporadic* is something that is *occurring occasionally*. Thus answer choice (D) is wrong. Only answer choice (C), *irregular*, truly gets at the same meaning as the given word.

8. **D**

Potential means *possible or conceivable*, so answer (D) is the correct choice.

9. **B**

The odd word *blacklisted* refers to an old way of keeping out undesired people by creating a list of banned individuals. Thus, answer (B) is the only true answer, as banned and *barred* are similar words.

10. **D**

Presumptuous means *taking liberties* with what's given. Similarly, it also means *overly assuming*.

11. **C**

A *memento* is defined as *something that serves to warn or remind*, and the answer choice (C), *souvenir*, fits this definition perfectly.

12. **A**

Someone's *legacy* is the effect they leave behind once they are finished or departed. In this case, the school president is concerned about his *memory*, answer (A).

13. **B**

Something put in *jeopardy* is placed at a point of peril or danger. Thus, answer choice (B), *danger*, is the clear choice.

14. **D**

Integrity means having *especially moral or artistic values*, so while togetherness is a fine thing, someone having *sincerity* is most likely to be described as having *integrity*.

15. **D**

The noun *infraction* means to *break a rule or code*. Therefore, among the answer choices, answer (D), *violation*, comes closest to the meaning of the given word.

16. A

A *collective* is a body of people with like-minded goals or values, so only choice (A), *group*, makes sense.

17. A

Identifying the meaning of this kind of word in context is a good strategy here. A *hoax* is a *trick by convincing someone what is false is true*. *The War of the Worlds* was a radio show in which Martians attacked the Earth. Clearly, convincing anyone that this was true was a *hoax*. Thus, answer (A) is correct. Even if you didn't know the true definition, you could probably have made a guess based on context clues.

18. C

From Latin, the word *genesis* means the *origin or coming into being* of something. From this, you can see that choice (C) is the only logical choice.

19. B

A *feud* is defined as a *quarrel that is often prolonged*, so of the answer choices given, only choice (B) seems to fulfill that definition.

20. B

Fraud is the *act of deceiving or misrepresenting*, so while something may be a deception and still be pretty, the true answer is choice (B), *fake*.

21. D

An *adept* person is someone highly skilled or well-trained, and while this person may be talkative, older, or cautious, the only correct answer is (D), *skilled*.

22. A

Ardent is the state of being *intense in feeling*, in other words outspoken, as in an *ardent champion* of a cause. *Testy* can be seen as argumentative or loudmouthed, but the best answer to this question is (A), *vocal*.

23. B

The word *rampant* implies an excess, or *without restraint*. Something *widespread* can be considered as having no boundaries. Also, given the context of the sentence, one can see that crime is out of control or at least very prevalent. Thus, choice (B) is the best answer.

24. D

Puny means *weak or without strength*, and *weak* is one of your answer choices, therefore choice (D) is correct.

25. D

Sinister is defined as *wicked or devious behavior*, and *evil* is another word for wicked. No other answer choice really fits the meaning of the given word.

26. C

The adjective *witty* is used to describe someone *characterized by cleverness*, definitely not someone sulking or careless. Only *clever* among the choices fits the definition.

27. A

An account said to "open the jury's eyes" would imply that it clarified or illuminated a situation. Thus, the last two choices are not appropriate, as they are negative responses. Of the other two, only choice (A) truly fits the definition as given by the context of the sentence.

28. A

To *relinquish* something is to *give it up*, so of the answer choices, only (A), *concede*, really fits.

29. C

Here's another good context question. The root of the given word *recur* is the prefix "re-," which means "again."

30. A

Incite means *to move to action*, and of the choices given, only (A), *induce*, gets that meaning across.

31. A

Similar to incite, the verb *implement* refers to *setting into motion or beginning*. While to *suggest* something might be to start a process, answer (A), *introduce*, can mean taking an action.

32. B

A *query* is a *question*. Therefore, answer choice (B) is correct.

33. B

Timid means *shy or lacking in courage*. While an animal that is scared may be dangerous if provoked, the correct answer choice is (B), *fearful*.

34. C

One's *colleague* is an *equal* or a *coworker*. Of the choices given, only *peer* is an acceptable answer. Choice (C) is correct.

35. D

Potent means *having or wielding authority or influence*. Another word for wielding influence would be *power*. Scanning the answer choices, only (D) is a possible answer.

PART 4: PARAGRAPH COMPREHENSION ANSWERS AND EXPLANATIONS

1. C

The question asks you to read the passage with an eye toward its use of examples. Here, the author very clearly sets up the theme that Conan Doyle's character Holmes is a logical character. To illustrate that, he brings up a recognized scientific contemporary. Choices (A) and (B) have no bearing on the paragraph. Choice (D) brings up the idea of Darwin's meticulous research abilities, but does not reference the main focus of the paragraph (Holmes). Only choice (C) includes both men.

2. B

This detail question asks you to focus on the specific relationship between cities and climate as illustrated in the text. Looking back, we see that the paragraph introduces its subject first, and then gives some description of the changes that might take place. The last sentence in the paragraph finally gives us the information we need. Structures and man-made items affect the weather. Of the answer choices, choice (B) is the clearest paraphrase of that sentence.

3. B

This question asks you to make assumptions and predictions based on information given to you in the paragraph. From the tone of the passage, you can tell that Marianne is a generally quiet woman thrust into a high-profile situation. We can't really know what she's thinking exactly, but we can make an assumption based on the tone of the piece that she is overwhelmed by the attention given to her newfound wealth. Choices (A) and (C) seem to highlight the idea that she is a gaudy or flamboyant person, an assumption that seems all wrong given what we're told in the final sentence. Choice (D) is not reflected in the passage. Only answer choice (B) seems a fair assessment for Marianne's future behavior.

4. D

Here all you have to do is head back to the original text and find the word in question. Examining closely the context within which the word *infamous* is found, we find the group was plotting to blow up the King and the Parliament but were foiled. The gist of the paragraph is that the conspirators were up to no good, quite the opposite of heroes, choice (A). Choices (B) and (C) make no sense whatsoever. Only choice (D), *notorious*, accurately describes the sentiment the author meant.

5. A

Here's a nice easy one for you! All you have to do is judge the tone of the paragraph. Simple, right? Not so fast. Take a second to look at the language choices used: *screamed, knocked, ran*. Now take a close look at the answer choices, too. Choice (A) makes sense, since the action is so vivid and aggressive. Looks good, but let's save it and check out all the choices first. Answer (B) seems totally wrong for our purposes. Nothing here is tender. Choice (C) seems possible, but the sense of the paragraph is not so much exciting as dangerous. Choice (D) is wrong. Looking back at (C) and (A), choice (A) seems like the more appropriate choice.

6. D

Eliminate answers that either disagree with the passage, or that may or may not be true based on the passage. Choice (A) cannot be correct because it contradicts the passage: The life cycle is a direct result of the rain levels. (B) may or may not be true: although the passage mentions "astounding" blooms, it doesn't say anything about their color specifically. Wildlife, (C), isn't mentioned in the passage at all. (D) is a near-paraphrase of what the passage says about desert plant life cycles, so it is the correct answer.

7. C

The passage argues that many famous writers had narrow life experiences, but vivid imaginations, so look for an answer choice that makes a specific contrast between the need for imagination and experience in a writer's life. (C) makes that contrast. (A) contradicts the example of Robert Louis Stevenson, who wrote about things outside of his social scene. (B) similarly contradicts the example of Jane Austen, who did not write adventure stories. Friends and family (D) are mentioned in the passage, but not advice from friends or family.

8. C

The passage tells us that Tania was a good actress and gives examples of her variety of roles, so acting *prowess* describes a quality of good actors that she possesses. (C) suggests the positive quality of her versatility. Eliminate (B) and (D) because they are negative words, whereas you're looking for a positive quality. Knowledge, (A), is positive, but is not necessarily related to acting versatility.

9. B

Eliminate any answer choices that do not have to be true based on the passage. The color of coral animals (A) is not mentioned in the passage at all. (B) is practically a paraphrase of sentence two, "Beneath the waves . . . is a fantastic and very beautiful world," so (B) is the correct answer. (C) may or may not be true based on the passage. (D) is contradicted by the last sentence, which says that vast numbers of animals—not volcanoes—form coral islands.

10. C

In a question about the passage as a whole, the wrong answers will often be either too broad or too narrow, or will mention subjects that aren't in the passage. Eliminate answer choices that don't fit the scope of the passage. (A) is too broad: The passage is about groups of immigrants in a particular area and time, not the whole history of immigration. (B) can't be right because cultural contributions aren't mentioned in the passage. (C) is the correct answer: The idea of assimilation is referred to throughout the passage. (D) is too narrow: the effect on cities is only mentioned in one sentence.

11. C

The passage says that the DAR thought that immigrants should "completely adopt American culture and customs." The rest of the paragraph about the DAR just gives examples of what they did to support that belief, so we're looking for an answer choice that describes how they thought immigrants should conform. (C) matches that idea most closely. Notice that, while other answer choices may or may not be true, they don't fit specifically with what the author is saying about the DAR in the passage.

12. A

In the second sentence, the passage says that an animal adapts "color, shape and behavior in order to blend into its environment." The rest of the paragraph is a list of examples about how different animals become "all but invisible" with camouflage, so we're looking for an answer that says camouflage makes animals hard to see. (A) matches that idea. The passage says nothing about nesting (B) or habitats (C), and most of the animals mentioned are prey animals, not predators (D).

13. C

The key to this question is in the first sentence: "… the biggest surprise … was the discovery … of intense volcanic activity." Choice (C), the correct answer, is a paraphrase of the sentence about surprise. Don't be distracted by the rest of the details listed in the paragraph or by the other answer choices. The key idea here is the observers' surprise.

14. **C**

In an "all are true *EXCEPT*" question, concentrate on eliminating any answer choices that are true according to the passage. Eliminate choice (A) because it is true according to the first sentence. The second sentence says that choice (B) is true, so eliminate it too. Sentence four says that adults enjoyed the early Hula Hoops, so (C) must be false. (C) is the correct answer. The last two sentences of the passage show how (D) must be true since they describe how the Hula Hoop was a hit for the "fledgling" toy company.

15. **B**

Eliminate answer choices that are too broad, too narrow, or not mentioned in the passage. (A) is too broad: the passage doesn't include any information on fads besides the Hula Hoop. (B) is the correct answer: The passage starts with the earliest origins of the hoop toy and ends up with the popularization of the Hula Hoop. (C) is too narrow: only one sentence in the passage explains how the name came about. The passage says that the Hula Hoop is popular, (D), but doesn't address why.

PART 5: MATHEMATICS KNOWLEDGE ANSWERS AND EXPLANATIONS

1. B

In order to render this equation manageable, first turn the mixed number into an improper fraction, and then multiply both sides of the equation by 12 to clear the denominators:

$$\frac{3}{4} + 1\frac{1}{3} = \frac{5}{6} - x$$

$$\frac{3}{4} + \frac{4}{3} = \frac{5}{6} - x$$

$$12\left(\frac{3}{4} + \frac{4}{3}\right) = 12\left(\frac{5}{6} - x\right)$$

$$9 + 16 = 10 - 12x$$

$$12x = 10 - 9 - 16$$

$$12x = -15$$

$$x = -\frac{15}{12} = -\frac{5}{4} = -1\frac{1}{4}.$$

2. C

Use FOIL:

$$(3a + 4)(4a - 3)$$

$$(3a \times 4a) + [3a \times (-3)] + (4 \times 4a) + [4 \times (-3)]$$

$$= 12a^2 - 9a + 16a - 12$$

$$= 12a^2 + 7a - 12$$

3. D

If $2m > 24$, then $m > 12$. But so are all the answer choices, so check out the other inequality. If $3m < 48$, then $m < 16$. Thus, (D), 16, could not be a possible value for m.

4. A

For starters, (D) is out. When you add square roots, you can't simply combine the sums under the radical sign, as (D) does. But what you can do is factor out perfect squares from the number under the radical signs, like so:

$$\sqrt{75} + \sqrt{108} =$$

$$\sqrt{25 \times 3} + \sqrt{36 \times 3} =$$

$$\sqrt{25} \times \sqrt{3} + \sqrt{36} \times \sqrt{3} =$$

$$5\sqrt{3} + 6\sqrt{3} = 11\sqrt{3}.$$

5. B

Since the lengths of each side of a square are the same, $PQ = PS$. Therefore:

$$3a + 2 = 2a + 7$$

$$a = 5.$$

So choice (B) is correct.

6. B

The three interior angles of any triangle add up to 180°, and the parts of the ratio here add up to $1 + 2 + 3 = 6$. So to know what to multiply the ratio part numbers by to get numbers that add up to 180, divide 180 by 6, which gives you 30. Now you know that the three angles have degree measures of $1 \times 30 = 30$, $2 \times 30 = 60$, and $3 \times 30 = 90$. So the difference in the degree measures between the largest and the smallest angles is $90 - 30 = 60$.

7. A

The Pythagorean theorem states that in a right triangle, $a^2 + b^2 = c^2$, where a and b are the two perpendicular side lengths, called the legs, and c is the length of the hypotenuse. To figure out the perimeter of this triangle, we need the length of the hypotenuse, so let's apply the Pythagorean theorem:

$$(3)^2 + (6)^2 = c^2$$
$$9 + 36 = c^2$$
$$45 = c^2$$
$$c = \sqrt{45} = \sqrt{9} \times \sqrt{5} = 3\sqrt{5}$$

So now you can add together the sides to get the perimeter: $3 + 6 + 3\sqrt{5} = 9 + 3\sqrt{5}$.

8. D

Since AE is a line segment, all the lengths are additive, so $AE = AD + DE$. We're told that $AD = 6$ and $AE = 8$. So $DE = AE - AD = 8 - 6 = 2$. We're also told that $BE = 6$. So $BD = BE - DE = 6 - 2 = 4$. We have the length of BD, but still need the length of BC. Since $CD = 3(BC)$, the situation looks like this:

Here x stands for the length of BC. Since $BD = 4$, we can write:

$$x + 3x = 4$$
$$4x = 4$$
$$x = 1$$

So $BC = 1$, answer choice (D).

9. B

The central rectangle shares a side with each of the four squares, and the four squares form the legs of the four right triangles. Two of the rectangle's sides have a length of 4, so the two squares that share these sides must also have sides of length 4. The other two sides of the rectangle have a length of 3, so the other two squares, which share these sides, must also have sides of length 3. Each triangle shares a side with a small square and a side with a large square, so the legs of each triangle have lengths of 3 and 4, respectively.

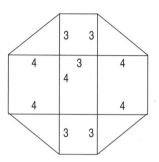

Since the legs are of length 3 and 4, the hypotenuse of each triangle must have a length of 5. The perimeter is the sum of the hypotenuses of the triangles and a side from each square:

$$\text{Perimeter} = 4(5) + 2(4) + 2(3)$$
$$= 20 + 8 + 6$$
$$= 34.$$

10. D

If $\dfrac{\sqrt{n}}{3}$ is an even integer, then $\dfrac{\sqrt{n}}{3} = 2k$, where k is an integer because any even integer is equal to 2 multiplied by an integer. Since $\dfrac{\sqrt{n}}{3} = 2k$, $\sqrt{n} = 6k$. Squaring both sides of $\sqrt{n} = 6k$, we have $(\sqrt{n})^2 = (6k)^2$, and $n = 36k^2$. So n must be a multiple of 36. Only choice (D), 144, is a multiple of 36. $144 = 4 \times 36$. Checking choice (D), $\dfrac{\sqrt{144}}{3} = \dfrac{12}{3} = 4$ and 4 is an even integer. Choice (D) is correct.

11. D

Here's a good opportunity to pick numbers. For instance, you could pick 10 for n, so that Gheri is 10 years old. In that case, Carl is 4 years old and Jean is 2 years old. So the sum of their ages is $10 + 4 + 2 = 16$. Now, if you plug 10 in for n into the answer choices, you get:

$3n + 4 = 3 \times 10 + 4 = 34$.   Too big.

$3n - 4 = 3 \times 10 - 4 = 26$.   No good.

$3n - 8 = 3 \times 10 - 8 = 22$.   Still too big.

$3n - 14 = 3 \times 10 - 14 = 16$.   That's more like it!

12. C

We hope you are comfortable with basic mathematical definitions. 2, 19, 37, and 67 are all prime. $51 = 3 \times 17$, so it is not prime. Knowing the *rules of divisibility* can help you when dealing with problems involving prime numbers, multiples, or factors. For instance, here one should be able to see quickly that 51 is divisible by 3, because its digits—5 and 1—add up to 6, which is a multiple of 3. (C) is correct.

13. B

The circumference of a circle $= 2\pi(\text{radius})$, so a circle with a circumference of 2π has a radius of 1. The area of a circle $= \pi(\text{radius})^2$ so the area of a circle with a radius of 1 is $\pi(1)^2 = \pi$.

14. D

To figure out the probability that a band member chosen at random will be a sophomore, you just have to apply the probability formula:

$$\text{Probability} = \frac{\text{Number of favorable outcomes}}{\text{Number of possible outcomes}},$$

or in this case,

$$\text{Probability} = \frac{\text{Number of sophomores}}{\text{Number of band members}}$$

$$= \frac{20}{13 + 20 + 16 + 15} = \frac{20}{64} = \frac{5}{16}.$$

Thus the correct answer is (D).

15. C

The key here is to realize that $a - b = -(b - a)$. So if $k - 3 = -\frac{5}{3}$, then $3 - k = -\left(-\frac{5}{3}\right) = \frac{5}{3}$.

16. A

Solve the equation $\frac{3x}{5} = 3x^2$ for x. Since $x \neq 0$, we can divide both sides by x. Then $\frac{3}{5} = 3x$. Dividing both sides by 3, we have $\frac{1}{5} = x$. Thus, $x = \frac{1}{5}$.

17. A

Here's another situation where you could pick numbers (otherwise you could use substitution). The key to picking numbers here is to know where to begin picking. Here the best place to start is with c and d. You're told that $4c = 3d$, so you make $c = 3$ and $d = 4$. So if $c = 3$ and $\frac{1}{2}b = c$, then $b = 6$. And if $b = 6$ and $a = 2b$, then $a = 12$. Therefore, using the numbers we picked $\frac{d}{a} = \frac{4}{12} = \frac{1}{3}$, choice (A).

18. B

Begin by converting the dimensions of the rectangular area to be covered to inches: 2 feet by 3 feet = 24 inches by 36 inches. 3 inches go into 24 inches 8 times, and 4 inches go into 36 inches 9 times, so to cover the area $8 \times 9 = 72$ tiles are needed.

19. A

$\frac{1}{4} = \frac{7}{28}$ and $\frac{1}{3} = \frac{7}{21}$, so the integer values for which $\frac{7}{x}$ will be greater than $\frac{1}{4}$ and less than $\frac{1}{3}$ are all the integers between 21 and 28. Play it safe and list them out: 22, 23, 24, 25, 26, 27, for a total of 6, choice (A).

20. B

The manhole cover has a diameter of 14 inches, so its radius is 7 inches and its area is $\pi(7)^2 = 49\pi$ square inches. The diameter of the hole is 12 square inches, so its radius is 6 inches and its area is $\pi(6)^2 = 36\pi$ square inches. Thus, the cover is $49\pi - 36\pi = 13\pi$ square inches greater than the area of the manhole.

21. C

Some answer choices you should be able to eliminate straight off the bat. $\frac{4}{7}$ is greater than $\frac{1}{2}$, so that's out, as is, for that matter, $\frac{1}{2}$. So you're left with $\frac{1}{3}$, which is about 0.333, and $\frac{3}{8}$, which is 0.375. Choice (C) is closest.

22. A

Since the question asks for the answer in dollars, start by converting cents to dollars. There are 100 cents in a dollar, so 39 cents = $\frac{39}{100}$ dollars. Since each peach costs $\frac{39}{100}$ dollars, y peaches cost $\frac{39}{100}y$ dollars. If x oranges cost as much as y peaches, x oranges also cost $\frac{39}{100}y$ dollars or $\frac{39y}{100}$ dollars.

Then one orange costs $\frac{1}{x}$ as much, or $\frac{39y}{100x}$ dollars.

This is an ideal problem to solve by picking numbers. Let's say that 5 oranges and 10 peaches cost the same; that is $x = 5$ and $y = 10$. If peaches are 39 cents each, 10 of them will cost $3.90, so that's the cost of 5 oranges. That means each orange costs $\frac{\$3.90}{5}$ or $0.78. We try our numbers in each answer choice:

Choice (A): $\frac{(39)(10)}{(100)(5)} = \frac{390}{500} = \frac{39}{50} = 0.78$. This may be our answer.

Choice (B): $\frac{(39)(5)}{(100)(10)} = \frac{195}{1,000}$. Discard.

Choice (C): $\frac{3,900}{(5)(10)} = \frac{3,900}{50} = 78$. This is 78 dollars, not 78 cents. Discard.

Choice (D): $\frac{(39)(5)}{10} = \frac{195}{10} = 19.5$. Again, discard.

Choice (A) it is!

23. C

To come up with the largest number of groups, you should minimize the number of students in each group. Each group must contain at least three students, so that means you could have a total of 12 groups with 3 students in them, and one final group with 4 students in it, for a total of 13 groups, choice (C).

24. C

The altitude to the base of the triangle is the same thing as the height of the triangle, and the area of a triangle = $\frac{1}{2}$(base)(height). So if the area of the triangle is 36 and its base is 9, the altitude is found as follows: $36 = \frac{1}{2}(9)$(altitude), so altitude = $\frac{36}{9} \times 2 = 4 \times 2 = 8$.

25. C

Just plug in -5 for x into the equation and solve:
$$2(-5)^2 - 6(-5) + 5 = 2(25) + 30 + 5 = 85.$$

PART 6: ELECTRONICS INFORMATION ANSWERS AND EXPLANATIONS

1. B

Voltage and current are directly proportional. Anytime voltage increases, current will also increase.

2. D

As electric current passes through a wire, a magnetic field is generated around the wire. The magnetic field can be made stronger by winding the wire into a coil.

3. B

Voltage can be given in a number of different units. Small voltages are expressed as millivolts (mV), which are the same as $\frac{1}{1,000}$ of a volt. Large voltages can be given in kilovolts (KV) or even megavolts (MV).

4. A

In the symbol, the number 1 indicates the base, which is the middle piece of semiconductor material inside a transistor.

5. C

For a simple parallel circuit with two resistors of equal value, divide the resistance of a single component by the total number of components. For this parallel circuit, we have two 750 ohm resistors, so 750 ohms $\sqrt{2}$ = 375 ohms.

6. C

When current first flows through a coil, the magnetic field builds relatively slowly. This is because the expanding magnetic field generates a voltage in the coil that opposes the original current flow. This is known as counter-emf, and it is produced by a process known as self-induction.

7. B

Calculating resistance is easy if you know the formula (R = E ÷ I) and can easily convert the factors in your equation. In this case, 5 mA should be made to be .005 A. The resistance comes out to be 50 V divided by .005 A, or 10,000 Ω of resistance. Remember to place your answer in the same form that the answer choices are given to you. Answer choice (B) is just a shortened way of saying 10,000 Ω.

8. B

If silicon is doped with elements that have three electrons in their valence shells (such as boron or indium), the result is a "hole" being left where an electron would normally reside in the crystalline structure. These holes can also migrate throughout the crystal. This takes place as an electron moves into a hole, thus creating a hole in the spot it previously occupied. As electrons flow in one direction, holes will flow in the opposite direction. P-type material is thus noted for its ability to conduct current by the movement of holes.

9. D

Since diodes are rated according to the maximum amount of current that can flow in the forward-bias direction without damaging them and are also rated according to their peak inverse voltage (PIV), the maximum amount of voltage that can be withstood in the reverse-bias direction, the answer is (D), both (A) and (B).

10. B

The crystalline structure of pure silicon is very stable. The four valence electrons in each silicon atom bond with the valence electrons in the atoms around it, so no free electrons exist to allow current flow. This can be changed by "doping" the silicon's crystal structure with either phosphorus, arsenic, or antimony. Since these elements all have five electrons in their valence shell, they will bond themselves to the other silicon atoms, but leave one free electron that is able to migrate throughout the crystal. This changes the silicon crystal into an N-type material. This new material is still electrically neutral, but is able to conduct electricity due to the presence of free electrons. The correct answer is (B).

11. C

There are two types of transistors: an NPN transistor, and a PNP transistor. An NPN transistor is made up of a thin piece of P-type material sandwiched between two pieces of N-type material. A PNP transistor is the opposite: two pieces of P-type material that have a piece of N-type material between them.

12. D

Choice (D) is the schematic symbol for a ground. Choice (A) is the general antenna symbol; (B) balanced antenna; (C) unshielded loop antenna.

13. D

All four choices are schematic symbols for audio devices, of which (D) is the symbol for an earphone. (A) represents a loudspeaker, (B) a microphone, and (C) a Piezo transducer.

14. C

Taking a quick look at the periodic chart will tell you that there are always two electrons in an element's inner shell and that the remaining electrons reside in what is called the valence shell. An element with an atomic number of 10, therefore, will have eight electrons in its valence shell.

15. C

More than four electrons in the valence shell means that the element is an insulator. Insulators do not conduct electricity, and therefore are useful for creating electrical barriers. Examples of insulators are rubber and plastic. Thus, an element with five electrons in its valence shell is (C), an insulator.

16. B

An ampere is defined as one coulomb of electrical charge flowing past a point in one second. One coulomb is the amount of charge in 6.25310^{18} electrons. This is the same as 6,250,000,000,000,000,000 electrons. If this many electrons flow past a point in a conductor in one second, one ampere of current is flowing.

17. D

Inductors work exactly opposite to capacitors, in the sense that they allow DC to pass easily, but resist the flow of AC. This is known as *inductive reactance,* and it will rise in direct proportion to the frequency of the current flowing through the inductor. Since both (A) and (B) are correct, the best answer choice is (D), (A) and (B) only.

18. B

The ground wire in an electrical cord is connected to the chassis (frame) of the equipment. Since earth ground is a zero voltage point, all "stray" electricity will go to it by following the path of least resistance through the copper ground conductor.

19. B

This is the circuit symbol for an ammeter, which is used to measure current.

20. C

Of the statements given about series circuits, only choice (C) is not true of series circuits. In a series circuit, *the current flow will be the same in all parts of the circuit*. The current that leaves the voltage source must return to the voltage source, and since there is only one path for current to follow in a series circuit, current will be the same throughout the circuit. Voltage measured across each of the components, on the other hand, may be different depending on their resistance.

PART 7: AUTOMOTIVE AND SHOP INFORMATION
ANSWERS AND EXPLANATIONS

1. A

Detonation is when an air-fuel mixture explodes, rather than burns. It can often take place when an engine's air-fuel mixture is lean.

2. C

The current that flows through the ignition primary winding builds a strong magnetic field that surrounds both it and the *secondary coil winding*. This is the device that creates high voltage for the spark plugs.

3. C

Engine coolant is normally made up of a 50/50 mix of antifreeze and water.

4. C

The most common drive tool for sockets is the ratchet, which turns the fastener in only one direction as the handle is moved back and forth through a narrow arc. Ratchets are reversible, so they can be set to tighten or loosen a fastener. Sockets can also be used with pneumatic (compressed air) power tools, such as an air impact wrench. The air impact wrench can remove fasteners quickly by applying tremendous amounts of torque (twisting force) using a "hammering" action that vibrates fasteners loose.

5. D

Automotive technicians will sometimes use a steel rule or tape measure to determine distances. When accuracy down to one-thousandths of an inch is required, an outside micrometer is used. The outside micrometer is made to measure the outside diameter of cylindrically shaped objects, as well as the thickness of flat objects.

6. B

This image depicts the exhaust stroke, which is the fourth stroke in the four-stroke cycle. In the exhaust stroke the spent gases in the combustion chamber are purged from the engine.

7. D

A fuel injector sprays fuel into the intake stream as it receives electrical signals from the Powertrain Control Module (PCM).

8. B

Carpenters often will use a *claw hammer*, which serves a dual purpose. The hammer head has two ends: one to drive nails and the other to remove nails. Claw hammers come in a variety of sizes, and these are determined by the weight of the hammer head. A general purpose claw hammer would have a 13 oz. head.

9. B

This is a center punch. Center punches are used to make small indentations that serve as starting marks for drilling operations. Making a small indentation with a center punch can help the drill bit stay on target long enough to get a hole started.

10. C

Spark plugs are threaded into the cylinder head where the spark plug protrudes into the combustion chamber and generates the spark to initiate combustion.

11. A

Automatic transmissions do all of the gear selection for the driver. This is done in the transmission using hydraulics and *planetary gear sets*. The newest automatic transmissions are controlled electronically by the vehicle's powertrain control module.

12. A

Brake systems are *hydraulically operated*. A pumping piston, located in the master cylinder, is operated by the brake pedal and puts pressure on the system's brake fluid.

13. B

A hacksaw, depicted in (B), is used for cutting metals such as steel, aluminum, or copper. The blades in a hacksaw are replaceable, and it is important to choose the right blade for the material that is going to be cut.

14. D

MIG welding is also known as *wire-feed welding* because the electrode used for the weld process is a wire that is automatically fed from a spool.

15. A

The carpenter's level has three level vials, which are mounted horizontally, vertically, and at a 45-degree angle. It is used in construction for checking for true vertical, true horizontal, and 45-degree angles.

16. D

None of the ignition systems listed would utilize contact points. Only older cars with breaker points would have contact points.

17. A

When working with wood, there are many occasions when it is necessary to remove a small amount of material to make a piece fit properly or to make a surface smooth. One tool that can be used for this purpose is a *plane*.

18. D

The *pitman arm* is a short lever arm connected to the steering gear that transmits the steering force from the cross shaft to the steering linkage system. Long-short arm suspensions most commonly use linkage steering to connect the steering column to the pitman arm, center link, and idler arm.

19. C

The catalytic converter is responsible for converting the toxic components of engine exhaust into relatively harmless compounds such as carbon dioxide and water and is, thus, part of both (A), the exhaust system, and (B), the emission control system.

20. C

The most common type of pliers is the *combination slip-joint*. These are adjustable at the joint of the two handles of the pliers. With two different positions to choose from, these pliers can grip objects in a wide range of sizes. Sometimes, this design also incorporates *a wire cutter* for increased versatility.

21. A

For higher engine speeds, the flame must be started *earlier* (A) in order to generate the most effective downward push on the piston. This is known as *advancing* the timing.

22. A

A ball peen hammer is used for forming soft metal, peening rivet heads, and striking metal in out-of-the-way places.

23. D

A common type of suspension system, long-short arm suspension systems include *ball joints*, *upper control arms*, and *lower control arms*, among other components.

24. D

The most common chisel is the *cold chisel*, which has a straight, sharp edge for cutting off bolt heads or separating two pieces of an assembly.

25. A

Of the given choices, only (A), worn engine bearings, would not be the cause of a loss of compression, as the engine bearings do not weigh in on compression issues.

PART 8: MECHANICAL COMPREHENSION ANSWERS AND EXPLANATIONS

1. B

Pulling the roller over the step requires less force than pulling it.

2. D

Work is accomplished when force is applied against an object. This is summarized by the formula $W = Fd$ where F is force in newtons (N), d is distance in meters (m), and W is work in joules (J).

3. B

Since the question asks which of the following are true, and since we always remember that *smaller* gears *always* turn faster, the answer is (B).

4. A

Any work that is done to accelerate an object at rest to speed v will be converted into the kinetic energy of that object. This principle is known as the work-energy theorem.

5. D

Performing work at the rate of 1 joule per second is the same as expending 1 watt of power.

6. C

There are several properties of liquids that are unchanging. First, they are effectively incompressible. Even when extremely high pressure is applied to a liquid, the volume of the liquid will decrease only a very small amount. This property makes liquids very effective for transmitting force. And the second overarching principle of hydraulics is that liquids conform themselves to the shape of their container. Whether in a pipe or a pump, liquids will always change their shape to fill the space completely. But not all liquids are by nature good lubricants. Here, the correct answer is (C).

7. C

Holding the handles close to the end, at point B, results in longer levers that place more force on the branch for the same amount of effort.

8. D

This one's just to see if you are paying attention. Using the formula for pressure $\left(P = \dfrac{F}{A} \right)$, if 100 pounds of force are applied over an area of 2 square inches, then the resulting pressure is 50 pounds per square inch. Another way of shortening this answer is to say it is 50 *psi*. So technically, (D) is the answer, as both (A) and (B) are correct.

9. D

Mechanical advantage is defined as "the advantage gained by the use of a mechanism in transmitting force." Using the proper equipment, it is possible to increase or even multiply force many times over what is initially applied.

10. C

The fulcrum is the point that the lever pivots on. When effort is applied to one end of the lever, it changes direction at the other end. The position of the fulcrum will define whether any mechanical advantage is gained. If the fulcrum is closer to the object being lifted, less effort is required to do the work.

11. B

Specific gravity is the weight of a liquid in comparison to the weight of water. The floats will rise higher in liquids with higher levels of specific gravity.

12. C

According to Newton's Second Law of Motion, when a net force acts on an object, the object will accelerate in the direction of the net force. The acceleration will be less if the mass of the object is greater.

13. A

Belted pulleys turn in the same direction.

14. A

The illustration shows a fixed pulley.

15. C

The load piston has a total surface area of 10 square inches. Using the formula $P = \dfrac{F}{A}$, 100 pounds ÷ 10 square inches = 10 pounds per square inch (psi) of pressure that should be applied to the load piston.

16. B

The force applied to the pumping piston is $\dfrac{1}{10}$ of the force that is developed at the load piston. The mechanical advantage gained with a system such as this is determined by the ratio of the surface areas of the pistons.

17. D

Note that in order to lift the load 1 foot, it is necessary to pull the rope a total of 4 feet. This is because each of the four rope links must shorten by 1 foot to get the lower block to move 1 foot. Neglecting friction, this gives a total mechanical advantage of 4:1, so if 4 pounds of force are required to lift a load, only 1 pound needs to be applied to the rope.

18. A

A child's teeter-totter is an example of a first-class lever.

19. C

In the example of the hockey puck sliding along an ice surface, while ice has much less friction than most surfaces, it will still exert a sliding frictional force on the puck that eventually causes it to stop moving.

20. A

Torque is *twisting force*. When a bolt is being tightened, torque is being applied to the bolt. For example, when tightening a fastener, if one uses a wrench that is one foot long, and applies a force of 100 pounds to the end of the wrench in a direction perpendicular to the wrench, 100 foot-pounds (ft-lb) of torque is being applied.

21. B

When tightening a fastener, if one uses a wrench that is 1 foot long, and applies a force of 100 pounds to the end of the wrench, 100 foot-pounds (ft-lb) of torque is being applied. Simply multiply the applied force by the length of the wrench to determine the torque.

22. A

Vacuum is highest at the most narrow or restricted part of the air passage. Therefore, vacuum gauge Y will indicate a vacuum that is higher than both X and Z.

23. C

Work is accomplished when force is applied against an object in motion. This is summarized by the formula

$$W = Fd$$

where F is force in newtons (N), d is distance in meters (m), and W is work in joules (J). These units are also part of the SI system of measurement. If a force of 100 N is applied to the box, and the box is moved 10 meters, then a total of 1,000 joules of work has been done.

24. A

According to Newton's Gravitational Law, since gravity exerts a force on bodies that pulls them together, this force causes an acceleration due to gravity, which is represented by the symbol g.

25. A

Gear B can only mesh with gear E because gear F is too short and gears A and D are in constant mesh.

PART 9: ASSEMBLING OBJECTS ANSWERS AND EXPLANATIONS

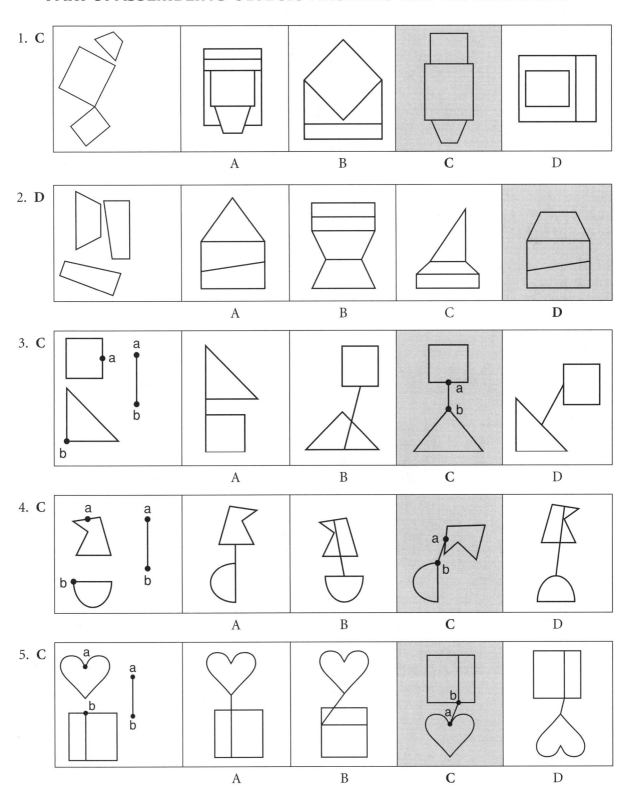

1. **C**

2. **D**

3. **C**

4. **C**

5. **C**

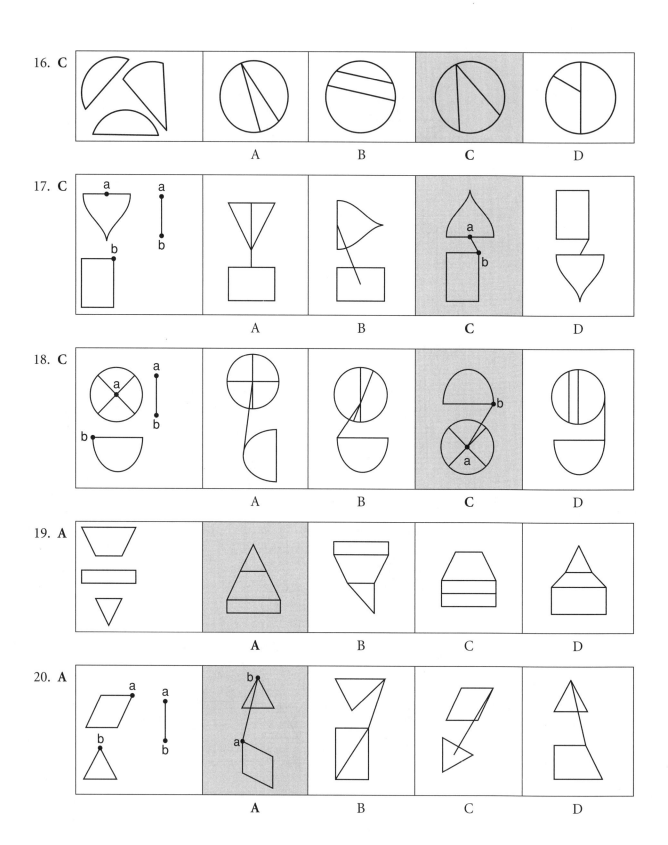

16. **C**

A   B   **C**   D

17. **C**

A   B   **C**   D

18. **C**

A   B   **C**   D

19. **A**

A   B   C   D

20. **A**

A   B   C   D

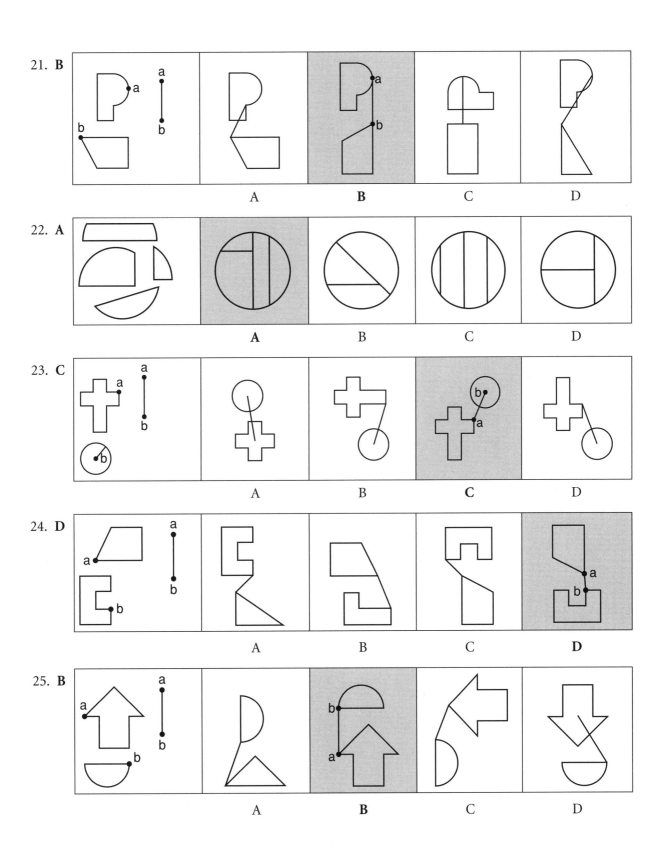

Index